PENGUIN BOOKS

The Dreadful Monster and its Poor Relations

'In this crisp, thoughtful and occasionally sardonic study, Hoppit follows the money ... fair-minded ... excellent' Ferdinand Mount, *London Review of Books*

'In 1707, England ceased to exist as an independent state, joining itself with Scotland and, roughly a century later (and less happily), with Ireland ... The fiscal dimensions of this story are superbly illuminated by Julian Hoppit' Brendan Simms, *Wall Street Journal*

'Famously, the UK lacks a codified constitution. Julian Hoppit's history of taxation from 1707 to 2021 points out that after the Second World War, the UK bequeathed the Germans a federal system and a written constitution. We just never thought to design one for ourselves' *Prospect*, Books of the Year

'His research has given him an unrivalled understanding of the money problems that lie at the heart of much of the current, and past, discontents about the Union' Roderick Floud, *History Today*

'Hoppit shows how the history of financial relations within the United Kingdom is profoundly relevant to the current constitutional debate ... he steers the reader deftly through complex historical statistics' Vernon Bogdanor, *Daily Telegraph*

ABOUT THE AUTHOR

Julian Hoppit is Astor Professor of British History emeritus at University College London. He is the author of *Risks and Failure in English Business, 1700–1800*, *A Land of Liberty?: England 1689–1727* and *Britain's Political Economies: Parliament and Economic Life, 1660–1800*.

JULIAN HOPPIT

The Dreadful Monster and its Poor Relations

Taxing, Spending and the United Kingdom, 1707–2021

PENGUIN BOOKS

PENGUIN BOOKS

UK | USA | Canada | Ireland | Australia
India | New Zealand | South Africa

Penguin Books is part of the Penguin Random House group of companies
whose addresses can be found at global.penguinrandomhouse.com.

First published in Great Britain by Allen Lane 2021
First published in Penguin Books 2022
001

Printed and bound in Great Britain by Clays Ltd, Elcograf S.p.A.

The authorized representative in the EEA is Penguin Random House Ireland,
Morrison Chambers, 32 Nassau Street, Dublin D02 YH68

A CIP catalogue record for this book is available from the British Library

ISBN: 978–0–141–99226–6

Contents

List of figures

List of tables

List of maps

List of images

Whence did this dreadfull Monster come?
Whose Son is he? Begot of whom?
How came he here? what plague on Earth
Produced this Portentous Birth . . .
About he goes with linked Pole,
A Bottle at his Button-hole,
A Rule, a Compass, and some Cork,
And other Instruments of Work . . .
Of Sacred things he loves no quibble,
Save his Compt-Book he knows no Bible . . .

Anon., *A Scots excise-man
described* ([Edinburgh, 1707?])

A poor relation – is the most irrelevant thing in nature, – a piece of impertinent correspondency, – an odious approximation, – a haunting conscience, – a preposterous shadow, lengthening in the noontide of your prosperity, – an unwelcome remembrancer, – a perpetually recurring mortification, – a drain on your purse, – a more intolerable dun upon your pride, – a drawback upon success, – a rebuke to your rising, – a stain in your blood, – a blot on your 'scutcheon, – a rent in your garment, – a death's head at your banquet, – Agathocles' pot, – a Mordecai in your gate, – a Lazarus at your door, – a lion in your path, – a frog in your chamber, – a fly in your ointment, – a mote in your eye, – a triumph to your enemy, an apology to your friends, – the one thing not needful, – the hail in harvest, – the ounce of sour in a pound of sweet.

Charles Lamb, 'Poor relations' (1818)

Preface

Writing a year after the French Revolution of 1789, Edmund Burke likened the British state to a venerable oak. Compared to constitutions newly imagined in Revolutionary America and France, he celebrated its natural strength, the growth of countless seasons fair and foul.[1] Perhaps that remains a useful analogy, though old oaks are often wizened and worn. Time has certainly taken its toll. The UK is a composite state of varied territories, comprising two kingdoms, a principality and two-thirds of the province of Ulster, where many of its people wish to be Irish not British. It has a splendidly decorative but constitutionally emasculated head of state – witness the Queen's inability to halt the Conservative government's illegal prorogation of parliament in late 2019. Her father was Emperor of India but the empire is gone, as has membership of the EU. Memories of both have proved deeply divisive.

It is striking that with the most recent phase of globalization, the UK has constitutionally become more insular and more riven by its internal fault lines, not least because it is governed through a complex and confusing constitution. Different devolution settlements have been reached with Northern Ireland, Scotland and Wales, but the division of responsibilities between all tiers of government is Byzantine. Moreover, compared with other Western nations, it is a highly centralized state with marked inequality between its regions, particularly because of London's unmatched prosperity. That is a recipe for discontent.

Although it unwise for historians to make predictions, Northern Ireland and Scotland are now closer to leaving the Union than at any time in over two hundred years. Doing so would involve referendums after protracted discussions about identity, democracy and sovereignty, but where questions around public finances will also loom large. They certainly did before the 2014 Scottish independence referendum when three questions stood out: whether Scotland could afford to go its own way given public expenditure per head was well above the UK average; whether it would be able to manage alone a financial crisis akin to the devastation wrought in 2008; and whether it would really be independent if it continued to use the pound sterling.[2] Less prominently, there were wider questions about the potential costs of Scottish independence, including to other parts of the UK, in terms of reduced economies of scale and new border arrangements.

It was not simply crude materiality that explained the importance of such matters, for taxation and public expenditure express fundamental aspects of a state's nature and raise in the minds of its people telling questions of the value of their political community. As the great nineteenth-century French political theorist Alexis de Tocqueville put it, 'there is almost no issue of public interest which does not derive from taxes or end up in taxes.'[3] Something similar was meant when Benjamin Franklin, borrowing from early eighteenth-century English authors, quipped about the inevitability of death and taxes.[4] But taxes are tricky as well as ubiquitous. As was suggested during the debates over the American constitution in 1787, 'It is well known that the subject of revenue is the most difficult and extensive in the science of government.'[5]

There is nothing new in the centrality of fiscal matters to the functioning of the UK. It has always been an amalgam of nations and regions, each with different resources, histories and hopes. A union state need not be a unitary state in many ways, but particular dynamics and doubts affect the sphere of public finances. Consequently, settling them was central to the unions of 1707 (between Scotland and England and Wales) and 1801 (between Britain and Ireland). They were prominent again with the partition of Ireland in 1921 and the establishment of the Irish Free State in the following year. Significantly, Northern Ireland's customs arrangements proved to be the main sticking point in implementing Brexit after the UK narrowly voted to leave the EU in 2016, because of the impossibility of maintaining the integrity of the UK as a customs union that could diverge from the EU while also avoiding a hard border between Northern Ireland and the Irish Republic. (As a prominent Ulster Unionist put it at the time, 'Trade borders have always run to the core of any nation.'[6]) Yet if these were all important turning points, they rarely settled questions about the territoriality of public finances for long: complaints that the Union as a fiscal compact was territorially inequitable have been raised repeatedly over the centuries. Whatever the ingenuity of politicians and civil servants, no balm has been able to soothe this itch for long. In the following chapters I show why that is, offering a historical perspective on important aspects of the UK's current discontents.

Crucially, the UK's public finances, considered geographically, have always struggled with two major imbalances: with England's much greater size and resources and with London as an unusually large and powerful capital tucked into its south-east corner, closer to Paris, Amsterdam and Brussels than to Edinburgh, Dublin or Newcastle. Furthermore, this was complicated because England's predominance and London's power were intimately tied to changing regional rather than national economic fortunes over time, through industrialization and then deindustrialization, tied as those processes were to the rise and fall of a global empire. This in the context that a distinctive English sense of national community has long been less well developed than is the case in Scotland or Wales – though that appears now to be changing.

At its simplest level, two competing myths have framed all of this. Soon after 1707 the crude piece of Scottish doggerel quoted at the outset of this book described the agents of the new tax state there as a 'dreadfull Monster', with London draining the nation through new and burdensome exactions.[7] Claims that, in public-finance terms, 'the leviathan maw' of London has impoverished distant provinces have been made repetitively ever since, in terms of both siphoning off tribute and tailoring policies to London's distinctive circumstances and preoccupations, in part because of central government's alleged ignorance of the UK's richly varied parts.[8] The opposing myth is that the provinces have been like parasitic poor relations, 'a drain on your purse, a more intolerable dun upon your pride, a drawback upon success, a rebuke to your rising', and that far from being a fantastical ogre London is a golden goose benefiting the whole Union.[9] This too has been a zombie idea, repeatedly rising from the dead, as in the wrong-headed and offensive claim from the 1980s that Scotland was a 'subsidy junkie'.[10]

Such myths about excessive centralization and free-riding are not mere fabrications, however, but ways of seeing, understanding and arguing about whether the UK has been worth it to the people of its nations and regions. In what follows I explore how it has and has not worked as a fiscal compact, of the balances struck between the centre and peripheries in terms of the flows of taxes and public expenditure. It is a study of ideas and principles as well as of numbers and practice. It reflects on the organic nature of the Union, but also the difficulty people have often had in clearly understanding where things stand. Partly that is because of problems of measurement, but more important is that settling the public finances of any union state involves grappling with several inescapable dilemmas or trade-offs. In particular, the quest for uniformity or equality can often come at the cost of fairness or equity. Which, then, should be preferred? And if some diversity or autonomy is to be allowed, how are accountability and responsibility to be maintained? But those challenges are also constrained by desires for frugality or economy and productivity or efficiency. Too much economy can lead to some people and places being 'left behind'; too much public spending on the grounds of equality and equity can erode competitiveness. This book, then, is centrally about the debates and decisions around the competing aims of equality and equity, framed by the constraints of autonomy and accountability and economy and efficiency.

Commonly the tension between equality and equity is considered in terms of differences between rich and poor – for which 'class' is often a shorthand. But where people lived also profoundly affected their relationship to public finances, because of differences in both material circumstances and culture. Should, therefore, contributions to and disbursements from the public purse be uniform across the state's extent, or should they vary geographically? If the latter, on what principles and within what, if any, limits?

Such questions are faced by most states. After all, complaints around paying too much to the centre were major causes of the American and French revolutions and have recently helped to generate moves for greater autonomy or independence in southern Brazil, northern Italy and Catalonia. But the UK has experienced rather different dynamics here: today strong separatist movements in Northern Ireland and Scotland go hand in hand with much greater public expenditure in those places than in Wales or, especially, England.[11] Does that help to explain why 55 per cent voted against Scottish independence in 2014? This book has two main strands, therefore: it sets out the geography of fiscal balances; and it considers how this has affected the operation and perceptions of the Union state.

The central problem is that while all states require some degree of unity, internal geographical variations often place considerable obstacles in the way. It will be easier for some parts to conform than others, because of environmental as well as cultural considerations, related to economic and demographic waxing and waning. After all, states are artificial not natural institutions and, as they evolve, decisions have to be made about what rights and obligations should be compulsory for all. Should the same language, laws and religion be required? Should all enjoy the same protection of their lives and property? Where should uniformity end and diversity begin and how does this relate to ideas of belonging, fairness, assimilation and unity? Answers to those questions may work for a time, only to be unsettled by changes in the economic geography of the state, especially in terms of public finances, the focus of this book.

This is, then, a study of aspects of the political economy of the UK over the last three centuries, of central questions around the public finances of a country that was and, just, remains a major power. Throughout, horse-trading was has been involved – of balancing the demands of different parts of the Union in relation to the core dilemmas I have outlined. Some of the frictions entailed were produced by the unions of 1707 and 1801 and the disunion of 1921–2 and can be thought of as 'national'. But government has also evolved by deciding what taxing and spending should be central and what should be local, in the context of economic changes that have largely been regional. Three interlocking 'frames' are therefore considered in later chapters: national, regional and local.

For many years after 1707, when spending on the military and war debts dominated public expenditure, some territorial variation in taxes was accepted on the grounds of equity. But efforts to apply taxes uniformly across the Union that began in 1707 eventually reached fruition in the 1850s. It was then hoped (by Gladstone and others) that the natural course of things, the iron rule of the market, would in those circumstances equitably equalize economic opportunities and rewards. Irish voices were raised long and loud against such thinking, while continued hardships in the Highlands towards the end of the nineteenth century led to public expenditure being used as the main tool in the attempt to make the fiscal regime fair. This was contemporaneous with the growth of welfare spending to mitigate some of the worst failures of the market mechanism. Wider regional policies expanded somewhat after 1930, but really flourished in the golden age of economic growth between 1945 and 1970. It was implicitly confirmed in the Barnett Formula of 1978, whereby changes in public expenditure in England automatically triggered proportionate changes in the other parts of the Union. But only a year later, with the election of Margaret Thatcher's Conservative government, regional economic policy was downgraded as the Victorian values of Gladstone from around 1850 were revived, straining the Union to breaking point in the process. Devolution in 1999 unsuccessfully attempted to heal that wound, in part because Scottish nationalists had been arguing that 'our oil' in the North Sea provided rich material foundations for independence. But providing a convincing answer to Scotland's own fiscal dilemmas was an important factor in leading to the rejection of independence in the 2014 referendum.

My focus in what follows is upon the ways different parts of the UK have viewed public finances territorially – of the balance of nations throughout, between central and local government since the early nineteenth century and after 1900 between newfangled regions. This pushes somewhat aside the British Empire that was such an important feature of the lives of so many in Britain and Ireland before the 1950s. But for much of its history the empire was, in terms of the UK's public balance sheet, largely self-financing, making few clear calls on domestic taxpayers and contributing directly to the Exchequer much less than might be thought. As so many of the costs of empire were exported, this allowed a certain insularity to infest the debates explored in this book. That said, clearly part of the 'dreadful monster' myth drew on the fact that the City of London was financially a close and active partner of the British state and the British Empire and this need to be recognized.[12] But while such connections have been emphasized by some, this has rarely been in terms of how they played upon the territoriality of Britain's public finances – doubtless in part because people from across the UK were active imperialists, indeed often disproportionately from those parts far removed from London. Consequently, these important dynamics are treated only in passing here.

This book covers a big topic over three centuries rather briefly, thereby foregrounding major questions and developments. While it rests on considerable primary sources, it also depends heavily on the work of many earlier scholars, as my endnotes make clear. But my aim is not synthesis. As with all intellectual endeavours, I adopt certain perspectives. In particular, I am interested in how the Union state has operated domestically, seeking to understand the challenges that it faced and the answers it provided. By attending to its fiscal dilemmas, the voices of both the 'centre' and the 'periphery' are important to what follows. Indeed, studying those dilemmas allows the Union to be understood more holistically than has sometimes been the case. While that will not satisfy either strong unionists or nationalists, it will hopefully allow everyone to understand better why fiscal equity has proved so elusive in the UK.

I

Introduction

States emerge and change in size and form as different balances are struck between enlargement and disunion, often in response to rival pressures for centralization and decentralization.[1] While the consolidation of states has been an important feature of European history in the period covered by this book – there were around five hundred in 1800 but only twenty in 1900 – seeing them only in terms of expansion is limiting and distorting, as some examples show.[2] The creation of an Iberia-wide Spain in the sixteenth century lasted until 1640 when Portugal regained its independence. Germany united in 1871, expanded under the Nazis, was divided in 1945 and united again in 1990. In 1814 the joint monarchy of Norway and Denmark gave way to one between Norway and Sweden, who then separated in 1905. And so on. In recent decades, forces for disunion have grown noticeably, dramatically affecting the Soviet Union and Yugoslavia, while independence movements thrive in Catalonia and Scotland.[3]

The history of the UK has also to be seen as one of splintering as well as merging, with the unions of 1707 and 1801 to be understood alongside the Irish Revolution of the early twentieth century, followed later by increasing calls for Welsh and Scottish independence. Leading studies of these processes tend to focus upon identity politics, constitutional arrangements and the role of empire, with matters of public finances featuring only at major turning points.[4] Such moments were certainly critical, but on a day-to-day basis the Union state also experienced fiscal forces at work that both encouraged and challenged its integrity, coherence and efficiency. Again, this is not a problem peculiar to it. Recently proposed increases in fuel duties sparked the febrile hostility of *les gilets jaunes* in *la France périphérique* to President Macron's central state.[5] Within the UK such challenges have often been framed in national terms – of the interests of England against those of the other parts of the Union. Yet the power of a vaguer anti-centralism, narrower regionalism and the proper balance between local and central government should not be underestimated as key considerations. After all, states are usually internally divided and if nationalist politicians ignore such features, the historian should not. Nations and states are both 'imagined communities' and more rarely coterminous than is commonly acknowledged.[6] The UK is quite like Belgium, Germany and Spain in that regard.

Running an enlarged state is rarely straightforward. A meaningful degree of unification has to be created from component parts that may vary significantly in physical size, resources, environment, population, culture and laws. In particular, differences of geography, memories and mores can put significant obstacles in the way of the smooth running of expanded states. Various ways have been tried to achieve that balancing act, most obviously through formal federalism. As Alexis de Tocqueville put it, the imperative here is that the 'federal system has been created to unite the various advantages that result from the large and the small sizes of nations'.[7] It is a reasoned way of balancing unequal parts within union states. Yet federalism is generally easier to achieve in republics than in monarchies (Germany between 1871 and 1918 is an instructive counter-example): the UK is just that, a collection of kingdoms where widespread and rather instinctive suspicion of federalism has a deep historical tap root. Usually this is ill-considered, such that opposition to federal developments in the EU has emphasized burgeoning centralization, whereas a more federal UK has tended to be damned in terms of excessive decentralization.[8]

A notable feature of the evolution of the UK is that the incorporating unions of 1707 and 1801 were bespoke and different compacts, achieved in the face of considerable opposition. In both cases, opponents were anxious not only about the loss of sovereignty and separate identity, but that the proposed unions would be costly and enervating because of England's undoubted demographic and economic superiority. Both unions were profoundly asymmetrical. And while settlements of a sort were reached at those unions, how the parts of the UK worked with one another subsequently has involved a lot of bumping and barging on the way – between its nations, between central and local government and, mainly in the twentieth century, between its regions. A critical aspect of this is money: where taxes have been raised and the money so collected spent. This raises fundamental questions about the extent to which subjects and citizens are treated uniformly across the state: in particular, significant regional differences have periodically reared their head with regard to whether taxes are light or heavy here and there, or public expenditure territorially discriminatory. Like all states, the UK has had to grapple with the question of how far geographical differences should be ignored and how far they should be managed.

How should such a question be addressed? This chapter provides various contexts for the substantive chapters that follow, particularly by introducing the main concepts used subsequently and by providing a general picture of the UK's different places and people as they changed over time.

UNIONS AND UNIFORMITY

When there are significant differences of circumstances and aims between the parties, forging political unions requires deciding how complete or how limited they should be. Federal solutions offer one way ahead, even if in practice they have taken various forms, with the central state usually responsible for certain general, often outward-looking functions such as diplomacy and defence, with others devolved to its regions or provinces, such as policing and education.[9] Commonly they depend on written constitutions setting out the division of responsibilities between the federal and state governments, with a supreme court adjudicating disputes between them. Fiscal federalism makes explicit how such clarity is to be funded. So, for example, initially the federal USA and Germany both depended heavily on customs duties, with other taxes collected by their component states.[10] But there are alternative arrangements for unions. Greater autonomy for constituent states is provided through confederations such as Sweden–Norway in the nineteenth century, hybrid federal–confederal states like Belgium today or other ad hoc arrangements such as

Spain's. But as the case of Quebec, Catalonia and the Basque Country show, heightened provincial autonomy does not preclude the existence of strong separatist movements. After all, the UN Charter asserts the right of people to self-determination in their political arrangements, without helping very much to answer the question 'Who are we the people?'

In its expansion and contraction, the UK eschewed following any constitutional model or historical example. But its unions and disunions were not stabs in the dark. They were produced by individuals who, as part of a Europe-wide culture, pondered the varied political arrangements of the ancient and medieval worlds, of the comings and goings of tribes, cities, states and empires. Around 1700 there were more immediate examples to hand, notably in Iberia, France, the Holy Roman Empire, the Dutch Republic and Poland–Lithuania, all of which had recently shifted shape and form.[11] The efflorescence of political thought that began in Renaissance Italy offered principled ways of thinking about such rich possibilities for state formation.

More directly, the regnal union of Scotland and England in 1603, when James VI of Scotland also became James I of England, led to concerted thinking about what form a fuller union between the two countries might take.[12] Similarly, various plans for a British–Irish union were sketched in the eighteenth century, while the growth of Britain's empire across the Atlantic encouraged many ideas for unifying colonies in some way, including James II's 'Dominion of New England' (1686–9) and, prompted by Benjamin Franklin, the Albany plan of union in 1754.[13] From the middle of the eighteenth century, written constitutions proliferated, with those of republican America and France leading the way, informed as they were by a close attention to political principles.[14] France's proximity was important here, but, as part of the anglophone world, America's federal constitution subtly influenced opinion in Britain, from its ratification in 1788 through to arguments for disunion that culminated in its civil war (1861–5) and beyond.[15] Importantly, in stark contrast to what it was prepared to contemplate at home, from the middle of the nineteenth century British governments began making constitutions for parts of its empire, often federal ones, such as Canada in 1867.[16] This is, to put it mildly, curious.

At their core, the unions of 1707 and 1801 were limited and markedly different 'incorporating unions', based on extending the jurisdiction and governance of the Westminster parliament over Scotland and then Ireland following the abolition of the parliaments at Edinburgh and Dublin. For most of its history since 1707, the sovereignty of the Westminster parliament has been the constitutional heart of the UK, centred on its statute-making powers (laws agreed to by monarch, peers and commons), subject to the justice of the courts. The evolutionary potential of new statutes and the near absence of fundamental laws have been prized by opponents of a written constitution in the UK, but advocacy of undivided parliamentary sovereignty has also been at the heart of resistance to devolution and membership of the EEC/EU.[17] Significantly, the Scottish National Party has supported the highly questionable view that Scotland's tradition of sovereignty is popular (based on the consent of the people) rather than parliamentary, supposedly demonstrating that the Union is incompatible with Scottish ways of doing things since time out of mind.[18]

A key difficulty of the UK's approach to its expansion and contraction is that this has often left unsettled points of principle central to political unions. Yet the unions and disunions that have produced the UK have had, nonetheless, to decide what rights and obligations should be common to all of its citizens. In turn, considerations about the extent of uniformity immediately lead to those about equality, a complex and politically contested ideal. As Amartya Sen has urged, it is important to be clear quite what equality is at issue given the wonderful range of human diversity – at the very least it is important to distinguish between equality before the law, equality of opportunity and economic equality. However, it is notable that questions about equality often divide opinion politically between enthusiasts for it on the left and critics of it on the right, fundamentally because they are closely bound to wider differences about the weight to be accorded in daily life to morality and the market.[19] Still, equality might suggest that all members of a state should be dealt with uniformly (or 'indiscriminately' in the language of the mid-nineteenth century), come what may – something that in turn can be seen as leading to assimilation. It is predicated on the belief that all citizens have some inherent rights, most obviously to the state's protection of their lives and property, and obligations, most obviously (given the concerns of this book) to pay taxes to meet the costs of those rights. The language of rights has itself developed significantly since the American Declaration of Independence of 1776.[20] Rights, it must be stressed, are acquired and exercised outside the market: they are inherently political.

Given the subject of this book, the complication here is that people's circumstances have varied geographically in Britain over time, waxing and waning with industrialization and deindustrialization – shifting prosperity on to and then away from the coalfields, for example.[21] Consequently, some people are more or less able to pay taxes and more or less needful of public goods, which is to say that a rigid approach to equality may be inequitable. Equity requires recognizing that people's circumstances can differ considerably and that public finances have to be tailored accordingly – that is, unequally – through redistribution to a greater or lesser extent, either by progressive taxation or targeted spending. Seemingly at issue here is the principle of derivation, of whether the people of particular areas should receive the same share of public expenditure as they have paid in taxes.[22] In practice, that has very rarely been the case. But it also relates to a fundamental question of whether states should seek to aid economically struggling communities over the very long term, or whether they should allow them to wither in the face of altered economic realities. After all, as the Austrian political economist Joseph Schumpeter argued, creative destruction is inherent in the development of capitalist economies.[23]

At one extreme are market fundamentalists, as in this example from 1798: 'It is in the interest of every man to engage in that line of business which is adapted to the circumstances in which he is placed, and not to force a business for carrying on of which every requisite is wanting.'[24] In a similar vein, in 2007 a Treasury paper questioned regional policies, stating that they run 'counter to the natural growth process and are difficult to justify on efficiency grounds'.[25] But the changing fortunes of places raise difficult questions about the relative weight to be given to the importance of individuals, families and communities. Famously, Norman Tebbit, Secretary of State for Employment, told the Conservative party conference in 1981 that in the 1930s his unemployed father 'didn't riot; he got on his bike and looked for work and he kept looking 'til he found it'. But this emphasis upon individual labour mobility pays little regard to the familial, social and cultural ties that bind many people to their locales.

As the reach of the state has grown, such considerations have been bound up with changes in public goods as recognized needs, such as schools, hospitals, utilities and infrastructure. Determining what is and what is not a need to be met publicly, and whether it should be met by central or local government, is, as in questions of equality and rights, fundamentally a political decision about reasonable standards of life and the distribution of costs and benefits.[26] As one economist supposedly wondered, 'What do you mean by need? Is a need just something you want, but aren't prepared to pay for?'[27] Unsurprisingly, such thinking feeds into the idea of 'unwarranted' subsidies from more to less prosperous regions or nations, rather than the more neutral language of supportive transfers and risk sharing as inherent benefits of a union state.

If the tension between equality and equity also raises issues of rights and needs, in practice public finances are also influenced by notions of economy and efficiency. These are rather less complicated to consider. It is easy to see why frugal governments are often welcomed and that wasting taxpayers' money is condemned, even if economists approach such matters very differently, with John Maynard Keynes and his followers arguing since the 1930s for the efficacy of macroeconomic management by central government, and neoliberals favouring limited intervention by the state in markets. More politically contentious are the effects of pursuing economic efficiency. If greater productivity seems highly desirable in a world of competitive markets, there may be a trade-off because the rewards are almost always shared unequally across society.[28] In many countries, industrialization eventually helped to reduce inequality in income and wealth, but since the 1980s that trend has gone into reverse in Britain and America, associated with a sectoral shift away from manufacturing towards services, as Tony Atkinson and Thomas Piketty have clearly shown.[29] On the other hand, policies designed to reduce inequality are argued by some to lead to less economic efficiency – as reflected in criticisms of nationalized industries. Ultimately, this is about the relative weight given to financial rather than social values.

As is starting to become clear, the question of whether the UK was worth it for its people is deceptively simple, but quickly involves weighty questions about balancing the scope of the market and the reach of politics. There are two final twists here. First, as already suggested, are 'people' to be considered individually or collectively? There is a strong presumption in economics (and law) to focus on the former, its clarity aiding particular types of logical analysis.[30] For example, two economists, one of them a former Governor of the Bank of England, have emphatically asserted that 'all taxes are ultimately taxes on individuals, and it is in this connection and only in this connection that considerations of equity enter the analysis of taxation. It simply makes no sense to talk about "fairness" between sectors of the economy, or industries, or between the personal and corporate sectors.'[31] Such thinking usually means paying little or no heed to territorial considerations. Geographers naturally demur, while political scientists with their interest in groups have to think about the territorial jurisdictions relevant to those groups.[32] Indeed, the following chapters are all about the interplay between evolving ideas of economics, geography and politics.

Yet if the analytical frame is the collective rather than the individual, then using the UK as a whole has seemed too broad to many, with its constituent nations, regions and cities offered up as alternatives. None of these are better, only different. Importantly, if a state has, Janus-like, to look both inwards and outwards, localities and regions are often hard for it to get into focus. In these ways, 'seeing like a state' is not at all straightforward.[33] Consequently, central government in London has found it much easier to deal with the constituent nations of the UK. Because of industrialization and urbanization, regions were reformulated in the nineteenth century and then got caught up with ideas about federalizing the UK that began to develop at the end of the nineteenth century, with Winston Churchill and the Fabians invoking the seven provinces of the Anglo-Saxon 'heptarchy', while in 1919 the geographer C. B. Fawcett proposed dividing the UK into fifteen provinces with their capitals, twelve in England and with the other nations each constituting one of the remaining three provinces (Map 1).[34] Such ideas got nowhere, but in the interwar period administrative necessity began to require central government and

Map 1. C. B. Fawcett's proposed provinces of England, 1919

some corporations to devise new regions, though never to any consistent template.

Secondly, for individuals or collectives to assess the value of the UK in public-finance terms seems simple enough on the face of it – what is the balance between how much they put in and how much they get out, directly and indirectly? But especially when collectives are at issue, it can be tricky to pin down the actual rather than the perceived effects of taxation and how one assesses the impacts of general expenditure. Additionally, the figures provided in official statistics available since the early eighteenth century have often not been broken down territorially to the extent that some contemporaries have wanted. Conceptual difficulties have melded with data limitations in the long debates over the dreadful monster and its poor relations.

The patchy nature of records about the territoriality of British public finances has important implications, not only for setting out what the actual situation was, but also for how it was perceived, creating a void that could be filled by guesswork, estimation and deduction. But that often meant that discussion was ill-founded, riddled with assumptions and misconceptions, and expressed assertively and polemically. It is, in any case, hard to assess what people think about central government taxes and spending. From time to time, discontent has boiled over, while now and then glimpses can be found of people's attitudes. But the silent majority is just that, while, at the extreme, smuggling and fraud are by their nature usually hidden from history and in any case more likely to be stimulated by the opportunities for illicit activities generated as a consequence of governments' demands than by principled hostility to taxation.

Moreover, the great growth of state activity in twentieth-century Britain, with complex sources of income and complex patterns of expenditure, has made it very hard for people to judge how far the state is working in their interests. Indeed, misperceptions have flourished. For example, in 2014 a poll found that people thought that 42 per cent of central government expenditure was on health, education, pensions and welfare, whereas the actual figure was 69 per cent. By contrast, people thought that the combined costs of central government, the EU and overseas aid was five times higher than was actually the case (4 rather than 20 per cent).[35] In fact, there is nothing new in this, 'because every one has a natural propensity to believe, that men who have the handling of public money will misapply it', as the Scottish agriculturalist and economist James Anderson wrote in 1792.[36] Such misperceptions are interesting in their own right, but 'real' in that they affect behaviour.

It is particularly important, then, not to fall into the trap of expecting or stereotyping certain types of behaviour. While attitudes can be gauged from public discourse through the period or deduced from election results, at least over the last century, this is just as likely to be misleading as insightful. For example, although it is commonly said that the US federal Internal Revenue Service and the taxes they administer are passionately disliked by many Americans, detailed studies have shown that many are proud to pay taxes.[37] Similarly, in late twentieth-century Britain, the British Social Attitudes surveys consistently found little support for reductions in government taxation and spending – though whether 'expressed preferences' are 'true' is another matter.[38]

TAXING AND SPENDING

At heart this book examines the relationship between changes in the internal economic geography of the UK and central government's taxing and spending considered geographically – including grants from central to local government. This involves exploring seemingly simple issues of first determining the territoriality of taxation and public spending and then uncovering the discussions that ensued. In practice, achieving the first part of that objective is far from straightforward. It is not just that the evidence is patchy – oddly, in certain respects it is better for the eighteenth than the nineteenth century – but that a number of definitional and conceptual matters have to be addressed.

Taxation provides the starting point for this book. A government must first collect revenue to spend, for public debts can only help get around that bind to a limited degree and for a limited time. Yet, while it might seem obvious enough what is meant by taxation, a little digging soon turns up some important features that have to be grasped. Take, for example, this definition by a leading scholar: 'taxes are compulsory payments, exacted by the state, that do not confer any direct individual entitlement to specific goods or services in return.'[39] Three central elements need to be considered here.

First, sovereignty is the basis of compulsion in taxation, though, reciprocally, taxes denote membership of the state by its taxpayers.[40] As one Scottish author noted in 1816, 'taxes are vitally essential in vindicating the rights, and maintaining the structure of civilized government', providing it with the wherewithal to maintain order.[41] But disagreements as to what government spends money on and the loss of income to taxpayers mean that taxation can be judged by some to be unacceptably coercive and economically damaging. Moreover, the inherently unequal relationship between the individual and the state necessarily widens as the latter grows in relative importance within society. Consequently, though tax rebellions may have been rare in Britain, smuggling has periodically been very significant and the wider question of 'tax morale' – attitudes around the willingness to pay – is an important consideration in the following chapters.[42]

Second, taxes are collected by the 'state'. A lot of ink has been spilled on defining such an institution, but here it means simply the successive governments of the UK. Yet since 1707 different tiers of those governments – central, county, boroughs and metropolitan districts, parishes – have imposed taxes with some transfers of receipts within the governmental hierarchy, especially from central to local administrations. To simplify matters, this book focuses mainly on what central government has done, though the changing fiscal balance between central and local government provides an important subsidiary theme from the middle of the nineteenth century.

Finally, when people are taxed they are not directly buying services, but contributing to the maintenance of the common good. Importantly, taxes differ from insurance payments to the state for particular welfare goods. Unlike many countries, such as Germany, the UK has come to make heavier use of taxation than insurance payments, blurring hypothecation – that is, the connection between particular revenue streams and particular public expenditures.[43] Even so, deciding on what constitutes the common good beyond the minimal provision of security is fraught, and easier to achieve when the procedures for doing so have wider legitimacy – returning discussion to the subject of tax morale. Subsequent chapters consider how that was done, initially under a highly exclusive and oligarchical political system, then from 1832 under a gradually reforming one until all adult women were given the vote in 1928.

Generally, historians have seen the impressive amounts of taxes that found their way to London over the last three centuries as reflecting the robust fiscal health of the wider state, as well as helping to explain its considerable military power. They have shown how much the relatively well-resourced 'fiscal-military state' of eighteenth-century England depended on efficiently collected duties on domestically produced goods by the excise service. That continued to play a part in the nineteenth century, but the historian Martin Daunton has powerfully argued that building trust between taxers and the taxed in Britain has rested on a range of moral and political as well as practical considerations, including rectitude and transparency.[44] An argument that I develop is that bringing the contested unions of 1707 and 1801 into the discussion raises important issues about both the legitimacy and power of the Union state that have previously been underappreciated.[45] As such it brings a historical perspective to a distinguished body of work by economists and political scientists (especially of Scotland) about the territoriality of public finances and the often confused workings of the UK since the late nineteenth century.[46]

Taxes come in different shapes and sizes and with different purposes – as suggested by the abundant synonyms for 'tax': duty, impost, levy, rate, tariff, tithe, toll, tribute. If direct taxes on individuals or entities are commonly distinguished from indirect taxes on goods and services, linked to the view that direct taxes tend to be 'progressive', falling more heavily on the better-off than indirect, 'regressive' ones, these are cruder categories than is often assumed. Much depends on what is being taxed: indirect taxes on luxuries such as caviar are clearly taxes on those with high disposable incomes.[47] More important for my concerns is that the impact of taxes can vary geographically. For example, introducing a tax on land in the 1690s had to grapple with the fact that rentals were much higher in and around London than in northern England. Similarly, taxation of many domestic outputs, such as bricks, coal and spirits, has to consider that they are neither produced nor consumed everywhere. Inescapably, taxing them has territorial considerations, as do certain import duties.

What is clear is that the number and types of taxes proliferated first in the eighteenth and then in the twentieth century, with many taxes abolished between 1815 and 1880. In 1707 it was very straightforward, with the main taxes in Britain consisting of just the direct land tax, and with duties on a handful of domestically produced commodities, chiefly beer and its raw materials, collected by the excise service and on imported goods collected by the customs service. Unquestionably, the number of different types of tax and the scope of taxation have increased significantly since then, to raise more money and to raise it from more points within society. But the matter is complicated because taxes sometimes aim to affect behaviour as well as to raise money. Customs duties can be tariffs to a greater or lesser extent, while taxes on alcohol, tobacco and air travel seek in part to reduce their consumption. Health, morals and economic objectives drive tax policy, along with the needs of the Exchequer. This raises fundamental questions about the grounds on which taxes should seek to be applied universally, and how selective they should be. It is easy to think about this in terms of different social groups – the rich, say – but, as already noted, taxing certain things may also involve territorial factors. For example, in 1763 a tax was introduced on cider, on the grounds that its consumption in some western and south-western counties of England meant that duties on beer and malt raised very little there: the aim was to ensure that alcohol was taxed to the same degree everywhere. But the cider counties complained loudly against a measure said to be 'exorbitant, unequal, partial', pointing up the many advantages, natural and man-made, enjoyed by the barley-growing (and therefore beer-swilling) counties of eastern England.[48]

Inevitably the growth in different types of taxes has involved debates over their relative merits, requiring criteria to be stated. Just as certainly, there is limited agreement on that. To Adam Smith, who discussed taxation at length in the *Wealth of Nations* (1776), and who was a Scottish customs commissioner for the last twelve years of his life, there were four fundamentals to good taxation: that they be proportionate to the ability to pay, certain, convenient and cheap to collect.[49] The last three of those 'canons' are largely uncontentious. But the question of the ability to pay is much more complicated. First is the difficulty of assessing ability, of how far and how thoroughly the state should inform itself about individual circumstances: distaste for an intrusive state has a long history in Britain.[50] Second, where taxes are levied, their formal incidence is not always where they finally fall – their effective incidence. If, say, land is taxed, it might first appear to fall only on landowners and their tenants, but it is easy to see how they might pass on some or all of such costs to their labourers, consumers and suppliers. Smith recognized this very considerable difficulty, usually thought of in terms of national social inequalities, though as will become clear there is an important territorial dimension to it. The first of Smith's four canons is also tricky because it strays into the subjective terrain of equity and whether what is fair is the same as what is efficient. Utilitarianism from the late eighteenth century, marginal utility theory a century later and today's 'optimal taxation' literature have each provided a way of resolving the conundrum. But it is wholly unrealistic to see all of this as only a matter of finances, for, as we have seen, it raises questions about individual rights, obligations, choices and the very nature of the relationship between a state and its people.

Another way of considering such issues is to think about what economists since 1974 have called the Laffer curve (Figure 1), named after the American economist Arthur Laffer – though, as we will see, the idea is much older in origin. It provides a useful simplification,

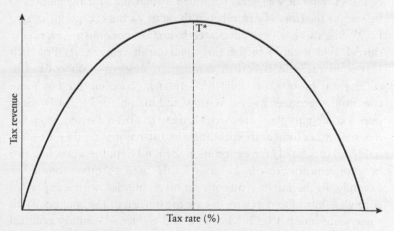

Figure 1. The Laffer curve

showing the curvilinear relationship between tax rates and income raised. Critically, beyond a certain point higher tax rates produce lower income because they discourage taxable activity or encourage avoidance, smuggling and fraud. But the optimal tax point (T*) is not the same for everyone. In particular, most taxes are inherently likely to bear more heavily on the poor than the rich. This might be a simple arithmetic relationship – that a person twice as rich as another can bear twice the level of taxation – but it might involve a more complex geometric relationship, for example that a person twice as rich can bear five times the level of taxation. The former seems more intuitive, but the latter is more likely. No less important, should we conceptualize about taxation in relation to individuals, families, communities, interests, societies or economies? That all depends on what is being addressed. As has been noted, while economists tend in such matters to look to the individual, other social scientists, including geographers, focus upon collectives of one sort or another. The following chapters unpick the history of some of these differences. How did people at the time think about the issues the Laffer curve points towards and how did that affect the public finances of the Union state?

Two further contextual elements are important in the appreciation and discussion of taxing and spending in the UK over the last three centuries. First, it was usual for much of that time for the market to be seen as the rule, as natural, and the state as the exception, as artifice. While this has been advocated by many economists – especially since David Ricardo in the early nineteenth century, via Friedrich Hayek in the mid twentieth century, to modern neoliberals – in continental Europe, particularly Germany, economic life has more commonly been seen as *both* natural and man-made.[51] Clearly wider norms come into play here. Second, there has been a strong tendency to separate taxation and expenditure in discussions. Yet they are inevitably related, partly for expectations around hypothecation but also because expenditure can be consciously used to offset taxes. For example, in the late seventeenth century bounties on the export of corn were introduced in part to ease the burden of the land tax. With some justification Joseph Massie, a mid-eighteenth-century political economist, called such largesse 'un-taxing'.[52] And benefits such as

mortgage tax relief allow claims of expenditure against tax liabilities –
what is termed 'tax expenditure'. Establishing a dividing line between
such indirect and more explicit public expenditure is not always easy
(and often pointless), though of course successful public expenditure
to aid the economy will often increase tax revenues. But even so, it is
also important to grasp how taxation and expenditure can be linked
in principle. Adam Smith, for example, subtly argued that the 'subjects of every state ought to contribute towards the support of the
Government, as nearly as possible, in proportion to their respective
abilities; that is, in proportion to the revenue which they respectively
enjoy under the protection of the State'.[53]

By linking taxation and expenditure, if only indirectly, Smith appears
rather different from the cartoonish depiction of him as the great liberal
advocate of the free market. Here Smith was adopting an important
position with respect to what is called 'distributional justice' – how
property is accumulated and dispersed within society. Samuel Fleischacker, a political philosopher, has suggested that Smith was proposing
something fairly new here, because it was commonly thought at the
time that poverty was needed to ensure people worked to avoid it or
because poverty was considered part of the divine order.[54] That may
be, but there have been major developments in the level of welfare and
economic management most expected the state to provide. The poor
law gave very basic welfare provision for much of the period, initially
in England and Wales until it was extended to Scotland and Ireland in
the mid-nineteenth century, but from the late nineteenth century education, pensions, unemployment benefits, health care and more were
introduced across the UK. Unemployment came to be seen less as the
consequence of personal failings than of capricious market forces, and
individual ill-health as a scourge linked to unavoidable poverty and
bad luck that the whole of society should address. Providing welfare
inevitably involved redistributing resources not only between social
groups but also between places. This has often, however, not addressed
the causes of inequalities, be they social or territorial.

Historians have shown how, in the twentieth century, central government spent heavily on both war and welfare, but then highlighted one
or the other to support different characterizations of the state.[55] However, in terms of the territoriality of public finances in relation to the

operation of the Union state, these were less important than significantly increased spending on infrastructure from the 1920s and regional aid from the 1930s. Within a markedly more democratic political system, both obviously raised questions about value for money, addressing which required cost-benefit analysis that had first been formalized in the nineteenth century. While there is an institutional and technocratic history to this – the Treasury's 'green book' setting out assessment criteria has gone through various iterations in its forty-year history – more significant here is that in considering spending on infrastructure and regional aid, quantitative financial and qualitative social conceptions of value have often been in tension, tied to how far market forces should be managed.[56]

Resolving such tensions politically has involved considerable horse-trading, to reduce which different types of funding formulas have been developed. This is most sophisticated in calculations of central government grants to local governments, but also, and more famously, includes the Barnett Formula of 1978, which sought to limit special pleading by Northern Ireland, Scotland and Wales in the annual budgetary processes. But it too has now become politically contested, while governments have understandably allowed for funding outside such formulas in special cases. This is always liable to raise two related aspects of 'poor relations' thinking. First, in a zero-sum way, that if a scheme in one place gets extra funding, then that is not available for spending elsewhere. This can be exacerbated because, usually for political reasons, some may find it helpful rhetorically to characterize public spending in such binary terms. Second, in a free-rider way, that extra spending in one place can result not from proven need but from excessive leverage, often political or corporate.

PLACE AND PEOPLE

There are several varieties of British exceptionalism, often resting on its island situation, just visible, off the European mainland. Supposedly, in the words of Shakespeare's John O'Gaunt, it is a 'precious stone set in the silver sea', 'the envy of less happier lands'. Such romantic patriotism mutated over the centuries – masking the decay and destruction inherent to economic change – while the island's size was later juxtaposed with the enormous extent of its global empire.[57] Surely, it was once thought, this spoke of the remarkable qualities of its people and institutions in forging power and influence from such limited means. Such comforting stories are obviously mythic, most relevantly here because usually no place is left for Ireland, while irritatingly England and Britain are often used interchangeably (though far from only by the English).

A foundational and much repeated error is that Britain is a small island, a 'little world' in John O'Gaunt's words again. It is not. By area it is the seventh largest island in the world fully outside the Arctic Circle, twice the size of Ireland, eight times that of Sicily and twenty times that of Jamaica, by far the largest of Britain's Caribbean islands at the high noon of empire. Malta is a small island and so is Singapore: neither Britain nor Ireland is. Moreover, France and Spain may be bigger than Britain, but they are also more compact: as the crow flies, it is further from the south-west to the north-east corner of mainland Britain than it is in those countries – greater still when including the Scilly and Northern Isles.[58] Similarly, Edinburgh is significantly further from London than Lyon from Paris, while Aberdeen is closer to Bergen in Norway than to London (Map 2). Consequently, the tyranny of distance, if eroded over time, has been a rather more important aspect of the Union state after 1707 than is usually allowed. London's position in the south-east of England enabled it powerfully to connect Britain with continental Europe, but as a capital city it was fairly remote from many of the island's regions. Haltwhistle, close to Hadrian's Wall in Northumberland, England's most northerly county, claims to be the geographic centre of the UK, but as the crow flies it is only seventy miles from Edinburgh yet 258 miles from London.

Quite apart from the productivity of the economic base, the physical size of a state, how compact it is, how densely populated, how concentrated in towns, all influence fiscal systems. Potential administrative economies of scale are a large part of that, in terms of both income and expenditure. Larger unified economies, with larger markets, also allow heightened productivity through greater extensions of the division of labour, which might again benefit both sides of public accounts. And with greater size comes greater opportunity for sharing

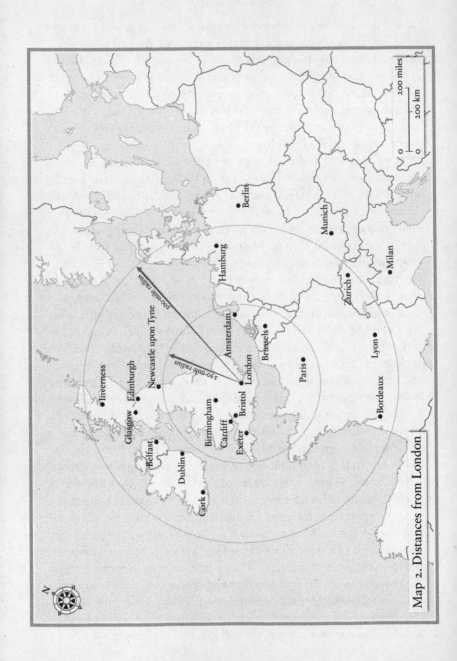

Map 2. Distances from London

risks – through what are in effect insurance schemes as well as more directly redistributive policies – increasing the chances for greater stability, be it social, economic or political.

Greater size is not, however, an unalloyed good, for it also matters how homogeneous a state is, and larger ones tend to have more diverse preferences to satisfy and more diverse cultures for the state to manage. With greater size comes greater distance, physical and often cultural, between the capital and the periphery, the core and the margins – such language is itself suggestive of division and disunity. Size, therefore, provides greater opportunities but also greater challenges. Getting the balance right is rarely easy, with clear implications in the case of Britain for thinking about the making and unmaking of the Union: at its greatest extent in the nineteenth century it was two and a half times the area of England (Table 1).[59]

Table 1. Areas of the territories of Britain and Ireland

| | Area km² | % of UK | | |
		1707–1800	1801–1922	1922–
England	130,000	57	40	53
Wales	21,000	9	6	9
Scotland	78,000	34	24	32
Ireland (whole island)	98,000		30	
Northern Ireland	14,000			6

If Britain is larger and less compact than is often imagined, it is also physically unusually varied. The wide span of latitudes means a significant range in hours of daylight between the southerly and northerly extremes, while tidal variations are also considerable, including the second greatest in the world at the mouth of the River Severn. The prevailing movement of the weather from west to east affects the geography of pastoral and arable agriculture – though the Gulf Stream has a more benign influence on western coasts than the chill North Sea on eastern ones.[60] However, these factors are secondary to geological variation, directly leading by one account to 44 distinct relief regions in Britain (10 in Scotland, 8 in Wales, the rest in England) and 16 in Ireland.[61] As much as France, Britain is awash with *terroirs*.

Geological variation within the UK has three main features that are relevant to this study. It explains why Scotland has around 900 coastal islands (97 inhabited) compared to 25 in England and Wales. This became an important issue with the growth in public goods from the late nineteenth century linked to changing norms of what constitutes the essentials of life. Many of the islands are sparsely populated and difficult to access, making the provision of public goods there more costly.

Geology manifests itself, secondly, in terms of variations in relief, with important consequences for differences in rainfall and temperature and the ability to provide infrastructure and utilities. With temperature decreasing by nearly 1 degree centigrade for every 100 metres in elevation, shorter growing seasons are an inescapable feature of upland Britain. With much more of their territory being hilly and mountainous, this particularly affects Scotland and Wales, encouraging forestry, pastoral farming and the cultivation of lower-value crops such as oats. Much of south-west England has a growing season of over 310 days, whereas in most of the Scottish Highlands it is under 210 days. Finally, the proximity of south-east England to the economies of continental Europe has also been a significant structural feature. As has been noted, 'ecology favoured the English'.[62] Industrialization, urbanization and globalization have weakened the significance of such variations in the UK, but they have not eradicated them.

Finally, coal-, oil- and gas fields have all been important to the economic fortunes of the Union state. In particular, the link between coal and industrialization in Britain is well attested.[63] In 1700 Britain was already globally distinctive for the large amounts of 'black gold' it produced and consumed, but in the age of steam (circa 1760–1914) there was a significant redistribution of a rapidly rising population on to or near to its coalfields, especially to south Wales, the Midlands, north-west England, Yorkshire's West Riding, Tyne-Tees and Scotland's central belt (Map 3). Tellingly, the first geological map of England, southern Scotland and Wales was produced in 1815, and for the whole of Scotland in 1836, speaking of the need of a rapidly industrializing society to understand its bedrock for mining, canals and railways.

As this suggests, an appreciation of the changes to the size and geographical distribution of population is foundational for what follows,

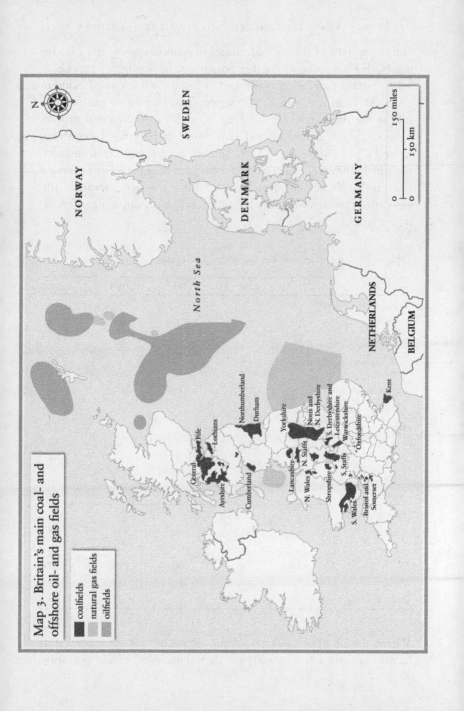

Map 3. Britain's main coal- and offshore oil- and gas fields

coalfields
natural gas fields
oilfields

NORWAY

SWEDEN

DENMARK

GERMANY

North Sea

NETHERLANDS

BELGIUM

Central
Fife
Lothians
Ayrshire
Cumberland
Northumberland
Durham
Yorkshire
Lancashire
N. Wales
N. Staffs
Notts and
N. Derbyshire
S. Derbyshire and
Leicestershire
Shropshire
S. Staffs
Warwickshire
Oxfordshire
Bristol and
Somerset
S. Wales
Kent

N

150 miles
150 km

indicating some of the core dynamics of economic geography. Fortunately, this is an area where it is possible to be reasonably precise, at least since the first census was taken in Britain in 1801 and Ireland in 1821. As Table 2 shows, Britain's population increased nearly ninefold in the three centuries since 1700, with especially rapid growth between the late eighteenth and early twentieth centuries. By contrast, Ireland's population grew very quickly in the eighteenth century, peaking in the early 1840s at over 8 million, before the Great Famine later in that decade killed perhaps 1 million through starvation and associated diseases. Massive emigration followed, shrinking its population further.

Table 2. Britain and Ireland's population, 1700–2001

	1700	1801	1901	2001
Population in millions				
England	5.0	8.4	30.1	49.1
Scotland	1.1	1.6	4.5	5.1
Wales	0.4	0.6	2.0	2.9
Britain	6.5	10.6	36.6	57.1
Ireland (whole island)	1.8	5.2	4.4	5.6
% of UK population				
England	77	53	73	84
Scotland	17	10	11	9
Wales	6	4	5	5
Ireland		33	11	
Northern Ireland				3
Persons per km²				
England	38	65	232	378
Scotland	14	21	58	65
Wales	19	29	95	138
Britain	28	46	160	249
Ireland (whole island)	18	53	45	57

Within the UK, England's population share has always exceeded its territorial share and is now greater than it has ever been. Importantly, the Union of 1707 has been followed by a gradual relative decline in population for Scotland, so that its share is now half what it had originally been and its population density is one-sixth that of England. More dramatically, from the 1840s Ireland's population declined significantly both absolutely and relatively, falling to one-third of its peak level. Wales, by contrast, has generally maintained its population share, crudely because industrialization on its coalfield was, relative to its population, more influential than in Scotland or Ireland. Although it is easy to think of it as a largely agrarian society, Wales is now twice as densely populated as Scotland. In many respects the consequences of Scotland and Ireland's relative decline in population provide a central thread in this book, because to the critics of the impact of the unions of 1707 and 1801 it powerfully attested to the growing appetite of the dreadful monster.

While England's population growth outstripped that of both Scotland and Wales, all three countries became urbanized more rapidly than most of the rest of Europe. Ireland, by contrast, remained much more rural and agricultural during its time within the Union.[64] Britain became a predominantly urban society in the middle of the nineteenth century, and by 1911 over 75 per cent of the population lived in urban districts.[65] This transformation began in earnest with London's extraordinary growth in the seventeenth century, becoming the largest city in Western Europe on the eve of the Union of 1707. Around then, England was over twice as urbanized as Scotland (13 and 5 per cent respectively), with Wales barely urbanized at all. In the first century of the Union, the rapid growth of Edinburgh and Glasgow in particular narrowed that gap, despite the mushrooming of centres of industry and trade in England. In 1801 England had 49 places with a population of over 10,000, Scotland had 8 and Wales had none.[66] Although Dublin was the second largest city in the Union in 1801, Ireland as a whole was and remained markedly more rural. From the early nineteenth century, although urbanization continued in Scotland it was more rapid in England and Wales, a pattern that continued into the twentieth century. However, though in 1951 England and Wales were 77 per cent urban and Scotland 60 per cent, the critical point is not that Scotland was less urbanized but that England and Wales were urbanized to an unusual extent compared to most of Western Europe.[67]

Britain's urbanization depended on the growth of many different types of towns and cities, but, throughout, London's enormous size has set it above and apart from the rest. For the past three centuries it has been many times larger than any other town or city in Britain (demographically, the second city was initially Edinburgh, then Manchester and then Birmingham). Yet, broadly speaking, demographically its fortunes since 1700 have risen, fallen and since the 1980s risen again (Figure 2). It is remarkable that as industrialization took hold on Britain's coalfields from the late seventeenth century, London was still able to loom so large economically and demographically. Industrialization did not pass it by; it took place within it and fed its greater growth, not least because of London's pivotal role in the increasingly global orientation of the British economy.[68] The coming of the railways, with London at the hub of many mainlines, enhanced this considerably; its population overtook Scotland's then, an advantage it has never surrendered. By contrast, London's relative decline – it lost 1.7 million people between 1951 and 1981 – was linked to the collapse of its port, the siphoning off of tens of thousands of people into satellite new towns and the heyday of regional economic planning by central government.[69] A consideration throughout this book is how far its fortunes have depended on its central place within the Union state and vice versa.

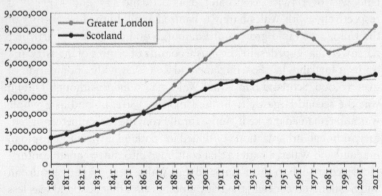

Note: There was no census in 1941, so the figures are estimated.

Figure 2. Population of Greater London and Scotland, 1801–2011

London's demographic potency reflects its restlessly evolving functionality. As a capital city of a multinational state and, for much of the period, a global empire, it was naturally the home of the royal court (with the monarch the head of the established religion) and executive government, parliament and central law courts. (Although Scotland retained its own separate legal system after 1707, centring on the Court of Session in Edinburgh, Scots used the House of Lords as a high court strikingly often.[70]) Such powerful centripetal forces have fed into and off London's wider economic and social role as a financial centre, as the UK's largest port until 1945, as a major site of industry and as a cultural powerhouse. Notoriously, however, London has had a dark underside. Cramped and unsanitary conditions wrought a terrible toll on lives in the eighteenth and nineteenth centuries. Consequently, London's growing population (0.6 million in 1700 and 6.2 million in 1901) often depended heavily on replenishing losses by attracting people from elsewhere, often to live in very poor districts. This was one way by which its demographic influence was far more pervasive than just its functional promiscuity and brute size suggest. And then, with the rise of commuting after 1850 and the burgeoning of satellite towns, especially since 1945, London has been essential to the growth of the wider south-east region even in the face of rapid industrialization elsewhere. This region is now far and away the UK's most prosperous.

Britain was a precocious industrializer, enabling it economically to outperform most of its international competitors for much of the eighteenth and nineteenth centuries. But this also rendered the UK's rural and agricultural economies less competitive, a realization encapsulated in the bitter debates over the protectionist Corn Laws between 1815 and 1846. Most dramatically, in the nineteenth century sustaining life in large parts of Ireland and the Highlands and Islands of Scotland became very difficult for many, leading to significant rural depopulation as people moved to towns and abroad. But as the historian Tom Devine has shown, the 'Clearances' significantly affected the Scottish Lowlands as well as the Highlands, while, as William Cobbett lamented at the time, in the first half of the nineteenth century England's agricultural counties, mainly in the south, south-west and east, lost through internal migration over 1 million people and counties with a mixture of agriculture and industry another 0.6 million people.[71] Such movements raised important questions about the relative strengths of the tax base of rural and urban parts of the UK and where central government's economic priorities should lie.

If being 'left behind' put rural regions during Britain's era of economic superiority into a very different position vis-à-vis the Union's fiscal state, times did eventually change. Deindustrialization as well as industrialization caused major changes to the Union state's economy and demography, especially when it began to bite hard in the interwar depression. Cotton, coal and shipbuilding, all once pillars of Britain's economic might, gradually withered across the UK, taking their toll on jobs and incomes. Consequently, since 1918 the population of Scotland, Wales and Northern Ireland have all either stagnated or declined relative to the UK as a whole, as has the population of the north of England.[72] Such an important change in the economic geography of the UK took place, moreover, as the state had begun to take on new responsibilities, requiring more taxing and spending, notably in this case with regard to unemployment benefits. This was bound to change key fiscal relationships and how they were perceived, by individuals as well as by communities.

THE STATE AND THE WEALTH OF NATIONS

Over the past three centuries, Britain has become a much more crowded and prosperous place. Population has grown ninefold, yet real per capita incomes have risen perhaps fifteenfold.[73] Such changes obviously pose very different challenges to government and opportunities for action. The state's scope has grown out of all recognition: central and local government expenditure, a rough measure of its overall activity, was probably no more than 5 per cent of GDP in 1700 but had grown ninefold by 1990 (Table 3).[74] In turn, this has been linked to a dramatic transformation in the functions of the state.

The growth of central government spending since 1707 has been far from smooth (Figure 3). Frequent wars were the main driver until Napoleon's final defeat at Waterloo in 1815, through direct military

Table 3. Government expenditure in the UK, 1700–1990

	% GDP	% central	% local
1700	5	85?	15?
1790	12	83	17
1910	12	50	50
1951	40	77	23
1990	46	69	31

expenditure, subsidies to allies and the repayment of war debts. Only about 10 per cent of central government expenditure in that period was not spent in those ways. And the wars became more and more costly, so that by 1815 central government expenditure was about 20 per cent of GDP. Indeed, fears of national bankruptcy began to be voiced loudly from the middle of the eighteenth century, even by such 'moderns' as David Hume and Adam Smith. This and associated doubts over the balance of the constitution, in the context of the failed effort to stop American independence, led to calls after 1779 for what was called at the time 'economical reform', especially cutting wasteful and constitutionally enervating expenditure. But long and bloody war with Revolutionary France after 1793 constrained the force of such cries, until they were unleashed at peace in 1815.[75]

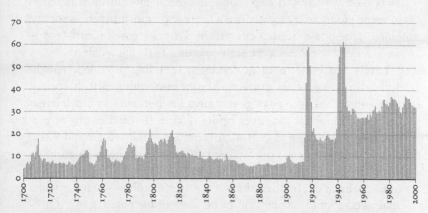

Figure 3. Central government expenditure relative to GDP, 1700–2000, %

'Cheap government' and 'liberal' sentiments, increasingly legitimized by Adam Smith's criticisms of excessive governmental economic intervention, became the guiding assumptions of much of the political elite in the nineteenth century. With few major wars between 1815 and 1914 and rapid economic growth, the state, central and local, shrank dramatically in relative size, to just 8 per cent of GDP in 1890. To some this 'night-watchman state' oversaw an age of high liberalism and free trade, involving itself little in people's lives. While this did not mean that, domestically, government was doing less and less in the nineteenth century – real per capita central government spending on civil items more than doubled – in the early twentieth century, state spending on civil matters (rather than on the military and war debts) began to grow more vigorously. There were three reasons for this: the need to tackle major social problems had risen up the political agenda; the extraordinary costs of two world wars took government spending and economic management to a wholly new level; and the challenges of the interwar depression were so great as to require considerable action by central government.

The publication in 1936 of Keynes's *The general theory of employment, interest and money* offered governments a persuasive rationale for such increased activity, activity demanded by the Second World War, the 1942 Beveridge Report into welfare provision and the stunning Labour party victory over Churchill's Conservatives in 1945. After 1945 there was another step change in central government willingness to spend money to try to produce a fairer and more prosperous society. Notably, despite concerted efforts, the Thatcher governments (1979–90) managed to roll back the state to only a fairly limited degree.

Levels and patterns of government spending provide a rough-and-ready sense of its growing significance within British society. Unquestionably, since 1939 government has become very much larger and more important than ever before (Figure 4). Another way of putting this is that in 1750 central government employed around 8,000 people, mainly revenue officers, or 0.1 per cent of the population. In 1905 there were 78,000 – all but 4,000 in England – or 0.9 per cent of the population. In 2012 there were over 8 million when the wider state is taken into account, or 13 per cent of the population.[76] Obviously this has profound implications for how people at the time

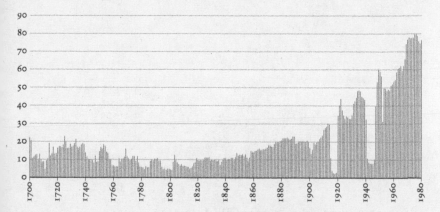

Figure 4. Civil share of central government expenditure, 1700–1980, %

viewed government action (and inaction). But those perceptions were also informed by changing expectations of what governments should properly aspire to do: there were plenty of complaints in the eighteenth century that the state was too intrusive and expensive, despite its limited manpower and civil expenditure. Clearly heed needs to be taken of both the numbers and the perceptions.

The scope of the state can, of course, also be thought about in terms of how and where it raises its money. Taxation is the most important element of this, having contributed the equivalent of 92 per cent of total central government expenditure between 1700 and 1980. Consequently, the geography of taxation is a central feature of this book. Yet, although central government borrowing was much less important, its general ebbs and flows since its formal institution in the 1690s also suggest some of the key dynamics in the growth of the Union state. There have been four broad phases in the history of the national debt (Figure 5): considerable growth from 1700 to 1822, entirely driven by wartime need; fairly steady decline thereafter to the eve of the First World War; driven upwards once more by the costs of that war but then for the first time growing significantly in peacetime – deep depression required central government to spend more than it could collect in taxes; and finally a huge surge of the national debt in and immediately after the Second World War, followed by a sharp

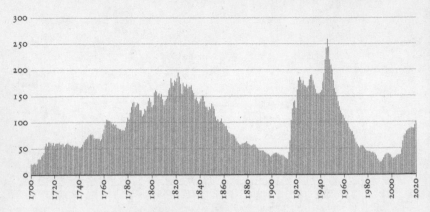

Figure 5. National debt relative to GDP, 1700–2020, %

decline to a low point in 1990. With the enormously damaging financial crisis of 2008 it began to grow again, though paying for the global pandemic of 2020–21 will cause it to rise much further still.

A key feature of the national debt is that it has always been organized in London, mainly through the Treasury and the Bank of England, but drawing upon and stimulating the City of London's growth as a global financial centre. With creditors being repaid with national taxes, it has been easy for some to imagine the national debt and its supporting institutions and complex financial instruments as a massive fiscal whirlpool, enriching London and the south-east through taxes levied on the rest of Britain. (Ireland had a separate debt from 1715 to 1817.)

The continuous solvency of the UK government has been one of its greatest achievements, even if it has been subjected to stressful financial crises – including the South Sea Bubble in 1720, the Bank of England's suspension of cash payments in 1797, effectively defaulting on a loan from the US in 1932, the massive IMF bailout in 1976 and the enormous cost of 'Black Wednesday' in 1992. It has been a survivor. The disruptions and dislocations of the unions of 1707 and 1801, the rise and fall of empire (including Irish independence), the stresses and strains of many bloody wars and dramatic changes in social expectations were, fiscally, coped with. Many other states have been less successful. State bankruptcy has afflicted some – the Dutch Republic and pre-Revolutionary France – invasion, desolation and dissolution others. Yet such a record has allowed its evolutionary development to continue relatively unchecked, affording less opportunity for a radical reconstitution of how it has balanced its fiscal dilemmas. Whether this has been for the good is doubtful given that today the UK is both a much more centralized state than other members of the OECD and a regionally very unequal one.[77]

In what follows, I explore the fiscal terms of the unions of 1707 and 1801, along with those of the disunion of 1921–2 and devolution in 1999, and how they then worked out in practice. I attend to the policies and the debates surrounding them as well as what the figures seem (and seemed) to show. Despite its obvious importance, historians have paid little attention to this facet of the Union state, and I hope, in viewing that state in fiscal terms, to show some of its fundamental developments and achievements, as well as limits and paradoxes, at the levels of both public policy and the lived experience. I explore in particular why very different views about the equity of the fiscal settlements emerged and how those disagreements played out. This was just as much part of the day-to-day experience of individuals living in the Union state as that revealed in those studies that have explored topics such as the Highland regiments of the British army or the domestic impact of the wider imperial economy.[78] Indeed, questions of public finances, taxation especially, had an unmatched immediacy and importance in people's lives that made them subject to constant political and public scrutiny.

As this chapter has shown, tackling this subject requires seeing how the varied material and cultural circumstances across the Union worked with a complex of often politically charged views of the priorities of a good society, views that were based on varied assumptions and rhetorical techniques. Clear resolution of the fiscal dilemmas was never likely. Quite apart from problems of evidence and method in deciding whether the Union state was worth it to its people, there are often good reasons for or against analytically privileging the individual not the collective, markets rather than morals, objectivity instead of subjectivity and undivided rather than divided sovereignty. The task in what follows is to show how such considerations were argued over, key choices made and what that then meant in practice. The story shows both the strengths and weaknesses in the Union state, suggesting why some of the current discontents are so hard to resolve.

The three chapters that follow each explore key moments of union and disunion considered fiscally and how these then worked out in, roughly speaking, the following century. In Chapter 2, it is Scotland's limited incorporation into the British state that is the focus. The limitation was not simply that the 1707 Union allowed Scotland to retain its own religion, laws and education system, but that, fiscally, incorporation was challenging to both partners and that even by 1800 Scotland's experience was significantly different from that of England. In Chapter 3, the fiscal terms and consequences of the Union of 1801 are examined, and in particular whether, as was hotly disputed at the time, Ireland was overtaxed both before and after the Great Famine. That story links closely with the Home Rule debates from the 1860s over whether the Union state should be reformulated along more federal lines, in the context of developments in central government's willingness to spend taxpayers' money to address pressing social questions. Chapter 4 starts with the disunion of 1921-2 that created the first devolved government (in Northern Ireland) within the smaller Union state. While in several ways this anticipated later debates and decisions about devolution for Scotland and Wales, its importance was overshadowed by world wars and deindustrialization. In particular, the latter foregrounded regional rather than national concerns for the first time, setting off some new dynamics in how the UK fiscal state worked, albeit ones that had been anticipated before the First World War in worries that Home Rule for Ireland, Scotland and Wales would be problematic if England was left undivided. In the final chapter, some of the consequences of devolution are considered in relation to how one might understand and address the fact that the UK remains so centralized and regionally unequal.

2

1707–1801: Scotland's challenge

In 1688 the Calvinist Dutch Republic invaded England to prevent it from joining a French alliance intent on destroying the republic. So began the Glorious Revolution of 1688–9 that set Britain and Ireland on a new course. The subsequent flight of the Catholic king James II to France was fictionalized as an abdication, followed by the joint crowning of William and Mary, the king's Dutch son-in-law (and Dutch head of state) and Anglican daughter. Consolidating that extraordinary dynastic settlement required wars against Scottish and Irish Jacobites, as James's supporters are known, memories of which still feed intolerance today. There were three far-reaching consequences to these earthquakes. First, it further subjugated and alienated the Catholic majority in Ireland. Second, it meant that Britain was now inextricably bound to a European alliance to thwart the expansionist ambitions of the Sun King, Louis XIV, involving it in two long wars until a lasting peace was eventually achieved in 1713. Repeated allied victories led by the Duke of Marlborough, famously at Blenheim in 1704, meant that Britain attained great power, a status it retained until after 1945 when it was diminished by the costs of two world wars, the collapse of its heavy industries and the loss of its global empire. Britain's attainment of great power status was only possible, thirdly, because parliament became established as central to political processes, underwriting a 'financial revolution', including the foundation of the Bank of England in 1694, that began significantly to expand the fiscal capacity of the state, allowing it to exert more military power than ever before. But with annual parliaments, propertied society across Britain now had access to sovereign power to further much more particular interests, undergirding profound economic changes already under way.[1]

The Union of 1707 was central to these developments, born of a dispute between England and Scotland dating back to the death in 1700 of the only remaining child of Anne, who succeeded William as monarch in 1702. Her poor health and the threat of a Jacobite restoration made the succession question an urgent one to Britain's dominant Protestant faiths – Anglicanism in England and Wales and Presbyterianism in Scotland. Joint action between the parliaments at Edinburgh and Westminster was needed given that the regnal union of 1603 had seen a king from Scotland's ancient house of Stewart succeed to the English throne. But, without consultation, English politicians plumped for the Hanoverians, inevitably offending Scottish pride and belittling the considerable independence Scotland enjoyed. Tensions mounted and tit-for-tat threats were made, all while Britain was mired in a bitter war. In London, fears mounted that Scotland might go its own way, perhaps, given the relative popularity of Jacobitism there, and even resurrect its 'auld alliance' with France. Developing the regnal union into a parliamentary one was designed to prevent that possibility, with Scotland finally agreeing to England's choice of the Hanoverians that bore fruit with the accession of George I in 1714. In return, Scotland was offered the valuable prize of full access to English markets, both at home and in its growing empire as part of an island-wide customs and currency union. If it retained its laws, religion and educational system, Scotland lost its parliament and its leading politicians now looked more to London than to Edinburgh.

Undeniably, Britain was placed on a new footing in 1707. But there were continuities. In an age of intense international rivalries, the state remained, like its neighbours, depressingly prone to bellicosity. A quarter of a century of relative peace after 1713 was followed by five major wars, culminating in the allied defeat of Napoleonic France at Waterloo in 1815. While European theatres remained central in these conflicts, fighting over territorial and commercial prizes spread globally, particularly in North America, the Caribbean and India. In the process Britain morphed from a colonial into an imperial power; indeed, after 1763 it was the greatest imperial power of the day despite American independence in 1776. Such power politics were underpinned first by a state that was much more successful than most of its competitors in taxing its citizens and enlarging the national debt in wartime. It enjoyed unmatched fiscal capacity. That rested, secondly, on an economy that had begun to improve markedly in the seventeenth century and was internationally distinctive in the eighteenth century, as what later came to be called the 'industrial revolution' took hold. Emblematically, canals, steam engines and cotton factories spread across a society whose agricultural base was already being transformed through new crop rotations, selective breeding and enclosure. Birmingham, Glasgow, Leeds, Manchester and Sheffield flourished as dynamic hubs of such developments, changing the economic geography of Britain in the process. All of this enabled rapid population growth from the 1760s, prompting Malthus in 1798 to worry about the sustainability of such dynamics. In Britain, though not Ireland, such anxieties proved exaggerated.

Union in 1707 set significant challenges to public finances in terms of extending to Scotland a system that had been developing in England and Wales since the 1640s, when excise taxes were first introduced on domestically produced goods.[2] This chapter explores the debates and resolutions over the fiscal terms of the Union, how they then played out in practice and how such developments might be explained. Critical here were significant differences in the size and productivity of the two partners, posing major challenges of reconciling commitments made in the treaty to the principles of equality and equity – that all should be taxed alike and subject to similar priorities for public expenditure, while acknowledging that there were marked inequalities in the geography of well-being. Throughout the eighteenth century, many in Scotland felt that they were being unreasonably burdened and their distinctive circumstances ignored by policy makers. In London, meanwhile, there were repeated concerns that Scotland was failing to pay its way. Nonetheless, Scotland's place within the fiscal union began to change significantly in the second half of the eighteenth century, though even by 1800 little of its taxes were sent south.

PUBLIC FINANCES IN THE UNION TREATY

The Union of 1707 was no bolt from the blue. Real efforts to bring it about began soon after the regnal union of 1603, were temporarily imposed by crude military might under Cromwell and were unsuccessfully tried again, this time through negotiation, soon after the Glorious Revolution. These repeated failures show the difficulties of marrying this odd couple: of different circumstances and capacities, after centuries of plundering and bloodshed, along with distinctive traditions, identities and beliefs. Particularly important was that Scotland was both smaller overall and less productive. This is suggested by the fact that in 1700 Edinburgh had around 55,000 inhabitants compared to London's 575,000. Nationally, Scotland's surface area was over one-half that of England's, yet it supported only one-fifth of the population. Scotland had failed to match the broad-based improvement in England's economy in the second half of the seventeenth century. Tellingly, in the 1690s catastrophic harvests caused widespread famine in Scotland, killing as much as 10 per cent of its population.[3] England hardly suffered in comparison and in fact was then undergoing its 'financial revolution'. Similarly, in the same decade Scotland's first concerted attempt at empire building by establishing a colony on the isthmus of Panama, the 'Darien scheme', failed ruinously whereas England's imperial efforts had over several decades provided a major fillip to its economy.[4] That failure attested to the fragility of Scotland's state, which much more often than in England and Wales had to grant privileges, delegate or contract out to get things done, in particular to the royal burghs in matters of trade and industry, to owners of hereditary ('heritable') jurisdictions for administering justice and to private tax collectors (usually called 'tacksmen' in Scotland or 'farmers' in England).[5]

Both before and after the Union, negotiators on both sides knew clearly, if only very impressionistically, that a significant gulf existed between England and Scotland in terms of society, the economy and the state. A key question for the Union negotiators in 1706 was what weight to give to such features in the context of the assumed desirability of an island-wide customs and currency union. At the time they compiled statistics of taxes raised on each side to focus matters, statistics that showed that for every pound collected in Scotland, thirty-six were collected in England and Wales.[6] To put it another way, on the eve of the Union Scotland's public revenue was under 3 per cent that of England and Wales, or, using modern population estimates, 14 per cent on a per capita basis. That was a considerable gap to bridge, but did it reflect real differences in the ability to pay (taxable capacity), the willingness to pay (tax morale), administrative efficiency or tax policy? Those are questions to be kept in mind throughout this chapter.

If, on the eve of the Union, England and Wales were known to be much more heavily taxed than Scotland, it understandably concerned the Scots that integration into a British-wide customs union might be immiserating or ruinous, not only through extra taxes but also because most Scottish farms and firms were believed to be less competitive. Indeed, it was claimed that Scotland was already too heavily taxed, while the London-based East India Company, enjoying a monopoly of trade with Asia, meant that Scottish merchants would now be excluded from this valuable commerce. William Black, the most effective critic of the treaty's fiscal terms and presumptions, believed free trade with England would turn out to be 'empty' and enslaving.[7]

Acting for the government in London, Daniel Defoe and others challenged claims that Scotland would be crippled by the new tax regime.[8] Not that difficulties would not be encountered. To the Scottish peer the Earl of Stair, 'If these English duties bite, and we do not deny that they will, remember none the less that in any kind of union involving free trade[,] equality of taxation is the mainstay on which the welfare of both countries depends.'[9] This emphasis on equality was significant, though both sides agreed that the new fiscal regime could not simply impose on Scotland what was already in place in England and Wales: the blow was to be softened by granting Scotland temporary exemptions on the taxation of salt, stamped paper, windows, coal and malt, while specific privileges were also confirmed (articles 6–8 and 10–13 of the treaty). It was recognized implicitly that Scotland's limited taxable capacity meant that full fiscal convergence would have to wait until those exemptions ended, though an important caveat was that future taxes were to be raised by paying 'due regard to the circumstances and abilities of every part of the United Kingdom' (article 14). Such equity was not the case with the land tax, where Scotland was pegged at a very low ratio relative to that in England and Wales (article 9).[10] Finally, Scotland was to be compensated, by the so-called 'Equivalent', for, among other things, post-Union taxes collected in Scotland to repay the pre-Union national debts of England and Wales it had previously not consented or contributed to. This took the form of both a £398,000 lump sum and, as payments consequent on expected increases in tax receipts in Scotland through heightened economic activity, the 'rising Equivalent' (article 15).[11]

All told, as far as taxes were concerned the treaty awkwardly enshrined principles of equality (or uniformity) and equity, failing to provide a clear means by which they might subsequently be reconciled: 'due regard' could mean many different things and was to be worked through by brute politics within an unequal union. (Scotland was to send to Westminster just 45 MPs and 16 representative peers to join the 513 English and Welsh MPs and roughly 200 peers already there, which meant that Scotland had less than one-half the representation suggested by its population share.) Some hoped and others expected that Scotland would fairly quickly become as prosperous as England, stimulated by the creation of a British free-trade area and Scotland's admittance into the imperial economy. That is to say, changing Scotland's political economy was expected to trump its natural disadvantages, a highly optimistic view, if in keeping with the powerful rhetoric of improvement that had developed since the mid seventeenth century.[12]

This incorporating union was, though, limited in certain ways. Scottish autonomy in law, religion and education was largely maintained. More importantly as far as public finances were concerned, there was no expectation that it should now operate the system of parochial poor relief, paid for out of local rates, that was in place in England and Wales. In that sense, Scots crossing the border after 1707 remained formally excluded from the possibility of relief.[13] In fact, England was unusual in European terms in this statutory requirement that local government had to aid those teetering on the edge of destitution. Such a division of responsibility heavily influenced the balance then struck in the nineteenth century between local and central government in meeting the social and environmental costs of urbanization and industrialization. But the Union of 1707 was largely inconsequential to that.

As a practical measure, in terms of public finances, the Union established a common currency and customs zone. One consequence was that colonial officials across the Atlantic were informed of the need now to treat 'Scotsmen ... as Englishmen to all intents and purposes' regarding their new rights within Britain's empire, especially trading rights.[14] But it also required the institution in Scotland of customs and excise services modelled on English and Welsh practices where the 'farming' of collection had ended before the Glorious Revolution. In the case of the excise, carefully calibrated practices and disciplined bureaucracies were run out of central offices in London.[15] Excise 'collections' and customs 'headports' across Scotland were now overseen from Edinburgh by two new boards of commissioners that reported to and took instructions from London, the Treasury in particular. English experts were sent to Scotland to fill some senior posts in these new services, although 97 per cent of those actually collecting excise duties remained Scottish.[16] On the ground, revenue officers employed English standards of weights and measures, which might rankle or confuse where traditional Scottish standards were the norm.[17] And a new Court of Exchequer was established in Edinburgh to deal with revenue disputes.

In all, while Scotland enjoyed some temporary fiscal exemptions and privileges to smooth the Union, the system of public finances created in 1707 sought uniformity of practice and equality of experience across Britain. Taxes raised in Scotland were to pay for the costs of government there, with surpluses sent to the Exchequer in London. Quite how much might be sent seems never to have been considered explicitly, however, leaving the door open for considerable disagreement on both sides over what then transpired. Differing views quickly emerged, often politically charged. One extreme view, from a supporter of the failed Jacobite rising of 1715, is worth quoting at length:

> Before the Union we have no Taxes but what were laid on by our own Parliaments, and those very easie, and spent within our own Country. Now we have not only the Cess or Land Tax, the Customs conform to the *English* book of Rates, near the Triple of what we formerly pay'd, and Excise, both most rigorously exacted by a Parcel of Strangers sent down upon us from *England*; But also the Malt-Tax, the Salt-Tax, the Leather-Tax, the Window-Tax, the Taxes upon Candles, Soap, Stearch

[*sic*], and almost a general Excise; and after all the Tax upon stamped Paper and Parchments, by which alone vast Sums of Money are levied from the Country: The most of all which Taxes are bound upon us for 64 and some of them for 99 years to come. And which is the heaviest Burden of all, we are for ever deprived of our own Parliament and Officers of State, being reduced in a Manner to a Province, and must every Year send up great Sums of Money to *London*, to maintain such of our Nobility and Gentry as the Court Faction think fit to chuse [*sic*] Members of the *English* Parliament, Tools and Instruments of still greater and greater Oppressions and Burdens to be laid upon us, for Payment of the *English* Debts, and for carrying on the Trade of Stock-jobbing; which in a short Time is like to be the only Trade in Britain. And besides all this, great Sums of Money, are yearly drawn out in discussing Appeals before the English Parliament, who know nothing of our Customs and Laws: So that we have better lose the Plea, or throw the Dice for it, than prosecute an Appeal at *London* before such Judges.[18]

Yet London was told a very different tale. Robert Harley, the chief minister between 1710 and 1714, received official reports on how little taxation was being collected in Scotland, leaving nothing to be sent south. The downturn in Scotland's trade in the wake of the Union (because of the disruptions caused by war and intensified competition from England) and the persistence there of various privileges only partially explained this. More worrying for Harley were accounts that establishing the new revenue system had met with passive resistance and heightened smuggling, encouraged by the reluctance of judges and juries to prosecute or convict. Higher than expected expenditure was laid at the door of proliferating offices to deal with 'voluminous & expensive' new regulations and paying down much higher than expected pre-Union Scottish public debts.[19]

THE GEOGRAPHY OF TAXATION IN EIGHTEENTH-CENTURY BRITAIN

Historians of the Union of 1707 and the forging of Britain that followed have paid very little attention to questions of public finances before the era of Home Rule in the late nineteenth century. The creation of a Britain-wide single market, encouraging productivity gains through greater economies of scale, has been stressed, especially in comparison to France, riddled as it was by regional fiscal duties, 'farming' and privileges.[20] Beyond that, many historians have happily followed Christopher Whatley's suggestion that the Union increased duties in Scotland fivefold, ruinously for daily life.[21] While numbers and rates of duties in Scotland rose with the Union, though the evidence for that seems never to have been set out clearly, it is untrue that the amounts of taxes actually collected there increased sharply immediately after the Union. In fact, they remained around the same level as in recent decades (Table 4).

Table 4. Annual average central government revenues collected in Scotland, 1686–1714, £

1686–8	168,000
1692–1700	147,000
1703–5	160,000
1708–14	156,760

Note: The figure for 1703–5 is for the 'Average as if levied in England', i.e. without accounting for the costs of farming some revenues; final receipts averaged £109,194.

Though it is possible that more tax was collected in 1708–14 than was reported – because of corruption or Jacobite infiltration of the revenue services – the amount is unlikely to have been large. Moreover, the Scottish figures for 1703–5 are net of various repayments. Doing the same for the post-Union figures reduces the net take to £121,000, nearly a quarter below the figures for 1703–5. Whichever way one looks at it, in terms of the actual tax take, clearly there was no fivefold rise because of the Union; indeed there was no rise at all and may even have been a fall. However, that is not to say that after 1707 the new tax regime was not in key respects disruptive, unwelcome and challenging. Farming revenue collection ended, to be replaced by state-appointed revenue officers; duties on trade with England were abolished; the collection of duties on trade with Asia were moved to London; and complex new regulations were introduced.

If the short-term impact of the Union on total tax receipts in Scotland was negligible, there were important longer-term developments. The best available evidence for this are the continuous runs of figures for amounts collected there of customs duties (on goods imported from abroad) and excise duties (initially wholly on domestically produced goods, but gradually on some imports also), excluding repayments made on re-exported goods and the like (Figure 6) – the basis for the following discussion.[22] These were much the most productive taxes in eighteenth-century Scotland.

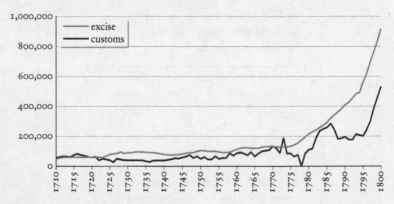

Figure 6. Customs and excise receipts in Scotland, net of repayments, 1710–1800 (five-year moving average), £

In the first fifty years of the Union, total customs and excise receipts in Scotland rose by just 16 per cent, with a decline in customs revenue more than offset by a rise in excise revenue. Over the next fifty years the combined rise was nearly tenfold, with customs receipts now also growing significantly. This was well ahead of population growth and, at a compound rate of 4.6 per cent per annum, despite burgeoning trade and industry, was certainly ahead of economic growth, though figures for that are only available for Britain as a whole. Clearly Scotland was becoming a much more heavily taxed society from 1760, especially after 1780. Of course, a rapid rise is easier from a low base, while comparing the situation in Scotland with the rest of Britain in the first century of the Union places developments in a broader context. There are different ways of representing this, which fed divergent perceptions of the fairness of public finances at the time. For example, in 1804, when annual official statistics of national shares of taxes began to be published, taxes collected in Scotland accounted for only 5 per cent of the whole. Yet the picture can be refined by taking population into account, as could be done after 1801 by drawing on the results from Britain's first census (Table 5).

Table 5. Total per capita tax collected in England and Wales and Scotland, 1703–5 and 1804, £

	England and Wales	Scotland	Scotland as % England and Wales
1703–5	1.07	0.15	14
1804	4.75	1.56	33
% growth	344	940	

The figures in Table 5 expose two apparently conflicting features of the taxing union: that, even after nearly a century, amounts collected in Scotland accounted for just one-twentieth of the British total, with Scots seeming to pay only a third of the per capita level of England and Wales; and yet taxes collected rose very much more rapidly in Scotland.

Simply comparing the two sides of the Union compact is rather crude. In the first place, the experience of taxation in eighteenth-century Wales shared more with that in Scotland than with that in England. Even taking its small population size into account, Wales became relatively less important as a source of excise revenue across the eighteenth century and, lacking significant ports, was never important for customs revenue – it was mainly served by Bristol and Liverpool, which were also major hubs for the valuable Anglo-Irish commerce.[23] If the land tax was relatively more productive in Wales than in Scotland, that spoke of the significance of the bargain that had been struck in 1707 in pegging that tax in Scotland at much lower levels.[24] When the income tax was introduced in 1799 across Britain, amounts collected in Scotland per head fell well short of those in

England, but they were slightly lower still in Wales.[25] Yet, if amounts of taxes collected in Wales were pretty meagre, this provoked little or no debate. It was Anglo-Scottish comparisons that dominated discourse. The nature of the compact between the countries shaped these attitudes fundamentally, with Wales long subsumed by the English state, whereas Scotland always remained a conscious and potentially wary partner.

A final stage in thinking about the geography of exaction in eighteenth-century Britain is to adopt a regional rather than a national frame. While most British taxes were collected in England, London and the south-east were fiscally the most productive English regions. Throughout the period, around one-third of the excise was collected in London, and about one-fifth in the south-east, or about one-half of these revenues in total. For customs the concentration was even more marked. While other ports in the south-east produced very little revenue, London's produced 80 per cent of Britain's customs revenue in 1710 and still over 50 per cent in 1829, despite the considerable growth in the ports and industrial hinterlands of Glasgow, Hull, Liverpool and Newcastle upon Tyne. Over 40 per cent of the land tax and about 35 per cent of the income tax were collected in London and south-east England. Such figures are out of all proportion to the distribution of population at the time. For example, in the 1780s London's per capita excise and customs receipts were respectively around 370 and 860 per cent of the British average. While historians have been right to stress the importance of the national reach of Britain's revenue collection, especially for the excise, this has significantly obscured its marked regional variability.[26] It was not just that the capital was home to the central offices of the revenue services, the Treasury and the Exchequer, but that it, alone or within the wider south-east, was far and away Britain's most important source of public income. Here, really, was the beating heart of British public income.[27]

In Scotland, too, some areas produced more taxes than others. In 1792 James Anderson rightly observed that 'the whole of the [Scottish] national revenue ... is obtained from the small but active and industrious division of it, on both sides of the ... Clyde and Forth, which abounds with manufactures and commerce.'[28] Between 58 and 76 per cent of all excise revenue collected in Scotland between 1752 and 1815 came from a narrow central belt running from Greenock in the west through Glasgow, Linlithgow and Edinburgh to Haddington in the east.[29] The Clyde's three customs ports – Greenock, Port Glasgow and Glasgow – collected 73 per cent of all Scotland's customs revenue, with Leith, Edinburgh's port, collecting 10 per cent.[30]

Clearly, while large national differences existed in the amounts of taxes collected, there were also large regional differences at work. The Thames and the Clyde, with the cities of London and Glasgow, were easily the most tax-productive parts of their respective countries. But it follows that there were also parts of Britain where very little tax was ever collected, indeed where costs of collection ate up much if not all of that which was collected. In the excise this was especially true of west Wales and Scotland's Highlands and Islands, and somewhat true of Cumberland and Northumberland, but the problem was more widespread in the case of customs duties: sixteen English 'headports' experienced net losses from 1710 to 1780, six of them in Kent and Sussex.[31]

Were these national and regional patterns of taxation mirrored by the geography of central government expenditure? Unfortunately it is impossible to be precise about this, for two main reasons. First, the good if patchy evidence of the geography of taxes is not mirrored on the expenditure side. Now and then, figures exist for a few items, but, because it did not excite political or public debate, reports were not produced in the same way as they were for the income side of public accounts. Secondly, the matter is complicated because public accounts inadequately separated the income and expenditure sides. In particular, before 1800 some duties collected by revenue officers might be paid out directly by them without showing up clearly in the summary national accounts. Three areas of spending were especially important: on repayments to merchants when they re-exported goods they had previously imported and on which they had paid duties – so-called 'drawbacks'; on subsidies to encourage certain areas of economic life, such as linen production – so-called 'bounties'; and finally on Scotland's civil, legal and ecclesiastical government. These need considering before looking at the three general areas of expenditure by the British government: the military, interest payments on the national debt and civil government.

Drawbacks and bounties were major items of local spending from gross receipts before remittances to London, overwhelmingly from customs rather than excises.[32] The former mainly repaid duties to encourage re-exports, hoping to stimulate the 'carrying trade', which was held – through the example of Dutch success in the seventeenth century – to be both economically and, because of the importance of naval resources, strategically valuable. Their 'cost' was therefore usually a direct product of the duty regime and so in practice often neutral: what the state raised from some imports it gave back on their re-export. Bounties mainly aimed to stimulate exports and import substitution, that is, the domestic production of goods to reduce reliance upon imports, thereby helping the balance of payments. Many bounties were certainly introduced on that basis, but it was sometimes claimed that some were effectively drawbacks, notably in regard to the sugar trade, or tax breaks.

Unquestionably, the economic significance of drawbacks and bounties was much greater in Scotland than in England, especially in the quarter century before the outbreak of the American Revolutionary War in 1775.[33] Drawbacks accounted for an astonishing 91 per cent of Scotland's gross customs receipts then, especially because of Glasgow's trade in American colonial tobacco, sending most of it on to markets in continental Europe.[34] Mercantilist regulations at the time, the so-called 'Navigation Acts', required the colonies to send their products to British ports, even if the final destination was elsewhere. Merchants, the shipping industry and the ports on the Clyde all flourished as a consequence, producing a mountain of paperwork, but little actual revenue. American independence was a body blow to this, exacerbated by new procedures subsequently introduced around warehousing re-exports intended to streamline procedures. But industrialization kept the region prospering on more secure foundations, requiring an imposing new customs house to be opened at Greenock in 1818. Scotland also did relatively well out of the bounties on fisheries and linen, in each case as a central government initiative to stimulate its economy. Whereas corn-export bounties were much more valuable in England (as a political counterbalance to the burdens of the land tax) than in Scotland, they tailed off quickly in the 1760s, whereas bounties on fisheries and linen that benefited Scotland in particular kept on flowing until they began to be killed off by the intense pressures for cheap government and free trade, especially in the 1820s.[35]

Spending on management charges was a second main area of expenditure made directly from revenues collected before they were sent to London, which, as will be shown later in the chapter, was greater in Scotland than in England.[36] Additionally, in Scotland, though not in England and Wales, money was also spent on: various costs of government administration; the central courts; the kirk; the Equivalent; and the Board of Trustees for Fisheries, Manufactures and Improvements, a body instituted to aid economic development as a trade-off to increased taxation on malt – more on which later. Perhaps three-quarters of these payments came from the excise, costing that revenue stream about £6 million from 1707 to 1815, or 14 per cent of net receipts.[37] In fact, such accounting oddities were common across Britain, but the important point here is that Scottish civil expenditure took place before remittances were made to London, making tax collection there look rather less productive compared to England and Wales than was actually the case.

For much of the first century of the Union state, little tax revenue was sent from Scotland to London, because much less was collected there and because of the relatively higher costs of management charges, drawbacks and bounties. Before the 1760s an annual average of around £25,000 was sent south, but then amounts grew, slowly at first and then rapidly. More than £100,000 was remitted for the first time in 1780 and more than a £1 million in 1800.[38] In this way, Scotland began to contribute significantly to the Exchequer in London only towards the very end of the eighteenth century. The evidence is very slight, but very little tax revenues from Wales appear to have been received in London until well after 1815.

GOVERNMENT SPENDING IN EIGHTEENTH-CENTURY BRITAIN

Frustratingly, while the geography of the income side of British public finances between the two unions can be set out fairly clearly, it is impossible to do the same for expenditure. As we saw in Chapter 1, the growth of that spending was concentrated in periods of war. Unsurprisingly, therefore, between 1707 and 1800 some 56 per cent of central government expenditure went on the military (half on the army and subsidies to allies, half on the navy), 35 per cent on interest payments on the national debt and, despite what some historians have misleadingly claimed, just 9 per cent on civil expenditure.[39] Although just where most of this money was spent is impossible to pin down, some important points can still be made.

The wars that drove British public expenditure in the eighteenth century became increasingly global and expensive, with rising shares of spending heading overseas, though the records do not allow those shares to be accurately calculated. This was directly on the British and imperial armed forces and indirectly via subsidies to allies. For example, at the end of the War of the Austrian Succession in 1748 some £350,000 was spent on imperial garrisons and their forces, £236,000 on re-imbursing four American colonies for their help in the war effort in Canada and £1,743,000 on subsidies to European allies.[40] Then there would have been the costs of British forces stationed overseas, but how much was spent is unclear. The point is that British public expenditure had interwoven domestic, European and imperial commitments.

There was more direct military spending on the Royal Navy than on the army, because of the greater capital and maintenance costs of its ships as well as a strong antipathy within Britain to a peacetime 'standing army', though some of the costs of the army were borne by the Irish to pay for troops barracked there.[41] It is striking, there-fore, that there were no state dockyards in Scotland before Rosyth in 1909, though Royal Navy ships were sometimes resupplied at Leith, Greenock and Stranraer.[42] Efforts were concentrated at Chatham, Plymouth, Portsmouth and Woolwich, all on England's south coast or near London – though a small Royal Navy dockyard was established at Milford Haven in Wales in 1809.[43] Yet before 1815 there were naval dockyards in the Caribbean (Jamaica and Antigua), in North America (Halifax, Nova Scotia) and the Mediterranean (Gibraltar).

If very little of Britain's vast spending on its navy took place in Scotland, some of its military expenditure did take place there. A key aspect of this was capital investment, in barracks, forts and infrastructure, in an attempt to construct a network of well-linked defences against both internal and external threats to the Hanoverian regime. For the first half century or so of the Union, the great stimulus here was Jacobitism, with the major risings of 1715 and 1745–6 both leading to considerable investment. Several barracks were built after the first of these, but in the 1745 rising all three forts along the Great Glen – William, Augustus and George – ignominiously fell to the Jacobites. All were rebuilt, with Fort George, housing 1,600 men, costing £200,000 (twice its estimate) by its completion in 1757 (Image 1). It was the largest building project in the Highlands until the Caledonian Canal opened in 1822, though its original purpose of defending access to Inverness and the Great Glen was never put to the test.[44] It was re-invented as a training centre for young men pouring out of the Highlands and into the British army, while its remoteness and security meant that it was considered as somewhere to exile Napoleon in 1815.[45]

Scotland was not alone in having barracks built in this period – in 1792 it had 12, England had 33 and Ireland 37 – but for much of the eighteenth century they were relatively more numerous there than in England (but not in Ireland).[46] In the early nineteenth century, with the threat of a French invasion of southern England, attention switched away from Scotland: defensive Martello towers were built at Leith and in the Orkneys, but dozens were erected on the coasts of Kent, Essex and Suffolk.[47] At the same time, many barracks were built around London, along the Thames estuary, and on the south coast, mainly near Portsmouth and Plymouth.[48] Of course, all of these buildings needed manning, but just how many men were placed in them is unknown. What is well known, however, is that there were Scottish regiments in the 'British' army before 1707, while after it there were more Scots in it than their share of the island's population, especially with the formation of Highland regiments from the 1740s: around a quarter of officers and rank and file were Scots.[49] But where regiments were stationed, and the amounts of money which flowed to them from London and from them to whom, has yet to be studied.

Although the construction and maintenance of roads was a local responsibility at the time, to allow easier movement of men and supplies through Scotland, especially in the Highlands, central government invested in over a thousand miles of 'military roads' and dozens of bridges there after 1724, hoping to aid commercial development in the process.[50] Importantly, almost all of these were east of the Great Glen and north of the central belt: the far north, the south and north-west of

Image 1. Fort George, completed in 1768 as a post-Culloden fortification.

Scotland remained largely untouched. The dual military and commercial purposes of such roads are suggested by the fact that central government spent £169,000 on Highland roads between 1760 and 1800, well after their military purpose became secondary, and they were now included as civil expenditure in the public accounts (Map 4).[51] Such initiatives were systematized and extended from 1803 when an act established a Commission for Highland Roads and Bridges, which spent £450,000 building 875 miles of road and several large bridges by 1816.[52] There was no comparable spending in England and Wales until the construction of the state-funded road from London to Holyhead after 1815 to improve communications with Ireland.[53]

If it is hard to pin down the geography of military spending in Britain in this period, it is even harder to make meaningful comments about the geography of interest payments on the national debt. That debt was highly centralized in London, mainly via the Treasury's dealings with the Bank of England, the East India Company and the South Sea Company (even after the disastrous failed attempt of the latter company to take over the whole of the debt in 1720). Where public creditors were based is unclear, though, in part because many owned homes in London as well as the country, or employed London-based intermediaries to act on their behalf. The best study we have of this question is of the years between the creation of the national debt in the 1690s and the start of the Seven Years War in 1756. It showed that there was a very heavy concentration of public creditors in and around London, usually 93 per cent or so. Beyond that region, the most significant were abroad, especially in the Dutch Republic, though there were some in Ireland.[54] In the 1780s, 87 per cent of holders of the national debt were in and around London.[55] A study of holders of East India Company stock for the period 1756–1830 (not exactly the same thing as public creditors, but close enough for these purposes) found that there were none at all in Scotland until 1783; in 1830, London and the Home Counties accounted for 60 per cent, Scotland 4 per cent and Wales just 0.3 per cent. There seems little doubt, therefore, that public creditors overwhelmingly lived in and around London, if not always permanently.[56] Wealth holders in Britain living outside London and its environs had therefore relatively little direct experience of the national debt, except, like the financially much less advantaged,

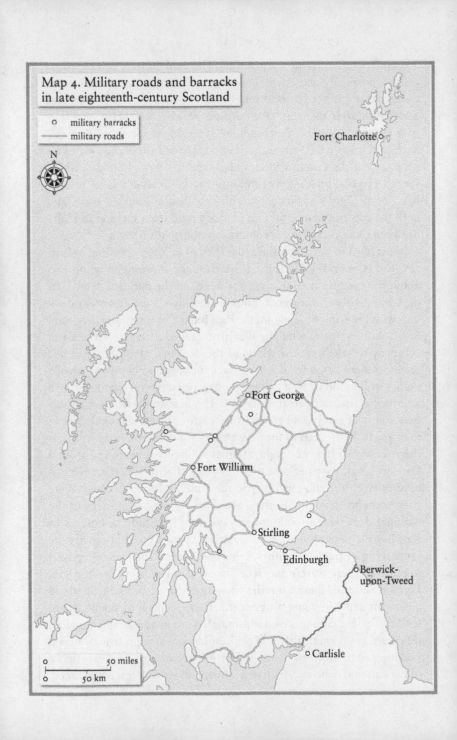

Map 4. Military roads and barracks
in late eighteenth-century Scotland

○ military barracks
╌╌╌ military roads

N

Fort Charlotte ○

○ Fort George

○ Fort William

○ Stirling

Edinburgh

○ Berwick-
upon-Tweed

○ Carlisle

○————— 50 miles
○————— 50 km

feeling the state dipping into their pockets for taxation to sustain the growing edifice of public credit. The criticisms of the growing national debt that resulted are discussed later in this chapter.

Central government spending in Scotland on barracks, garrisons, forces and roads sought to ensure that the country posed no threat to the Union state. Five other items of expenditure stand out as London sought to strengthen Scotland's economy, closing the gap with England and directly demonstrating some benefits from the Union. In 1727 the Board of Trustees for Fisheries, Manufactures and Improvements was established as a concerted attempt to stimulate Scotland's economy, especially its linen industry and fisheries. It was funded partly under the terms of the 1707 treaty, partly under negotiations for ending the rising Equivalent and partly to sweeten the pill of collecting the malt tax from 1725. It spent over £400,000 before 1815 on the linen and flax industries, aiding their considerable growth in Scotland.[57] Secondly, the 1745 rising led to £152,000 being spent on buying out the private ('heritable') owners of districts of legal administration. This was done to make the practice of justice in Scotland closer to that in England and Wales, in the hope that its society would become both more orderly and more prosperous.[58] Thirdly, revenue from the seized estates of Jacobites was put to public use in Scotland, mainly between 1755 and 1784 through a Board for Annexed Estates. Revenue was spent directly on Scotland's infrastructure, mainly in the Highlands, and substantial sums were lent for the Forth and Clyde and Crinan canals, as well as for the improvement of Leith's harbour.[59] (In 1784 the estates that had not been sold off or transferred were 'disannexed' and returned to their original owners or their heirs.) Fourthly, in 1803 taxpayers' money began to be ploughed into the Caledonian Canal, totalling over £900,000 by the time it was opened in 1822 – this despite the enormous costs of the Napoleonic Wars. This was aimed at generating trade and opportunities that would forestall emigration from the region, with little success, a failure that came to haunt advocates of greater public expenditure for decades to come.[60] Finally, monies were spent to buy out the remaining revenue privileges that had been protected in 1707, including £70,000 in 1767 to the Duke of Atholl for his rights over the Isle of Man's customs collection, aiming to end the island's role as a vibrant smuggling entrepôt.[61]

What distinguished this spending in Scotland from ad hoc central government expenditure in England was that it all attempted to stimulate significant parts of Scotland's economy, usually by seeking to mould it according to English expectations. The heavy emphasis on infrastructural improvements in Scotland was in part driven by the idea that market forces, market integration and market size could be improved and increased, with attendant productivity increases heightening commercial assimilation across Britain. Such commerce was expected to help pacify and 'civilize' what politicians in London (and often in Edinburgh) viewed as unruly districts. Although no grand plan was followed, the tenor of developments was clear. By contrast, spending in England lacked such apparent objectives. Among other spending, sporadically rewards were given to inventors, compensation was paid to those whose cattle were destroyed to stop the spread of disease, and the creditors of the Levant Company were paid off to ease its dissolution. But this was all ad hoc, driven by notions of fairness and immediate necessity rather than some plan of national improvement. Paradoxically, a consequence of attempting to bring Scotland's economy more into line with England's was to emphasize differences and diversity: that on the expenditure side meaningful flexibility of approach was needed, not some overarching uniformity.

CONTEMPORARY VIEWS ON TAXATION IN GENERAL

As is clear, because public expenditure was largely driven by the related needs of European interstate rivalry and empire building, this had fairly modest consequences for the geographical balance of spending among the territories of the British Union state. Consequently, when contemporaries looked, as they often did, at the geography of its public finances, it was the distribution of taxation that caught their eye. They were not always pleased with what they saw. In considering their views, it is helpful to identify four broad areas, each linked to the other: tax policy; the ability to pay; the willingness to pay; and tax administration. These need to be considered in relation to the patterns established earlier: of the modest impact of the Union upon the tax take in Scotland until the second half of the eighteenth century; and of the heavy focus of collection in London and south-east England.

It would be wrong to suppose that opinions about the geography of public finances were evenly balanced between the two main partners of the Union. There was markedly more discussion and debate in Scotland than in England. Partly that was because in England much took place within the corridors of power, while in Scotland it was a staple topic of the 'science of man' explored within the Scottish Enlightenment that flourished in a society where universities, debating clubs and publishing were so interlinked. Such an imbalance in how and where questions about the geography of taxation were addressed was itself bound to cause some confusion, with voices in Scotland and England as likely to speak past as to each other. But there is also a more general sense in which understandings of taxation in eighteenth-century Britain were in a state of flux, with new ideas jostling for space and acceptance. This section focuses on the thought and policy of central government, while in the next section Scottish positions are considered.

English views of Scotland's fiscal place within the Union state were expressed intermittently and usually only at the general level. But from the early days successive leading ministers in London worried about the low tax take and high public expenditure in Scotland: Sidney Godolphin, Robert Harley, Robert Walpole and Henry Pelham each turned their mind to such considerations, eliciting information, generating proposals and issuing directives. The tenor of ministerial views of the operation of the fiscal state in Scotland is suggested by the Duke of Newcastle's observation, in the midst of the crisis over the malt tax in 1725, to General Wade, the military commander in Scotland, that it was 'high time' Scots were 'brought under an equal obedience to the laws, with the fellow subjects in this part of Britain'.[62] Such thinking was brought sharply into focus by the participation of some Scottish revenue officers in the 1745 rising and the cost to England of suppressing it. To English eyes the challenge was clear: in 1752 Lord Chancellor Hardwicke, the main architect of policies aimed at eradicating the Jacobite threat, complained in parliament of 'the insufficient manner in which the taxes had been collected in that northern quarter of the kingdom: some method, to be sure, should be taken to make Scotland pay her taxes; but could any ministry ever hit upon that method?'[63]

As taxes mounted from the middle of the century, so English worries about their collection in Scotland occasionally resurfaced, including that smuggling was especially prevalent on the Scotland's west and south-west coasts. Worries were also expressed about the cost of bounties, especially on fisheries. Official statistics and reports became common in the 1780s, occasionally throwing more clearly into relief national differences in the operation of the fiscal state. This could raise tempers, especially when concerns were laid before parliament. In 1790 Walter Stanhope, an English MP, having pored over official statistics, thought that 'in England the Excise was the best collected system of taxes in the country, and in Scotland, from what he had read ... he feared it was the worst.'[64] (In response, Scotland's excise commissioners strongly defended their record to the Treasury.[65]) This was a view fuelled by occasional complaints from English businesses that inadequate collection and lower tax rates in Scotland competitively advantaged Scottish licit and illicit competitors within the British common market.[66] From such perspectives, too many Scottish businesses were not 'fair traders'.

Such views fed into the development of tax policy in London in the period, but framed within and often subservient to more general considerations. These need outlining. As already shown, the Union awkwardly enshrined the principles of both equality and equity, without making sufficiently clear how they were to be put into practice. An important contextual point is that, even before the Union, politicians in London had puzzled over questions of territorial equity in taxation. In the 1690s John Houghton and Charles Davenant tabulated acreages and various taxes collected in the seventeenth century in England, county by county, in the context of establishing the land tax, which became the most important direct tax in the eighteenth century.[67] By this tax, counties in southern and eastern England were more heavily taxed than those in the north and the west – in recognition of significantly different regional land valuations. This imbalance was widely understood and, if sometimes commented on and tabulations reprinted, remained unchanged in the period. Sometimes this was regretted, not least because of rising prosperity from industrialization in the Midlands and the north of England, which made the land tax increasingly ill-founded territorially, but it was politically so difficult to address this that the land tax was left untouched until 1798.

A second contextual factor was that propertied society in eighteenth-century England stood firmly against giving central government significant police powers. In the late seventeenth century a standing army under royal authority was widely viewed as a potential tool of arbitrary authority, while in the middle of the eighteenth century instituting even a civil militia was bitterly contested.[68] Such worries were also expressed about the growing power of excise officers to enter premises to make their assessments, challenging the sanctity of private property and individual liberty. On such grounds, in 1733 a storm of protest successfully saw off Walpole's proposal to rationalize aspects of revenue collection by shifting some of it on to the excise.[69] It speaks volumes that in 1763 two future prime ministers described the excise as 'odious' to parliament.[70] Not that the customs service escaped censure. Because many of its officers were political appointments, they could be viewed as exerting undue influence by the centre, threatening local independence in general and parliamentary elections in particular, irrespective of whether sinecurists were likely to be competent. Such criticisms were part of a long political tradition in England of calling simply for less government expenditure, from the so-called 'Country party', including both Whigs and Tories in other contexts, in the early decades of the Revolution constitution of 1688–9, through the 'patriot' opposition in the heyday of Whig one-party rule (circa 1714–60). They were re-energized by the costly debacle of the American Revolutionary War, in movements to address wasteful and costly spending, patronage and sinecures. Initially this took the form of calls for 'economical reform', morphing into assaults on 'old corruption'. Wider radical and liberal critiques of the bellicosity of the British state in the aftermath of the French Revolution were regarded as particularly challenging by central government.[71] But everyone could see that the revenue laws were voluminous, convoluted and contradictory, leaving citizens potentially open to the arbitrary whims of the state's officers.

This begins to give a sense of some of the constraints within which taxation developed in eighteenth-century Britain. It also needs to be seen as an era of some, often unsuccessful, experimentation regarding taxes. Between the Glorious Revolution and the Union of 1707 there were seven major taxes that were tried and failed, including a poll tax. Similarly, William Pitt the Younger introduced and then abandoned twelve taxes in his first period as prime minister from 1783 to 1801, including on theatres, gloves and clocks.[72] None of these failures had much of a territorial dimension to them. But two others did.

A particularly significant debate broke out in 1763 over a proposal to tax cider. The circumstances were that Britain had just emerged from the Seven Years War, having triumphed over France, extending its empire in North America and India in the process. Yet this came at great cost. The unredeemed national debt had nearly doubled to £133 million, giving rise to acute anxieties over the prospect of national bankruptcy. Increasing public income was needed to address such concerns. But what particularly motivated the cider tax was the belief that in England's western counties cider, which was then duty free, was often preferred to taxed beer. The proposal attempted therefore to ensure that all who enjoyed alcoholic drinks were taxed alike. But this caused a storm of protest, which some, in the manner of the rampant Scotophobia of the period, aimed at the Scottish prime minister, Lord Bute – that he was an Etonian who lived much of his life in England seemed irrelevant.[73] Far from equalizing taxes, the cider tax was said to be 'exorbitant, unequal, partial' because it was to be levied at twice the rate of beer, while the cider counties allegedly lacked the natural advantages of the barley counties of eastern England, which also benefited from bounties on corn exports.[74] Numbers were produced purporting to show conclusively that Devon and other cider counties were already more heavily taxed than counties in the Midlands and north of England. As William Dowdeswell, an MP for a cider county and a future Chancellor of the Exchequer, declaimed: 'Such is the *Equality* of this Tax!'[75] And such was the force of this reaction that the tax was soon moderated before being abandoned.[76] In 1784 similar arguments were advanced against a proposed brick tax – that places with plentiful supplies of stone and timber would be able to avoid it.[77] But with central government more financially desperate than ever and brick making widely spread, opposition failed.

Much more momentous were attempts, simultaneously and over the next decade, to make the North American colonies contribute slightly greater amounts to the costs of their defence. Everything the government in London tried there, be it stamp duties or levies on external trade, met with the same response of resistance and rejection, leading ultimately to the Declaration of Independence and the defeat of Britain in war. This tale about taxation and representation as a central cause of the American Revolutionary War has been told many times before. Less well known is that there was also a more detailed discussion about the merits of taxes on overseas trade against those levied internally, both in relation to the ability to pay.[78] Significant here is that America's rejection of London's taxes, including Britain's humiliating and expensive defeat in war (the national debt in 1783 stood at £233 million), raised important questions about fiscal legitimacy in enlarged states that could not be ignored in the metropole. Central diktat, no matter how well based it seemed to those responsible, had significant limits when strongly held local sentiments thought otherwise. Meaningful authority often had to be rather carefully negotiated between the parts of such a dispersed and disparate empire.[79]

Failed taxes in eighteenth-century Britain say something important, therefore, about the nature of authority. But they also betray some of the confusions over the principles of taxation, including those underpinning what we now call the Laffer curve.[80] Undoubtedly those principles were recognized early in the life of the Union state. In 1728 Jonathan Swift, the great commentator on contemporary affairs in Britain and Ireland, opposed a suggestion made in a pamphlet to increase taxes in Ireland by pointing out

> a Secret, which I learned many years ago from the Commissioners of the Customs in *London*. They said, when any Comodity [*sic*] appeared to be taxed above a moderate Rate, the Consequence was to lessen that Branch of the Revenue by one half, and ... that the mistake of Parliaments on such occasions was owing to an Errour [*sic*] of computing two and two to make Four. Whereas in the Business of laying heavy Impositions, two and two never made more than One, which happend [*sic*] by lessening the Import, and the Strong Temptation to Running [i.e. smuggling] such Goods as payed high Duties.[81]

Yet if this was understood at the top of a key revenue service in London, the lesson could be forgotten. Famously, increased duties on tea led to a surge of smuggling in the middle of the century. This connection was well understood, but the bold and, as it proved, correct step that reducing duties should increase revenue was not taken until 1784 by Pitt the Younger when he cut rates from 119 to 12.5 per cent.[82] That was important, but Pitt went further by thinking of such considerations territorially. Just the following year, in the debate over liberalizing trade between Britain and Ireland, Pitt suggested – he cannot have had hard evidence – that a country half as wealthy, populous and commercial as another could bear only one-tenth of the taxation because a poorer nation has less disposable income overall that can be taxed.[83] In the context, that raised serious questions over whether Scotland was really, as some alleged, under-taxed.

It is impossible to know how Pitt came to appreciate the complicated connections between tax policy, taxable capacity and the willingness to pay, as it stemmed either from conversations or from documents that have not survived, but interestingly a few months later Thomas Jefferson, on his way from Paris to Fontainebleau, had very similar thoughts about such a 'geometrical progression'.[84] Perhaps both had drawn much the same lessons about taxation and the American Revolutionary War, but perhaps they had both also imbibed some of the latest thinking about taxation, especially the latest thinking from Scotland.

CONTEMPORARY VIEWS ON TAXATION IN SCOTLAND

In the decades after 1707 there was widespread popular resistance to revenue officers in Scotland. In many places 'official were overwhelmed, as indeed sometimes was the military sent in to protect them. In this regard Scotland was, simply, ungovernable; in England guerrilla war of this kind – resisting and routing customs officers – was far more localised.'[85] It reached a climax in the 'Porteous riot' of 1736 in Edinburgh, when a captain of the city guard, John Porteous, awaiting punishment for murder in suppressing a riot, was lynched by an Edinburgh mob fearing that he was about to be pardoned. This barbarity was the starting point for Sir Walter Scott's *The heart of Mid-Lothian* (1818) – and painted by his friend James Skene. Scott acknowledged the anarchy of smuggling and how it undermined legal traders but thought that it 'was almost universal in Scotland in the reigns of George I. and II. [1714–60]; for the people, unaccustomed to imposts, and regarding them as an unjust aggression upon their ancient liberties, made no scruple to elude them wherever it was possible to do so'.[86]

Such initial opposition may have rested in part on nostalgia for a world that had been lost, but it was articulated in terms of the greater intrusiveness, excessive exactitude and unbearable burdens of the new revenue regime (linked to beliefs about English ignorance of Scottish circumstances), draining Scottish money to London just as forewarned by the political theorist Andrew Fletcher before the Union.[87] As already shown, in the decades after the Union such a dreadful monster was more imagined than real, but it was a natural position for Jacobites to adopt, rejecting as they did every aspect of the Hanoverian state.

Obviously the potency of such Jacobite rhetoric lost its force after the movement's brutal defeat at Culloden in 1746, but new ideas of 'rights', empowered by the American and French revolutions, allowed criticisms to be reiterated, if in somewhat new garb. James Callender, an autodidact and satirist, was inspired by the one-time excise officer Thomas Paine, whose *The rights of man* (1791) had decried the violence of the British imperial state and the enormous and regressive costs of frequent wars. But Callender thought that Scotland especially suffered as a consequence: its MPs 'feel the total insignificance of their situation, and behave accordingly'; English taxes were bleeding its industries dry; and Scotland's liberties were being lost to the power of tyrannical revenue laws. Relative Scottish poverty could therefore be explained as a consequence of London's actions rather than something inherent in the country's geography and economy. By his lights, England was a nation of hypocrites, preaching liberty but practising oppression, especially upon Ireland, Scotland and Wales.[88]

It is hardly surprising that those who loathed the Hanoverian state lambasted its sustaining system of public finances. What is more striking is that in Scotland some of the state's servants also found grounds for sharp criticism. Reay Sabourn, a solicitor of the Scottish Court of Exchequer, a body set up in 1708 to deal with revenue cases, complained in 1729 of the oppressive and arbitrary proceedings of the revenue officers that undermined the liberty and property supposedly protected by the Revolution constitution of 1688–9.[89] Such views became more potent through the establishment of a vicious spiral of rising wartime costs leading to higher duties, which increased both smuggling and ever greater legal powers of enforcement. This led in 1790 to Andrew Hamilton, an excise commissioner in Edinburgh who must have known Adam Smith, denouncing the evils of 'over-taxing'.[90] In effect, to his mind tax rates were still being set well beyond the optimal point on the Laffer curve as far as Scotland was concerned.

Sabourn and Hamilton's points about the oppressive aspects of the revenue services were informed by their administrative experience. But it says a lot that they were able to speak out so forcefully. In fact, they should be seen as part of a wider and searching attempt to improve Scotland's place within the Union state. Many historians have emphasized the vitality of a 'Scottish Enlightenment' that was at once nationalist and unionist.[91] Within this, fiscal topics were commonly considered by the influential Scottish debating clubs of the period – the Select Society most famously – and a growing print culture. It is telling that the most important analyses in Britain of taxation in this period came from the pens of Scottish authors, exploring the principles upon which a just and sustainable tax regime should rest. In the 1770s, Lord Kames and Adam Smith grasped that the relationship between incomes and taxes was geometric not arithmetic. As Smith put it, 'It is not very unreasonable that the rich should contribute to the publick expence [sic], not only in proportion to their revenue, but something more than in that proportion.'[92]

Scottish authors were also at the forefront of considerations of the growing national debt. David Hume and Adam Smith are the best known of these – they were highly critical – but there were significant and often more strident contributions from many other authors, including several peers.[93] In the main, these interventions decried the national debt as siphoning off provincial vitality to support metropolitan excess while indebting generations to come. Aware of Scotland's economic weakness relative to England, discussions of taxation and the national debt can therefore be viewed as an aspect of the so-called 'rich country–poor country' debate of the time, of how Scotland could prosper given it was so closely bound to the political economy of a much larger and wealthier neighbour.[94]

It would be wrong to suppose that such voices were unrelentingly hostile to all aspects of British public finances. Smith, for all of his unease about government influence over economic life, was clear that a strong state was a basic requirement for that life to exist at all – a Hobbesian point. In 1719 the General Assembly of the Church of Scotland, echoing a recent statute, denounced smuggling in Scotland, invoking biblical precepts on the justness of taxes and instructing ministers across Scotland to read out their 'act' on the subject.[95] Moreover, such voices sought to influence, not just lament, often addressing Scottish and English audiences simultaneously. That necessarily required employing rhetorical modes that would work in both England and Scotland. Most importantly, many Scots engaged purposefully with improving the state of affairs, especially from the 1740s.[96]

At the institutional level, the Convention of the Royal Burghs, the Highland Society, and the chambers of commerce at Edinburgh and Glasgow sought to explain Scotland's views on fiscal matters to London in the hope of tempering policy. Individual engagement by Scots in the British fiscal state was also important. To the cases already mentioned of Sabourn and Hamilton can be added those of Duncan Forbes (Lord Advocate), John Clerke and John Dalrymple (both Barons of the Exchequer in Scotland), and Adam Smith, who worked with leading English politicians (Charles Townshend and Lord North) and influenced others (the Earl of Shelburne and Pitt the Younger). In 1785, after seven years as a customs commissioner, Smith celebrated a recent fourfold rise in the amounts collected in Scotland, while seeing the scope for further rises.[97]

Smith was certainly a particularly important Scottish voice within the evolution of British political economy. But it is important to recognize the concerted attempts made by many other Scots in the 1780s and 1790s to demonstrate to central government in London where Scotland was ill-served by the British fiscal state and the reasonable efforts made by the revenue services in Scotland to do their best with the poor tools they were provided with. Two voices provide examples of such efforts and which should be seen as part of a wider process of active engagement with Britain.[98]

James Anderson was an agriculturalist in Aberdeenshire, a political economist who published extensively, a correspondent of both Jeremy Bentham, the Utilitarian, and George Washington, first president of the USA, and an adviser to the Treasury on the state of the fisheries and wider economy of the Highlands and Islands. In this last task, undertaken in 1784, he refined his earlier thinking about Scotland's economy and the influence on it of taxes, bounties and regulations. He questioned the wisdom of imposing high taxes on poor districts, because it simply encouraged smuggling where cost-effective revenue collection was physically impossible. Indeed, he believed that 'taxes are in general levied with much greater rigour in Scotland than in England' and that, relative to the amount of market exchange in the region, the burden of taxation was in fact much higher than elsewhere.[99] This was a vital point about the optimal tax point being different from one part of Britain to another and one he built upon in 1792 when he discussed the effects of the tax on coastwise coal shipments, a tax that had been devised before the Union to exploit London's dependence on coal from north-east England. He warned against such metropolitanism in fiscal policy, risking as it did taxes that would keep poor provinces poor. Because of 'the dictates of natural equity', wise legislators should 'mitigate every burden imposed, as to be exactly proportioned to the circumstances of the district, and abilities of the people' – that is, territorially variable tax rates.[100] To his way of thinking, therefore, where taxes were concerned the principle of equity trumped uniformity or equality.

In part, Anderson developed his case by looking at official data on taxes collected in the Highlands and Islands. This was within an older tradition of 'political arithmetic' that, under influences from Germany, was being reborn as 'statistics' in the late eighteenth century. Public finances, including their territoriality, seemed naturally suited to such a method. It is in this light that Sir John Sinclair's studies of British public revenue should be viewed. Sinclair was an improving Caithness landowner, a leading light of the Highland Society, an MP for thirty years, the promoter of a semi-official Board of Agriculture and organizer of a monumental parish-by-parish survey published as the *Statistical account of Scotland* (1791–9). As Anderson recognized, Sinclair's enormous energy sometimes ran ahead of his powers of reasoning, but Sinclair was the first student of many of the concerns of this book.[101]

In 1785 Sinclair published his *A history of the public revenue of the British Empire*, with further editions in 1790 and 1803–4, expanding them from one to three volumes to become the standard, internationally recognized work. Here Sinclair, often using official figures, set out the evolution, strengths and weaknesses of the British fiscal state, including how these affected the two main nations of the Union. He was resolutely pro-Union and questioned the wholly negative view many (especially Scots) had painted of the national debt, arguing instead that it drew idle money into circulation, fertilizing economic life. But he also fought against the misunderstandings of English politicians of Scotland's wherewithal, if often by synthesizing in his own writing the ideas of others: of the different capacities of the agricultural economy of each country; the difficulties of collecting revenue in many parts of Scotland; that many foreign commodities consumed there were taxed in London; and that some income from Scotland was being spent by its elite living in London. He concluded that it was astonishing 'how so much, rather than how so little' Scotland was paying into the Exchequer, quite apart from the stream of young men flowing south into the British army.[102]

As the examples of Anderson and Sinclair show, the developing engagement by Scots in the British fiscal state was at once positive and critical, seeking better to inform policy makers of Scotland's particular circumstances, especially where they led to Scotland being less favourably treated by the revenue laws. Such views became much more influential with the political supremacy of Henry Dundas over Scottish affairs at the end of the eighteenth and very start of the nineteenth century. His initial position on the taxing union was stark; he declared in 1782 that 'the public revenues in Scotland are ill-collected, ill-managed and ... of those collected a sufficient proportion does not reach the Treasury in England.'[103] Establishing a close relationship with prime minister Pitt the Younger, Dundas was able to transmit some Scottish suggestions for Britain's fiscal state to the heart of government, a relationship mischievously captured by the caricaturist James Gillray in 1796, where a drunken Pitt – well known to like his drink – is supported by a convivial Dundas, draped in tartan (Image 2).

As we saw earlier, towards the end of the eighteenth century, the

Image 2. James Gillray, 'The wine duty; – or – the triumph of Bacchus & Silenus; with John Bulls remonstrance', 1796. The prime minister, Pitt the Younger, sits drunkenly in a barrel of wine, exclaiming about the tax on wine, supported by Henry Dundas, then at the height of his power in Scotland. John Bull on the right complains of the burdens of heavy taxes put upon him.

years of Dundas's political pre-eminence, the amounts of taxes collected in Scotland rose sharply.

TWO TAXES

Having set out the main features of views on taxation in London and Scotland in this period, looking at two attempts to extract more revenue from Scotland – on malt and whisky – helps to show how balancing equality and equity was attempted in practice.

Before the Union, the tax on malt was very lucrative in England because it was a key raw material in the huge industry of beer brewing, with malt production very hard to keep from the prying eyes of revenue officers. But, at the Union, Scotland was explicitly exempted from the tax during the ongoing War of the Spanish Succession (1702–13).[104] Yet before that war was formally concluded, though well after Britain had effectively given up the fight, central government decided to extend the malt tax to Scotland. Given that government in London had in other ways antagonized significant bodies of opinion in Scotland, this was a final straw and pressure for disunion boiled over, seen off in a vote in the House of Lords by the narrowest of margins.[105] The tax was regarded by many Scots as being forced on their country by a parliament with 'a mind to Ruin us'.[106] A common Scottish view was that 'it was a burden which they cou'd nowise bear' on the grounds of fairness, while the English felt that 'taxes shoud [sic] be equal' across Britain.[107]

Such was the furore in 1713 that little attempt was made to collect the malt tax in Scotland until 1725. When that happened, loud and forceful complaints were renewed. The tax was said to be a 'Bully from a foreign Land', its collectors 'Worse than the Plague, the Pestilence or Pox'.[108] Rioters in Glasgow, a 'great mobb' crying 'No Malt Tax', sacked the home of a local MP supposed to have supported the measure.[109] Glasgow's fearful authorities made little effort to suppress this powerful expression of popular opinion, which found less violent allies in a number of other Scottish towns and cities, notably among Edinburgh's brewers, where the 'mutinous Disposition and Ferment' was said to have become 'universal among us'.[110] Discussion in pamphlets of what was at issue recognized that the Union rested on the principle of equality of trade and taxation across Britain, but that 'all Laws, in the Execution, are to be regulated by Equity'.[111] Yet the authorities did not flinch from using force to restore order or to collect the tax, albeit with the surplus being invested in Scotland's fishery and linen industries. Such a posture and policy meant that, at the extreme, England's treatment of Scotland was likened to Egypt's enslavement of the Israelites.[112] Yet, although Scottish voices opposing the tax were occasionally raised thereafter, as 'a Burden beyond our Ability to bear' that 'must compleat our Ruin', the tax was nonetheless collected and the uproar subsided.[113]

Four main arguments were made by Scots against taxing their malt. First, that parliament should not tax any economy's pivotal 'staple goods', which in England meant wool and in Scotland barley, malt's raw material. Secondly, that taxing malt would impoverish an already vulnerable Scottish economy because its inferior quality made its production much more financially doubtful than in England. This was exacerbated, thirdly, by local taxes on ale particular to many Scottish burghs. Finally, Scotland's relative poverty within Britain allegedly provided greater opportunities for trouble makers 'to work up the spirits of the people to tumults & outrageous riots'.[114] The weakness of these positions was that the tax on malt in England had long been a key foundation of public revenues and to attack it on negative grounds alone raised important implicit questions about policy making. Should British tax policy be determined by the island's poorest or richest parts? Should Scotland be treated differently? How should tax morale be built and maintained in Britain's poorer parts?

Answers to those questions began to emerge from the middle of the eighteenth century, but are nicely illustrated by discussions about the taxing of whisky (for which barley is again a key raw material).[115] Importantly, although reliable statistics are wanting, whisky production in Scotland appears to have grown rapidly from around the middle of the eighteenth century, in the process supplanting beer as the national drink.[116] Two main reasons were given for this: a decline in the consumption of beer, partly because of the exploding fashion for tea, partly because of the spread of municipal taxes on ale, which encouraged the growth of distilling (presumably as an outlet for cheaper barley); and that the rise of whisky consumption was driven by a patriotic zeal not to consume illegally imported spirits, in the context of the state's concerted and somewhat successful attempts to reduce smuggling around the Irish Sea.[117] Endorsed by Robert Burns (himself a one-time excise officer), whisky, especially Highland whisky, came to be lauded as a national drink in Scotland, an association that has flourished ever since. It was said to be a wholesome guard against the country's challenging environment, where, as its earlier name of 'aqua vitae' suggests, it was said to be 'rather a necessary article than a luxury of life'.[118]

Much Scottish spirit production took place in numerous small portable stills in the Highlands, where revenue officers were few and far between. With barley a relatively more important crop in Scotland than in England, such production was part of the economy of make-shifts by which the poor tried to get by – significant emigration in the late 1770s, near famine in the early 1780s and the beginning of the Clearances there are all evidence of the region's precarious economy. One large producer was at Ferintosh, near Inverness, whose duty-free status had been confirmed at the Union. This obviously gave it an advantage, but in 1736 other Scottish spirit producers were also exempted from new (but not old) duties collected in England, an arrangement that lasted for several decades.

If in Scotland most spirit production was done on a small scale, in England a significant share of total distilling was undertaken by six capital-intensive producers in London, whose difficulties in evading duties were offset, to some degree at least, by the influence they exerted over revenue policy. As production in Scotland mounted, the temptation to smuggle output into England increased, raising the ire of London's big six. Consequently, in the 1770s the sharply rising costs of the American Revolutionary War prompted the Treasury in London to think about how better to extract revenue from the High-lands and the equity of continuing Ferintosh's privilege and wider Scottish exemptions from spirit duties. Stiffening enforcement and punishment was one response – thousands of stills were seized and condemned in the 1780s in Scotland – but plenty there thought that this was socially and politically corrosive and that tax policy needed to fit Scottish circumstances better.[119]

In the early and mid 1780s, Scottish landowners and literati gave concerted thought to whisky duties, seeking to influence parliamentary investigations into the question. This included Sir John Dalrymple, a figure of some importance within the Scottish Enlightenment, but also a Baron of the Exchequer.[120] He deplored the mutual hostility in Scotland between traders and revenue officers caused by the current laws and helped to develop new thinking on how Scotland's distillers might better be taxed.[121] Tellingly, in late 1785 and early 1786 general meetings of landowners in Scotland developed an alternative policy, with the aim that 'every part of the United Kingdom will be put upon a fair and equal footing in the common market of Great Britain' – that is, better aligning equality and equity. Yet, while they proposed, as Dalrymple had, the levying of duties on stills rather than output, along with the outlawing of small stills that were easily moved to avoid detection by the revenue officers, they also proposed lower rates in the Highlands than elsewhere. It was argued that this would bring Highland distilling, the superiority of whose product was widely claimed, within the law.[122] It says much that the Treasury and parliament adopted these proposals, if after some amendment, notably that Highland whisky would be taxed at 66 per cent of the duty elsewhere in Scotland and small stills outlawed. (The Ferintosh privilege was also bought out in 1784 for over £21,000.[123]) In doing so, they accepted the argument that the Highland economy struggled to be viable and needed state aid, but that its total exclusion from the duty regime was unfair within a British context.

While critical of past policy, the Scottish discussion of the taxing of whisky in the 1780s was markedly more positive in outlook than earlier debates over the malt tax. But the new policy ruptured opinion in Scotland, mainly between the Highland and Lowland areas. One aspect of that was the justness of outlawing small stills, which some, such as Burns, saw as an assault on freedom and forcing the poor into crime.[124] More widely, an unintended consequence of the new policy was that it created the market for internal smuggling from the Highlands to the rest of Scotland and Britain, exacerbated by the fact that differences in duties widened, so that by 1797 Highland spirits were charged at just 12 per cent of the Lowland rate.[125] Such smuggling was morally reprehensible to many outside the Highlands, but it also raised larger questions about the core principles of public revenue. On the one hand, some argued that the Highlands deserved 'some indulgence' because of its 'unfavourable' climate, limited infrastructure and lack of cheap fuel.[126] But to others 'It is an universal principle, that no man, or set of men, in Great Britain, are entitled to any preference in the payment of public duties, whether directly or indirectly, so as to enable them to undersell other traders.'[127] This brought into sharp relief the difficulties of reconciling uniformity with equity. A solution attempted in 1797 was to refine Scotland's tax zones by introducing a new intermediate area (Map 5). But this did nothing to satisfy the more heavily taxed Lowlanders, who argued that parts of the intermediate zone were as naturally fertile and productive as anywhere in the country.[128]

More broadly, explicit territorial variations in rates of six major taxes constituted a central feature of British public revenue in this period: taxes on malt, spirits, salt, coastal coal movements, land and incomes were or came to be applied at lower rates in Scotland than in England. Plainly London was not insensitive to the difficulties Scotland faced in being part of a British tax regime. Yet questions over how best to tax Highland whisky also raised doubts about the wider application of moderating the principle of equal taxation in this way. If Lowlanders doubted the justice of privileging the Highlands, then it raised obvious questions about whether Scotland as a whole should enjoy similar benefits regarding other taxes compared to England. Of course, arguments were made that it should – that salt was more necessary in Scotland (for curing and preserving fish especially) or that the physical limits to inland canals in Scotland meant that much more of the coal it consumed was taxed because it had to be shipped coastwise. But this was nonetheless a type of special pleading that Adam Smith had condemned. (It is notable, however, that formal interest groups proliferated across the whole of Britain from about 1780, including in Scotland the Highland Society and the Edinburgh and Glasgow Chambers of Commerce, all founded 1783–5.) And such arguments began to take root, with some denying the power of government to 'equalize the irregular distribution of Nature' and that the only sustainable policy was a 'liberal [one] of suffering the current of Trade to seek its own level'.[129] Arguments for the parity of duty

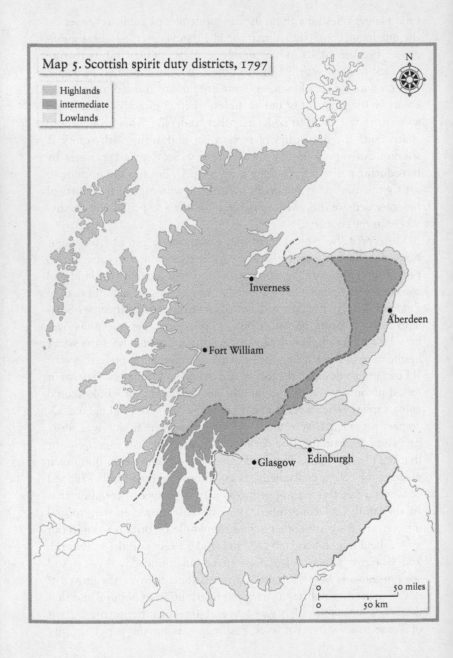

Map 5. Scottish spirit duty districts, 1797

Highlands
intermediate
Lowlands

N

Inverness

Aberdeen

Fort William

Glasgow   Edinburgh

0   50 miles
0   50 km

rates across Britain became common from the 1790s, though equalization of spirit duties in Scotland only took place in 1816 and of all duties across the UK's four nations in 1858.[130]

THE FIRST BRITISH FISCAL STATE

In deciding where to break into the relationship between central government taxation and spending, it makes more sense to start with the latter, because rises in the needs of central government were the key motor. Given the importance of this to executive authority, international relations and military might, national differences within Britain were of secondary significance. With most central government spending directed at the military and war debts, the approach was overwhelmingly a British one, if usually taken by English politicians viewing international and imperial relations in English terms. But differences in spending between England and Scotland consequent upon that were important only in two main ways: because of the far greater importance of Scotland to Jacobitism in the first forty years of the Union; and, relatedly, a general acknowledgement that Scotland's society and economy were less commercial than England's. As shown earlier, the first led directly to spending on forts and roads in Scotland, especially in the Highlands, and the second to various types of direct investment in economic projects as well as the abolition of heritable jurisdictions and other privileges.

Central government in London countenanced direct aid to Scotland's economy to a much greater extent than it did for England. Whether this had the effects it hoped for is quite another matter, though not one it worried unduly about, at least before the nineteenth century. As we have seen, the situation was quite different on the income side of public accounts, where worries that Scotland was not paying its way were raised across English political society from time to time. It is this that needs to be looked at in more detail.

As many Scots believed, there is no question but that British tax policy was largely developed with reference to English (and often metropolitan English) circumstances. Even so, many revenue policies had little or no particular territorial dimension to them, such as the reluctance to tax exports. Yet a significant point raised by some Scots was the difference between the formal and effective incidence of taxes, between where taxes were collected and where ultimately they were paid. Throughout the period, this was vital with regard to the monopoly of the London-based East India Company over British trade with Asia – the monopoly was significantly reduced in 1813 and ended completely in 1833. For example, almost all legal tea imports and attendant duties from the east were at the Port of London, even though tea drinking became island-wide, with consumers paying their share of the duties through higher prices. This was, however, part of a wider phenomenon by which Britain's central government became increasingly reliant on taxing imported goods, especially in London. The heavy concentration of customs collection at London has already been noted. What has often not been grasped is that in the second half of the eighteenth century central government shifted the collection of a number of key imports from customs to excise. In 1796, 64 per cent of the excise collected in London was on imported goods, compared to just 5 per cent elsewhere.[131]

London's role as Britain's dominant port for both overseas and coastal trade meant that taxes could be collected there that were ultimately paid for across the island, while the tax on the coastal trade in coal was particularly directed towards the capital's huge consumption.[132] Significant administrative efficiencies resulted from this. London's economic vitality was, therefore, hugely important to British public income. The contrast here with most other European capitals is marked. As one historian has observed: 'Of all the major European powers, only Great Britain – and to a less concentrated degree the Dutch Republic – possessed a metropolis of trade and population that was also its centre of power.'[133] The contrast between London and Paris is especially striking here. When travelling in France in the late 1780s, Arthur Young noted the quietness of the roads around Paris compared to London as evidence of its lesser economic significance. Paris was somewhat smaller, within a larger nation (geographically and demographically), with indirect access to coastal and oceanic trading.[134] It could not play as large a role as London. This was contemplated by Jacques Necker, the Swiss-born one-time French finance minister, who somewhat enviously noted 'the re-union in

London of almost all the [nation's] specie [i.e. money]; that city being at once a sea-port, the capital of the kingdom, the chief trading-town, and the place where almost all the exchange operations are made'.[135] London's economic importance, both in its own right and in terms of its connections with the rest of Britain, allowed Britons to be much more easily and heavily taxed.

London's significance to tax collection across Britain had the important consequence of obscuring the actual contribution made to the public purse by non-metropolitan areas. In national terms, perhaps only Scottish whisky was a significant counter-tendency. Ultimately, adjusting figures of the formal incidence to reflect better the effective incidence is nothing more than guesswork. In 1803 Sinclair estimated that a total of £150,000 of duties paid in England should be thought of as Scottish, raising Scotland's total income by nearly 6 per cent and reducing England and Wales's by under 1 per cent.[136] In 1810 the Scottish Lord Advocate undertook a similar exercise, which similarly improved Scotland's tax take without much altering Scotland's per capita share of the British whole.[137]

A second key feature of tax policy was the decision to levy some duties at lower rates in Scotland than in England. Understandably this was not something Scots dwelt upon and it is impossible to know how much additional revenue would have been collected in Scotland had rates been equal – there was a constant worry that such increases would only lead to more smuggling and fraud. The most significant difference was with the land tax, where Scotland was very lightly burdened. But overall probably differential duty rates restrained Scotland's contribution to the public purse only modestly.

The key driver of unequal duties in the first century of the Union state was the general impression that Scotland's economy was both smaller and weaker than England's. (Interestingly, Wales was not accorded any such similar treatment: it had been in the Union since 1536, had no separate legal code, parliament or universities, while the Council of the Marches had been abolished without fuss in 1689 and few Jacobites raised their heads there.) It is impossible to pin down the differences precisely, but Scotland's declining share of Britain's population across the period, from about 17 to 15 per cent, and its lower real wages at the end of the eighteenth century, are suggestive.[138] Similarly, some statistics indicate that Scotland's economy performed less well: towards the end of the period, Scotland's share of figures for Britain was 11 per cent of shipping tonnage, 6 per cent of official trade values, 11 per cent of coal output, 9 per cent of spending on roads, 14 per cent of printed calicoes and muslins and 5 per cent of pig iron output.[139] Similarly, between 1803 and 1814 Scotland contributed 9 per cent of income tax receipts.[140] It is impossible to know how representative such numbers are, but if in 1800 Scotland's economy accounted for 11 per cent of the British whole but 15 per cent of the island's population, then by implication Scotland's productivity was about 73 per cent of Britain's.[141] That seems plausible, though the gap would have been even wider around the time of the Union. Following the view of Pitt in 1785 discussed earlier, this might in itself have meant much less tax being collected in Scotland.

Having considered tax policy and taxable capacity, the next step in understanding the geography of taxation in eighteenth-century Britain is to turn to questions of tax administration. There is no doubt that in Scotland the introduction of the customs and excise services at the Union on the basis of those south of the border posed serious challenges of organization, recruitment and management of revenue officers, though very few English officers replaced Scottish ones on the front line of collection.[142] One way of summarizing how well they were met is to consider spending on collection (salaries and incidental costs) relative to gross income (Figure 7).

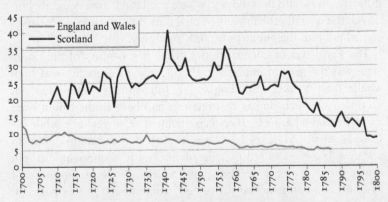

Figure 7. Excise management charges relative to gross receipts, 1700–1800, %

It is notable that in Scotland excise management charges rose on trend for decades after 1707, only clearly starting to fall from about 1760. Despite that, as late as 1800 management charges for all taxes were 9 per cent in Scotland but only 4 per cent in England and Wales.[143]

There were obviously good reasons why it was costlier to collect taxes in Scotland than in the rest of Britain: administrative scale economies were reduced by lower population density, productivity and output. Regarding the first of those, in the middle of the eighteenth century compared to England each excise officer in Scotland covered on average four times the area and two-thirds more people; indeed, later the excise was farmed in some of the Northern Isles.[144] But the quality of the accounts kept by the customs and excise services, the volume of correspondence that flowed from commissioners in Edinburgh to officers around the country, and the speed with which requests and directives from London were dealt with, also speaks to the efforts that were made, especially from the middle of the century. As already noted, English criticisms of lax tax collection in Scotland were strenuously disputed in the late eighteenth century. Anderson and Sinclair were not alone in believing that 'every tax is levied regularly, and full as strictly as in England, by careful, attentive boards and officers.'[145] The official records certainly suggest that.

It would be wrong, however, to argue that there were no problems with the administration of tax collection in Scotland (or in England, for that matter). After Culloden many more concerted steps were taken to improve matters in Scotland, including weeding out Jacobites from the revenue services, establishing a pension scheme for loyal excise officers in 1748, instituting new forms of record keeping and buying out various tax privileges mentioned earlier.[146] More and more revenue officers were appointed, against a backdrop of an expanding economy, helping to explain the surge in revenues from the 1780s.

Yet administrative limitations remained. Internally, significant arrears of payments from revenue officers were fairly common – in 1815 the excise commissioners in Edinburgh were still awaiting many payments from around the country stretching back decades, indeed in one case to 1714.[147] Often these were plainly unrecoverable bad debts, but slow payments were endemic: commonly about half the land tax was collected in a given year, with most of the rest arriving in the second or third year.[148] Seasonal patterns of financial flows linked to the underlying agrarian economy partly explain such arrears, but a culture of slow payment appears to have been usual – though how different this was to England and Wales is unclear.[149] Worse still was the widespread failure to collect the window tax introduced in 1749, commonly because the costs were expected to exceed the receipts; finding collectors was initially impossible in many Scottish counties.[150] If this was more resistance than revolt among propertied society, it is striking even so.

The difficulties of central government in finding collectors of the window tax in Scotland was consistent with the failure of Scottish justices of the peace (JPs) always to support revenue officers in applying the law. This had been especially the case in the early decades of the Union when a paucity of JPs had been identified as a structural weakness, exacerbated by the fact that juries were reluctant to convict those charged with revenue offences – the introduction of sheriff deputes after the 1745 rising helped.[151] This raises the important question of how far wider society actively evaded tax collection, either through smuggling or fraud. The willingness to pay taxes is the fourth general variable in understanding amounts of taxes collected.

It is inherently difficult to make secure judgements about the extent of illicit economic activity in any society. It certainly existed in many parts of the British Isles in this period. Hidden from view, it nonetheless attracts considerable speculation about its extent, not least in the Scottish case with its 'Wide and ill-guarded' coastline and sparsely populated remote inland districts.[152] Fundamental to its extent is its profitability, the cost of duties and the costs and risks inherent to illicit activity, in the context of the other legal opportunities available to people to make ends meet. Thus the black economy was more likely to thrive in some parts of Britain than in others: where there were fewer risks – because revenue officers were thinner on the ground or society more accepting of it; where opportunities for making a living legally were less available or where poverty was greater; and where charity and relief were harder to find. In all three of those regards, the black economy was likely to be more prevalent in Scotland than in England and in the Highlands to a greater extent than in the

Lowlands. Scotland's relative economic weakness, the fact that the revenue laws were mainly constituted with English not Scottish circumstances in mind, and the absence in Scotland of the system of poor relief used in England and Wales were all important in this respect. Indeed, several Scots celebrated the lack of statutory relief on the grounds that it encouraged independence and hard work. To Anderson, statutory poor relief was costly, had a 'natural tendency to enervate industry', corrupted people's morals and caused depopulation.[153] But it seems likely that, with such heightened independence in Scotland, came a greater willingness to partake of illicit opportunities, especially in the economically precarious Highlands and Islands.

Scotland's lower contribution to the British fiscal state had several causes. Less important were the inevitably high costs of collection there. In fact, the care with which commissioners in Edinburgh kept their records suggests the revenue services did well in difficult circumstances. More important, indeed central, was Scotland's less efficient economy. If there had been no other differences between the partners of the Union, that would have produced no more, and probably rather less, than three-quarters of the per capita tax take. In fact, despite Scotland's formally weak political voice – it had few members of either of the Houses of Parliament, while the Scottish Privy Council and Scottish Secretary were abolished in 1708 and 1746 respectively – it still prompted government in London to levy some taxes at lower rates in Scotland and to make more concerted efforts to stimulate its economy. This was encouraged, especially from the 1770s, by the active engagement of many Scots in improving the British fiscal state. Such political realism on all sides strengthened the authority of the British fiscal state in Scotland. And, after all, Glasgow's merchants had shown that the new economic opportunities presented by the Union could be very lucrative, easily outweighing the loss of an independent trade to Asia. Even so, the willingness to pay taxes was probably weak beyond Scotland's central belt. Taxing whisky clearly showed the difficulties faced by central government in collecting taxes across Scottish society as a whole, though of course the precepts of the British fiscal state sat ill wherever there was greater poverty and self-sufficiency.

CONCLUSION

These were important lessons more generally for the evolution of the UK, for when talk of a union between Britain and Ireland began to gain headway in the 1790s the Scottish experience over the previous ninety years was sometimes offered up to support rival positions for and against such a venture.

In 1799 one critique of the metropolitanism of the British fiscal state claimed that everything was subjugated to the interests of London – English regions as well as the Scottish nation. A rhetorical question asked at the time, 'Has Scotland found in the British legislature, the fostering hand of a natural parent, or the neglect of a step mother?', was answered emphatically by the capital's inattentiveness and lack of sympathy towards its territories. Scotland was said to have been starved of investment capital, leading its people to spread over Britain's empire, to freeze at the poles and burn at the equator 'in the pursuit of that subsistence which their country is unable to afford'.[154] To another author, Scotland had been degraded by the Union.[155] More moderately, John Foster, Speaker of the Irish House of Commons, declaimed in a four-hour speech that, while England's impact on Scotland had been mixed, Ireland had prospered economically to a greater extent *outside* a union. He stated that Scotland's linen production had increased by a factor of twenty-three since 1707, but by a factor of ninety-three in Ireland.[156] By his reckoning, the Union had not served Scotland particularly well.

Foster's use of official statistics was strongly contested, forming part of a wider positive assessment of benefits Scotland was said to have had gained from the Union, especially the growth of trade and industry associated with burgeoning Scottish towns and cities – it was hard to deny that Glasgow's trade had flourished or that there was heavy investment in Edinburgh's 'New Town'. Policy towards Scotland was improbably claimed to have been 'thoroughly liberal, disinterested and humane'.[157] Notably, Dundas and the Duke of Portland commissioned John Bruce to investigate the effect of the union of Scotland with England.[158] His lengthy report considered the range of opinions discussed in the debates leading to the Union of 1707 and delved into the comparative contributions of England and Scotland to the public purse. These showed that around 95 per cent was raised in England (and Wales), which only slightly underplayed the contribution from Scotland. His conclusion was that the Union had produced considerable economic benefits across Britain without greatly burdening Scotland; it was hoped that the same would happen with a Union of Britain and Ireland.[159]

These rival views in the late 1790s of the effects of the Union of 1707 nicely capture the disagreements, imbalances and special pleading that were at the heart of the first British fiscal state. There is no question of England's dominance within it: policies were mainly established with its capacities and needs in mind; the overwhelming majority of tax revenue was raised there; and relatively little central government expenditure was in Scotland and virtually none in Wales. Yet Scotland was, despite what is often asserted, an object of interest and concern to English politicians from the earliest days of the Union. And in practice they followed the Union treaty by paying at least some regard to the principles both of equality and of equity. Geographical variations in key tax rates and in central government spending were the main ways in which this was achieved. What drove such decisions was often a pragmatism about what was achievable, especially in collecting taxes, but there were also real hopes that Scotland could be improved by following England's lead. Among English politicians there was certainly considerable arrogance behind this, but, from their perspective, for much of the period Scotland was far from paying its way.

A marked feature of this was the extent to which politicians in London worried about Scotland's place within the British fiscal state, but paid no heed to that of Wales or to poor English districts. Partly that was because, compared to Wales, Scotland's greater size and population certainly made it seem to have greater potential. But it also reflected the strength of Scotland's conditional autonomy within the Union state: the greater prevalence of Jacobitism there; its cultural distinctiveness; the authority of Presbyterianism; its own law; and a well-developed culture of public discourse and intellectual enquiry. London could ignore Wales and English peripheral regions safely enough, but ignoring Scotland ran huge risks.

The territoriality of the first British fiscal state can, not altogether clearly, be divided into three sub-periods. In the first, lasting from the Union to the 1745 rising, Scotland's economy struggled to make much headway, struggled with the new duty regime and struggled to send any money to London. Tensions, frictions and suspicions seemed ever present. Central government did not ignore these, but except for the malt tax it made little effort to address them. In the second, from the 1745 rising to the end of the American Revolutionary War in 1783, this changed. Jacobitism was to be extirpated, not only through brute force but by bringing local administration more into line with English practices and offering even greater encouragement to commercial life in Scotland. Yet, if this began to improve the tax take in Scotland, progress was still very slow. Finally, from the early 1780s central government in London much more concertedly attempted to trim the fiscal state to fit Scottish circumstances. An important feature of this was the increasing use that was made of parliamentary investigations into key taxes and bounties, allowing opinions and evidence to be collected from near and far. And it says much about England's politicians that they often listened to, and were sometimes persuaded by, what they read and heard. Key policy amendments followed: some forfeited estates were returned to families; tax privileges were ended; payments in Scotland on linen, fisheries and roads were maintained or increased; and differential rates of duty applied on an extended range of goods. Although some divisions between England and Scotland remained, these were weakening and further undermined by opposition between the Lowlands and the Highlands over the taxing of whisky. Something approaching a cohesive fiscal state was established. A financially desperate British state was surely pleased with the steep rise in taxes collected in Scotland from the 1780s.

Even so, in 1804 the per capita tax take in Scotland was only 33 per cent of that of England and Wales. Yet, as has been seen, there were usually very good reasons for this, to do with different natural circumstances, regional differences in patterns of prosperity and poverty, geographically varied tax rates and the particular difficulties of collecting revenue in remote and thinly inhabited areas. But it is quite wrong to see such considerations in wholly national terms. The importance of London and south-east England to tax collection was huge, reflecting their economic vitality and the ways in which central government was able to exploit the capital's entrepôt role, both within and beyond Britain. A significant gap existed between the formal and the effective incidence of taxes and it was one that central government used to the full.

It is interesting to note that the same pattern of what might be called 'metropolitanism' can be found in the incidence of capital punishment, which was much more common in and around London, fading away as the miles from the capital mounted up. Both the fiscal state and the criminal code in practice focused heavily on London.[160] That reflected not only that city's importance, but also the nature of government in more distant provinces, where central diktats had much less force and local administrators and power brokers much more influence, requiring much less parliamentary legislation.[161] Only when the state's very existence was threatened – by Jacobitism and rights-based radicalism – was the military routinely used. Given that central government was already sensitive to the different fiscal capacities of Scotland and England, this speaks powerfully to the nature of the Union state at the time: England dominated the minds of ministers and officials in London, but they appreciated that to a considerable extent the state's legitimacy in Scotland depended on acknowledging its different circumstances, indulging in some give and take and not unduly imposing upon a people, a society and an economy that were less prosperous than those of England. Despite the rapid rises in the tax take in Scotland from 1780, there was no revolt or rising there. America had been lost in part because of London's tax policies towards it. The French Revolution arose from the bankruptcy of the French state. In Scotland, there was nothing of the kind. Ireland, though, was to be a very different story.

3

1801–1914: Ireland's challenge

In the nineteenth-century Britain wielded more power than at any other time in its history. To some historians it was an 'age of improvement', an 'expanding society', a 'victorious century'.[1] Industrial muscle, free trade and the gold standard allowed Britons to be ambitious, mighty and global. The Great Exhibition of 1851 and Victoria's invention as Empress of India in 1876 perhaps epitomize those achievements, but they were hard won. Britain's burgeoning factories and mushrooming cities left a trail of short and stunted lives. In Ireland, a million died in the Great Famine. And carving out the largest empire in human history robbed many of their lives and even more of their liberties. Such ambiguities alert us to profound strains at the time between old and new values and the struggles over where to draw the boundary between public life and personal responsibility, all revolving around the flawed Union of 1801.

Given the huge differences between Britain and Ireland – environmental, economic, political, religious and cultural – the Union of 1801 was an even greater leap of faith than that of 1707 and one which satisfied few for long. Across the nineteenth century, many in Ireland saw the Union as the latest iteration of England's kleptomania, reducing what had been a prospering semi-independent island to impoverished colonial status. Some in Scotland, now clearly prospering as never before, came to view Ireland as unduly favoured and the Union state as too centralized in London. England tried different solutions to the 'Irish question', finding none that worked for long. And, all the while, Wales generally went quietly about its own business. There were many reasons for these different experiences, but debates over public finances was one way in which they were knitted together, providing not only an important point of reference but, to those wedded to political economy, utilitarianism and hard facts, a seemingly objective way of judging the success of the expanded United Kingdom. Most in Ireland were certain that fiscal policies failed properly to balance the principles of equality and equity, whatever adjustments were made; many in Britain believed Ireland avoided its obligations, indeed threatened to ruin carefully constructed imperial budgets.

Questions about the territoriality of public finances after 1801 were fundamentally framed by the Union of Britain and Ireland, but were significantly influenced by three other major developments.

First, the regional and local incidence of a century of profound economic and demographic developments saw much less industrialization and urbanization in Ireland than in Britain or, more precisely, parts of Britain. In this, Britain was just as anomalous as Ireland: England and Scotland became Europe's most urbanized and industrialized societies while Ireland remained highly agrarian – though Dublin grew impressively and there was significant industrialization in and around Belfast. Yet in London it was Britain's experience that seemed normal, with industry supplanting agriculture as the nation's most prized asset. Moreover, because of emigration and the Great Famine, Ireland's diminishing heft within the Union continuously challenged the perceptions of politicians and observers. Such misunderstandings were at the heart of the Union state.

Second, although this was an era of small government, growing responsibilities were put on the shoulders of local authorities, which only became bearable by directing significant amounts of UK tax receipts to aid hard-pressed local ratepayers. This redrew the nature of government and required a reimagining of the proper territorial units of government, with major local government reforms in 1835 and 1888. These developments took place, moreover, in the context of significant parliamentary reform such that the basis of representation changed from one of confusion and exclusion to one based by 1884 on a significantly expanded male franchise, the secret ballot and recognizably modern political parties.

Finally, fundamental tensions were generated by emerging ideas of nationhood – in Ireland especially, but also in Scotland – grating with the dictates of a newly ascendant political economy, with its incapacity for dealing analytically with anything between a single individual and the UK as a whole.

SIGNS OF THE TIMES

After 1815, thinking about how to make the 1801 Union pay took place in response to the material conditions produced by a quarter century of major warfare. Even before the French Revolution, Edmund Burke and others had called for reduced government spending, administrative reform and greater fiscal accountability. But the huge costs and administrative expansion of the wars against Revolutionary and Napoleonic France transformed the problem through rising taxes and a national debt to GDP ratio that was not surpassed until the Second World War.[2] Consequently, violent calls for 'cheap government' and ending 'old corruption' gained considerable purchase across society. William Cobbett's unbridled, bigoted and anti-Semitic criticisms of London as an 'all-devouring *Wen*' were particularly striking.[3] But both the propertied and the poor wanted central government to bear far less heavily upon them. This led to cost cutting, lower taxes, a heightened scrutiny of public finances and a determination to regularize and simplify the political framework of economic life. Across the classes, from rich to poor, there was a general belief in the efficacy of less not more government and in the fundamental virtue of 'economy' – that is, frugality and minimal public expenditure: this was the liberal order.[4] Such beliefs remained potent for most of the following century, though occasionally large spending was countenanced, as in the £20 million paid to achieve the abolition of slavery within the British Empire – total central government expenditure at the time was around £50 million per year – by compensating previous owners, or spending millions of pounds in the 1860s on the (immediately redundant) coastal defences, the 'Palmerston forts'. William Gladstone, that towering figure of nineteenth-century politics, four times prime minister, four times Chancellor of the Exchequer, proclaimed in 1859 that 'Economy is the first and great article . . . in my financial creed.'[5] This had important implications as it limited available discretionary spending to mitigate unintended inequity produced through applying taxes universally. Tellingly, on the eve of the First World War an influential editor of Adam Smith concluded that 'of the two principles, Equity and Economy, Equity is ultimately the weaker'.[6]

This tone was set very early, with over 370 petitions sent in to the House of Commons in February and March 1816 calling for the abolition of the income tax in a period of acute deflation. Peace might have been welcome, but, because Britain had been at war for so long, it was shocking in its own way. Soldiers and sailors flooded the labour market, while those injured and traumatized by the fighting struggled to find aid, with the propertied intent on slashing not just taxation but the local rates that funded poor relief. Landlords and farmers struggled too. Prices had risen sharply in wartime, encouraging costly investment in enclosure, drainage and canals. But prices then began to fall precipitously from their peak in 1812, squeezing margins. Rent arrears mounted; debts went unpaid. The business of large-scale contracting that had grown up to support the massive wartime military also had now to be dismantled and peacetime markets refashioned. Peace, too, was a challenge for financial markets that had grown accustomed to a burgeoning national debt and the Bank of England's suspension of cash payments (that is, the requirement to back its notes with gold). All these factors were very challenging, but they were exacerbated by new technology that was now clearly beginning to sweep aside traditional skills. Cartwright's power loom may have been patented in 1785, but it was not until the 1820s that the fatally lower productivity of skilled handloom weavers became apparent, with shrinking work and lower wages.

In 1829 Thomas Carlyle, a Scottish social critic, reflected on this cauldron of social, economic and political change in his essay 'Signs of the Times'. To his mind, the defining characteristic of the era was that it was 'mechanical'. But while the new technology at the heart of the first industrial revolution was part of this, he insisted that people were now also 'mechanical in head and heart'.[7] Older values of community, care and craft were being trodden underfoot by the materialism of new economic thinking, utilitarianism and empiricism. If, polemicist that he was, Carlyle exaggerated his case, he was certainly right about the growing influence of this unholy trinity. Especially through the work of Adam Smith, Thomas Robert Malthus and David Ricardo, the founders of classical economics in Britain, the invisible hand of the market was argued to allocate scarce resources much more efficiently than the visible hand of government. Free trade, with fewer, lower and more uniform duties and fewer distorting subsidies and bounties, was held to be a sound basis, optimizing taxes by reducing room for disincentives, evasion and fraud.[8] It helped that giving free rein to the natural course of things could also be squared with Christian notions of a divine order. Jeremy Bentham was a key figure in arguing the utilitarian case. In 1776 he had taken to task William Blackstone's defence of England's notoriously complex and chaotic laws. An arch-rationalist, Bentham sought order, clarity and certainty and for the costs and benefits of any chosen course to be assessed in terms of the greatest happiness for the greatest number. Finally, there was a growing belief in facts, in the power of numbers, surveys and enquiries: the first census was taken in 1801 and every ten years thereafter (from 1821 in Ireland), royal commissions proliferated and statistical societies were established in London, Manchester and Dublin. Thomas Gradgrind, Dickens's demagogic enthusiast for facts in *Hard times* (1854), was plainly a caricature, but Robert Peel, who had served as Chief Secretary in Ireland and who, as prime minister from 1841 to 1846, repealed the Corn Laws and split the Tories, exclaimed, 'There is nothing like a fact'; facts, he maintained, were 'ten times more valuable than declamations'.[9]

An important feature of this worldview was that it crossed between academia, market makers and politicians. It was also vigorously expressed through lectures, quarterlies such as the *Edinburgh Review* (1802) and *Westminster Review* (1824), and conscious attempts at popularization by Harriet Martineau and others. *The Times* and *The Economist*, established in 1785 and 1843 respectively, became especially powerful articulations of what would now be called 'establishment' views. It would be wrong, though, to suppose that there could not be major differences of opinion expressed within political society and between it and society as a whole over pressing questions. The furore over the Corn Laws before their final repeal in 1846, or over Home Rule from the 1880s, is clear enough evidence of that. Much as *The Times* might thunder against Irish beggary or, in a disapproving sense, Scottish 'jobs', it was sometimes challenged in its own pages by letters to the editors and reports of different sides of parliamentary debates. What was different between this world of ideas and its eighteenth-century antecedents was the status attained by the likes of *The Times* and their ability, in an age of railways and steamships, to find their way quickly into the hands of readers across the UK. By 1850 the tyranny of distance was reducing and the nature of the public sphere being redrawn.

An enthusiasm for cheap and restricted central government and for the importance of self-help exerted a powerful influence between 1815 and 1914. Once the dead of Waterloo had been buried, expensive warfare was mainly kept off the UK's public balance sheets until the outbreak of the First World War (Figure 8). This may have been the UK's peak of imperial power, but many of its costs were met by the defeated and the colonized, allowing people within the UK to enjoy lower prices and less oppressive rule.[10] The Crimean War (1853–6) and the Boer War (1899–1902) were important exceptions, but the decades after 1815 saw the relative cost of central government shrink significantly. Whereas its expenditure had peaked at over 20 per cent of GDP in 1814, by the 1870s it was around just 5 per cent. Consequently, as A. V. Dicey, a leading constitutional lawyer, put it in 1887, 'It is hardly an exaggeration to assert that even now we have . . . nothing like what foreigners mean by an administration.'[11] In fact, that was an exaggeration, but he had a point.

Such 'cheap government' grated against the growing realization that rapid population growth, urbanization and industrialization were creating serious socially corrosive problems that needed addressing: dealing with poverty, crime, public health, conditions of employment

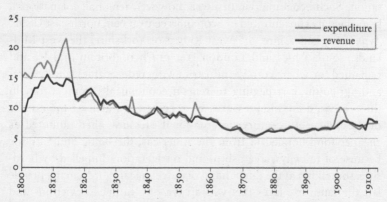

Figure 8. Central government finances relative to GDP, 1800–1913, %

and lack of education. This was no age of laissez-faire. But, because central government lacked the wherewithal to meet these challenges, local authorities had to do much of the heavy lifting involved.[12] This allowed central government to be kept small and for a time a pretty immediate relationship maintained between those who were paying for the new services, overwhelmingly propertied ratepayers, and those actually spending such funds – local administrators. But the weakness of this arrangement was that poorer areas had fewer resources and greater needs, despite significant reform of municipal corporations in 1835 and county councils in 1888. Where the relative lack of rate-payer income was severe, the only permanent solution was for central government to help local authorities, by loans and, especially, general financial support through grants-in-aid. This profoundly changed the balance of the constitution, with two key relationships becoming much fuzzier: of local to central government; and between them and rate- and taxpayers. As will be seen, quite what were and what were not fiscal 'entities' became very confused in the process.

Fundamental to the relatively low costs of the UK's central government in the nineteenth century was rapid industrialization, commercialization, urbanization and population growth. British goods and British capital reached across the globe, remaining potent even after the dramatic expansion of the American and German economies in the late nineteenth century. Underpinned by free trade and the gold standard, Britain's economy was unusually international in its orientation. Such economic vitality was, however, regional not national, being heavily concentrated in Scotland's central belt, north-east Ulster, Tyne-Tees, Lancashire, the West Riding of Yorkshire, the west Midlands, south Wales and London. Yet much of Britain and Ireland remained (or, where cottage industries withered, became) wholly rural and agricultural, struggling to remain economically competitive. In those areas, domestic pressures were acute until at least the middle of the nineteenth century; international pressures then mounted as cheaper food flooded in from the Americas, the Baltic and Ukraine because of railways, steamships and refrigeration. Impelled by hardship, sometimes at the direct hand of unfeeling landlords, many people left the land: in places this was an era of clearances, evictions and depopulation.[13] Such vulnerabilities were felt in many parts of Britain, but most acutely in Ireland, where rapid population growth throughout much of the eighteenth century had been sustained not by a major sectoral shift towards commerce and industry, but through subdividing the land and becoming more dependent on growing potatoes. Ireland's relative share of the UK population began to shrink from the first years of the Union and 1 million emigrated between 1801 and 1845, but dreadful famine in the late 1840s brought on by potato blight introduced a step change through immediate deaths (starvation and associated disease) and decades of emigration to Britain and America: Ireland's population halved between the Great Famine and the First World War (from 8 million to 4 million in very round numbers). In 1801 Ireland accounted for nearly one-third of the UK's total population; by 1911 it was one-tenth.[14]

The geography of economic and demographic changes was linked to a heightening of regional identities. Elizabeth Gaskell's novel of 1855, *North and South*, expressed a fundamental cleavage that had opened up, though industrialization's specific locales saw distinct areas emerge, such as the Black Country, the Potteries and the Welsh valleys. In this age of 'great cities', particular urban identities might be forged: Newcastle had its 'Geordies', Liverpool its 'Scousers' and London its 'Cockneys', terms which all came of age in the nineteenth century. All this rather complicates usual views of national identities flourishing in Europe after the French Revolution.[15] Certainly 'Struggles for national self-determination were characteristic of the age', but while such struggles were loud in Ireland, they were more softly spoken in Scotland and merely muttered in Wales and England – though the use of 'England' as a synonym for 'Britain' was common enough among the English.[16] Many within the UK certainly held to an imperial identity, but four-nation identities developed in complex and distinctive ways, rarely to the same timescale. A heightened sense of Scottish nationhood developed in the early nineteenth century – with Walter Scott especially important in articulating key supporting myths about history, landscape, culture and character, not least when George IV visited Scotland in 1822 (Image 3). Yet Scotland's economy became increasingly like that of England, while its people eagerly participated in Britain's expanding empire. Britain was, therefore, simultaneously united, bifurcated and fissured. Adding Ireland to the

Image 3. Alexander Carse, 'George IV landing at Leith', 1822. This was the first visit by a monarch to Scotland since 1651. The building behind him, with two flags aloft, is the customs house.

mix made this an even headier brew, complicated by Ireland's size and potential: in 1801 its population was more than three times that of Scotland. But, as it was a poorer society, the amount of taxes collected in Ireland was only slightly higher than in Scotland. Such material circumstances sat alongside profound differences between Britain and Ireland in terms of religion, politics, economy and civil society. This was in no meaningful sense a new 'Greater Britain', but, in terminology that then became common, a new home 'empire'.[17]

The dominant centre of that home empire was England, dwarfing in size and significance the other nations of the Union. That structural and inescapable inequality led inexorably to questions about how the

Union should work. So, to take the most relevant instance, tackling the 'Irish question' assumed that Ireland was the problem that needed correcting, not England or Britain as a whole. As Lord Rosebery, the Scottish peer and future prime minister, put it in 1882, 'Every part of the United Kingdom must be English because it is a part of the United Kingdom.'[18] Moreover, such haughtiness was seen by some as integral to national character – to Matthew Arnold 'a disposition to hardness is perhaps the special fault and danger of our English race in general, going along with our merits of energy and honesty.'[19] To one French economist and politician, the English had an 'unbending' temperament, wanting everything to be in their image.[20] Only from the 1860s did that temperament begin to become somewhat more flexible, but even then presumptions of racial difference between Celts and Anglo-Saxons was sometimes more than a casual underlying assumption.

Such differences were bound to make balancing equality and equity in the public finances of the expanded Union hard to get right. Yet the struggles over that balance were, with questions of class, central to contemporary debates over public finances and to the viability of the Union state. Save for some works on Ireland, including Alice Murray's groundbreaking book of 1903, these are not questions to which historians of the nineteenth century, either of the Union state or of public finances, have given sustained attention.[21] And it is to the fiscal terms of the 1801 Union that discussion turns next, followed by the patterns of taxation and expenditure across the period and how best to explain them. The discontents engendered, however, raised loud calls for devolution and disunion that came to a head in debates over Home Rule that ran through much of the period from 1870. They are considered in the final section of this chapter.

THE FISCAL UNION MADE, AND REMADE

The United Kingdom of Great Britain and Ireland rested on acts passed by their respective parliaments that came into force on 1 January 1801.[22] As in 1707, it was an incorporating union, with the Dublin parliament abolished and that at Westminster expanded – by 100 Irish MPs and 32 peers (28 lay and 4 spiritual). With Scotland having only 45 MPs and Wales just 24, this appeared to be an impressive block of representation and one that eventually came to wield considerable power, even though England had 489 MPs. However, whereas England and Wales had one MP for every 17,000 persons and Scotland one for every 36,000, in Ireland the figure was just one per 52,000 people.[23] While the Union's framers lacked accurate population totals to make such calculations, they knew they had created a significant imbalance, which was implicitly justified on the grounds that many Irish were politically untrustworthy – evidenced in their eyes by various factors: a major republican-inspired independence rebellion in 1798; the unreliability even of its largely Protestant landowning class; the continuing adherence of about 80 per cent of Ireland's population to Catholicism despite a century of 'penal laws' excluding them from formal political life; and greater poverty. This was underscored by George III's refusal to countenance removing political restrictions on Catholics, even though Pitt the Younger and other leading ministers thought much greater toleration was essential to making the Union work. Even more than in 1707, the Union of 1801 was one of unequals, with less negotiation and more diktat (though just as much bribery). It did not help matters that Westminster's idea of liberty had become increasingly archaic in the face of emerging ideas on rights that had proved so important in the American and French revolutions. As in 1707, however, the larger leading partner mainly sought unity for reasons of wartime national security that had been seriously threatened in the rebellion of 1798, supported as it was by a French invasion, though in the process changing and challenging national identities. Enough of the politically dominant Protestant elite in Ireland thought the same. To Lord Byron, the Union was one of 'the shark with its prey', swallowing its victim to become 'one and indivisible'.[24]

Whereas in 1707 there was some mutual respect between England and Scotland, in 1801 there were large bodies of opinion in Britain and Ireland who viewed one another with a mixture of suspicion and fear. While mostly sharing the same language, many Irish saw the English (much more rarely the British) as self-righteous, hypocritical autocrats, while many English damned the Irish as superstitious, feckless thugs. Such views, which had existed for centuries, had been heightened by the 1798 rebellion, with its attempt to overthrow the political and economic order there. The ambition of creating a fully independent and republican Ireland clearly drew its inspiration from Britain's arch-enemy, Revolutionary France. But the operation of the Union state after 1707 had also taught British negotiators – William Pitt the Younger, Henry Dundas, Lord Castlereagh and other leading ministers – some important lessons about what to seek and not to seek from uniting with Ireland. Some of those lessons were Anglo-Scottish, notably avoiding the fiscal limitations of the 1707 Union, but some were formed by the long-term use and abuse of Ireland by

Britain. Britain had, in some meaningful, if often ineffective way, governed Ireland for many years before 1801, despite the independence of the Dublin parliament since 1782. It had executive officers, including a viceroy, at Dublin castle (retained after the Union), it had long restricted Ireland's economy to suit England and, to satisfy English cries of 'no standing army', it had barracked troops in Ireland that were paid for by Irish taxpayers.[25] Critically, here, Ireland had a fiscal regime sharing some features with Britain, especially concerning customs and excise. But, fiscally, Ireland was also distinctive. Several taxes in Britain were not collected there – on land and luxuries, for example – while the hearth tax, abolished in England in 1689 as a badge of slavery, was collected in Ireland until 1822.

In the eighteenth century, Ireland's central government revenue totalled £65 million and Britain's £928 million, a ratio of 1:14.[26] But there were important changes over time, from two main directions. Across that century, tax receipts had increased about fivefold in Ireland, but sevenfold in Britain, both because of the greater fertility of Britain's economy and the more rapid development of taxes there, especially on the wealthy's items of conspicuous consumption. And, because the population was growing much more rapidly in Ireland, the per capita tax burden fell sharply relative to Britain, from a ratio of under 1:2 in 1700 to 1:7 on the eve of the Union.[27] Had those dynamics been understood by the framers of the Union, then perhaps the worst of the fiscal problems that arose in Ireland subsequently might have been avoided. Ministers in London certainly did not set out to fleece Ireland. Arguably they sought to be 'kind, generous, and friendly', certainly to make arrangements that they thought were 'fair'.[28] They honestly believed that the final terms rested on solid evidence and sound reasoning. But key decisions were made on the basis of tax and trade data for just one year, 1798–9, with little consideration of how typical that wartime year was – up-to-date figures were presumed to be the best and the papers of Castlereagh, Chief Secretary for Ireland at the time, are full of them.[29] Nor was much effort made to relate the figures collected to the relative size of the economy and population of each nation. William Playfair's stunning invention of graphs in 1786 to depict Britain's developing trade and public revenues since 1688 might have been compared with R. V. Clarendon's similarly conceived graphs of Irish public revenues published in 1791.[30] But they were not: this was a government with a small administration that had been stretched to breaking point by years of war and domestic disquiet.[31] Finally, there was a profound intellectual misstep regarding issues around the Laffer curve. Even though in 1798 Pitt recalled that taxes 'nominally equal might apply very differently in the two countries', when it came to the crunch this was given little weight.[32] Instead, ministers embraced beguilingly simple arithmetic: Ireland's fiscal capacity relative to the UK as a whole would determine its share of the UK's total taxes, no more, no less.

Despite the magnificence of the new customs house opened in Dublin in 1791 and patriotic optimism about Ireland's economic prospects, opinion in Ireland in 1799 and 1800 was overwhelmingly that the Union would introduce a financially oppressive and *'provincializing System'*.[33] Differences between the two islands were stressed: 'the inhabitants of no two countries on the face of the globe are so essentially different' was the view of the Irish 4th Earl of Darnley, an avid cricketer in Kent, where he lived.[34] Bellicosity, with all of its human and financial costs, seemed to run through Britain's marrow. If Ireland was to be much more closely hitched to that, surely it would suffer, it was argued, the more so given the tensions that raising taxes in Ireland had generated in the 1790s.[35] A cartoon of the period by Isaac Cruikshank caught this nicely (Image 4). Here on the right is calm femininity, Miss Hibernia; facing her on the far left is her suitor, a ruddy, gesturing John Bull, perhaps in his cups. Between them are his family, identified as various taxes that struggle to sate the appetite of the central 'dreadfull Monster', the new income tax. Understandably, Hibernia rejects marrying into such a dysfunctional household: 'Really Mr. Bull . . . I fear I must decline all thoughts of the intended Union – your family is so very large.'[36] Such views were commonplace. John Foster, Speaker of the Irish House of Commons, put it bluntly to his MPs: though Pitt was a great finance minister, 'he wants your purse and your trade'.[37]

In the Union debates, politicians in Ireland offered detailed challenges to the proposed fixed 2/17th share of joint expenditure the island was to meet. By their reckoning that was unsustainable. Henry Grattan, the leading Irish politician of his generation, issued a stark

Image 4. Isaac Cruikshank, 'Miss Hibernia at John Bulls family dinner!!',
1799. Between John Bull on the far left and Miss Hibernia on the far right
are various taxes, rendered as the children of John Bull, of which much the
largest and most voracious is the new income tax in the middle.

have some more!

saac Income!!

Really Mr Bull notwithstanding you have done me the Honor of placing me at the head of your Table to day... I fear I must decline all thoughts of the intended *Union* ... your Family is so very large & so enormously expensive, that I fear my small Dowry will scarcely suffice Master *Income* alone, for *one meal*... besides I understand these are but a small part of your numerous Family & that you have several Junior branches still in the Nursery

Dont be so boisterous, there is enough for us all

Abraham ———— Hat Stamp

Hannah Heier Tax

Simon Soap Tax

Tommy Dble Tax

Pub^d of Caricatures lent out for the Evening

LLS FAMILY DINNER!!

warning: 'Colour it as you please, she [Ireland] will pay more than she is able; and she will pay for a force, not to protect, but to enslave.'[38] The shortfall would have to be met by borrowing on a scale well beyond the capacity of Ireland's money markets – the Irish debt was already a matter of some concern there, leading to a ruinous drain of money to London. Echoing David Hume in the 1750s, critics predicted that its debts would escalate, ending ultimately in bankruptcy.[39] Ministers in London certainly heard such concerns, but, mainly for reasons of national security, were intent on pushing through a limited incorporating union.

It was not that the Union's negotiators ignored the fact that Ireland's weaker economy lacked the coal and iron so essential to Britain's increasingly potent industrialization, or that the relative fortunes of the two islands might change. It was agreed that the fiscal terms (articles six and seven) might be revised every twenty years, to adjust for changes. The baseline, however, was to require Ireland to contribute 2/17ths (just under 12 per cent) to joint – what was now called 'imperial' – expenditure. Castlereagh rather plumped for that proportion, without thinking it through carefully.[40] In a similar vein, while some trade barriers between Britain and Ireland were removed in 1801, this was incomplete. In language reeking of mercantilism, dozens of goods were 'enumerated', subject to 'countervailing duties' when traded between the two islands. In part this sought to produce a more level playing field given differences between the two islands regarding what was taxed and at what rate. But there was also some sensitivity to perceived vulnerabilities within Ireland's industrial sector, its young cotton industry being afforded gradually diminishing protection. Such an incomplete Union was also required because of the commitment that the partners should maintain separate national debts. That was meant to ensure that British taxpayers did not have to pay for the extravagance of Irish politicians, but it proved to be a fatal decision.

In key essentials, the fiscal terms of the 1707 and 1801 unions were very different, in three main ways.[41] First, in 1707 a new British financial entity had been created. In 1801 Britain and Ireland were to continue as fiscally linked but distinct. There was no currency union. The requirement that Ireland pay a fixed share of total expenditure was designed to avoid the complaints that it was failing to pay its way that had dogged Scotland since 1707. Ireland was also allowed to collect revenues much as it had done for years – there was to be no plague of English excise men swarming through Irish villages levying previously unheard-of taxes. This meant taxes on income, land and eight major excised goods, all very lucrative in Britain, were not extended to Ireland, which also enjoyed lower rates of duties on five other excised goods.[42] Secondly, allowing Ireland to maintain a separate public debt, while paying taxes to help support the British national debt, obviated the need for any discussion of compensatory 'equivalents' that had been impossible to manage satisfactorily in the Scottish case. Finally, a somewhat separate Irish currency and weights and measures could be maintained. And while there was to be freer trade between Britain and Ireland, this was far less complete than what had been agreed in 1707. All told, Ireland and Britain were to maintain separate annual budgets, exchequers and revenue services, if now subject to a single parliament that had to be sensitive to the need for 'particular exemptions and abatements' in taxes for both Ireland and Scotland. This was certainly not, as 1707 had been, a full customs and currency union. Conditions were set out by which full fiscal unity might be achieved in the future, however, whereby taxes would be applied 'indiscriminately' across the islands and their debts merged. This depended either on the liquidation of their national debts, or the relative size of the two debts reaching the same 2/17ths shares required for joint expenditure. It was not said when significant changes might happen, but twenty years hence appears to have been in mind when, simultaneously, hefty subsidies at pre-Union levels for encouraging Ireland's economy were to end and a revision of the share of the burdens was to be reconsidered.

Fiscally, the main weakness of the 1801 Union was that no one could know what future imperial expenditure would be. With the French Revolutionary Wars (1792–1802) inching towards their end, the hope was that the Union would coincide with an era of peace and prosperity. Pitt and others anticipated that in such circumstances both islands would prosper as, employing Scottish ideas, reduced regulatory friction between them, along with greater 'liberality' in Ireland's governance, would enhance the commercial opportunities for farmers and landlords, merchants and manufacturers, with everyone ultimately enjoying the fruits of less bridled capitalism.[43] The ruinously expensive Napoleonic Wars (1803–15) smashed such optimism. Whereas the Revolutionary Wars had been much the most expensive that Britain had yet fought, annual costs to central government were in real terms half as much again in the Napoleonic Wars. It quickly became clear that, despite expanding the tax base, including equalizing British and Irish customs duties by 1814, Ireland could meet its fixed share of UK public expenditure only by borrowing more and more, which soon became overwhelming.[44] And so from 1817 the fiscal terms of the Union were rewritten: Ireland's separate exchequer and debt were merged into one for the UK as a whole; the 2/17ths share was effectively pushed aside; over the next decade significant further steps were taken to harmonize duties between Britain and Ireland; and in 1823 the revenue commissioners in Ireland and Scotland were both abolished, with UK collection now overseen from London alone. In a similar vein, in 1824 the imperial system of weights and measures was introduced across the UK and in 1826 Ireland's currency became the pound sterling. By 1830 Ireland's position within the Union had shifted towards that of Scotland immediately after 1707.[45] But abandoning the 2/17ths share and equalizing most taxes between Britain and Ireland meant that how much Ireland should now send to the Exchequer in London was unknown and liable to disagreement about what was fair. In 1801 fiscal equality had been sacrificed to a particular view of equity. But the ruinous premise of Ireland's 2/17ths share required a radical rethink in favour of greater equality, with less regard paid to Ireland's specific circumstances.

With apologies to Wales, the Union of 1801 changed Britain's composite state from a bilateral to a trilateral one, with Ireland supplanting Scotland as England's largest partner, politically, territorially and demographically. As we saw in the last chapter, the Union of Britain and Ireland took place soon after Scotland began to contribute very much more revenue to the Exchequer in London. Fiscally, its industrialization and urbanization, along with policy tweaks, meant that it was at long last being fully incorporated into the Union state. From London's perspective, it was a fiscal problem that was at long last being solved; from Scotland's perspective, the Union now seemed to be paying. Ireland was, though, a very different prospect: in London it was seen as popish, populous and poor.

Between 1801 and 1914, it was Irish discontents that dominated discussions of the territoriality of the UK's finances. Indeed, these were far more frequent, concerted and unyielding than the Scottish disquiets explored in the last chapter. From early complaints that Ireland was being bankrupted by the Union, through calls for repeal in the 1830s and the crisis of the Great Famine, to the Home Rule debates about devolution and federalism, the fiscal relationship of Ireland to the Union state was repeatedly and publicly argued over. In Ireland a wide array of critics – the clergy, corporations, radicals, political economists and commentators – all joined the fray, given focus by Irish politicians in Westminster. As such, they were met publicly, not just in parliamentary debates, royal commissions and by politicians on the stump in Britain, but by the London press, financial analysts and cartoonists. Equality and equity were in perpetual tension in these debates, the resolution of which was impossible because of changing ideas of nationhood and a widespread attachment to the spirit of 'economy'.

A TAXING UNION

Beginning in the 1780s there were major improvements in the keeping and publication of central government's financial accounts, to aid transparency and accountability, to reduce waste and to purge the constitution. Very much in the spirit of this age of facts, from 1804 annual accounts were published among the mountainous volumes of parliamentary 'blue books'. These distinguished the UK's three kingdoms until 1851; but from 1852 until 1889, only UK-wide figures were published at the time – itself evidence of an official preference to treat the UK holistically, without reference to national shares. Happily, in the 1890s, amid heated debates over reconstituting the relationship of the UK's nations, some historical reconstructions of national shares of the UK public accounts were made – though Wales was always lumped in with England through this period. From 1889 there was a return to the pre-1851 system of reporting, though now with expenditure also apportioned territorially, again evidencing a new willingness to treat the three kingdoms as somewhat separate financial entities.

Over the whole period, England and Wales dominated the UK's public finances.[46] Never less than 76 per cent of taxation for central government was collected there, though also never more than 86 per cent. Very roughly, the remaining shares were divided equally between Ireland and Scotland. These patterns were fundamental to perceptions of the relative importance of the different nations of the UK: to central government England loomed very large; reciprocally, the other nations of the Union could easily believe that they were given little thought. But these must be related to significant population change, with per capita figures showing a very different dynamic: Scotland and Wales accounted for a fairly steady share of the UK population, but Ireland's fell significantly and England's rose.

There are two closely related but distinguishable stories to be told from Figure 9. One is of significant divergence early in the Union giving way to greater convergence in the late nineteenth century, followed by some divergence again. The second is of the different paths taken by the three kingdoms: of declining per capita taxes collected in England and Wales for much of the nineteenth century; of burdens in Scotland falling only briefly after 1815, followed by slow rises for most of the rest of the period; and of burdens falling in Ireland for several decades after Waterloo, to be followed by decades of rises.

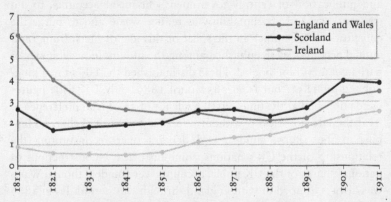

Figure 9. Tax collected, per capita £, by nation, 1811–1911

Especially notable is that taxes collected in Scotland were, on a per capita basis, marginally higher than in England and Wales from around 1860 until the eve of the First World War. By contrast, amounts collected in Ireland were, apart from the 1880s and 1890s, always clearly less than in Britain. But Ireland's tax burdens need to be put more clearly into the context of its significant population decline after the census of 1841 (Figure 10).

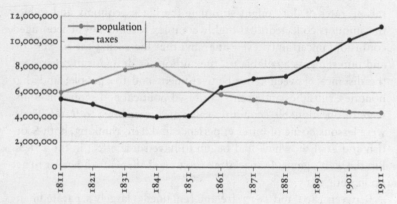

Figure 10. Ireland's population in millions and total taxes in millions of £, 1811–1911

Ireland's population was growing quickly in the decades leading to the Great Famine of 1846–9, though less rapidly than Britain's. Over the same period, the taxes collected in Ireland fell. But soon after the Famine, those trajectories were reversed; far from the Famine and high levels of emigration through the rest of the century ushering in an era of falling revenues in Ireland, quite the opposite happened. A major feature of the Union state was its ability to extract more revenue from Ireland's shrinking society, both absolutely and relatively. It did this with a tax regime that was markedly more regressive there, with a much higher dependence upon indirect taxes on excised and imported goods. This dependence gradually grew, so that in 1911 customs and excise provided 78 per cent of central government revenues in Ireland, compared with 62 per cent in Scotland and 41 per cent in England and Wales.

As in the last chapter, these patterns are to be understood as the outcome of the interplay of tax policy, taxable capacity and the tax gap, the last itself a function of administrative efficiency relative to tax morale, the willingness or not to pay taxes, itself somewhat unpredictably influenced by public expenditure, as will be discussed in the following section.

By 1801 framers of tax policies could draw on many decades of hard-won experience with which to move forward. They knew that raising rates of duty might stimulate the black economy and reduce the amounts collected; that highly complex revenue laws encouraged confusion, uncertainty, even anarchy; that increasing the powers of, and punishments available to, the authorities dramatically increased the distance between central government and the people; and that bounties, subsidies and grants confused political and economic aims, were of questionable economic value and were lures to fraud. These were lessons borne of bitter experience and hard thinking, both Scottish and English, which had begun to have some effect in the 1780s. But the wars against France after 1793 made them much harder to act upon until 1815.

Between 1801 and 1817, Ireland remained a largely separate financial entity, often carrying on with the taxes that had been collected before the Union. Consequently, there was no immediate widespread resistance to the revenue regime as there had been in Scotland after 1707. Certainly this was an era of near open warfare between the authorities and peasant distillers, especially in north-west Ireland.[47] This, though, had origins dating back to the 1780s when new duties and harsh new penalties were introduced, including the notorious 'townland fines', where a whole district could be fined for any illicit distilling that was successfully prosecuted for taking place there. If this and the violence between the authorities and distillers and their communities was more extreme than simultaneous struggles over taxing whisky in Scotland's Highlands and Islands, a similar cause was at work: an attempt by central government to tax a very poor people because all were meant to contribute something to the public purse. But those poor enjoyed whisky (or 'whiskey' in Ireland) as an essential part of an everyday life of considerable hardship, where any attempt at taxation was liable to be seen as burdensome at best, enslaving at worst.[48] (Much later, whisky was by both the Scots and Irish likened to 'ichor', the blood of Greek gods, and a 'panacea'.[49])

There was, though, a more or less immediate reaction in Ireland to the fiscal aspects of the Union through complaints that the 2/17ths share was excessive, requiring exhausting amounts of taxes to be collected and unsustainable amounts of debts to be contracted. It was argued that this was beyond the island's capacity, despite the best efforts of its revenue services. Moreover, because Ireland had its own Chancellor of the Exchequer who presented his annual budget to the House of Commons in Westminster until 1817, these were points that were well aired. Evidence of substantial rises both in the tax take in Ireland and in its debt was there in black and white for all to see. What it showed was that, with the heavy costs of the Napoleonic Wars, the shortfall of income to expenditure, producing increasing indebtedness, was greater in Ireland; Britain's debt doubled between 1801 and 1817, but Ireland's quadrupled.[50] From one perspective, this might be put down to Ireland being spared various taxes, notably on incomes, or the inefficiencies of its administration, or both. From another, it was evidence that Ireland's economy was faltering under the pressures of the Union in general, including overtaxation, because of the demands of the 2/17ths share. Writing from exile in America, the Irish radicals William MacNeven and Thomas Emmet argued that the Irish were taxed at three times the rate of their new homeland, with the Irish having been subjected to 'political slavery'.[51] Yet as Figure 9 showed, in 1811 the per capita tax take in Ireland was only one-sixth of that in England and Wales and about one-third of that in Scotland.

As already noted, between 1817 and 1830 there was considerable erosion of Ireland's distinctive fiscal treatment. Particularly relevant here was that customs and stamp duty were harmonized between the two islands, along with many excise duties. There were certainly complaints about this in and on behalf of Ireland. The merger of stamp duty in 1830 triggered seventy-five petitions to parliament from Ireland, all berating a tax that would fall heavily on newspapers, invoking in the process the principles of the freedom of the press and the injustice of taxing knowledge. Daniel O'Connell, who did so much to mobilize Irish opposition to the Union state from the 1820s until his death in

1847, complained in 1830 that 'England has thrown off millions of taxation this year, while Ireland, which by many degrees [is] more depressed, is to be saddled with an increase of £300,000 of taxation.'[52] Four years later he denounced 'the most shameful robbery of Ireland'.[53]

In 1830 O'Connell drew attention to a key dynamic at work alongside moves towards fiscal assimilation: the abolition of many duties ('remission', as it was called at the time). In both Britain and Ireland, absolute amounts of taxes collected fell between 1815 and 1842 as hundreds of low-yielding duties were abolished on the grounds of 'economy' and the liberalization of trade. Additionally, two highly lucrative duties were also abolished, on incomes in 1816 and on beer in 1830, the former because of the selfish pressures of the political classes, the latter to try to make the tax regime less regressive. All told, these tax cuts were worth £48 million. Yet, while in the climate of the times these were widely welcomed, there was a marked territoriality to them, which caused dissent, especially in Ireland. In 1843 official statistics showed that 95 per cent of remitted taxes aided Britain and only 5 per cent Ireland. Especially notable was that £17 million of the cuts were due to the abolition of the income tax and nearly £4 million on beer, neither of which had been levied on Ireland.[54] In fact, many of the reductions and repeals of taxes helped to harmonize further the fiscal regime across the UK: greater equality was part of the aim. But, because the now untaxed beer was much more heavily consumed in England whereas the Scottish and Irish favoured taxed spirits, the benefits of tax cuts were clearly nationally unbalanced.[55]

The reintroduction of the income tax in 1842 was a countervailing development, with Peel not extending it to Ireland, fearing it would be too burdensome and administratively challenging given that Ireland's landowners, unlike their counterparts in Britain, had never collected the land tax.[56] He later explicitly rejected calls to apply taxes indiscriminately across the UK: fiscal equality he viewed as a crude 'iron rule'; it was, he thought, 'impossible to disregard the peculiar situation of different parts of the United Kingdom'.[57] In holding that view, he was invoking a clause in the Act of Union which said that future taxes had to be mindful of the different circumstances of Ireland and of Scotland. Perhaps, given his experience in Ireland, he also accepted the conjecture of Pitt the Younger from 1785 that a society half as prosperous as another might only be able to support one-tenth of the taxation. He had certainly earlier appreciated that in certain circumstances it was sometimes necessary to set aside the ordinary principles of political economy.[58] There may have been political calculus in Peel's position, in terms of keeping the Protestant Ascendancy (the generally Anglo-Irish elite) on side in Ireland, but probably Peel was more swayed by arguments that to tax income would remove capital from an economy often said to have been starved of investment – in 1842 the Loyal National Repeal Association petitioned parliament on the heavy and unjust taxation of Ireland.[59]

Unsurprisingly, Ireland's exclusion from the income tax after 1842 attracted critical comment in turn from British MPs. In 1845 there was an explicit motion in the Commons for the tax to be extended to Ireland. William Williams, a radical and Welsh-born MP, calculated that taxation collected in Ireland relative to the UK as a whole had been falling on trend since 1817 and was now only 7 per cent, meaning, he concluded, that 'in regard to taxation [Ireland] was in a most remarkable degree protected'.[60] In this he was following the argument of the Dubliner Robert Montgomery Martin, a founder of what became the Royal Statistical Society, who in 1843 had published a lengthy analysis of changing economic fortunes in his book *Ireland before and after the Union*. By his reckoning, Ireland 'was one of the least taxed countries in Europe'. Moreover, while Scotland was much more heavily taxed, it was flourishing while Ireland was not.[61] On this occasion, the argument for equality of taxation across the UK was successfully met by an argument for inequality. As the Irish MP Richard Sheil put it, Ireland would be much more governable and lucrative if, 'instead of adapting Ireland to your institutions, you do but try to adapt your institutions to Ireland'.[62] Although the 1845 motion was defeated, the question of how to treat Ireland fiscally did not go away and the income tax was extended to Ireland in 1853.

Several factors allowed the question of Ireland's exemption from the income tax to fester. One was the wider political contentions of the 'hungry forties': the Conservative party split over Peel's repeal of the Corn Laws in 1846; Chartist calls for a radical redrawing of the political and economic order, including more direct taxation, climaxed in 1848, the year of revolutions in Europe (including a minor rising in Ireland); and lobbying by the likes of the Financial Reform Association, established in Liverpool in 1848, again for greater direct taxation.[63] So, for example, in 1852 Glasgow's chief magistrate called a meeting which then petitioned parliament to reduce customs and excise, replaced by a 'general income tax', which was said to be simple and equitable, as well as the only system of taxation wholly consistent with true free trade.[64] Anti-Catholicism also had its part to play. In 1845 Peel's proposal to increase Treasury support for the Catholic seminary at Maynooth in Ireland led to a storm of protest, with a petition against it signed by 1 million people.[65]

But it was the Great Famine in Ireland which led some to conclude that the best way of addressing the structural limitations that had repeatedly rendered Irish society economically precarious was to apply Britain's political economy more forcefully upon it. There were voices in Ireland calling for such an approach: Martin's book was published in a new edition in 1848 and William Neilson Hancock, professor of political economy at Trinity College Dublin and a founder of the Dublin Statistical Society, argued strongly in 1847 for adhering to the principles of political economy.[66] And had not O'Connell himself called for 'an identity of laws, an identity of institutions, and an identity of liberties' between the two islands?[67] A key voice, however, was the Englishman Charles Trevelyan, the main Treasury official charged with making and directing central government's financial management of the Famine – discussed later in this chapter. He articulated more clearly than most of his predecessors a 'Treasury view' of public finances intent on allowing the market free rein through limited taxation and public expenditure.

If Gladstone saw Trevelyan as 'rash and uncompromising', 'blunt almost to roughness', his ideas at this time were in key respects very similar.[68] In 1853, as Chancellor of the Exchequer, he extended the income tax to Ireland, attempting to sugar the pill by cancelling £8 million of public loans that had been made to Ireland during the Famine. In his budget speech he acknowledged that Ireland had just been 'visited by an awful calamity', but he argued that taxes should be applied equally across the state. Echoing J. R. McCulloch, the classical economist, he opined that 'the exemption of one man means the extra taxation of another – and the exemption of one country means the extra taxation of another.'[69] He viewed questions of sub-UK territoriality as irrelevant: it was individuals, not communities, that were taxed. And the income tax affected the rich not the poor, while he believed that indirect taxes could be avoided through the consumption of non-taxed goods.[70] All in all, Gladstone sought to reset public finances in Ireland in terms of far greater equality across the UK. What, he thought, would be the harm in that?

There was considerable support in parliament for extending the income tax to Ireland. To Richard Cobden, a leading free trader, 'There must be perfect equality between the two countries, and every tax paid by this country must be paid by Ireland', though he hoped tax burdens would fall. The lack of an income tax in Ireland gave its businesses, in his view, an unfair commercial advantage.[71] This was a line repeated by *The Economist*, which also argued that Ireland's exemption from the income tax meant that people there were too disconnected from the consequences of public-finance policy. Introducing the income tax in Ireland would supposedly strengthen the bonds of the Union.[72] Against this it was argued that Ireland was already overtaxed relative to its economy, making it all the harder to recover from the calamity of the Famine. Free trade was said to have damaged Ireland's agricultural economy by opening it up to stiff competition from abroad. All in all, Britain 'chose to govern [Ireland] in a manner opposed to the wishes of the people', requiring the state to use much more brute force than in Britain, 'for the repression of the people of Ireland'.[73]

Extending the income tax to Ireland was a further step on the road of greater equality of taxation between Britain and Ireland set in train by the ill-judged terms of the fiscal union of 1801. Further major steps were taken in 1855 and 1858 by Gladstone's successors as Chancellor, George Cornewall Lewis and Benjamin Disraeli, with lucrative spirit duties becoming uniform across the whole UK only in 1858 (Figure 11).

Disraeli's reasoning for equalizing spirit duties in 1858 spliced the arguments of Cobden and Gladstone, emphasizing the benefits of free trade, perhaps suggesting that in financial matters Disraeli was more principled than is often allowed, though Disraeli also pointed out that Irish politicians sometimes wanted equality, sometimes not, mainly, he was implying, for self-interested reasons.[74]

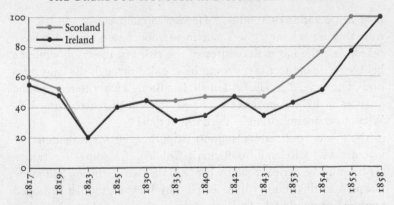

Figure 11. Scottish and Irish spirit duty rates relative to England and Wales, 1817–58, %

Taken together, the territorially equalizing budgets of 1853, 1855 and 1858 marked a new phase in the UK's financial relations – though Ireland continued to be exempt from the taxes collected in Britain on land, various coaches and carriages, horses and railways. There were changes to tax policy subsequently, notably the reintroduction of a tax on beer in 1880 – though the Scots and Irish argued it was taxed at a very low rate relative to its proof measure – and the extension of inheritance taxes. But the changes of the 1850s were those that set the agenda for debate up until 1914 by provoking a new era of concerted and detailed Irish complaints of the 'taxing union'. First Irish Conservatives and then nationalists repeatedly raised objections in the House of Commons, including at a significant Select Committee in 1864–5.[75] The extension of the income tax to Ireland and the cancelling of publicly funded debts there was called a 'swindle', leading Ireland to be continuously heavily overtaxed, which was said to be ruining its economy by diverting funds from capital investment while 'demoralizing' individuals by subjecting them to unbearable amounts of taxes.[76] An identity of taxation across the Union did not, it was claimed, equalize the burden of taxation.[77] Such imposts were merely 'tribute exacted by the richer and more powerful country from the poorer and weaker'.[78] Looking back from 1897, one survey of these discontents complained that 'No greater sophistry was ever preached than that of "equalized taxation". It was the greatest engine of oppression in Ireland during the second half of the nineteenth century.'[79] The Treasury came in for repeated criticism, including for controlling the information with which to assess the burdens of taxation.

Claims that Ireland was overtaxed were provoked by the indisputable facts that the country was poorer than Britain and losing population. But this was a rough-and-ready line of causation, liable to the counter charge that levels of taxation reflected reasonably accurately the individual's consumption, income and wealth. By such reasoning, if people were poorer, they bought fewer taxed goods and were not liable for the income tax. As *The Times* put it, 'No man ... pays one penny more, in direct or indirect taxation, because he lives in Ireland instead of living in England or Scotland.'[80] Consequently, it was 'metaphysical rubbish' to argue that any part of the UK was a separate taxable entity.[81] To try to settle matters, calculating Ireland's alleged overtaxation had to be attempted.

Calculations of Ireland's taxable capacity relative to Britain's were undertaken now and then throughout the nineteenth century. In 1801, as we have seen, it was put at 2/17ths (12 per cent). In the 1860s and 1870s, figures of between 5 and 7 per cent were proposed by Irish politicians, with the amounts of taxes raised put at 11 per cent.[82] But because these emanated from interested parties, they were liable to be dismissed as special pleading. The need for disinterested calculations became imperative once Home Rule became a major political question for the UK in the 1880s.

A critical contribution was made by Robert Giffen in 1886. A Scot, he was a fierce advocate of free trade, for a time working for both *The Economist* and *The Times*. A highly skilled and highly placed governmental statistician, Giffen calculated, in a widely read piece of journalism published around the time of the first Home Rule bill, that Ireland was taxed about twice as much in relation to its total income compared to Britain, though he also calculated that this was more than offset by central government expenditure in Ireland.[83] For such an 'establishment' figure to conclude that Ireland was indeed overtaxed energized the debate. Given the ructions over Home Rule – Giffen was a critic of Gladstone's financial proposals in 1886 – this helped to stimulate the establishment of a royal commission in 1894 to investigate Ireland's financial relations with the UK. But, issuing its final report two years later, it failed to settle matters. With its original chairman dying before his draft report was finalized, the surviving commissioners could not agree among themselves. Some calculated that Ireland was heavily overtaxed, at the other extreme that ideologically it was quite wrong to treat any part of the UK as a separate financial entity.[84] Ultimately politics trumped statistics: nationalists insisted that the commission had established that Ireland was overtaxed, while commentators such as *The Times* concluded just the opposite.[85] But if Ireland had been overtaxed, then the accumulated value of this might be huge. Antony MacDonnell, a Home Ruler who had been Under-Secretary of Ireland, asserted that since 1817 Ireland had sent to Britain £325 million as, in his words, 'tribute', over and above the cost of Ireland's administration.[86] As we will see in the next chapter, such calculations reverberated up until 1930.

Modern studies certainly show that, although Ireland's economy grew between 1861 and 1911, perhaps by about a fifth, the other three countries of the Union grew many times faster. Demographically and economically, Ireland was shrinking in relative importance within the UK, with a more agrarian (and increasingly pastoral) economy that depended even more than Britain on external trade. Based on the rapid growth of the heavy industries of its central belt, Scotland was as industrial as England by 1850. As was later noted, 'Scotland has held her own in the modern race of material progress.'[87] If Wales lagged, the dramatic expansion of steel making and coal mining in south Wales meant it was a key node of the UK economy by 1914. By contrast, in 1906 Ireland accounted for only 4 per cent of UK industrial production.[88] The 1894–6 royal commission stated that 26 per cent of Ireland's population was urbanized, compared to 71 per cent in Britain.[89] Such figures suggest that by the late nineteenth century more tax was taken out of Ireland relative to its GDP compared to Britain – just when taxation levels in England, Ireland and Scotland were at their closest before 1914.[90] As noted earlier, taxation in Ireland was also more regressive than in Britain.

Thinking in national terms like this gives only a general impression, however, because economic growth in every country of the Union varied regionally.[91] Importantly, industrial Ulster was growing much more rapidly than the rest of Ireland in the half century before the First World War. By 1914 its economy was similar to that in parts of industrial Britain.[92] Consequently, customs duties collected in Belfast had accounted for only 17 per cent of the total for Ireland up to the 1850s (Dublin was usually 43 per cent), but by 1910 Belfast accounted for 67 per cent and Dublin just 17 per cent.[93] Suggestively, in terms of public finances this heartland of unionism became increasingly important to the UK government in the era of Home Rule.

The final aspect of the taxing union to be considered is the tax gap, of how effective the revenue administration was in relation to the willingness to pay taxes. Soon after the Union of 1801 it was claimed that the 'Irish, of all ranks and religions, are remarkably jealous of taxation, and pay these imposts with reluctance. No subject throws them into greater irritation.'[94] Such irritation, however, has to be placed in the context of feelings about how burdensome these taxes were seen to be and the legitimacy of the taxing authority: as Henry Grattan had earlier put it, 'In Ireland, the iron hand of poverty limits the omnipotence of Parliament.'[95] What is clear is that the Union of 1801 happened at a time when the black economy was flourishing, encouraged by the high duties needed to fund the war effort. After 1815 that began to change. A primary cause was the huge reduction in the number of customs and excise duties levied and lowering some duties on those goods still taxed. Free trade, or at least freer trade, cut the ground from underneath smuggling. Having rooted out a huge amount of waste from the customs service, it then became possible to limit its responsibilities solely to internationally traded goods, with the excise solely responsible for the domestic sphere, paving the way to the creation of an Inland Revenue service in 1849. A little later the customs service crowed that the 'smuggler is no longer an object of general sympathy or a hero of romance', though it admitted that there was still illicit trade in tobacco, spirits and watches.[96] A secondary cause was the gradual institution of a significantly resourced UK-wide coastguard. A Preventive Waterguard was established in 1809 and a Coast Blockade in 1819, the rationalization of both of which led to the Coastguard in 1822.[97] In the 1840s this force numbered over 6,000 on 70 cruisers at a cost of £0.5 million annually.[98]

These developments affected all four nations of the Union. But obviously the Union of 1801 and the recasting of the fiscal compact after 1817 posed specific challenges for Ireland. A particular battle-ground was over duties on spirits. The taxation of alcohol meant that not all consumers were treated alike across the Union, with little weight being accorded to preferences that were culturally distinctive. In this way, the integration of the UK clearly had its limits. This was further shown by the introduction exclusively in Ireland of a 'Revenue Police' force in 1818, paid for and managed by the excise.[99] This replaced military support, which had been an important element in the war over illicit distilling that had been raging. At its peak, the Revenue Police had over 1,000 men – exceeding the number of excise officers in Ireland – operating from barracks concentrated where illicit distilling was believed to be most common, with 42 per cent of the force in the three north-western counties of Donegal, Sligo and Mayo.[100] There were two main reasons behind the creation of the force. One was the difficulty of reducing spirit taxes in Ireland given significantly lower duties already applied there, in the context of general moves towards, not away from, greater equalization of duties. Cutting duties, which would have rendered illicit distilling less profitable, would have been an ideologically uncomfortable step for London to have taken. Force seemed, therefore, the only way.

This was part, secondly, of a wider perception of the desperate need to establish the rule of law in Ireland. Policy makers in London already held strongly to the view that extreme lawlessness was endemic in Ireland. Early in the Union, frequent reports received in London informed and sustained such views, culminating in 1836 in a major book on the history of agrarian disorders in Ireland by George Cornewall Lewis, a future Chancellor of the Exchequer.[101] The consequence was that, in the midst of moves for greater fiscal assimilation, Ireland was in this important regard treated separately and distinctively: the Irish were to be forced into conformity rather than working with their preferences. At this stage Cornewall Lewis questioned such choices: 'The statute-book has been loaded with the severest laws; the country has been covered with military and police; capital punishment has been unsparingly inflicted; Australia has been crowded with trans-ported convicts; and all to no purpose.'[102] But even after the abolition of Ireland's Revenue Police in 1857, the Royal Irish Constabulary loomed much larger and more forcefully – and at greater cost – in Irish lives than its counterparts in Britain. Even so, illicit distilling was probably much more common in Ireland than Britain right up until 1914. In the five years from 1907 to 1911 there were only 21 seizures and detections of illicit stills in Britain, but nearly 5,400 in Ireland, where consumers regarded 'parliamentary' whiskey as too weak.[103]

AN ECONOMIZING UNION

In the eighteenth century, repeated and ever more costly wars drove central government spending upwards, peaking at over 20 per cent of GDP towards the end of the Napoleonic Wars. As we have seen, that ratio trended downwards from 1815 to 1870, but then edged upwards again. Even so, such expenditure was still relatively modest on the eve of the First World War, at under 10 per cent. Behind these general figures there was an important shift in the distribution of spending, away from debt charges and towards civil items, to over 20 per cent of the total by the 1880s and nearly 30 per cent on the eve of the First World War. Some of those new civil expenses were on governing a dramatically larger society and dramatically larger empire. The nineteenth-century architecture of imperial London speaks power-fully to this. Yet the spirit of 'economy' remained a potent one. Only from the 1870s did central government start to accept that to main-tain reasonable legitimacy and social order it needed to spend more money directly itself and indirectly through grants to local authori-ties. By investing heavily in solving questions of economic insecurity in Ireland, and to a lesser extent in the Scottish Highlands, requiring rudimentary education for all and introducing state-funded old-age pensions in 1908, the fiscal priorities of central government were fun-damentally changed and an important step towards centralization taken.[104] As early as 1883, George Goschen, a future Chancellor of the Exchequer, was bemoaning the end of laissez-faire; the age of economy was drawing to a close.[105]

Almost from the outset of the 1801 Union, it was easy enough for those willing to take the trouble to pore over tables in the relevant annual blue books published by parliament to see some fundamentals of the territoriality of central government taxation. But such categories were largely eschewed on the expenditure side of public accounts until 1889. General figures were produced distinguishing Britain and Ireland until 1817, but from then until the era of Home Rule, most expenditure was thought of as 'imperial'. Only then did official accounts identify central government spending that was directed specifically at each of the UK's three kingdoms. That in itself is telling: central government, and commentaries thereon, was generally more concerned with the territoriality of taxation than of public expenditure. However, that did not make it immune to criticism. Much so-called 'imperial' expenditure within the UK took place in London and southern England. To the centre that looked like a sensible reaping of economies of scale and concentration. But, because it was supported by taxes collected across the UK, the substantial transfers involved were always liable to be queried.

After Waterloo there was considerable pressure on central government scrupulously to account for its expenditure, down to the very candle ends, to pay off the national debt and to unfetter the pressures of supply and demand. Yet it was recognized that not everything could be left to markets to resolve and that some public goods had to be provided. In line with the growing power of political economy, a key development was a commitment to central government providing loans. But this important shift of emphasis away from grants was also a response to a major piece of civil expenditure by the government (briefly alluded to in the previous chapter) that quickly came to be viewed as a white elephant.

The Caledonian Canal, which made the Great Glen in Scotland a navigable waterway from Fort William to Inverness (Image 5), was legislated for in 1803 to aid a Highland economy suffering serious depopulation and to provide a much shorter and safer passage for commercial and naval vessels between Scotland's east and west coasts. Designed and constructed by the Scot Thomas Telford, the leading engineer of his generation, and supported by the Highland Society of Scotland, its benefits were expected to be 'incalculably great'.[106] Taking twenty years to complete, it cost UK taxpayers over £900,000, three times more than the initial estimates, mostly spent as the huge burdens of the Napoleonic Wars were also being shouldered. Even

Image 5. Neptune's Staircase, Banavie, close to the start of the Caledonian Canal, completed in 1824. Built to aid the economy around the Great Glen, the canal was criticized as an expensive white elephant for much of the nineteenth century.

before it was opened, it was damned as a 'Scotch job', a charge that stuck when it became clear that the canal would never carry enough traffic to generate much revenue and was badly built in places.[107] To many, the canal was a glorious folly, conclusively showing the costly inability of government to undertake effective direct investment, open, as it always was, to the demands of vested interests and back-room deals.[108] Tellingly, it was held up as an example of what not to do at the height of the Great Famine in Ireland; and the foundation of the Scottish Office in 1885 was said by its critics to be the worst 'Scotch job' since the Caledonian Canal.[109]

It was in this climate of changing principles, worries over the unfin-ished Caledonian Canal's future utility, and the post-war depression that, in 1817, a Public Works Loan Board was instituted, directing funds across the UK (though Ireland had its own commissioners as a Board of Works from 1831).[110] Still operating, it has been a key means by which, where private financial markets fall short, UK taxpayers fund capital projects, usually undertaken by local authorities. In its early years it lent money for civic improvement, infrastructure (around the UK, including the London to Holyhead road) and mines. But in the mid nineteenth century a rising share of the Board's loans were made to Ireland, reaching 38 per cent of the £9 million total between 1835 and 1859, mainly to fund railways and the building of workhouses under the poor law introduced there in 1838. Loans then grew substantially (to £28 million between 1860 and 1876) particularly because of the statutory requirements put in place in 1870–75 for the universal provision of elementary education, water and sewage. To pay for those requirements local authorities often had to borrow heavily but which some struggled to repay, especially in Ireland. From 1801 to 1886, Ireland received over £42 million in central government loans, 38 per cent of the total, but was responsible for 73 per cent of the £14 million in loans that were written off as irrecoverable debts.[111]

The Public Works Loan Board reflected an important development in governance across the UK in the nineteenth century whereby local authorities increasingly undertook work that was either permitted or required by a minimally resourced central government. In certain respects this was a well-established principle, dating back to the foundation of the old poor law in 1599–1601. But it was followed enthusiastically in the nineteenth century in the realms of poor relief, public health, 'disturnpiking' (abolishing toll roads and bringing them back under public control), policing and education to meet the social, environmental and economic costs of industrialization and urbanization. But the bind here was that poor places often struggled to raise enough by the rates because of their higher levels of expenditure on public goods. In the late nineteenth century, as the UK's national debt continued to fall, local government debt rose significantly. That poor districts lacked sufficient rate income to meet their statutory commitments had been understood since at least the early eighteenth century, but in the nineteenth century it increasingly required central government to provide local authorities with grants-in-aid. For most of the period to 1914, this was done out of general taxation, with particular shares of costs provided for new obligations placed upon local authorities, but with some national taxes being put into a specific fund for grants.[112] In this way, UK taxpayers supported local ratepayers – though Sir Edward Hamilton, the Permanent Secretary to the Treasury, remarked that 'the allocation of the money proceeds on no uniform or equitable principle', confusing the borderland between local and national services.[113] With hindsight, however, this played out very clearly in national terms, with Ireland receiving a much higher relative share (Figure 12).[114]

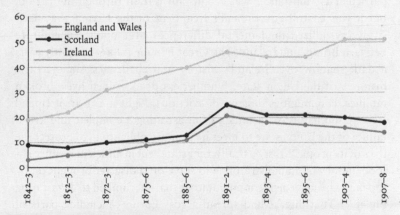

Figure 12. Share of local government expenditure met by UK Exchequer, by nations, 1842–1908, %

The greater dependence in Ireland on grants-in-aid reflected its relative lack of ratepayer income, especially after the Famine.[115] Mainly this was because its economy could not keep pace with Britain's, though a common complaint was that Ireland's landowners were escaping fiscal responsibilities attached to the source of their wealth: certainly there was greater opposition to paying for the poor law there through local rates.[116] A second aspect of this dependency, however, was that the rise of local government spending in Britain was mainly a response to problems which affected Ireland to a much lesser extent: the urban disamenities of Britain's great cities dwarfed in scale those in Ireland. The requirement that certain welfare goods such as education and old-age pensions should be uniform across the UK inevitably meant higher taxation everywhere. But, in Ireland particularly, doubts were raised about the additional burdens this implied there, with Lloyd George's old-age pensions of 1908 decried as 'the kind of blunder which the Union encourages', even though Ireland had a higher proportion of old people. As a leading former Treasury official put it in 1912, 'England has regulated Irish expenditure on the lavish scale of her own expenditure' – though in fact many Irish, including some who clearly were not old enough, rushed to claim the benefit.[117]

Complaining that public policy paid insufficient regard to Ireland's particular circumstances was a constant refrain through the period, but it was central government's treatment of the Famine that decisively crystallized fundamental differences over public expenditure between Britain and Ireland. The Great Famine (1846–9) rightly casts a dark shadow over Ireland's history and challenges Anglo-centric histories of the Union state. Numberless dead, ruined lives, broken families, communities destroyed, evictions, flight and fear: it ripped Ireland and its history asunder, demonstrating a complete and awful failure of the Union state to meet its primary obligation, to protect the lives of its people. Most basically, that state sent insufficient resources – food, money or administrators – to stave off a disaster brought on by too many being dependent on potatoes that succumbed to devastating blight.[118] That disease had spread across Europe, including parts of Britain, but only in Ireland did it lead to catastrophe. Why did the Union state not avert it?

Fundamental was a state of antipathy, often based on racial tropes, between the two islands: a running theme was that each thought the other should have been doing much more. But things were much less straightforward than this: strong differences of opinion existed on either side and there were significant common points between the two, while ideas changed as the Famine progressed.[119] This last point was crucial to the state's failure. In 1846 one *Punch* cartoon, 'Union is strength', shows a portly John Bull giving an emaciated and despairing Irish family a basket of bread with one hand and with the other a spade (or peat cutter) with which to become productive (Image 6). Here are the benefits of a composite state, with one part aiding another in its hour of need. In contrast, three years later *Punch* depicted a scrawny English labourer struggling to shoulder a jubilant Irishman, who, despite carrying a bag with £50,000, wears patched clothing (Image 7). Here are some of the dangers of free-riding to a composite state. In both prints, England is represented as strong, able and selfless, with Ireland as dependent, excusably so in the first, but not in the second.

Central government in London reacted pretty effectively to the first signs of severe food shortages in Ireland, distributing imported food, paid for by UK taxpayers. But thereafter it became increasingly concerned to ensure that its actions did not distort food markets that, with the repeal of the Corn Laws in 1846, had just been significantly liberalized. Its faith in those markets was excessive. It was also determined to avoid encouraging a dependency culture among both Ireland's poor and landowners (who were often accused of shirking their social, moral and local duties) – lines that had been peddled by *The Times*

Image 6. 'Union is strength', *Punch*, 17 October 1846. Illustrating the risk-sharing benefits of the Union.

Image 7. 'The English labourer's burden', *Punch*, 24 February 1849.
Illustrating changing attitudes in Britain towards Irish need in the Great
Famine.

for some time and which in 1847 had branded Irish landowners as
'the spoilt pets of the State'.[120] Hence after 1847 central government's
reaction was to provide loans funded by UK taxpayers, to extend
locally financed poor law provision and to direct some local rate
income from more to less prosperous parts of Ireland: grants and gifts
from Britain were mainly to come from private charity. This was
animated by the same ideas that lay behind the Public Works Loan

Commission and the reformed poor laws of the 1830s as well as by the fact that Ireland was exempted from several taxes in Britain that brought in over £12 million annually.[121] Because the potato crop had failed significantly before, nothing was to be done to hinder market forces leveraging a structural change in the most vulnerable parts of Ireland's rural economy, mainly in the west.

Despite what is sometimes claimed, there was no genocidal intent in these policies, though policy makers and administrators in London were certainly short of basic humanitarian instincts.[122] There was an appalling failure of comprehension, leading to a catastrophic failure of appropriate action. It is difficult to argue against the view that had the famine hit populous parts of mainland Britain, more generous policies would have been attempted. (Famine threatened in the Scottish Highlands at the same time but was on a smaller scale and so mainly averted by local action.[123]) But four major factors encouraged central government inaction: British taxpayers were very reluctant to see more of their money sent to 'unthrifty' Ireland;[124] Peel had dramatically split the Tory party over repealing the Corn Laws such that after the general election of 1847 a group of around eighty hardened laissez-faire MPs held the parliamentary balance of power and pressed for fiscal retrenchment even in these circumstances; a severe financial crisis in 1847 made it hard to raise the money to meet an unexpectedly prolonged emergency – repeatedly small and poor potato crops in the late 1840s surprised everyone; and thirty years of 'cheap government' had left Whitehall administratively stunted.[125]

At the Treasury, an enormous burden of famine relief fell on Charles Trevelyan, its Assistant Secretary. As has been already noted, he was certainly rigidly attached to the verities of political economy – of self-help and small government, of local responsibility and loans – but he was not uncaring or idle. He was dangerous not only because he held fast to his economic beliefs, but because of his unremitting energy within a perilously small central government.[126] That government struggled to make sense of what it was faced with, including sifting through the mountains of information it received in order to assess what was truly needed (in the context of ultimately being accountable to UK taxpayers who knew that Ireland was exempt from some key taxes). Observers of the famine in Ireland did not in fact speak with one voice. To many the problem was not a national but a local or regional one, not of Ireland but of the west and south-west of Ireland. And, as was noted earlier, there were those in Ireland who also strongly favoured adhering to the principles of political economy, if moderated by a Christian duty towards charity. The Irish political economist William Neilson Hancock was certain those principles would make Ireland's situation better and that relief was very hard to apply without generating an enervating dependency culture.[127]

A key feature of the central government's response to the Famine was to treat Ireland as fiscally largely self-contained but regionally varied. Its poorest districts could temporarily be supported by loans financed by UK taxpayers, but they were also to depend heavily on transfers of rates collected only in Ireland. By emphasizing the need for local responses to the Famine, central government in London denied that significant permanent transfer payments should be made from Britain to Ireland. This highlights the belief that local authorities should undertake some of the work of the state, that Ireland was in certain respects a distinctive fiscal entity, and an unwillingness by central government to regard risk sharing as integral to the Union. The issue of risk sharing was not clearly addressed until Home Rule became a key political battleground, by which time there was much more territorial equality of taxation. Whether or not one was a supporter of some degree of devolution or federalism, questions of public financed loomed large, in increasingly 'three kingdom' terms.

Many in Ireland viewed Britain's response to the Famine as somewhere on the spectrum from the mean to the murderous. Many in Britain believed that sending more resources to Ireland to meet the challenge of the Famine would be a waste of hard-earned money. Scottish as well as English voices were raised in complaint. At the first meeting of the National Association for the Vindication of Scottish Rights, held in Edinburgh in November 1853, after the decision to extend the income tax to Ireland had been taken, it was claimed that Scotland contributed £5.7 million to the imperial exchequer, but Ireland only £153,000, despite the fact that Ireland's agricultural economy was twice the size of Scotland's. Further, Ireland had received £8 million from central government for Famine relief whereas the 'poor Highlander was left to perish on his native heath'.[128] Ireland's political voice was said to be drowning out Scotland's; a realignment was needed.[129] With Scottish industry and trade booming, there was little appetite in Scotland for dissolving the Union.[130] But, in public expenditure terms particularly, the Union was now being seen by a sizeable section of Scottish political society as unfair. Complaints were loudly voiced against centralization, against an 'Anglicising mania' and 'the leviathan maw of the English Metropolis'.[131] Spending in Scotland fell well short of that in England on royal palaces, harbours of refuge, the improvement of London (parks, museums and government buildings) and policing.[132]

There was, indeed, a huge wave of spending on imperial buildings in London from the 1840s that was paid for by taxpayers across the UK. The new Houses of Parliament began to be constructed in 1840, eventually coming in, like the Caledonian Canal, at three times over budget. Other expensive buildings and public spaces followed in and around Whitehall in the decades up until 1914, including the Public Record Office, the Foreign Office, the Royal Courts of Justice and the War Office. The total cost of £9.5 million was a major stimulus to London's economy, but tellingly was justified by Trevelyan on the grounds that a concentration of purpose-built accommodation for government and civil servants would increase their efficiency and economize on expensive rented office space – in 1904–5, 95 per cent of all UK civil servants worked in London.[133] This was also, he thought, befitting the capital of a modern imperial power, 'a mother of nations'. All of this spending in London was paid for by taxpayers across the UK.[134] The building of Balmoral Castle in the Scottish Highlands, completed in 1856, was symbolically significant, but fiscally inconsequential as it was paid for by Prince Albert's own funds.

Investing heavily in the infrastructure of the Union state from the 1840s reflected the global vitality of Britain's economy but also an increasing realization that government had to provide more public goods and to invest more in making the private economy work more fairly. Many of these initiatives, such as those relating to public health and education, were UK-wide. But there was an increasing acceptance in central government that parts of the UK were needier than others. By 1870 Gladstone, who continued to believe that Ireland should be taxed to much the same extent as the rest of the UK, had come to recognize that it had particular problems relating to land ownership and tenancy that required attention. The Land Act of that year was followed by several others over the next quarter of a century that finally grasped the nettle of absenteeism and insecurity of tenure as major brakes on Ireland's agrarian economy. Enormous resources, backed by UK taxpayers, were then mobilized for the task.[135]

Solving the Irish land question was a clear expression of the modern system of producing territorial equity: taxes are equally applied across the state's domain (more or less), but public expenditure is not. In this case, it took the form of the provision of state-backed loans at preferential rates rather than direct spending. The scale of this was extraordinary, totalling nearly £100 million by the time of the Irish Revolution (1916–21) – or perhaps 60 per cent of Ireland's GDP then – unsurprisingly leading to complaints in London about Irish poor relations.[136] Nonetheless, it marked an important change towards fiscal territoriality, but not one limited to Ireland alone. Rioting within Scottish crofting communities in the early 1880s – over evictions, excessive rates and poverty – also led to significant governmental funds being directed there.[137] In 1897 a Congested Districts Board was instituted in Scotland, modelled on that introduced into Ireland in 1891. Both can be seen as regional development boards, created by central government (though partly locally funded) to nurture areas that market forces alone seemed unable to do. The founder of the Irish Board, Arthur Balfour, owner of 187,000 acres in Scotland, who served as Scottish Secretary (1886–7), Chief Secretary in Ireland (1887–91) and prime minister (1902–5), believed that by improving the infrastructure of remote coastal and, to his mind, overpopulated districts, market forces would aid their fishing industries and encourage emigration, lifting those remaining out of the 'demoralizing slough of insolvency' – though in both Ireland and Scotland the boards were also a response to social disorder.[138] The total expenditure of Ireland's Congested Districts Board was much larger at £12.6 million, but in Scotland's Highlands and Islands thousands of grants totalling over £0.5 million were made for the purchase of land and to fund, or help to fund, infrastructure, mainly roads, piers and harbours and local industry (including tweed making in the Outer Hebrides). The Scottish Board was ended in 1912, the Irish Board in 1923.

HOME RULE FINANCE

Balfour's creation of the Congested Districts Board for Ireland in 1891 was an expression of 'constructive unionism', of attempting to kill Home Rule with kindness. Home Rule had begun to be powerfully voiced by Isaac Butt in 1870 as a constitutional expression of the need to redraw the Union compact. The aim was a degree of Irish self-government, with the restitution of some sort of assembly or parliament at Dublin, powerfully expressed by many Irish MPs acting as a bloc to disrupt the normal workings of the House of Commons. It was, then, very different to the calls for Irish independence that were voiced with more or less anger and violence throughout the nineteenth century. Eventually and famously, Gladstone converted to Home Rule in 1885 and then put his enormous energies and abilities behind it, introducing a bill in 1886 which failed in the Commons and another in 1893 which passed that hurdle only to fall in the Lords. He split his Liberal party over it, with the Conservatives now becoming the home of out-and-out unionists. In 1912 Herbert Asquith's Liberals tried again, this time succeeding to pass the act in 1914, but whose implementation was postponed because of the outbreak of the First World War. In 1916 the Easter Rising in Ireland was an armed attempt to establish an independent Irish republic. Its quick and brutal suppression significantly stimulated support in Ireland for independence, leading to the landslide election of seventy-three Sinn Féin MPs in 1918, who refused to take their seats. With Ireland now ungovernable, warfare followed – part an independence struggle, part civil war – resulting in the partition of Ireland in 1921, with six of Ulster's nine counties adhering to Britain, and the creation of the Irish Free State in 1922.

Questions about Home Rule were repeatedly and loudly raised in the Union state between 1870 and 1914. A fundamental one was whether this constitutional adjustment should be limited to Ireland or applied across the UK ('Home Rule all round'), perhaps by constructing an explicitly federal compact. In particular, Ireland's claims for distinctive treatment fomented Scottish calls for Home Rule, with a Scottish Home Rule Association established in 1886.[139] After all,

Scotland was contributing fully to the imperial order. Its politicians were often at the forefront of the Union state (irking some in Ireland), its economy was at its industrial and commercial zenith, it was a net contributor to the Exchequer in London and it caused little trouble.[140] Little wonder then that calls in Scotland for more attention to be directed to its needs and in favour of decentralization began to be made.[141] London, it was said, was too distant from and ignorant of its circumstances to ensure good government in a nation with a proud history. Why should Ireland have its own executive government when Scotland did not? Predictably, *The Times* bemoaned such 'fostering of prejudices within the island', but in 1885 a Scottish Office, headed by a Scottish Secretary, was instituted to ensure that Scotland's needs were better articulated and understood at the highest levels of government.[142] It was a fairly short step from that to calling for Home Rule for Scotland. When Gladstone, then an MP for Midlothian in central Scotland, introduced his Home Rule bill in 1886, he recognized the need for there to be political equality in the treatment of the three (not four) nations of the Union.[143]

Obviously the failure of the 1886 Home Rule bill failed to settle matters. To try to take some of the sting out of calls for special treatment by each of the home nations where public finances were concerned, in 1888 George Goschen, the Chancellor of the Exchequer, determined that some funding, initially from probate duties, was to be distributed according to set proportions: 80 per cent to England and Wales; 11 per cent to Scotland; and 9 per cent to Ireland. It is unclear how those shares were arrived at and they were not always followed, but the proportions were widely employed for government spending until 1958.[144] As a forerunner of the Barnett Formula of 1978, Goschen's ratios recognized that the different countries of the Union had in certain fiscal respects to be dealt with separately.

Given the profound difficulties the government was facing in tackling the 'Irish question', it prioritized dealing with Irish over Scottish Home Rule, but, linked with acute unease about the structures and financing of local government, it raised the fundamental question of what territorial units could and could not legitimately call for greater self-government. At last, the voice of Wales began to be raised. In 1892 Samuel Evans, the MP for Mid Glamorgan, now a thriving industrial centre, asked why Wales should not be treated as a separate entity like Ireland and Scotland, asserting that it too 'is not treated fairly or equitably in the matter of . . . financial relations with England'. Goschen had no truck with such arguments: Wales had been fiscally indivisible from England for centuries. He wondered why, if Wales were to be treated separately, English counties or cities might not make the same claims. Practicality, he argued, required fiscal entities to be large enough to warrant distinctive assessment and treatment in the Union state: the population of Wales in 1891 was 892,000, as against London's 4.2 million, Lancashire's 3.9 million, the West Riding of Yorkshire's 2.5 million and County Durham and Staffordshire's 1 million.[145] On these grounds, Goschen concluded sharply, 'We cannot accept Wales . . . as a separate financial entity in our fiscal system.'[146] And that was that for many years.

Calls for Home Rule required deciding on what powers should and should not be devolved and what should be the fiscal relationship between the imperial and the national power. The second of those proved to be extremely difficult to answer in practice. The financial aspects of all three Home Rule bills were quickly found to be seriously flawed and confusing.[147] Those of the second were said to be 'extremely involved', and of the third 'a masterpiece of freak finance'.[148] It was not that it was necessarily so difficult to decide what Ireland should keep its own monies for or how much it should pay for imperial services; rather it proved very difficult to pin down what its true tax receipts were and what should properly be called imperial expenditure. Thus was revived the now well-established question of the formal and effective incidence of taxation (in the language of the period 'as collected' and 'true'). Ultimately this was decided upon by the UK Treasury, whose control over the account books was viewed by many in Ireland as unreliable and far from disinterested. On the expenditure side, major differences of opinion were expressed over what it was reasonable to be paid for by a government in Dublin and a superior government in London. An important ambition of Gladstone and others was that, through Home Rule, to reduce expenditure in Ireland to improve imperial balance sheets. Unsurprisingly, Irish Home Rulers, seeking to relieve taxpayers there, wanted the UK government to continue to pay for as much in Ireland as possible. Unionists, on the other hand, stressed that Home Rule for Ireland would be an act of 'financial suicide' there.[149] Moreover, these difficulties took place against the backdrop of Ireland's generally diminishing demographic and material weight within the Union – Scotland's population overtook that of Ireland in 1901 – and of rising UK civil expenditure (for old-age pensions particularly) requiring more central aid than ever to Ireland.

Acceding to the principle of Home Rule meant qualifying the principle of equality in public finances, meaning as it did that differences between the nature and desires of different parts of the Union required distinctive fiscal arrangements to satisfy people and maintain the legitimacy of government. Such greater complexity would necessarily complicate the relationship between the taxpayer (and ratepayer) and government, for sometimes their money would go to the devolved government, sometimes to the imperial government, not always in a clearly distinguishable way. Gladstone had for years held strongly to the belief that levying few taxes was central to the compact between a government and the people, because the taxes would then be clearly 'felt' and more directly linked to the uses to which they were put, aiding thereby economy. Others doubted the wisdom of such narrowness (Goschen stated in 1889 that 'simplicity of taxation' had been taken 'to a point beyond which you cannot carry it without danger'), but Home Rule and increasing central government expenditure involved a refashioning of that fundamental.[150] In the process the status of taxpayers changed. Analytically, liberal political economy considered taxpayers without regard to geography and only in respect to how rich or poor they were. Now the political Liberalism of Home Rule required a reconceptualization of taxpayers as members of national communities. To *The Times* this 'new-fangled doctrine' was 'preposterous'.[151] To many in Ireland and some in Scotland, it seemed only right and proper.

CONCLUSION

Unquestionably, the 1801 Union was poorly engineered. A lot of attention has been paid to the failure to grant religious and political rights to Catholics, but the financial terms were also fundamentally flawed. It is understandable, then, that its history is traced by moving from one bitter conflict to another over Catholic emancipation; O'Connell's repeal movement; the Great Famine; disestablishment of the Church of Ireland and its tithes; the land question; and, not least here, public finances. Unquestionably, under the Union Ireland's population plummeted, its economy struggled and its long-strained political community fractured badly. Many of its people were never reconciled to a union state viewed as alien, oppressive and extractive. As A. V. Dicey put it, 'It will always remain a paradox that the nation which has built up the British Empire (with vast help, it may be added, from Ireland) has combined extraordinary talent for legislation with a singular incapacity for consolidating subject races or nations into one State.'[152]

Two peculiarities are inherent in such views, however. The first is about judging the Union from the standpoint of its component nations. With nationalism such an important feature of European history in the period, that is understandable. But it is particular. Geopolitically, the Union should also be judged both holistically and regionally. Using those frameworks, the Union's successes, judged materially, significantly outweighed its evident failures. The second peculiarity is exploring the history of the nineteenth-century Union state in terms of the causes of Irish independence – that is, focusing on what broke it up.[153] Again, that is understandable, but it runs the risk of underappreciating common and often integrative aspects of the Union, including parliament, the Post Office, the British army, a global empire and, after 1817, a single Exchequer. On this last point, people across the UK eventually came to be taxed in much the same way, with significant amounts raised near and far. Certainly in Ireland this often involved much more brute force than in Britain, but the fact is that year after year central government used a permanent administration spread across Ireland to extract some of its precious resources. Relatedly, smuggling in most parts of the UK also decreased considerably across the century. Forms, revenue officers and flows of money were all part of the web spun by the Treasury over the whole of the UK. But the flows could be multilateral and human, not simply bilateral and material. Administrators, such as Anthony Trollope, the novelist and Post Office employee, moved around the Union. Maurice

Walsh, the County Kerry-born author of 'The quiet man' (1933), was an excise officer from 1901 and was sometimes posted to the Scottish Highlands, where he came across another revenue officer, Neil Gunn, a leading Scottish nationalist and socialist.[154] Or then there was William Gardner, who began working for the customs service in 1827 in Yorkshire, but had numerous postings from Colchester to Carlisle in England, before ending up at Leith via Waterford.[155]

The vivid contrast between Scotland and Ireland's experiences of British public finances says much about the fiscal arrangements between both nations and the Union state. A century after the 1707 Union, the amount of taxes collected in Scotland per person was well under a half that in England and Wales. By the middle of the nineteenth century, that gap had been closed completely, with remarkably little fuss. Convergence between the taxation of Britain and Ireland also took place in the nineteenth century, but the gap was never closed and after 1853 Irish complaints about overtaxation were frequent and loud. Those complaints stressed how poorly tailored policies were towards Ireland, including doing lasting damage through London's hopeless and allegedly malicious reaction to the Famine. But the widespread desire for equality, economy, small government and free trade encouraged indiscriminate taxation across the Union. Such policies suited industrial Britain reasonably well. But agriculturalists berated the eviscerations ushered in by free trade. Such laments were voiced in parts of Britain, but across most of Ireland, with its much more heavily agrarian economy. As one Irish unionist put it, 'The Irish people have suffered severely by Free Trade. The "Curse of Cobden" has replaced in Ireland the "Curse of Cromwell".'[156]

A fundamental aspect of the public-finance disputes of the Union state was about the rightness and universality of the principles of political economy. For many years these held sway, reaching a pitch with the reform of the poor laws across the UK, the Treasury response to the Great Famine, the equalizing tax measures of the 1850s and the triumph of free trade. Fundamentally, this was ideological, with other possibilities readily to hand. While socialist alternatives to the precepts of political economy were developed in Europe during this period – Marx and Engels's *Communist Manifesto* was published in 1848 – and Carlyle damned the '*dismal science*', Irish hostility was more visceral.[157] The *Nation* newspaper, founded in Dublin in 1842, was an important early fount of this, which was soon picked up more widely. In 1846 the *Limerick Examiner* newspaper, dismissing the 'theorems of a doubtful science', lambasted political economy as 'Political audacity and treachery!'[158] To John Mitchel in 1861, political economists had turned the arrival of the blight in 1845 into a murderous and epic famine. This was at one with Irish accounts of the might of the Treasury. An iron discipline and an iron administration rode roughshod over all: 'For over a century in Ireland we have defied the laws of political economy, but they have conquered us at last,' wrote Erskine Childers on the eve of the First World War.[159]

Mitchel and Childers were polemicists, exaggerating in two main respects here. The first (and less important) was that the Treasury was far from omnipotent. Its function was to control spending within policies set down by other departments and ministers.[160] It was more a brake than an engine. More importantly, the dominance of a fairly crude form of political economy began to wane soon after 1860. Partly that was because of wider intellectual developments, especially a questioning of its abstractions in the face of the lessons of history.[161] But also in practice it sowed the seeds of its own diminution. Irish exclamations against the equalizing tax policies of the 1850s were one of a number of causes of Gladstone's realization that Ireland had to be treated distinctively within the Union state. His Home Rule bills were, in part, a denial of the universality of a single political economy in public policy. As he put it when introducing the first Home Rule bill, 'Are we to give up the fiscal unity of the Empire? I sometimes see it argued that, in giving up the fiscal unity of the Empire, we should give up the unity of the Empire. To that argument I do not subscribe. The unity of the Empire rests upon the supremacy of Parliament, and on considerations much higher than considerations merely fiscal.'[162] Such a view was adapted by Unionists through policies, such as instituting the Congested District Boards, that sought to kill Home Rule with kindness.

These developments were linked to a structural limitation within the liberalism that was such an important guiding force of the Union state. Liberalism favoured the consolidation of states, yet also small central government and decentralization 'to counteract the centralization inherent in its imposition of national standards'. In the UK case, the rub was that 'Scotland, Wales and Ireland were rather good-sized units where national and regional criteria fitted together quite well; it was England that was the problem. The extent to which Home Rule was primarily an English problem – in the sense of raising questions about English identity – has been underestimated.'[163] The importance of this is hard to exaggerate. Presumptions among many leading politicians about the inviolability of English unity have proved very persistent ever since.

Two other important contests were bound up in the evolution of fiscal policy in this period. Gladstone's acceptance that Ireland was in some respects a separate fiscal entity involved a closely related shift in assessing policies away from the consequences for individuals towards consequences for communities. But that opened up in turn the question of which communities were relevant, to which there was no simple answer. Nations were one, of course, but the changing relationship between central and local government, as well as between taxpayers and ratepayers, meant that counties and, especially, cities also came to loom larger in the political consciousness through the reforms of 1835 and 1888. A growing regional sensibility was a vital development that moderated the importance of nations within the Union, albeit, as Goschen put it in 1871, 'we have a chaos as regards authorities, a chaos as regards rates, and a worse chaos than all as regards areas.'[164]

Fiscally the Union state, and Ireland's place within it more particularly, changed considerably between 1801 and 1914: in 1801 Ireland supplanted Scotland in relative importance within the fiscal union; by 1830 Scotland had taken that palm. On the eve of the Famine, Scotland was clearly flourishing within a political economy which, since the 1780s, it had helped to frame. But if policy makers in London had learned from the Scottish Enlightenment and Henry Dundas, they were generally reluctant to take on board complaints that their system was ill-suited to Ireland's distinctive circumstances. With the rising tax take from Ireland after the Famine, that was somewhat understandable. A high degree of equality of taxation was, from one perspective, clearly successful. But complaints that this was inequitable to Ireland did gradually make an impact. The response, though, was not to change the tax regime, but to maintain a notably more preferential balance between UK taxpayers and local ratepayers in Ireland, while underwriting enormous UK loans on the land question, especially, again, in Ireland. This, though, failed to convince many in Ireland that the taxing union was anywhere near fair. To them, equal taxation produced a tax regime that was markedly more regressive than in Britain, and creaming off ever more taxation while Ireland's population shrank just seemed plain wrong. In those circumstances, quite apart from the other major factors of the Anglo-Irish connection, agreement was impossible. The fiscal union of 1801 had, simultaneously, worked and failed.

4

1914–1999: Regions and nations

The First World War changed utterly the contexts underpinning the territoriality of Britain's public finances. Waging the war and paying for it undermined old certainties about the size, ambitions and policies of government. But this was more than simply the consequences of the economics of total war. The Irish Revolution of 1916–22 was the first major stage in the almost complete collapse of the British Empire that took place over the next forty years. That inevitably compromised the international order that had sustained Britain's industrial economy before 1914, but this was worsened by heightening competition from abroad. Deindustrialization had begun its deadly crawl across the UK. While the pre-1914 political economy of the gold standard and free trade was more or less restored in 1925, this only made matters worse by increasing the price of Britain's exports and allowing competition from more efficient producers from overseas. From 1931 that order was abandoned and a managed national economy began to be forged, requiring new ways for central government to see, understand and act, encouraged by the extension of the vote to all adult men and women in 1918 and 1928.[1]

With greater welfare provision, the peacetime state was from the 1930s becoming a Leviathan. The Second World War and the election of the Labour government in 1945 deepened and refined these developments, which were broadly accepted for thirty years. But the Thatcher revolution from 1979 to 1990 stimulated growth in and around London, marginalized regionalism, ignored growing calls for devolution in Scotland and Wales and shredded the conventional relationship between central and local government without having much success in diminishing the overall size of the state. By the end of the twentieth century, central government spending as a proportion of

GDP was over four times the pre-1914 level. New Labour in 1997 courageously seized the nettle of devolution, with its many consequences for the fiscal balances to be struck between the UK's parts, but its solution was hopelessly incoherent and incomplete.

Much higher public spending naturally required many more taxes, but also posed big questions about spending priorities and whether money was well spent. An optimism about the potency of planning was one part of this, though it was quickly associated with the dangers of an autarkic 'new mercantilism' and heightened centralization. It is telling, therefore, that the utility of the Goschen ratios waned after 1945 but that they were refashioned in 1978 by Joel Barnett, Chief Secretary to the Treasury. This bore witness to the power of Scottish and Welsh special pleading within central government and the rising tide of Scottish and Welsh nationalism outside it, seeking to show that the government would increase spending in those nations in line with increases in England. Yet if the Barnett Formula was born of political expediency – it failed even to warrant a mention in its creator's memoirs – it has remained, even after Scottish and Welsh devolution got under way in 1999, the key determinant ever since of apportioning changes in public expenditure among the nations of the Union.[2]

Fundamentally, the battles over public finances in this period, considered geographically, were over a potentially much larger prize, but subject to many more competing claims within and outside government. This took place in the context of democratic and interest-group pressures for accountability, equity and efficiency that encouraged the growth of increasingly technocratic government. Government became not just very much larger, collecting and spending very much more money, but bewilderingly complex, with ordinary citizens often no longer able to comprehend how taxes and public spending actually affected them. Given the new authority of the ballot box, this encouraged those seeking power, perhaps especially nationalists in different parts of the UK, to make highly simplified and frequently misleading claims about the dreadful monster and its poor relations.

THE IRISH REVOLUTION AND
THE PUBLIC FINANCES OF THE
UNITED KINGDOM

Victorious, perhaps, but after the First World War the UK was left badly diminished and depressed. If, a century later, the war's murderous toll still lingers in the national memory, its economic and financial consequences were hardly less significant. As a total war, with resources mobilized on an unprecedented scale, necessity shattered conventional precepts of fiscal restraint. The national debt nominally rose from £707 million in 1913 to £7,777 million in 1920, or from 28 to 140 per cent of GDP. On the revenue side, taxes were 8 per cent of GDP on the eve of war and reached 16 per cent in 1918. But, while war debts were gradually repaid, after 1918 the state remained much larger and more active than before 1914: taxes averaged 20 per cent of GDP between the wars and 31 per cent in the second half of the century.[3] Gladstone's world of 'economy' had long gone. The refashioning of the state is the focus of much of this chapter.

No less important for the subject of this book, however, was the fact the First World War was critical to setting in train the Irish Revolution, in three stages: the War of Independence in Ireland (1919–21); partition of the island in 1921 by carving off six of Ulster's nine counties to form Northern Ireland; and the founding of the independent Irish Free State in the following year (with an associated civil war, 1922–3). Although the Free State remained formally within the British Empire until 1937, its establishment represented a profound contraction of the Union state. Such ruptures involved heavy direct costs and led to the first devolved government within the UK. Yet none of this solved the Irish question. Devolved government in Northern Ireland rarely worked well and was suspended during the Troubles (1968–98), really a civil war, while in the debates around how the UK was to leave the EU after 2016 the nature of the border between the Irish Republic (established in 1949) and Ulster proved to be the fundamental sticking point.

A third bill for Irish Home Rule was introduced into parliament in 1912, once again by the Liberal party. As with its predecessors, it was passionately opposed, for going too far by unionists, especially in Ulster, and for not going far enough by Irish nationalists. Eventually, in September 1914, the measure was forced through parliament. But it was quickly suspended so that central government in London could concentrate on prosecuting the recently declared war against the Central Powers in Europe. The frustration at this in much of Ireland, after nearly half a century of pressure for Home Rule, was palpable, prompting nationalists to risk an armed rebellion. The Easter Rising in 1916 was quickly and brutally suppressed by the authorities, but it triggered the Irish Revolution. It is hard to overstate the significance of this to the UK as well as to Ireland. Here, as with American independence in 1776, was a catastrophic failure of the Westminster constitution and Westminster politics. Most relevantly here, it had important long-term implications for the UK's public finances, both structural and particular.

At a crude level, Irish independence shrank the population of the UK by 8 per cent and its territory by 21 per cent. As Adam Smith had appreciated, a smaller UK domestic economy reduced the scope for some productivity gains, while creating the UK's first land border produced the conditions for smuggling between Ireland and Northern Ireland which even membership of the European Economic Community (EEC) and its successor the European Union (EU) did not eradicate – both Ireland and the UK joined in 1973.[4] But it was also the case that the UK lost regions that were significantly more agrarian and less prosperous, while, reciprocally, partition meant that the Irish Free State was damaged by losing the most industrial part of the island of Ireland: in 1922, GDP per head in the Irish Free State was around a half that in the UK.[5] Initially, therefore, Northern Ireland's economy, centring on industrial Belfast, was much closer in structure to that of the rest of the UK. Consequently, with Irish independence the UK's revenue regime became better aligned to the economic life of more of its population. Many in Britain had also been alarmed at the high cost (and the sheer frustration) of governing Ireland before 1914, especially on the land question, law and order, old-age pensions and local authorities. Irish independence may have conjured up to some the alluring prospect of reducing average public expenditure per head in the UK. Irish independence appeared, wrongly, as we will see, to make the Union economically and fiscally more coherent.

The creation of the Irish Free State also provided lessons about what it took to leave the UK, while changing the parameters for advocates of devolution or independence in Scotland and Wales. A notable feature is that since 1923 there has generally been freer movement of people between Ireland and the UK than with other countries, morphing in recent decades into a Common Travel Area that is continuing after Brexit. This includes rights to education, welfare and voting for citizens of one country living in the other.[6] But public finances proved harder to settle. If there were some prospects of UK public finances being improved by Irish independence, it was also the case that establishing the Irish Free State was bound to be costly and disruptive. This was not easy given the destruction of war in Ireland – including the IRA's symbolic torching of the Custom House in Dublin in 1921 (Image 8) – and the need to erect a new public-finance regime. This

Image 8. The burning of the Custom House in Dublin in 1921 by the IRA as a key symbol of British rule. The building survived, but much of its historic archive did not.

proved fraught, suggested by the fact that the Irish pound was for many years pegged to sterling while tax receipts for the Irish Free State prevented it from spending as much on welfare as the UK. Nor did independence soon lead to an improvement in Ireland's economic prospects. Whereas population in the UK grew steadily after 1921, in Ireland it stagnated until the 1960s, while per capita GDP in Ireland remained stubbornly one-half that of the UK into the 1950s: it was joining the EEC that saw Ireland's economic fortunes improve significantly.[7] To unionists across the UK these were valuable lessons that might be used to counter claims for Scottish and Welsh independence.

More specific consequences of Irish independence for UK public finances were also important. As with Brexit, a clean break was politically and diplomatically unfeasible. Several financial obligations loomed large in negotiations. The UK pressed Ireland to contribute towards three big costs: pre-1921 national debts; the Irish land annuities that had funded the land settlement; and war pensions. David Lloyd George, prime minister, in language characteristic of the casual anti-Semitism at the time, sought 'something fair between the two countries, not a Jew bargain'.[8] Predictably there were loud cries in Ireland that such demands would be just another form of tribute exacted to maintain a semi-colonial relationship. In the end, the national debt obligations were written off, but the others remained. The war pensions were costed at a lump sum of nearly £13 million and the land annuities at £5 million per annum, though they would gradually diminish over the coming decades. With the burden of the latter said to be relatively greater than German reparations to the Allies after 1918, they were a major source of friction between the Irish Free State and the UK, contributing eventually to an economic war between them from 1932 to 1938. Strikingly, from this unequal trial of strength, Ireland emerged in credit. One of the peace terms compounded the £100 million of capital on the land annuities into a single £10 million lump sum.[9] In crude financial terms, Irish independence cost the UK Exchequer millions of pounds in lost revenue alongside tens of millions of pounds of unpaid debts, all while its coffers were badly stretched. UK taxpayers unwillingly and indirectly helped to lay some of the foundations of the public finances of the infant Irish Free State.

Fiscally, Irish independence made clear to the UK government three fundamentals: that allowing the language of overtaxation and inequity to gain hold fed separatism – and it is significant that it has been little used by Scottish or Welsh nationalists subsequently; that disunion involved considerable economic and fiscal dislocation to both sides; and that, while Treasury spending in Ireland ended, there were heavy direct costs in reaching a final settlement, involving an economic war. On the other hand, while Ireland gained a reasonable degree of political liberty in 1922, economic prosperity took much longer to achieve and, paradoxically, rested heavily on entering into another union, this time with Europe, whose political economy was much more favourable to agrarian economies such as Ireland.[10] As will be shown later in this chapter, all of these lessons were to be reworked in the debates around Scottish and Welsh independence after 1950. These were not, however, the only general lessons to be learned.

A major consequence of the Irish Revolution – though unwanted by nationalist revolutionaries – was that it established Northern Ireland as a province within the UK; it was (and remains) smaller than Wales or Yorkshire in both territory and population – though, because of bitter sectarian and political divisions, less united than either. Critically, it was a province with a devolved assembly at Stormont from 1921 to 1972 (with an executive headed by a prime minister), establishing which required agreeing a division of powers, financial and otherwise, with Westminster. In that way, creating Stormont addressed fundamental questions about equality and equity in public finances that echoed those leading to 1707 and 1801 and which prefigured debates over devolution at the end of the twentieth century in the other nations of the Union. Indeed, Northern Ireland effectively got Home Rule. Given the extension of devolved government to Scotland and Wales in 1999, the question arises as to what lessons, both of practice and of principle, the devolution in Northern Ireland provided.[11]

In 1920 the Government of Ireland Act sought to establish parliaments in Dublin and Belfast, as part of a solution to keep a divided Ireland within the Union. All Ireland would continue to send MPs to Westminster because it was to remain subject to 'imperial' policy, but some government was now reserved for its own two parliaments. A division of responsibilities and resources had to be determined for this to stand any chance of success. It was decided that MPs for Ireland's Westminster constituencies could vote there on purely British matters, raising obvious enough doubts about the alignment of power and responsibility that were raised later in the century over Scottish devolution as the so-called 'West Lothian Question'. Financial relations also had to be contracted. Initially Ireland was to pay £18 million to London as an 'imperial contribution' – 56 per cent from the south and 44 per cent from the north, an index of sorts of their respective economic vitality given that the population shares were 70 and 30 per cent respectively. Irish independence cancelled all of this, but Northern Ireland remained liable both to send money and MPs to London and to run the Union's first devolved government. Northern Ireland was defined as a separate fiscal entity, with supporting administration, able to raise some of its own taxes if it chose, but required to continue to collect imperial customs, excise and income taxes. A Joint Exchequer Board, with membership from both Belfast and London, was to manage the financial relationship. But a critical earlier decision made by another committee established that Northern Ireland was to be provided with a standard of local service equal to the average standard obtaining in Britain – called initially 'step-by-step' and later 'parity'.[12] This unionist policy ensured that Northern Ireland's experience diverged from that of the Irish Free State, but also had important implications for the principle of territorial uniformity on the expenditure side of public accounts, privileging equality and equity over economy and efficiency.

The principle that, with regard to welfare spending, the Westminster and Stormont parliaments were to move together had important implications given that Northern Ireland's taxable capacity fell well short of Britain's. Throughout the interwar years, unemployment in Northern Ireland was substantially above that in Britain, significantly reducing tax receipts and boosting welfare expenditure: in 1929–30 the per capita yield of customs and excise in Northern Ireland was 62 per cent of the level in Britain and for the income tax only 41 per cent.[13] Consequently, parity meant Northern Ireland was committed to heavy expenditure, consuming what it might otherwise have sent to the imperial exchequer. Initially that contribution had been 49 per cent of its expenditure but after 1923 it fell to around 8 per cent, where it remained until the Second World War.[14] Unsurprisingly, this provoked some in Britain to question the justness of the financial arrangements of devolution and whether self-government was more notional than real. To one commentator, Northern Ireland was nothing more than a 'petitioner for uncovenanted subsidies and guarantees' such that 'Partition, so far as Northern Ireland is concerned, has proved an economic failure of the first magnitude.'[15] When, in the Second World War, conscription was not extended to Northern Ireland so as not to aggravate the nationalist community there (Ireland was neutral through the war), this allowed for complaints to be made about the province's failure to make a 'proper contribution' to the imperial exchequer while receiving generous 'subsidies'.[16] Here we have classic versions of the 'poor relations' argument. But nationalists and republicans in Ulster could also criticize the subsidization of the province by Britain as a means of propping up a reconstituted Protestant Ascendancy, an 'absolute freehold' underwritten by 'another blank cheque . . . guaranteed on the part of the unconsulted taxpayers of Great Britain'.[17]

There was, of course, a wider worry here given that Irish independence changed the national dynamics of power within the UK: four nations became three, hitched to a province across the Irish Sea. Changing population shares show this nicely. England gained markedly, rising from 78 to 83 per cent of the UK population, Scotland from 10 to 11 and Wales and Northern Ireland increasing only slightly: such is the power of big numbers – Irish independence increased England's weight within an already ill-balanced union. Moreover, geographical majoritarianism became a real and present danger as a genuinely mass electorate was established through the extension of votes to women. Politically, there was an understandable anxiety in Scotland and Wales after 1918 that England's voice and English assumptions within the political economy of the UK were more potent than ever before. What mattered here was the application of the national frame given, as one Scottish observer noted, 'Every democratic system involves the outvoting of minorities by majorities . . . In an independent Scotland, that Lowlands would undoubtedly outvote the less populous Highlands. No process of subdivision, however far it be carried, can ever entirely eliminate such "injustices", since they are an intrinsic feature of democratic government.'[18]

Consequently, the Irish Revolution encouraged calls for devolution or independence in Scotland and Wales. Those claims re-emerged quickly after 1918 – a second Scottish Home Rule Association existed from 1918 to 1927 – and were subsequently refreshed, revised and refashioned. Among many others, Plaid Cymru, the Welsh National Party, was founded in 1925 and the Scottish National Party (SNP) in 1934, with both committed to independence and, more immediately, viewing their nations as separate entities within the UK each deserving of distinctive treatment. Yet, while they often employed similar arguments to those used by Irish nationalists and painted the Union as limiting their national well-being (socially and culturally as well as politically and economically), there were important differences because the unions they looked to end were much older, the religious and cultural differences were less significant, the countries were physically smaller and, sharing the same island with England, were more closely interwoven with its economy. The last two points have proved crucial: could Scotland and Wales support their own currencies; how would trade across new land borders be managed if taxes and duties in the separated states began to diverge; could such small states maintain welfare provision; and how would the cost of losing administrative – and governmental – scale economies be met? In the nature of things, many different answers to those questions have been offered, while such materialism has in any case played a larger part in the so-called 'Scottish question'; in Wales the greater emphasis on culture, language especially, along with its much smaller size, has hindered the development of an equally potent 'Welsh question'.[19]

LEVIATHAN RISING

An unremarked consequence of Irish independence was that it led central government in London to stop routinely distinguishing the three kingdoms in its published annual summaries of public finances. It was as if, to the official mind, nationalist Ireland had been the only source of disputes over the territoriality of those finances. Here, perhaps, was the rebirth of Gladstone's view from the 1850s that fiscal uniformity across the UK was highly desirable. But the post-1918 order was very different, with the state growing in size and responsibility for three general reasons: by following through on new social and economic priorities in the form of the expanding welfare state; industrial and regional policies that began to emerge in the 1930s; and Keynesian demand management from the 1940s. All of this required more knowledge and expertise as well as revenue and administration. Yet, when the first official national income estimate was drawn up in 1941, it was for the UK as a whole, while complaints about the inadequacy of regional data were voiced until the 1990s. In fact, public-finance accounts were not always UK-wide. First, it was important that Northern Ireland was treated as a separate fiscal entity for fifty years after 1922. Secondly, between 1921 and 1955 seven annual accounts were published that, as a minimum, distinguished Scotland from England and Wales. Thirdly, Scottish and Welsh nationalists produced figures purporting to show how UK public finances adversely affected their countries. Even if these numbers might be questionable, conceiving of Scotland and Wales as distinguishable if dependent financial entities helped to frame wider debates about how the UK's public finances should operate.[20] Finally, from the 1970s pressures for devolution (regional and national) led to more frequent and systematic reports, particularly the annual Government Expenditure and Revenue in Scotland (GERS) since 1991 – a Scottish Statistical Office had existed since 1952. All of this is helpful, if compiled using different methods, sources and categories. An old difficulty exacerbated by much greater welfare spending was how to allocate geographically the expenditure side of public accounts. Some spending, such as that by the Foreign Office or Ministry of Defence, could not easily be distributed among the home nations, while spending by the Scottish and Welsh secretaries was sometimes discretionary and sometimes not.

The general pattern of central government finances in this period is very clear (Figure 13): exceptional growth in both of the world wars also ratcheted up peacetime levels to new highs. In real terms, this was a twentyfold rise between 1910 and 1995.[21] Before 1914, central government spending was usually under 10 per cent of GDP; between the wars, it was generally a little under 20 per cent; and after 1945 it was under 30 per cent until edging up in the 1960s. In the period of the

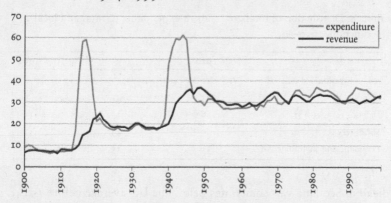

Figure 13. Central government income and expenditure relative to GDP, 1900–1999, %

Conservative governments under Margaret Thatcher and John Major respectively (1979–97), with their emphasis on rolling back the state and on fiscal restraint, the ratio averaged over 34 per cent, a little higher than the Labour governments of 1974–9. By this measure, central government activity rose fourfold across the century. This was associated with a major shift in both income and spending from local to central government. In 1910 about 31 per cent of total government revenue was collected locally; by 1995 it was just 3 per cent.[22] In 1910 local government accounted for nearly 40 per cent of all government spending; by 1995 it was just 18 per cent and had come to depend much more heavily on grants from central government rather than locally raised income – business rates had been 'nationalized' out of local authority hands in 1990.[23]

These changes were driven mainly by increased spending on education, health, pensions and welfare benefits (Table 6) – while defence spending remained high for some time after 1945, the suggestive label 'warfare state' is somewhat misleading.[24]

The end of empire, an ageing population, economic vicissitudes and changing societal values about the proper actions of the state fed these developments. But they did not play out equally across the UK. In purely national terms, spending per capita was lower in England than elsewhere, a difference that has persisted in almost all years since the early interwar period. As discussed earlier, public expenditure per

Table 6. Distribution of total government expenditure (central and local), by function, 1910–90, %

	1910	1951	1990
Administration and other	22	7	8
National debt	15	11	9
Defence	28	25	11
Social services	20	43	57
Economic and environmental	15	15	15

head in Scotland was sometimes below the UK average before 1914, but always above it thereafter: by 12 per cent in 1928/9; 16 per cent in 1948/9; 34 per cent in 1968/9; and 19 per cent in 1988/9.[25] Using different sample years, figures for Wales were lower than these, and for Northern Ireland higher, often significantly (Table 7).[26]

Table 7. Distribution of territorially identified public expenditure by nation, 1972–96. UK = 100 at given dates

	1972–3	1979–80	1995–6
Northern Ireland	127	144	133
Scotland	127	119	120
Wales	110	112	114
England	96	96	96

Higher public expenditure in Northern Ireland, Scotland and Wales went hand in hand with lower tax receipts, driven in each case by a weaker economy than in England. This was especially marked in Northern Ireland and Wales, which remained more rural than England and Scotland, though not in some of their regions. However, even in Scotland GDP per head was 80–90 per cent that of Britain after 1945, only rising above that level from the 1970s with the growth of the service sector and the bounties of North Sea oil.[27]

Important as the national framework was, key economic developments played out regionally rather than nationally. While hopes that after 1918 the pre-war economy might be restored were patently over-optimistic, few anticipated just how difficult adjusting to the new world order was going to be. Certainly there were deep roots to the interwar malaise. After 1865, rapid industrialization in the USA, Germany and elsewhere had eroded Britain's economic primacy, while rising cheap food imports undercut its much-prized agriculture: the age of great estates and great houses was closing. Yet before 1914 these changes were manageable, although there had been bitter battles over 'tariff reform' (that is, increases) linked to giving preference to imperial imports. After 1918 they were not. The dollar, not the pound, was now the premier international currency. A short-lived post-war boom was followed by years of struggle, decline and depression, exacerbated between 1925 and 1931 by a misguided and backward-looking return to the gold standard and relatively free trade. This hit hard in those places that had been the main locales of British industrialization, especially in central Scotland, Tyne-Tees, west Cumbria, north-west England and south Wales. Unemployment was the most potent sign of this collapse, movingly demonstrated by the Jarrow March (1936) and George Orwell's *Road to Wigan Pier* (1937). Such powerful voices were buttressed by the state's own regional unemployment figures, which had become available with the introduction of unemployment insurance from 1911. Here was a new and potent index of the geography of economic collapse, much more frequently updated than the decennial census data that previously had roughly indicated the geography of economic change (Table 8).

In 1932, at the height of the interwar depression, the unemployment rate in what has been called 'outer Britain' was around double that in London and the south-east. While unemployment began to fall in the 1930s, it remained very much higher where shipbuilding, iron and steel, coal mining and cotton industries had once given Britain considerable economic power: but now these were 'distressed', 'depressed' and even, acknowledging the permanence of the change, 'derelict' areas.[28]

Unemployment led, of course, to problems of acute poverty, as well as encouraging the mobile to move to find work, hollowing out the communities they left behind – 'the murder of whole townships', in the words of Hugh Dalton, a leading Labour politician of the period.[29] Between the wars, depopulation was, however, a rural as well as an industrial problem, particularly affecting Mid Wales and the Highlands

Table 8. Insured unemployment rate, 1923–38, %

	1923	1932	1938
England			
London	10.1	13.5	8.0
South-east	9.2	14.3	8.0
South-west	10.6	17.1	8.2
Midlands	10.7	20.1	10.3
North-east	12.2	28.5	13.6
North-west	14.5	25.8	17.9
Scotland	14.3	27.7	16.4
Wales	6.4	36.5	24.8
Northern Ireland	18.2	27.4	28.3

and Islands. To some, multiple regional crises coalesced as national ones, though this did not happen in England, because it was too large, or Northern Ireland, because it was too small. Depopulation in the Highlands was turning it into a barren 'Sahara' according to one report from 1939, while Scotland as a whole was described in 1937 as 'gradually being emptied of its population, its spirit, its wealth, industry, art, intellect, and innate character' – its population actually declining in the 1920s.[30] (The population of Wales also fell in the 1920s but, unlike Scotland, also contracted in the 1930s.) Before 1914 Scotland's tax receipts had been buoyant; after 1918 they were not, while the welfare bill there rose.[31] Little surprise that its depiction as a poor relation was revived. As one Scot put it in 1935, 'The conception of a partnership from which both countries derive benefit has been displaced by that of a parasitic relationship in which one country is advised, with a greater or lesser degree of shamelessness, to content itself with being a beggar.'[32]

Changes in the geography of economic prosperity that took place so rapidly between the wars have proved very persistent. The shift towards a much more service-based economy in London and south-east England took place alongside the declining relative importance of agriculture in many areas and the absolute collapse of coal mining, shipbuilding and manufacturing. Deindustrialization had begun in the 1920s, but accelerated from the mid 1950s.[33] If this meant that

Scotland's population further declined in the 1970s and 1980s, it has also meant that per capita public expenditure exceeded public revenue in England's south-west and far north as well as in Northern Ireland, Scotland and Wales. On the other side of that coin, there were English regions where the reverse was substantially true, especially the west Midlands and the south-east.[34] Since 1945 these patterns have proved hard to change.

After 1945 a much-enlarged state was heavily involved with significant regional transfers of public funds, from the more to the less economically prosperous parts. This was one consequence of a broader political economy of redistribution via direct taxation of higher incomes and wealth that had begun before the First World War. Death duties and inheritance taxes were a part of this, but the transformation of the income tax after 1914 had more general consequences. Although that tax was permanent in Britain from 1842 and in Ireland from 1853, its burdens were generally light until the early twentieth century. Only then did the number of payers exceed 1 million, mostly at very low rates: Lloyd George's People's Budget of 1909 raised the top rate to just 8 per cent. Immediately before the First World War the income tax provided about 29 per cent of central government revenue, but customs and excise 46 per cent.[35] That war required a major expansion of the income tax, overtaking in importance customs and excise, but in 1939 it was paid by only 25 per cent of the working population – prompting one correspondent to *The Times* to ask: 'Is it sound policy to allow almost nine out of every ten voters to feel that Budgets are no concern of theirs'?[36] (The 1930s also saw the final abandonment of free trade, increasing the potential for customs duties to be relatively more significant.) It was the Second World War that saw it extended to most of the rest, linked to the full introduction of Pay As You Earn in 1944.[37] (Under the same pressure to pay for greater welfare provision, National Insurance was made universal and compulsory in the same period.) As the income tax spread, so it was applied at higher rates. In 1976 the top rate was 83 per cent and the standard rate 33 per cent, significantly higher than in France, Germany and the USA.[38]

All told, between 1918 and 1979 the income tax provided 42 per cent of central government revenue and customs and excise 37 per cent.[39] A more progressive tax regime was central to the expanded welfare state: inequality of taxation was viewed by many as essential to producing a more equal and equitable society. The picture was not a steady one, however. Before 1914, regressive indirect taxes were the most important to central government; between 1918 and 1979, progressive direct taxes were more important; but after 1979 the Conservative governments of Thatcher and Major looked to restore the *ancien régime* by cutting income tax and raising VAT. By 1989 customs and excise was producing significantly more revenue for central government than the income tax. The importance of such shifts needs to be emphasized. In general, in the first half of the century increased taxation redefined the British state and the nature of civil society, not least because general, centrally controlled, taxation paid a more important – and social insurance a less important – role in funding welfare in the UK than in France and Germany.[40] More particularly, the relative importance of direct and redistributive taxation related to the desired balance of economic power between the state and the individual and of that between welfare and self-help. As we will see, this had important territorial dimensions.

There is no question that the growth of the UK's public finances in the twentieth century has been associated with significant regional variations in the balance between taxes and spending. The excess of spending over taxation has been widest for Northern Ireland, followed by Scotland, northern England and Wales, whereas in London and south-east England taxation has exceeded expenditure. There is no question that the geography of economic change was the main reason for these patterns. Yet if that has often been recognized, plenty have invoked the two central myths that frame this book. To explore how, we need first to examine some general considerations before turning to looking at key moments.

SPEAKING TERRITORIALLY AND ECONOMICALLY, 1918–1979

In the late nineteenth century, the German economist Adolph Wagner coined his 'law' – really an observation – that in mature industrial societies the growth of public expenditure exceeded economic growth, a trend he predicted would continue in the future. Mainly he put this down to increasingly complex economies requiring more governance, to the need for state action to mitigate the negative consequences of urbanization and because of rising demand for public goods such as disaster relief, welfare provision and research and development that were too costly or risky for the private sector to provide. Such general ideas help to frame the particular developments within the UK in the twentieth century where historians have tended to explain the changing boundaries of state action in terms of the impact of war and welfare.[41] Understandably, these have broadly been approached as UK-wide undertakings: welfare provision was uniform while two total wars involved all, if not quite all, equally. (As a teenager in wartime Aberdeen, my mother recalls eating fish most days despite the privations of rationing.) Yet even welfare and warfare involved some lumpy expenditure, benefiting some places but not others. Indeed the rise of central government's expensive capital projects – including (beyond war and welfare) on major roads, airports, nuclear power, industry, new universities and housing (including new towns) – had to be spread over time and space. Priorities had to be established, costs and benefits – social and political as well as economic – weighed, and rates of return and depreciation calculated, leading to hundreds of questions, asked by old interests and new.[42] How such questions were resolved and what their consequences were will be considered in later sections, but here we need to consider how territorial dynamics helped to raise public expenditure more generally after 1918.

If important decisions had to be made as to whether increasing government spending should be applied equally across the UK, some principles had to be invoked. There was little dispute that cash payments, like unemployment benefits and pensions, should go to individuals or families wherever they were, but it became more complicated when capital costs were involved. For example, although the National Health Service was indeed national, and UK-wide requirements for certain levels of educational provision have existed since 1870, there are practical difficulties in providing hospitals and schools where people are thinly scattered and distant from towns and cities. If cottage hospitals and village schools helped to answer such needs, to central government accountants they became less viable as standards and costs rose. Unsurprisingly, taxpayers and electors usually thought that they had a right to enjoy such improvements, wherever they lived. But this could look to some like writing a blank cheque. As Sir Robert Hall, economic adviser to the Conservative government in 1958, put it: 'if people live in an inaccessible place they must expect to pay for it', by which he meant either forgoing some public goods or personally paying to have access to them.[43] Government provision of roads nicely illustrates the questions raised here.

Since the sixteenth century, local government has had some responsibility for road maintenance. But it only became a fundamental concern of central government in the first decades of the twentieth century as motor transport took off: a Road Fund was instituted in 1909; the Ministry of Transport dates from 1919; the main A roads were numbered in 1923 and central government took over their care in 1937.[44] The nature of these responsibilities depended on settling some key questions. Most fundamental was which roads should the government, local and central, be responsible for and to what standard? In particular, should good roads be provided to even the most remote settlements? An extreme Treasury view from 1957, contributing to a debate over relative levels of spending on roads in England and Scotland, noted that 'the only criteria the Chancellor can accept for heavier investment in roads is [sic] their industrial importance and potential economic return.'[45] Many assumptions are bound up in such views, quite apart from the difficulties of undertaking the cost-benefit analysis to which they seemingly lead. Indeed, others might place equal or greater emphasis on social criteria, on the requirement for the road network to be available to all communities. In any case, if the government would not provide people with access to good roads, was it fair for the taxes that paid for such roads to be applied to everyone? And what of people who lived on islands, unconnected to the mainland road network? Should they too have to pay road taxes at the full rate and should ferries linking them to the mainland be paid for privately, publicly or some mixture of the two?

For some communities these were very pressing considerations. An extreme case was the fate of St Kilda, one hundred miles off the Scottish mainland, whose final permanent inhabitants were evacuated in

1930, showing how remote communities might wither in the face of economic and medical developments beyond their reach.[46] As this suggests, such questions often played out in national terms. While thinly populated and remote districts are to be found in England and Wales, they are much more prevalent in Scotland, where the demand for ferries is raised by long firths and many inhabited islands. This has certainly coloured central government thinking, which has provided roads throughout the UK, built bridges over major estuaries and subsidized ferries with taxpayers' money. The case of ferries illustrates the complicated types of reasoning involved. In 1974, Roy Pedersen developed an important principle that later came to influence the costly government support of ferries in Scotland – over £200 million in 2017.[47] The 'Road Tax Equivalent' recognized that islanders paying national road tax cannot directly access most of the UK road network 'without paying a substantial ferry surcharge'. In Pedersen's analysis, equity requires charging such ferry users the cost of travelling an equivalent length of road, with the shortfall of the actual cost of providing the ferry service met from general taxation. He has argued, however, that this has encouraged significant inefficiencies on many Scottish ferry routes, to the cost of the general taxpayer.[48]

Applying these considerations more broadly, increases in government spending in the twentieth century were always liable to encourage various interests to claim that they were particularly deserving cases: that in their area a hospital, a bridge, a school or an industrial estate was urgently needed – more urgently, by implication, than elsewhere. Three general factors were liable to underpin such claims. First, after Ireland's independence the Goschen ratios continued to be used for the rest of the UK until the late 1950s, sometimes being articulated both as a right and as a minimum starting point in negotiations – as a floor not a ceiling.[49] Secondly, different parts of the UK might claim that they were not enjoying equal treatment to other parts of Britain and ought to be brought up to that level: none, of course, ever argued for cuts to take them down to the average. Finally, that special circumstances in some places required levels of spending above those elsewhere in Britain – perhaps because of the depth of industrial dislocation, the scale of slum housing, poor infrastructure connections or the cost of providing public goods to thinly populated districts.

Increased spending in response to the second or third of these points could encourage public expenditure to spiral upwards, for, if other parts of the UK successfully argued that their special circumstances warranted more spending, then the average would rise, requiring increases to those places now below the average.

Reinforcing these arguments were institutional pressures, especially from the Scottish Office. Over thirty years old in 1918, it saw one of its key roles as fighting for Scotland's corner with central government, especially over funding. It developed a high level of expertise with dedicated civil servants working after 1926 under a full Secretary of State able to put Scotland's case in the cabinet and across Whitehall. Some Scots bemoaned these arrangements as involving excessive centralization or dependency, making Scotland a 'Crown colony', in the words of the Duke of Montrose.[50] There was some truth to that, with the Scottish Office operating as a general clearing house, but it meant that central government in London heard certain Scottish voices loud and clear: a Welsh Office was not created until 1964, while devolved government in Northern Ireland from 1921 to 1972 also meant its finances were little discussed within Whitehall.[51] Often enough, the Scottish Office was good at squeezing more money from London, or at least at resisting cuts. But there were dangers in overplaying its hand. George Pottinger, a leading Scottish civil servant who was jailed for corrupt distribution of public contracts, commented that 'the Scottish Office record is not a discreditable one, but it does not help when other Departments become weary of the sound of the piper.'[52] In a similar vein, one Treasury wag in 1961 suggested that 'In matters of money the fault of the Scots is asking too often and asking for lots.'[53] Indeed, from at least the 1950s complaints began to be aired in the Treasury that Scotland was getting more than its fair share of public expenditure, which could be conceived, as one official suggested in 1962, as a 'drain on the more economically efficient and prosperous parts of Great Britain'.[54]

Calls for independence or devolution provided an important context for these developments. After 1918 renewed attention to the Irish question provoked, as in 1886, concerns about constitutional relations across the UK. In 1919 a Speaker's Conference at Westminster addressed, to little effect, the possibility of devolution across the whole Union. Both Plaid Cymru and the SNP gained support from the fact that after 1918 the Union was unable to restore past economic glories. If the Union had generally served their economies well in the half century before 1914, that was clearly far from the case after 1918. This was vital grist to the independence mills but it has also meant that since the 1930s scrutiny by Plaid and the SNP has helped to ensure that central government views their nations as key units for assessing policy prescriptions and practice, while their rising electoral fortunes in the 1970s encouraged London into new iterations of 'killing Home Rule with kindness'. Both Labour and Conservative governments were willing to spend extra public money in Scotland and Wales to demonstrate the value of the Union there, even if those in some of England's poorest regions viewed this as rewarding the Union's critics and enemies.

As this suggests, thinking about Home Rule in purely national terms was challenged by England's very much greater size – territorially, demographically and economically. Some believed that a balanced 'Home Rule all round' required England to be divided regionally. This tension between regional and national frameworks only intensified after 1918: the regional frame was commonly used to make sense of and to address the geography of industrial depression; the national frame was fed by the rise of the corporate economy and economic nationalism abroad, most obviously in Nazi Germany and Soviet Russia. But thinking regionally was a major development in British geopolitics after 1918.

In the generation before the First World War there had been important advances among academic geographers about thinking regionally, including by Halford Mackinder, a founder and later director of the London School of Economics. Probably a more important figure, however, was Paul Vidal de La Blache in France, whose ideas informed the Scots polymath Patrick Geddes, a charismatic leader in the emerging town-planning movement that gained a fillip after 1918 when urban renewal became a social and political priority. In this way of thinking, 'every society is a complex web, with its relatively fixed geographical and historical conditions, its regional warp, as the very basis of its fluent economic and political woof. Economics is thus fundamentally regional, since sources of food, materials and power, conditions of transport and more, are of Nature's making, which we utilize more than we modify.'[55] Here was an explicit challenge to the inability of many economists to consider questions of territoriality. But there was also a political challenge, viewing regionalism as an antidote to over-centralization – 'London is not England' – in the context of an extended franchise: 'Democracy demands devolution.'[56] Altogether, the geographer's conception of society might be very different from the economist's, with greater regard to environmental, social and cultural considerations – and, with it, greater public expenditure.

Thinking regionally was closely related to an appreciation of the geography of interwar depression and the realization by the early 1930s that allowing market forces alone to produce a new equilibrium would take many years and involve 'an immense waste of', a key new concept, 'social capital'.[57] In 1934 even *The Times* could publish a series of reports on these themes – although anonymous, they were by a future Conservative Home Secretary, Henry Brooke.[58] In the context of mass politics and the power of the wider Labour movement, action not inaction, spending rather than retrenchment, was seen as desirable across the political spectrum: they were very much part of the thinking then of Oswald Mosley, founder of the British Union of Fascists, Harold Macmillan, future Conservative prime minister, and Hugh Dalton, future Labour Chancellor of the Exchequer. Macmillan even claimed in 1936 that politics was no longer 'the old business of playing off the Left against the Right'.[59] This meant, though, not Keynesian macroeconomic management – his *General theory* was not published until 1936 and only began to be influential to government in the Second World War – but 'planning', of urban renewal, major infrastructure projects and influencing the mobility of both industry and labour.[60] As early as 1935, *The Times* declared that, despite its seeming foreignness, planning was 'the keynote of the age in which we are passing'.[61] Some inspiration was provided by Soviet Russia's first Five Year Plan in 1928, Roosevelt's New Deal in America in 1933, especially the Tennessee Valley Authority, and Nazi Germany's Four Year Plan in 1936, though an explicit UK 'National Plan' had to wait for the Labour government of 1965.[62]

Identifying certain regions as requiring special measures was part of the politics of central government thinking from 1934 to 1979, even if the boundaries shifted and the terminology morphed from 'special' into 'distressed', 'development' and even 'intermediate' areas (Map 6). Important in this was identifying particular locales as suffering from inherited and intractable problems, ranging from uneconomic factories or depleted coal mines to dilapidated housing and poor social amenities within 'congested' districts in London, Glasgow and other major cities – unwittingly echoing the late nineteenth-century terminology applied to remote and poor districts in Ireland and Scotland. Regional bodies were required to draw up and implement plans, often within the framework of ten 'standard' regions invented by central government – though other regions were defined by many others, including the NHS and electricity boards. In doing so, as in the introduction of the Scottish and Welsh Offices, it not only assigned responsibilities but it created institutionalized inter-ests (through a bewildering proliferation and subsequent rethinking (and rebranding) of development bodies) that sought to get a bigger slice of the cake of public expenditure.

For the purposes of practical political economy, conceiving the UK as a collection of regions as well as nations was a major interwar development whose lasting significance challenges the dominance of the national frame. But that was due to a belief not that there was no growth within the wider economy, but that growth was geographically unbalanced: absent from the depressed areas and unduly concentrated in London, south-east England and the west Midlands where new industries such as electrical engineering and motor manufacturing flourished. It was clear at the time that there was some truth in this.[63] Between 1932 and 1938 there were over 1,400 new manufacturing plants employing 25 or more people in Greater London but fewer than 200 for Scotland and Wales combined.[64] An important dynamic was the growing importance of electrical and oil-based energy, liberating firms from proximity to coalfields, while new consumer-goods indus-tries were often located nearer their more prosperous markets than the site of raw materials or cheaper labour.[65] Such rationales could not prevent condemnations of the 'all-devouring Wen' to be recast in mod-ern guise, emphasizing the inequity – 'stark lunacy', in the words of the Labour party – of siting new factories well away from the deep pools of the unemployed.[66] This line was enthusiastically pursued by a

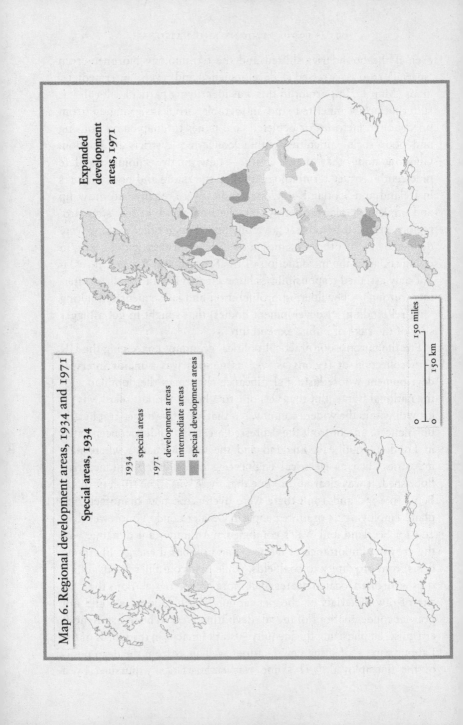

Map 6. Regional development areas, 1934 and 1971

Special areas, 1934

Expanded development areas, 1971

1934
▨ special areas

1971
▨ development areas
▨ intermediate areas
▨ special development areas

0 150 km
0 150 miles

number of Scottish commentators. To one academic at the time, 'Scotland is never likely to revive unless the growth of the London octopus is checked.'[67] There were consequently heavy pressures for public expenditure to be used to resist 'the drift South'.[68]

Such claims were partly fed by a belief that the organization of economic life across the UK was becoming more concentrated in London.[69] An early development was the rise of the corporate economy, operating across regions or nations, a rise that had begun before 1914 but was accelerated by the First World War. Important examples of this were railway amalgamation in 1923 and the creation of the Central Electricity Board in 1927 with its 'national grid'. These were major practical developments which raised grave worries to some that boardrooms in London were viewing the lives of people across Britain purely in balance-sheet terms. The Labour MP for Jarrow, Ellen Wilkinson, reflected that 'Anyone who takes the trouble to study the new forces at work in our urban civilization cannot deny the dangerous trend towards over-centralization that cheap power and quick transport have brought into this tiny country.'[70] (Here is the small-island myth again.) Similarly, to one Scottish nationalist, railway amalgamation was, amazingly, 'the most spectacular piece of national [that is, Scottish] debasement since the Union'.[71]

The scale economy imperatives of big business and new technology took place alongside the growing influence of national trade unions, often seeking to negotiate national wages and conditions – as in the General Strike of 1926. Nationalization of key industries by the Labour government of 1945 – coal, railways, gas, electricity, iron and steel – encouraged that further; this could be viewed as 'Londonization' while the terminology of 'nationalization', not 'socialization', is suggestive.[72] Other governmental initiatives were similarly national in scope: the establishment of the Forestry Commission in 1919; the classification of major roads in 1923; the first crown charter of the BBC in 1927 ('the greatest murderer yet of the Welsh way of life', according to one later critic); and government taking over responsibility for trunk roads in 1936.[73] The Second World War was also a great force for centralization and nationalization, symbolized by the first official estimates of national income calculated in 1941 and the growing influence of Keynes's ideas. His field of view, like that of the economists he sought to supplant, was the UK economy as a whole: monetary policy, general taxation and external trade. And implementing the Beveridge Report of 1942 proposed UK-wide solutions for slaying the five giants of want, disease, ignorance, squalor and idleness, most famously via the National Health Service and the substitution of the locally organized poor law by universal social benefits (both 1948).

Importantly, within the official mind there developed in the twentieth century a resort to both the regional and national scale in forming, implementing and judging questions of public finances. However, this was not just about regions as a subset of the nation; that would have been too straightforward, too suggestive of some more or less logical federalism. On the one hand, defining regions was never straightforward: their boundaries were rarely natural and uncomplicated, epitomized by the border created between Northern Ireland and Ireland, severing the province of Ulster in the process. Not least was the problem that, while Scotland and Wales might be treated as regions, they were usually called nations. Yet economically they remained strikingly diverse. It was, for example, commonly argued that the entire Highlands and Islands were economically distinctive within both Scotland and the wider UK, while at times the Northern Isles emphasized their own remoteness and separate Nordic heritage from both Gaelic and Lowland Scotland.[74] Though such considerations were liable to be obscured by the rise of national parties seeking devolution or independence, such differences mattered in implementing public policies, usually on technocratic grounds rather than some ambition to divide and rule. To understand how all this played upon public finances, it is helpful to divide the period between the First World War and devolution in 1999 into three: the interwar years, 1918 to 1939; from 1939 to 1970; and 1970 to 1999. The fundamental question is how the growth of public finances and rising calls for devolution or independence for Scotland and Wales were related.

1918–1939: HARD LESSONS

The financial costs of the First World War were enormous, requiring new and higher taxes and much more government borrowing than at any time since 1815. This was a costly legacy that had to be managed and for more than a decade most of the political class sought the restoration of the pre-war order of limited government, free trade and the gold standard. By these lights, the Treasury was, in the words of the historian Peter Clarke, a 'national housekeeper' not a 'national breadwinner', intent on keeping expenditure down by scrutinizing policies and budgets: the Permanent Secretary to the Treasury was made head of the civil service in 1919, while in 1927 the Treasury was said to be 'the one permanent institution which stands between the country and national bankruptcy'.[75] In this it was, for some years, supported by wider sentiment. As at the end of the Napoleonic Wars in 1815, after 1918 shrill demands for economy in public expenditure were made. One notification of the formation of an 'Anti-Waste League' in 1921 was even headed with a picture of that great prophet of economy, William Gladstone. Lord Rothermere, owner of the *Daily Mail* and a key voice of the League, attacked 'Squandermania' while the League's success in three parliamentary by-elections showed the popular purchase of such polemics.[76] It was in this context that the notorious 'Geddes axe' of 1922 – named after Sir Eric Geddes, the chairman of a committee charged with finding large savings in public expenditure – was wielded, cutting unemployment welfare especially. As Stanley Baldwin, Conservative Chancellor of the Exchequer, said at the time, 'money taken for government purposes is money taken away from trade, and borrowing will thus tend to depress trade and increase unemployment.'[77]

It says much that Philip Snowden, one-time excise officer (from Orkney in the north to Plymouth in the south) and first Labour Chancellor of the Exchequer from 1929 to 1931, followed Baldwin's thinking. Winston Churchill likened Snowden to a Gladstonian radical, meanly claiming that the 'Treasury mind and the Snowden mind embraced each other with the fervour of two long-separated kindred lizards' – though, characteristically, Churchill was ignoring his own attachment to economy at the time.[78] Towards the end of Snowden's tenure as Chancellor, the House of Commons established a Committee on Public Expenditure to consider how to reduce public spending further. While it did its work, a 'National Campaign for Economy' met at Manchester's Free Trade Hall, as if this embodiment of past glories legitimated the campaign's outdated solutions for new problems. While recognizing that increased expenditure was due to a 'quickening of the social conscience', a return to the spirit of Gladstone and Goschen was nonetheless demanded by many.[79] Such views held sway among most members of the Committee on Public Expenditure that reported in July 1931 (the May Report), stressing the need for heavy cuts in public expenditure to restore pre-war prosperity and the conditions for reducing unemployment. But the majority report of the committee also stressed the influence of mass democracy in encouraging politicians to win votes by advertising generous spending plans. Politically, the dice were 'heavily loaded ... in favour of expenditure'.[80]

Potent though cries for economy were after 1918, the growth of the state before and during the war was associated with a countervailing realization of the need to harness the power of collective action to address 'the haphazard methods' inherent to a free market economy.[81] After all, the First World War as much as the Boer War had established the poor physical state of much of the population: the lesson for many was that the days of unbridled capitalism were over and that heavy public spending was needed to provide better social amenities and to protect people from economic dislocations beyond their control.[82] No less a person than the owner of the *Daily Telegraph*, Lord Burnham, asserted as early as 1916 that 'Until recent years, the theory of individualism was accepted as gospel ... Today no theory is more hopelessly discredited ... Trade as a science is the order of the day; the talk is of association and cooperation; of enlightened State guidance and control.'[83] Keynes made a related point in 1924: 'The world is not so governed from above that private and social interests always coincide.'[84] Quite what communities should replace the individual was left open here, but the general shift, which plenty contested, had been under way for several decades, profoundly influencing the policies and priorities of government both during and after the First World War – extending, for example, the reach of the state into the provision of council housing from 1919, locally provided but centrally directed.[85] By 1939 over 1 million houses had been built by the state, making it, it was claimed in 1945, 'the outstanding peace time experiment in state intervention in this country in the provision of a necessity of life'.[86] (Public housing was especially important in Scotland.[87]) While peace in 1918 saw the scope of the state shrink, it remained larger and much more consequential than in the fin-de-siècle days of Edwardian Britain: a similar ratchet effect was to be experienced after 1945.

The links between growing public expenditure and a mass electorate were clear enough. But the politics of public expenditure was changing in other important ways. Naturally, when public expenditure aimed at national betterment, often including advantage over other nations, this could be characterized as economic nationalism, a 'new mercantilism'. This was consistent with the abandonment of the gold standard and free trade in 1931. Even Keynes, a dyed-in-the-wool liberal, acknowledged links between his priorities – government management of the macroeconomy by using public expenditure to hinder wild swings in total demand within the economy – and those of a pre-liberal order, recognizing an 'element of scientific truth' in the mercantilist doctrines of the seventeenth century.[88] More to the point, though, was that rising public expenditure increased the importance of expertise and specialist knowledge within and outside government. Government became permanently more bureaucratic and technocratic, while increasingly targeted by proliferating pressure groups – eventually brilliantly captured in the comic *Yes Minister* TV series (1980–84). For example, in the 1930s the Lancashire cotton industry, faced by increasing pressure from cheaper producers in India, argued that Britain should not be subject to competition from its empire.[89]

The end of free trade between the wars and the rise of economic autarky in most industrial economies provided an important new context in which central government sought to address the profound structural limitations of the UK economy's dependence upon coal, cotton and shipbuilding. It had to contemplate direct action at home in ways previously thought unimaginable and now had more scope to do so. At the general level, the question relevant to the concerns of this book was what role the state should play in the location of people and work in a changing economy: should work be taken to workers, should workers be taken to work or should both workers and work be moved? Most simply, answers depended on one's views of the relative power of market forces as against the power of government and of the weight attached to economic as opposed to social values. But if no action was taken at all, then what was to become of the people and their communities who were left behind?

Starting from one end, we can recall Norman Tebbit's boast at the 1981 Conservative party conference that in the 1930s his father did not riot, he got on his bike to look for work. By doing so, he was advocating the primacy of personal responsibility and market forces, not state aid, in dealing with structural economic change. Such thinking had been central to the new poor law of 1834 which continued to operate up until 1948, albeit in amended form. For example, in 1935 Horace Wilson, a prominent civil servant, thought moving work to workers was 'make-believe' and that 'people who wish to work must go where the work is'.[90] Wilson presumably thought that the 'must' would be achieved by market forces, but political diktat was contemplated by some. As with wider discussion about public expenditure amid depression, this was not simply right versus left. Huw Edwards, a leading Welsh trade unionist and Labour politician, suggested in 1944 that one-quarter of the population of the south Wales valleys, where unemployment had been so high before the war, should be compelled to move out by the state.[91] Plenty disagreed with such ideas, including the Conservative Francis Pym, who, rebuking Tebbit, thought it was ridiculous to tell three million people to get on their bike.[92] It was not just a question of scale, however. As James Griffiths, the first Welsh Secretary, noted, a high incidence of owner-occupation in the Welsh valleys, alongside a powerful attachment to both local community and local landscape, rested on very different values to those later expounded by Tebbit. Their cry was 'bring us new industries. We have done our share of the nation's hard work and deserve a break. We want to keep the old place going and live out our lives with our neighbours.'[93] Here we have a celebration of an idea of society to set against Thatcher's scepticism that there was such a thing as society at all.

It was in response to such contrasting views that interwar government began tentatively to develop regional policies rather than those directed only at the four constituent territories of the UK.[94] This was done with real commitment by some, by others only because it was viewed as politically expedient in terms of appearing reasonably concerned when facing depressingly long dole queues, active trade unions and a mass electorate. Significantly, this initially took the form of trying to move workers to the work, through the Industrial Transference Board of 1928. This provided grants to help workers – coal miners were especially targeted – to move, with political pressure also applied to employers elsewhere to take labour from the most depressed regions. Some 141,000 were moved by government schemes between 1931 and 1938, two-thirds of them from north-east England and south Wales. Although this was a fairly cheap option, problems with the policy soon became evident. Many returned home, shunning alien worlds of work, life and even language. Those who left tended to be younger, fitter and more able, weakening the pool of labour left behind while reducing the rate income in those areas, worsening the ability of local councils to deal with already challenging circumstances.[95] The policy was abandoned and attempts to clear 'congested' districts were generally linked to the new town movement after 1945.

Two other regional policies also sought to address the uniquely hard times of the interwar period. First, in 1929 'de-rating' business rates by three-quarters in some areas was hoped to encourage firms at least to carry on rather than fold, though Neville Chamberlain worried that it would reduce the incentives of local business people to involve themselves in local government.[96] This dull-sounding initiative did not come cheap, costing £26 million by 1931, but the stimulus – very clearly a subsidy – had little apparent effect and was judged to be too costly.[97] Secondly, in 1934 four regions of Britain were designated as 'special areas' under the watchful eye of two commissioners, nascent economic 'viceroys'. Appointed to direct efforts, the fact that one was responsible for Scotland and the other for England and Wales suggests official recognition of the unsuitability of a British-wide approach.[98] But they were given tiny budgets – £2 million initially, compared to a subsidy just for sugar beet of £4.9 million at the time – and spent more time assessing and reporting on problems, seeking to wring as much value as possible out of existing resources, than doing something fundamentally new. (Lord Nuffield, founder of Morris Motors, privately gave £2 million to bolster the scheme.) As Lloyd George sarcastically observed at the time, 'The age of miracles is past. You cannot feed the multitude with two

Commissioners and five sub-Commissioners.' It says something that different ends of the political spectrum could both conclude that the two commissioners lacked influence, funds and powers: on the left, Aneurin Bevan, once briefly a coal miner and now an up-and-coming Labour politician, rubbished 'an idle and empty farce'; on the right, the *Spectator* damned the policy as a 'betrayal'. In any case, the commissioners were themselves doubtful of the wisdom of a very much more intrusive state. Modest, ameliorative and targeted action rather than something more ambitious and general was what they sought.[99]

Even apart from deep questions over government policies towards the four 'special areas' was the important claim that Scotland's Highlands and Islands constituted a fifth area whose problems were, not for the first time, said to be unique. A Highland Development League was formed in 1936, one of whose founders called for a 'new deal' for the region, on the grounds that it had 'been sacrificed on the altars of the British Empire for two centuries' and of 'the duty of the State to equalize public benefits among its subjects'. But, as he arrestingly put it, to do so the 'official mind must be Hebridised'.[100] In parliament, debating a motion on the alleged 'complete breakdown of the social economy' of the region, equity, not charity, was invoked in claiming a fair deal.[101] In 1938 a major non-governmental assessment, the Hilleary Report, stressed that the region was being left behind and continuing to lose population fast. It emphasized the 'natural desire' of those in the region 'to share in the general social advance', suggesting ideas of common expectations, perhaps even of rights. But it was argued that, with the region's people unable to afford that themselves, central government had to step in more heavily than elsewhere, investing in industries 'in harmony with the Highland temperament' and the distinctive 'outlook in the islands' so as to build up 'a strong, healthy and virile race'.[102] The Scottish Secretary welcomed the report, but pointed out that the government was already investing heavily in the region – £2 million in the previous year – and could persuade the Chancellor to find only an additional £65,000, a sum understandably derided by many Scottish commentators.[103]

Although there were strong arguments for the unique problems confronting the Highlands and Islands between the wars, similar arguments were used with reference to Scotland as a whole. Soaring unemployment and declining population fed disquiet in Scotland about financial relations with central government in London. Some called for better statistics on Scotland's financial relations with England, but in their absence the dreadful monster was easily invoked for most of the period: in 1925 it was claimed that 'many millions of pounds sterling raised by taxation in Scotland are every year taken into England to be spent in giving employment to the people there' and in 1933 that 'There was no country in the world more heavily taxed than Scotland.'[104] If the former statement had some truth to it, the second had none, but it was on the expenditure side that opinion concentrated. While there remained those who were set against 'any form of State Subsidy with its corollary of State interference and control' – as a point of general principle as well as of geopolitics – it was more commonly complained that public expenditure in Scotland was too low.[105] On the eve of the Second World War there were several Scottish complaints that if £10 million could be found by the UK government to support Czechoslovakia in the face of threats from Nazi Germany, then more money could also be found to spend north of the Tweed.[106]

In truth, public finances were only able to mitigate to a limited extent some of the deeply damaging effects of the economic dislocations of the interwar period: the forces for structural economic change were too great, those of government too weak. The designation of special areas was an important administrative step on the road towards later regional development councils, while the commissioners did identify the importance of state investment in infrastructure and industrial estates to seek to attract new industries to the old industrial heartlands. Yet this was not enough to prevent some parts of the UK feeling ignored, left behind or abandoned. Such sentiments were seized on by Scottish and Welsh nationalists, yet were also felt just as keenly regionally across the UK.

1939–1970: THE AGE OF PLANNING

In the Second World War central government came to manage the British economy more broadly and deeply than at any other time in its history.[107] Requisitioning and rationing were felt everywhere, towards a single, clear and accepted aim. That Britain was only one cog in the Allied war machine did not prevent (and has not prevented) the effort involved from being told in stirring one-nation terms. It certainly showed the potential for large-scale collective effort and that, with peace, bolder state initiatives might be tried. The creation of the National Health Service in 1947 and the nationalization of several major industries such as coal, railways and electricity around the same time realized such thinking. Yet while UK-wide, these big-ticket items of public expenditure had important territorial consequences to put alongside a significant expansion of explicitly regional initiatives – while considerable centralization also took place. The Labour governments of 1945–51 and 1964–70 enthusiastically put their shoulder to this wheel, but some Tories also embraced greater state interventionism: Harold Macmillan, Conservative prime minister from 1957 to 1963, had represented Stockton-on-Tees in the 1920s, leading him to support the idea of a larger and more active state as a modernization of traditional one-nation Toryism. By 1970, however, changing contexts and worsening public finances led to new approaches being adopted.

As in 1918, victory in 1945 came at a very great cost. Paying for the war had seen taxes double as a proportion of GDP but expenditure tripled to 60 per cent, the shortfall being met by a massively expanded national debt. In the face of rising independence movements, soon enough Britain was unable to sustain its global empire. Changing domestic priorities also played their part, most famously through costly increases in welfare provision and the nationalization of industries. While the Beveridge Report proposed funding the former mainly by social insurance not general taxation, so that the state did not 'stifle incentive, opportunity, responsibility', fairly quickly this fell by the wayside, not least because of the need to iron out geographical variations in local authority resources.[108] The initial budget of the NHS was £437 million, with significant ongoing costs that have almost always marched inexorably upward. Total compensation paid to private owners for nationalization came in at £2,639 million, with some of the nationalized industries requiring significant continuing subsidies.[109]

As these number suggest, both the NHS and nationalization were explicitly centralist initiatives on a grand scale: nationalization directly involved 2.4 million workers and indirectly many more.[110] London was very much at the centre of this new order, with Bevan, the political architect of the NHS, famously declaiming that 'if a hospital bedpan is dropped in a hospital corridor in Tredegar [Wales], the reverberations should echo around Whitehall.'[111] Such exaggerations aside, it also needs noting that three separate acts established the NHS, one each for England and Wales (1946), Scotland and Northern Ireland (both 1947), reflecting the enduring differences in political and administrative arrangements within the UK. A key difference was that in England and Wales the NHS was the responsibility of the Secretary of State for Health, but in Scotland the Scottish Secretary, increasing that office's importance. Moreover, patterns of spending have differed regionally as well as nationally. Since the 1950s spending on the NHS per head in England has usually been lower than in other countries of the Union – its higher population density helping lower delivery costs while on average its population has also been healthier.[112]

The nationalization of some industries, such as electricity and railways, was partly driven by the belief that only governmental action could reduce the perils they posed to consumers as natural monopolies – though even larger monopolies were created in many cases. But nationalization of coal, iron and steel and shipbuilding was driven by the belief that these were fundamental and, while localized, strategically important national resources – often articulated as 'real' industries in a way in which consumer goods and service industries were not. Bringing them under public ownership emphasized their general value to the Union while preventing them from falling prey to the rising tide of multinational corporations. To support them through nationalization opened up the prospect that public revenue might be redistributed regionally away from the tax-rich south-east to the coalfields and the shipbuilding centres such as Barrow-in-Furness, Clydeside and Tyneside. Where the nationalized industries broke even, little or no redistribution was involved, yet over time some became less clearly financially viable as they were squeezed between growing international competition and worsening industrial relations. Detailed

studies showed that the nationalized industries were generally efficient by the 1960s, but then often faltered, though other commentators,
not just enthusiasts for the market, were more critical.[113] The railways
were a clear case where revenue stagnated while costs rose; similarly
the coal industry, having to mine increasingly poor seams in places,
sometimes for political reasons, was in precipitous decline from the
late 1950s. Subsidies were sometimes needed to keep mines going,
constituting important regional transfers in: 957 deep coal mines
have closed since 1947, 39 per cent under Labour governments, 61
per cent under the Conservatives.[114]

Compelling certain industries to be publicly owned could partly be
justified on the grounds that they were nationally important to all citizens as consumers as well as important to some citizens in particular
places, as vital props to local communities. But spending so much
taxpayers' money on nationalization also needs to be seen within a
wider ambition to regenerate economic life that had begun during the
Second World War. The Barlow Report of 1940, named after the
chairman, Sir Alan Barlow, of the royal commission that produced it,
was a key articulation of how state action after the war could address
the fundamental regional imbalances of the economy that had become
painfully apparent. While overshadowed by the Beveridge Report, it
was to some a 'great state paper' in analysing the need for central government to direct the geographical distribution of future economic
change, especially through policies for industrial location and new
towns.[115] As such, it was to some an alternative to the more celebrated
Keynesian revolution in economic management, attracting determined support from Hugh Dalton and others, though Keynesianism
soon became the main preoccupation.[116] The Distribution of Industry
Act of 1945 set out the commitment of central government to direct
industrial location for the national good by employing social as well
as economic criteria – by designating development areas to which
government directed industries. As has been said, 'Regionalism had a
good war.'[117]

The Barlow Report stressed the need to approach planning more
holistically, especially through its enthusiasm for new towns with
their economic, social and geographical ambitions, with developments already under way before the Allied victory over Germany and

Japan in 1945. A central figure in this was Patrick Abercrombie, a practical as well as academic urban planner. He had been encouraged by Patrick Geddes to develop a plan for Dublin during the First World War and went on to produce many others in a long career, including those for Greater London in 1944 and the Clyde Valley in 1946. What distinguished those two plans was that their regional scope required resources well beyond the capacity of local authorities to implement. For example, the Clyde Valley Plan proposed a new type of mass clearance, seeking to move 500,000 from Glasgow's slums, many into four new satellite towns.[118] Here was the opportunity for central government to make a direct impact on lives and landscapes.

The New Towns Act of 1946 led to the designation of 14 new towns – usually expansions of existing settlements – over the next four years and, after further legislation, 27 in total by 1970, including 20 in England, 5 in Scotland and 2 in Wales. Initially they were particularly designed to alleviate urban slums and industrial decay, managing urban sprawl in the process, but in the 1960s their purpose shifted towards trying to harness the rising tide of new technology. By 1969 their collective populations had doubled to 1.4 million people, with a final aim of reaching 2.8 million. None of this came cheap. In 1949 it was estimated that a new town of 50,000 people would cost £46 million, with nearly 80 per cent provided by taxpayers. Initially £50 million was made available, increased to £150 million in 1953. But by 1969 the outstanding advances to the 27 towns totalled over £630 million. Understandably, all this led to questions about value for money, with the Treasury playing its assigned role of throwing cold water over what it saw as unaffordable utopianism. But, as so often, it was reacting to policies made elsewhere according to ambitions that were not purely financial or economic. To Harold Macmillan in 1952 'the creation of the new towns is an exceptional, indeed, unique process and needs to be acknowledged and treated as such within the complex of government policy of which it forms a part.'[119]

The new-towns policy can be put alongside other major investments made by central government at the same time, such as the building of nuclear power plants on coastal sites around Britain – Northern Ireland was again spared. While the particular location of these strategic projects provoked considerable discussion, because the investment was territorially dispersed and the dangers and costs of nuclear fuel were underappreciated, this did not much feed separatist or unionist feeling. (An important counter-example, though this time more through the efforts of local authorities, was the flooding of Welsh valleys to provide English conurbations with ample water supplies – 'sheer robbery' of a poorer people, in the eyes of Welsh nationalists.[120]) In fact, more generally central government understood that, as its expenditure rose, so its spending ought, where possible, to be geographically diffuse, in the context of the extra burdens of 'London weighting' for the salaries of civil servants, introduced in 1920. For example, it sought to address criticisms, especially from Scottish and Welsh nationalists, that a mushrooming civil service was unduly concentrated in London and south-east England. Many Scottish Office staff were moved to a new building in Edinburgh on the eve of the Second World War. In 1962 *The Economist* suggested that, as in Australia, Brazil, Turkey and the USA, a new purpose-built capital might be constructed in Yorkshire, roughly equidistant between the Thames and the Clyde.[121] More realistically, in 1963 a Location of Offices Bureau was established, charged with moving many civil servants out of London. Much dispersal was in fact only within the larger south-east region, masked somewhat by a few headline-grabbing moves: in 1965 the Driver and Vehicle Licensing Agency (DVLA) was established at Swansea; in 1968 the Mint was moved to Llantrisant in south Wales; and major offices of National Savings and the Inland Revenue were established in and near Glasgow.[122] Competition between regions and nations was part and parcel of this process. For example, moving the Royal Mint, following soon after the election of Plaid Cymru's first MP and the SNP's second, disappointed the hopes in the north-east of England that it would be sited there, prompting the leading local Labour politician T. Dan Smith (later jailed for corruption) to suggest that 'What we need here is a couple of Nationalists.'[123]

Smith's complaint that England's north-east suffered in its dealings with central government compared to Scotland and Wales also needs to be put into the context of the creation of the Highlands and Islands Development Board in 1965. As already noted, something like it had been proposed in 1938 and after 1945 calls to halt the depopulation of the region began again. In 1949 Arthur, son of Patrick Geddes and a geographer at Edinburgh University, argued strongly that the region needed something along the lines of the Tennessee Valley Authority, with investment from the more prosperous parts of Britain to help the region to become economically viable. The subtitle of his later work on the Outer Hebrides is telling: 'a study in British community'.[124] White papers were published in 1950 and 1959, with a primary aim of addressing depopulation. In the 1950s government spending per head in the Highlands was twice that available to the rest of the country, spent on roads and communications as usual, but particularly on improving housing, water, sewage, electricity and television coverage. But this did not arrest the outflow of people.[125] The Highlands and Islands Development Board (HIDB) was established in response to this failure, in the hope that, in the words of its first annual report, its 'very great powers' were 'concordant with the intractable character of the problems involved'.[126] Those powers were partly political, partly administrative and partly financial. As in the creation of the Scottish Office in 1885, the HIDB established a significant interest group inside government that fought hard for its corner. But it also encouraged coordination of efforts in the region and applied significant new funding, especially for investment, to the extent that in 1971 its chairman, Andrew Gilchrist, suggested that 'In some respects, the Board resembles a small merchant bank.'[127] He thought that this spending represented good value for money, and by 1990 the HIDB was claiming that because of its efforts the region was now much more economically robust.[128] Wider factors were also at work – the growth of tourism and facilities for the North Sea oil industry especially – but for the first time in 150 years the population of the region stabilized, if at a lower level of prosperity compared to the rest of the UK.[129]

With the creation of both the HIDB and the Labour government's National Plan, 1965 represented the high-water mark of post-war enthusiasm for planning and heavy government investment in major new technologies (Image 9). But a devaluation crisis ruined the National Plan within a year, while corruption, graft and costly failed projects began to erode public support for big, interventionist and redistributive government. It is notable that, after six years of escalating development costs, the TSR-2 bomber was cancelled in 1965, with

Image 9. George Brown launching Britain's only ever national plan, 1965, as Secretary of State for Economic Affairs.

Denis Healey, future Labour Chancellor of the Exchequer, having likened the project to the scandalous South Sea Bubble of 1720.[130] But the £160 million largely wasted on TSR-2 paled into insignificance alongside the joint UK–French project to build Concorde, a supersonic commercial passenger airliner. The total bill to both governments was around £2,000 million, well over ten times earlier high-end estimates, while only nine were ever sold, to state-owned companies.[131] Though its cutting-edge design drew admirers, it was a white elephant financially and funding it saw poorer taxpayers subsidize a largely rich clientele. Such national failures can be put alongside decisions by central government to pull the plug on loss-making ventures of regional significance – 'lame ducks' from one perspective, vital social and economic assets from another – such as the aluminium smelter at Invergordon (1981) and the pulp mill at Corpach (1983), both in the Highlands. The closure of the former cost UK taxpayers £21 million in debt write-offs.[132] The collapse of the DeLorean car company in Northern Ireland in 1983, which swallowed up over £100 million in government funding, really gripped the public imagination in terms of the difficulties central government had in directly aiding industries, especially when government was eager to help troubled parts of the country.[133]

Government faced much less resistance to road building and, mundane though it may seem, much more important battles over territorial expenditure raged here, with rising volumes of traffic producing a new geography of congested districts as key roads became clogged. Ever-increasing road use after 1945 made government responsibility grow sharply, with more and more funds being spent on major road and bridge projects. The building of motorways fanning out from London – part of the M1 was opened in 1959 – was consistent with the heavy cuts in the rail network because of falling freight and passenger numbers, a rationalization that had taken some steps forward even before Dr Beeching, who spent much of his career in industry, produced his technocratic report of 1963 with its unwavering eye on the bottom line: rail mileage was reduced by about one-third.[134] While the idea of producing a coherent and financially viable national infrastructure lay behind both the expansion of major roads and the contraction of the railways, each had to fight its way through dense thickets of interests, including different conceptions of the national.

In such contests, particular grand projects could assume considerable importance, notably calls for suspension bridges across the Forth, the Humber and the Severn. In such duels between national and regional interests, the dates of the opening of the bridges is suggestive of their respective strengths as well as perceptions of need: the Forth Road Bridge near Edinburgh was opened in 1964; the Severn Bridge between England and Wales in 1966; and the Humber Bridge between Yorkshire and Lincolnshire in England in 1981. (Additionally, a major non-suspension bridge across the Tay in Scotland was opened in 1966.) Proponents obviously argued on the basis of need, potential and viability, sometimes being prepared to countenance costs being met by tolls implemented over decades rather than general taxation – though tolls were sometimes fiercely resisted, as when Skye was linked by bridge to the mainland for the first time.[135] But the criteria were not merely financial. Nicholas Edwards (Lord Crickhowell), the Welsh Secretary under Margaret Thatcher, observed in his memoirs that

'Cost-benefit analysis has an important part to play in decisions of this kind; but it cannot be used as a substitute for common sense.' Quite what 'common sense' meant, however, is implied by his lament that 'the politics of roads and estuarial crossings would haunt me throughout my time as an MP and minister' (1970–87).[136] What mattered was the interplay of need, finance and politics.

An important development by the time that Edwards became an MP was that the Goschen ratios for distributing central government expenditure among Britain's three nations had fallen out of use – by the late 1950s, in fact. Coinciding with structurally higher public expenditure, this created many more opportunities for bargaining over the spoils. Civil servants could only do so much in such circumstances, not least because for many years ministerial ambitions tended to run ahead of the realization that the UK economy was declining relative to other leading economies and that the growth of services rather than industry was the most productive path ahead for it in a globalizing world. More generally, the growth of government provoked the creation of many more think tanks, lobbyists, academic reports and charities, altogether producing a much more intricate ecology of politics. If this aided good decision making in many ways, there were downsides. Increased complexity, detail and interests could make particular decisions over spending less comprehensible or electorally accountable. This could be broadened out to a general criticism that, as one early critic put it, planning was 'inherently an attack upon the democratic principle'.[137] Aside from planning there was, moreover, an inherent asymmetry to the influence of interests within democratic politics. As the American economist and political scientist Mancur Olson influentially argued in the 1960s, because of the free-rider problem it is usually much harder for the general population to articulate common interests regarding particular policies than, say, car or drug makers.[138] Industrial policy in particular created opportunities for weak forms of pork-barrel politics and what economists call rent seeking, looking to use government regulations and finances for competitive advantage.[139] In this, the voices of Northern Ireland, Scotland and Wales could be very influential.

If the practice of politics raised particular questions about what was spent where, there were general criticisms of the expansion of the state. After all, the growth of collectivism – be it socialism, Keynesian social democracy or one-nation Conservatism – was explicitly a reaction to the ideology of individualism. It was hardly to be expected that adherents of that ideology would simply leave the field of battle. Though ripostes to collectivism began much earlier, Friedrich Hayek's *Road to serfdom*, published in 1944, was the best-known and most influential of them: Margaret Thatcher, aged nineteen when it was published, later enthusiastically embraced its message. Others of his ilk rubbished economic planning as 'an attempt to build another Tower of Babel'.[140] At a high level of abstraction, the actions of a larger state were argued to cost significant amounts of individual liberty, raised questions of rights and allocated resources less efficiently than did market forces. These were the fundamental tenets of neoliberalism as it developed in the second half of the twentieth century.

What gave such principles a territorial dimension was when they were related to the more practical matter of the desirable degree of centralization within government in an era when it significantly increased spending, in part to address regional inequalities. There were two key tensions here. One, which particularly affected Conservativism, was that an enthusiasm for decentralization might conflict with an enthusiasm for the Union. In 1950 the Conservative general election manifesto promised a rolling back of state control, claiming that 'Centralized control which ignores national characteristics is an essential part of Socialism. Until the Socialist Government is removed neither Scotland nor Wales will be able to strike away the fetters of centralization and be free to develop their own way of life.'[141] (Liberals too condemned the oppressive force of centralization as 'metropolitan encephalitis'.[142]) If this was compatible with Mr Podsnap's declamation in Dickens's *Our mutual friend* (1865) – 'Centralization. No. Never with my consent. Not English' – it nonetheless implicitly questioned the sovereignty of the Westminster parliament and the traditional opposition of the Conservatives to devolution. Undivided sovereignty and centralization went hand in hand and leading Labour politicians were well aware of the link between centralization and authoritarianism, 'the evil, incarnate in the great Leviathan'.[143] Secondly, there was a tension between the desirability of uniformity of standards for certain public goods across the union – education, health and welfare especially – and the desirability of taking account of local circumstances. 'The Headquarters official says: How can we ensure, with a minimum of interference and control, a uniform standard over the whole country? The provincial official asks: How can we escape from all this deadening red-tape, from the superfluous rules and regulations, from constant inspection and interference in matters which can only be satisfactorily settled locally?'[144] Centralization tended towards uniformity; decentralization towards diversity.[145]

This renewed confusion of principles was made pressing because centralization appeared to many to exacerbate age-old perceptions that London was physically and culturally remote from and ignorant of distant parts of the UK. It is worth remembering that George Orwell's *1984* (1949), a brilliant denunciation of a domineering state, was largely written on the Scottish island of Jura. And Labour's Thomas Johnston, Scottish Secretary from 1941 to 1945, who passionately and successfully argued Scotland's case in Whitehall, concluded that 'centralisation must stop south of the Cheviots'.[146] Clearly, then, the centralization–decentralization dichotomy did not simply reflect party politics: centralists and decentralists were found on both the left and the right. All of this confusion of principles and politics inevitably allowed for considerable rhetorical opportunism when it came to discussing the territoriality of UK public finances, particularly by Scottish and Welsh nationalists, whose voices became much louder and more effective from the late 1960s.

1970–1999: CHANGING WORLDS

Although there certainly was a 'Thatcher revolution' following the election of her Conservative government in 1979, with its determination to roll back the state and place more emphasis on individual responsibility, the public finances of the UK had been changing significantly for around a decade, including greater fiscal stringency. Circumstances were also changing significantly, with some electoral success for Plaid Cymru and the SNP in the late 1960s, the discovery of oil and gas in the North Sea soon after, entry into the EEC in 1973, growing problems over local government finance and the creation of the Barnett Formula in 1978. Despite the last of these developments, tensions over Scotland's place within the UK's system of public finances grew considerably, which the Conservative governments of 1979–97 only just contained and which the succeeding Labour government addressed through devolution that redrew the Union compact more significantly than at any time since 1922.

In the 1950 general election, 28 million votes were cast, but Plaid Cymru and the SNP secured only 27,000 votes between them, equivalent to roughly the population of one small town. In the general election of 1970, 28 million votes were again cast, but now the Scottish and Welsh nationalists obtained 480,000 votes. Like most small parties in a first-past-the-post system, such growing support resulted in just one MP, for the SNP. But it was already clear that a significant minority of voters in Scotland, Wales and Northern Ireland, where the Troubles were now raging, were deeply unhappy with their place within the UK. There were many causes of that, but one was certainly disquiet with the financial relations within the UK and a perception that attempts over many decades to improve their economic life had failed to reduce significantly their higher levels of unemployment.[147]

Harold Wilson's Labour government had already grasped some of the significance of this by instituting in 1969 a royal commission on the constitution that concluded in 1973 – the Kilbrandon Report, named after the chairman of the commission, Lord Kilbrandon. While recommending devolution for Scotland and Wales, the report argued against instituting a federal solution, on the grounds that it often worked poorly in practice elsewhere and defied 'common sense', a line supported in the same debate by Wilson, who thought a federal UK would be 'artificial, arbitrary and highly legalistic', and Margaret Thatcher.[148] After much delay, legislation to introduce devolved government into Scotland and Wales was passed by parliament, but referendums in 1979 lacked sufficient support for them to be implemented: 52 per cent voted in favour in Scotland, but this fell short of the required threshold of 40 per cent of the electorate; in Wales only 20 per cent voted in favour of devolution. The Conservative governments of 1979–97 were set against such constitutional change, but with the election of Blair's Labour government in 1997, efforts were soon resumed.

Despite the slowness with which devolution was obtained, powerful winds of change were blowing from the late 1960s that profoundly changed the debate over the Union's public finances in the interim. Three were critical. The first was the invention of the Barnett Formula for the territorial apportionment of some of that expenditure – initially to Scotland in 1978, then to Northern Ireland in 1979 and Wales the following year. Designed by Treasury officials to aid the Chief Secretary, Joel Barnett, in bearing down on public spending in Scotland, it has remained in place ever since. Critically, the Barnett Formula is based on the principle that change in spending in England is the base, the norm, from which a block grant for discretionary spending in the other countries is calculated – an example is given in the next chapter. The formula has been tweaked now and then, especially in 1992 to factor in changes in population distribution within the UK, but it still operates much as it did when it was first introduced.[149] So if the formula has lowered the heat in cabinet over the distribution of public spending among the nations of the Union and has the benefit of being simple, transparent and (roughly) comprehensible, it has done so on the basis that it is policy changes in England which drive things. Because of the way the formula works, England's rising relative population within the Union has had the effect of perpetuating higher levels of public expenditure in the other nations, while helping to heighten there the sense that their needs are secondary to those of England. Plainly this is not a recipe for peace and quiet.[150]

Confirming this, a year *after* the Barnett Formula was coined, the Treasury sought to establish empirically what spending the particular circumstances of different parts of the Union required with its so-called 'needs assessment'. It noted 'a long-established principle that all areas of the UK are entitled to broadly the same level of public services and that the expenditure on them should be allocated according to their relative needs'. Using England as the average, it concluded that, taking population along with many other factors into account, Scotland and Northern Ireland enjoyed 'excess' spending above need of 6 and 4 per cent respectively, while Wales suffered from 3 per cent too little.[151] Treasury figures in 1984 showed such variations continuing, leading Scottish Office officials to mount a major and largely successful counteroffensive. In their eyes, the whole methodology was fundamentally flawed and rested on the English nationalist assumptions of Treasury statisticians in London, summed up, for one Scottish civil servant at least, by Flanders and Swann's 'A song of patriotic prejudice':

> The rottenest bits of these islands of ours
> We've left in the hands of three unfriendly powers
> Examine the Irishman, Welshman or Scot
> You'll find he's a stinker as likely as not.
>
> . . .
>
> The English, the English, the English are best
> I wouldn't give tuppence for all of the rest.[152]

A second key development was the discovery of gas and oil in the North Sea. Exploration began in the mid 1960s, with profitable extraction beginning in 1969. It was quickly appreciated that this might be transformative – but for whom? Scottish nationalists were determined that the benefits should not be siphoned off to the Treasury in London or multinationals abroad. Because of the location of the fields, 'It's our oil' became, despite some opposition from the Northern Isles, a rallying cry of the SNP, who believed that this natural resource would help Scotland to escape the constraints of the past, both economic and political.[153] Naturally, unionists damned efforts to divide the British sector of the North Sea between Scotland and England, even apart from the practical matter of where any border might be drawn: due east from Berwick-upon-Tweed, in which case almost all of the oilfields could be called Scottish, or by continuing the direction of the border north-eastwards, in which case the share fell somewhat?[154] Because this question was not formally resolved until 1999, it enabled the SNP to argue that oil revenues from Scotland meant that it was certainly paying its way within the Union, indeed propping up Thatcherism instead of being invested for Scotland's future benefit, a charge that Nigel Lawson, Chancellor of the Exchequer from 1983 to 1989, rejected as a 'canard'.[155]

The impact of North Sea oil on debates over Britain's public finances coincided with the UK's entry into the EEC in 1973. Supporters of this move, both at the time and in the referendum of 1975 about whether to confirm membership, mainly stressed the economic benefits that might be expected to the UK as a whole – it would also help that Ireland joined at the same time. Costs were involved, obviously, including sending relatively small amounts of UK taxes to Brussels, including from the newly introduced VAT sales tax. And there was some loss of political independence. Indeed, the SNP opposed joining the EEC, on the grounds that the increasing centralization it entailed threatened Scottish nationhood.[156] Against such thinking, becoming part of a larger common market was expected to aid economic growth. But not any old economic growth. An insufficiently noted feature of the EEC from its foundation was that it would use its powers and resources to, in the words of the foundational Treaty of Rome (1957), reduce 'the differences existing between the various regions and the backwardness of the less favoured regions'.[157] If this was in keeping with regional policy within the UK since 1945, it nonetheless led to further serious debate about the purpose and fairness of the EEC. Given the UK was one of the EEC's more prosperous members, its 'less favoured regions' would not necessarily have powerful enough claims for aid compared with, say, southern Italy. Moreover, with around 70 per cent of the EEC's budget spent on the Common Agricultural Policy until reform early in the new millennium, and the UK being one of the least agricultural of the member states, it was to be expected that worries began to be expressed in Britain about the alleged inefficiencies of supposedly quasi-peasant agriculture in France and Italy.

In 1985 Margaret Thatcher successfully negotiated a significant rebate on the UK's contribution to the EEC. Her claim was that the UK was overtaxed by the EEC, because the method of calculating contributions from member states hit the UK unreasonably hard and because relatively little of the EEC's budget was spent in the UK. Here, with unrecognized irony, were echoes of age-old 'dreadful monster' arguments long banded about in Ireland and Scotland as they experienced membership of the UK. The consistency in Thatcher's position regarding the public finances of the UK and EEC was her desire for smaller, cheaper and less indebted government: the values of household thrift writ large.[158] She argued, for example, that successive UK governments, Labour and Conservative, had been unable to solve

Scotland's structural economic problems since 1930 'not by doing too little, but by promising too much'.[159] In fact, her government's efforts to roll back the state led to particularly pointed attacks on the relatively high public expenditure in Scotland – on its supposedly debilitating dependency culture, a veritable subsidy junkie as it was called by some of her ilk.[160] It followed that she viewed the prospect of devolved government in Scotland as adding another layer of unnecessary and costly government, sapping individual initiative, while undermining the UK. With a populist twist, she sought 'Not devolution to politicians and bureaucrats – but devolution to the Scottish people themselves. Devolution of housing [i.e. selling off council housing], devolution of education, devolution of share ownership and devolution of state-run industries to individuals [i.e. privatization].'[161]

At one level, Thatcher's position on devolution was consistent with traditional Conservative views on the diffusion of power, but it was revolutionary because she and her governments were profoundly suspicious of much of local government, especially of Labour party strongholds in the large cities, rejecting interwar Conservative enthusiasm for 'Town Hall, not Whitehall'.[162] In this very important sense, she was, despite all of the rhetoric to the contrary, a great centralizer. Consequently, in the 1980s central government was more critical of regional policies and bore down on local government's independence, including over rates, shifting the relative burdens towards UK taxpayers and aggregating power in London. Not that aiding those places worst hit by deindustrialization was ruled out. An important initiative of the early 1980s was establishing about a dozen enterprise zones, free of some normal regulation and local taxation, to encourage regeneration via the market rather than direct state intervention. (While this was consistent with neoliberal thinking, going back to ideas about free ports put about in the eighteenth century, intriguingly it had some origins among 1960s counterculture urban planners.) Most famously, this transformed London's docklands, but the initiative had an important impact on towns and cities across Britain, including Belfast, Birmingham, Glasgow, Hartlepool, Liverpool, Newcastle, Salford and Swansea.[163]

In fact, local government finance and its relations to the centre led Thatcher to her greatest political miscalculation. Problems over funding local government had mounted since 1945 as it became responsible for much higher levels of spending on housing, education and welfare, exposing the eternal problem of how to pay for such things where income from the rates fell short (Table 9). Equalization of the resources of local government via redistribution had received a major fillip in 1948, but this grated with Thatcherite presumptions.[164]

Table 9. The growth of UK local government, 1900–1980

	Total expenditure £m	Central government grant £m	Grants as % total expenditure	Total employed
1900	101	12	12	550,000
1930	424	108	26	541,000
1960	1,886	706	38	639,000
1980	18,669	11,846	63	931,000

Complaints that local rates were unfair were well established before Thatcher became prime minister, on two main grounds. First, that as a property tax some home owners could, in an era of rapidly rising house prices, have considerable equity but little income. Second, that rates were paid by a minority of those benefiting from local government expenditure. Deep into her premiership, she attempted to grasp the nettle by looking to replace rates with a poll tax, officially called the Community Charge, a single, flat-rate per capita tax on every adult. (A local sales tax was, reasonably enough, thought unlikely to work because local authorities were so small that smuggling between them was bound to occur.) In Scotland the more regular revaluation of rates made Conservatives there keen for the new tax to be introduced as quickly as possible. While Scotland was not being treated as a guinea pig, the Scottish Secretary was an enthusiast for the tax and, in a speech there in 1988, Thatcher had attacked 'the old, outdated, arbitrary and unfair system of local rates', paid by only one-quarter of the electorate in Scotland. The other three-quarters were free-riders in her view: 'Where is the fairness in that?' she asked.[165]

In the teeth of stiff opposition, the poll tax was introduced into Scotland in 1989 and into England and Wales the following year, paid for by direct invoice rather than, as was the case for most with the income tax, PAYE. With 27 million people losing from the tax and only 8 million gaining, it was little wonder that non-compliance quickly escalated against a tax viewed as a highly regressive and dangerously blunt instrument – 20 per cent were not paying in the summer of 1990.[166] By the end of 1989 there were over 1,000 local Anti-Poll Tax Unions in Britain asking, *pace* Thatcher, where was the fairness in the same tax being levelled on a peer or a business tycoon as well as a care worker or plumber?[167] Civil disobedience on such a scale across the UK was joined by major rioting in London in March 1990, leading the government humiliatingly to announce the abolition of the tax in 1991, though its replacement took two years to roll out.

Leading Tories have seen the poll tax debacle as the greatest failure of Thatcher's premiership, hastening her resignation in November 1990.[168] While her successor, John Major, kept the Conservatives in power until 1997, there is no question that the tax reopened major questions about equality and equity in UK public finances in three main regards. At the general level, by looking to tax most adults, the poll tax sought to raise more money from poorer areas than had been achieved through rates, reducing the need for transfers from richer areas. The tax was both socially and geographically regressive, running against some of the territorially redistributive aspects inherent to a union state. Secondly, the tax confirmed the centralizing bent of the Conservative government since 1979 in terms of imposing a UK-wide solution. More particularly, thirdly, its earlier introduction into Scotland where levels of public expenditure were higher, including on local authority housing, allowed it to be portrayed as one designed to challenge Scottish ways of doing things. In a way, though the parallel does not appear to have been made, perceptions in Scotland of governmental arrogance and condescension were at one with how the imposition of the precepts of political economy upon mid-nineteenth-century Ireland was regarded by the Irish. And whereas Ireland's dependence on the potato was plainly problematic to its sustainability, late twentieth-century Scotland was being energized by the growth of services and North Sea oil, significantly weakening the dead hand of its industrial past. Unsurprisingly, numbers of Tory MPs in Scotland fell sharply, from twenty-three in 1979 to zero in 1997 and just one seat in each of the next four general elections.

CONCLUSION

Despite the enormous costs to the UK of two world wars, the almost total collapse of its empire and significant deindustrialization, the growth of its public finances in the twentieth century opened up huge potential for improving society. Here was a particular form of the challenge of affluence, and, while there were heated debates over how that good was to be done, since the early years of the century some central direction and resource redistribution have been acknowledged by almost all as a necessary part of the policy agenda. The issue has been how much. Such redistribution has mainly been conceived and considered in terms of hierarchies of income and wealth, largely irrespective of geography. But, as this chapter has shown, questions about regions as well as nations have often loomed large as a consequence of significant geographical variations in economic fortunes within the UK. Without an explicit federal framework, neither the Goschen ratios nor the Barnett Formula could do much more than offer broad parameters within which to address such issues, leaving much to the interplay of politics and interests in their myriad forms. On the eve of devolution in 1999, the upshot was that there were strongly divergent views as to the proper forms and levels of redistribution from the more to the less prosperous.

Undoubtedly, the fundamental economic reordering within the UK since 1918 has to be considered geographically, with winners and losers often bunching in particular areas. This has been closely linked to significant transfers of tax revenues over most of the period, particularly into Northern Ireland, much of Scotland, south Wales and north-east England. Two main questions follow. The first is one of equity, where thinking terminologically in terms of 'transfer' not 'subsidy' is the best way of understanding what was involved. Quite apart from the fact that, as S. R. Dennison put it in 1939, it was 'impossible to allocate responsibility for changing location' – or why some places are more needful of public expenditure than others – Gavin McCrone, an economist and former Scottish civil servant, has set out the broader principles with characteristic cogency:

Fiscal transfers between regions in a modern state are of course to be expected, where there is a uniform system of taxation and a commitment to comparable standards of service. Expenditure is unrelated to tax revenue raised in a particular area ... Whichever the direction of the transfers, they arise not from a conscious decision to subsidise anything but from the automatic operation of the tax system and national public expenditure decisions.[169]

The key commitment to uniformity of taxation was made in the mid nineteenth century. That regarding standards of expenditure was made explicitly in Northern Ireland in the 1920s, but was felt implicitly by most within the UK at the time that the welfare state was being forged.

A second fundamental aspect of the significant territorial transfers that have characterized UK public finances since the 1930s is that they have proved so persistent. In part that was because heavy spending on welfare, which made up the bulk of the transfers involved, has been essentially ameliorative in purpose, incapable by itself of altering structural territorial inequalities. It has been regional policy rather than welfare spending that has directly sought remedies, requiring particular regions to be identified as problematic and needy. Such an administrative necessity is inherently divisive, particularly by unintentionally fomenting the identity politics of needy places. By 1971 all of Scotland and Wales beyond Edinburgh and Cardiff had been designated as either 'development' or 'special development' areas, encouraging support for nationalist politics there. This was exacerbated, as it was for other poorer parts of the UK, by the difficulties of reconciling different strands of unionist fiscal rhetoric given that transfers in practice often struggled to dispel economic gloom.[170] If the Union was such a boon, nationalists wondered why unemployment continued to be well above the UK average in large parts of Northern Ireland, Scotland and Wales.

Identifying certain areas as particularly needy by central government reflected the injection of social and geographical thinking into its policy processes. If this did not end the dominance of economic thinking, it did dilute the tendency of such thinking to privilege the experience of individuals. Put another way, geographers, political scientists and sociologists with their ideas about communities now came to exert some influence. (Of course, UK politics had always had a geographical framework – after all, MPs represented particular locales first and foremost, a point strengthened by extensions of the franchise.) This was not straightforward, however, for deciding what among many options constituted the best community for political action to address – in geographical terms, should it be a village, locale, region or nation? – raised a host of tricky questions that those pre-occupied with individual action were untroubled by. Margaret Thatcher famously doubted the utility of the concept of society; but defining society meaningfully as more than a sum of individuals does require plenty of tricky questions to be addressed.[171] Fundamentally, this helps to explain why the territorial dimension to UK public finances became so much more complex in this period.

The great growth of central government peacetime spending, first after 1918 and again after 1945, involved a dramatic increase in the number of particular purposes to which it was put. Certainly public expenditure was dominated by the costs of the NHS, education and social welfare where a reasonable degree of uniformity of standards across the Union was sought. But there were now many more outlets for taxpayers' money where diversity of need was at issue. All of this stimulated the growth of interest groups and expertise, making debate deeper and richer. Yet, alongside a burgeoning culture of audit and accountability, this made for policy decisions to become bewilderingly complex and incomprehensible to most citizens: senses of illegitimacy or disempowerment were possible reactions, reactions that were especially dangerous to those parts of the UK where nationalist sentiment was especially vibrant. It was in this context that devolution was finally introduced within Britain.

5

1999–2021: Conclusion

Before the 1970s most Westminster politicians were loath to consider holding referendums, except very occasionally on what were considered to be local matters. It is easy to see why. Referendums attempt to overcome some of parliament's limitations in addressing fiercely contested policies, effectively diluting its sovereignty by handing it momentarily to the people: they are a last resort in managing deep divisions. Enough saw the early years of the Troubles as such a juncture, with a referendum held in 1973 over whether Northern Ireland should remain within the Union. Revealingly, while twelve others have followed, nine asked questions about devolution. Only three have been UK-wide – those in 1975 and 2016 over membership of the EEC/EU and one in 2011 over the voting system in general elections. But all bear witness to serious splits over the nature of the Union, its place in the international order and the conduct of its politics. Few, however, settled matters well. The first was boycotted by the nationalist community in Northern Ireland and the last, after a campaign conducted with little attention to truth or reason, showed that most people in Scotland and Northern Ireland voted to remain in the EU, with most in England and Wales voting to leave. Division has been the watchword of this period, with mounting pressures for disunion which have only been contained by major constitutional restructuring focusing upon what is generally called devolution but which until recently was more akin to delegation. This has not been well ordered. The UK constitution is now a Heath Robinson contraption, over-elaborate, poorly engineered and steam driven, rather than a precision tool befitting a leading global economy facing grave threats. Although for now the Union has held, its fragility is palpable, its future uncertain.

Such developments unavoidably led to renewed questions about the proper boundary between uniformity and diversity in the UK's public finances. For example, from the mid 1990s complaints have ballooned of a 'postcode lottery' regarding the quality, quantity and cost of public services. For the sake of their children's education, some parents have been prepared to do anything to move to live within a 'good' school's catchment area. But geographical variations in NHS provision are more pervasive and important. Some places have no NHS dental care available; hospital treatment waiting times and success rates have varied significantly from one trust to another; and prescription charges differ between the nations of the Union. Such diversity is generally regretted because it reeks of inequality and inequity. Two developments have been crucial to this. First, awareness of variation has been increased because since the 1980s governments have imposed certain performance indicators on many public services on the grounds of accountability and incentivization. As a result, simple league tables, whatever their limitations, are seized on by the media and provided ready ammunition for political struggles. More importantly, devolved administrations have mainly been able to express their ambitions on the expenditure rather than the revenue side of public accounts. The significance of this should not be underestimated: such diversity helps to legitimate those administrations' existence, particularly in Scotland, where it is often said that heightened egalitarianism feeds expectations of better public services than in England, even if the supporting evidence for this is rather modest.[1]

By definition, devolution is intended to allow diversion from once common standards, raising fresh questions about whether such arrangements are equitable. Autonomy, even only partial autonomy, also unsettles lines of accountability, both political and financial. In the UK these have been further complicated because devolution has varied from case to case, with no agreed common end point in view, let alone a plan. Bespoke agreements with Northern Ireland, Scotland and Wales were followed by limited devolution to a minority of English areas such as Greater Manchester, creating a crazy patchwork of governance. Far from satisfying grievances, such haphazardness has tended to inflame them, culminating in the Scottish independence referendum of 2014 and the expression of disaffection by so many voting to leave the EU in 2016.

DISORDERED DEVOLUTION

Continually in power between 1979 and 1997, the Conservatives stood strongly against devolution to Scotland and Wales, let alone their independence. Maintaining the status quo was justified in terms of avoiding an additional tier of government to be paid for through higher taxes, continuing the benefits of sharing risks and resources across the whole of the UK, avoiding the West Lothian Question and allowing no room for separatist tendencies to develop. Why, it was asked, break up a successful union?[2] However, to its critics the Union was failing, often badly. Deindustrialization was being felt sorely, without much compensating service sector growth in the worst-affected areas; England's demographic weight within the Union continued to grow; and the poll tax debacle showed to some that London was at best insensitive to distinctive circumstances beyond its immediate ken. In 1986 Jim Sillars, who had moved, like many in Scotland, from the Labour party to the SNP, deplored recent 'hammer blows' to the 'main pillars of Scottish economic life', while arguing that the relative prosperity of south-east England was due to the presence of central government there.[3] Welsh nationalists such as Gwynfor Evans had argued much the same before.[4] This confusion of cause and effect, as this book shows, would have been familiar three centuries ago. As usual, it does not explain why the reduction of London's vitality would increase that of other parts of the Union. It also gives the complaint a national framework which ignores the many areas of England that also severely lag behind London.

With the election of Tony Blair's New Labour government in 1997, the prospects for devolution changed overnight, despite his admission that, although Scottish by birth and schooling, he was never passionate about the constitutional overhaul he set in train.[5] Perhaps that explains the terrible muddle his government produced. Devolution referendums were quickly held in Scotland and Wales. This was strongly supported in Scotland (74 per cent of the vote), but Wales was badly divided, with a bare majority, 50.3 per cent, voting in favour – just 25 per cent of registered voters. Nonetheless, the government pushed ahead pell-mell on both fronts, establishing in 1999 a parliament in Scotland and an assembly in Wales. Meanwhile, in 1998 the Good Friday Agreement in Northern Ireland was signed, an extraordinary achievement that ended thirty years of Troubles and revived devolved government at Stormont on new terms. A referendum in Northern Ireland overwhelmingly supported the agreement (71 per cent). Within three years, the Union state's constitution had been transformed.

While devolution to Belfast, Cardiff and Edinburgh were major achievements of compromise politics, they obviously left untouched England's demographic, economic and political heft within the Union state. This posed what has been called the 'English question', really the paradox of its importance despite its constitutional non-existence, a 'stateless nation'.[6] Originally this was to be addressed by English regional devolution, beginning with the creation of the Greater London Authority in 2000, after 72 per cent had already supported the idea in a referendum. But the plan for wider devolution within England was shattered when, against expectations, in 2004 a crushing 78 per cent of the people of north-east England voted against establishing regional government there – after a 'no' campaign decrying the idea of adding more politicians to people's lives and tax bills.[7] That rolling out regional government across England to balance devolution in the other nations in the Union had failed so early exposed the very different attitudes towards government across the UK and the uncertainties of regional identities within England. Further significant regional devolution in England had to wait until 2011, when the Greater Manchester Combined Authority was established, followed by eight others towards the end of that decade. After the debacle of the 2004 referendum, none were put to the people to decide. What resulted were curious combinations of authorities, mostly large conurbations, such as the west Midlands and Sheffield, sometimes not, such as Cambridgeshire and Peterborough. All sought to enhance local economic planning, without much regard to issues of regional identity or changing the fundamental fiscal imbalance between central and local taxation. Like the Conservative government it replaced, New Labour was rather more attentive to the imperatives of globalization than to overhauling and reinvigorating older regional policies.

Devolution in parts of the UK sought to satisfy a long-established belief that government needed to move closer to the people, helping to rebalance Britain's economic geography. Beyond that, bespoke arrangements rather than adherence to any coherent plan was the order of the day. The 'chaos of areas', bemoaned by Goschen over a century before, increased significantly.[8] Two-thirds of England's people remained governed as before, while those who were not shared no common characteristics. It is telling that in England local government is organized around five main types of authorities: county councils, district councils, unitary authorities, metropolitan districts and London boroughs. In the north of England this has been judged to be a 'bewildering and underwhelming path – leading to complexity, experimentation, fragmentation and incoherence with largely negative implications for territorial equity and justice'.[9] Such inconsistencies took a different form with devolution to the other nations of the Union. Scotland and Northern Ireland enjoyed much greater powers than Wales. Common to devolution across the UK, however, was that initially the new authorities were given few new powers to raise money, depending for about 90 per cent of the revenue on block grants from London, with the Barnett Formula used much as before – Scotland was able to vary income tax by plus or minus 3 per cent.[10] What devolved administrations did get was greater discretion over certain areas of public expenditure, such as health and education, but not in the twelve main areas of responsibility reserved to the UK government, such as macroeconomic management, defence, foreign policy and immigration.[11] Today, in addition to a common body of 11 main areas of devolved responsibilities, Northern Ireland has a further 9, Scotland 12 and Wales 8. Variation is the order of the day.

In 1999 Vernon Bogdanor argued that 'Finance is the spinal cord of devolution, for it is the financial arrangements which will largely determine the degree of autonomy enjoyed by the devolved administrations.'[12] Yet until 2016 devolution in the UK did not dramatically influence the territoriality of British public finances. On the revenue side, the overwhelming majority continued to be collected in England. But in per capita terms more was collected in Scotland if one uses, as seems right, a geographic rather than population-based share of North Sea revenues (Table 10).

Table 10. HM Revenue and Customs tax receipts by nation, 2011

	% of total geographic share	£ per capita geographic share	£ per capita population share
England	85	7,564	7,700
Northern Ireland	2	5,663	5,836
Scotland	10	8,535	7,020
Wales	3	5,160	5,330

Irrespective of how North Sea revenues are distributed, the geography of UK taxes divides England and Scotland on the one hand, producing a greater share of taxation than their population, from Northern Ireland and Wales on the other, with population shares above the tax shares. This is often overlooked because per capita public expenditure in Scotland is significantly higher than in England – nearly 13 per cent in 2013, allowing greater spending on costly items such as education and health as well as less costly ones such as agriculture, forestry and transport.[13] However, as Table 11 shows, levels of public expenditure in Northern Ireland and Wales were significantly higher still, leading free-market advocates to chastise such 'near "iron-curtain" spending ratios in', perhaps patronizingly, 'some of the UK's peripheral regions'.[14]

Table 11. General government expenditure in selected areas relative to GDP and public sector employment, 2012–13, %

	Ratio to GDP	Public sector employment
England	41	16
Northern Ireland	68	25
Scotland	53	21
Wales	66	21
London	27	14
South-east England	34	15
North-east England	62	20

Devolution has also not significantly changed the relative economic strength of the UK's parts. Looking at figures for 'gross value added', a measure of productivity, captures this well, while bringing in some English regional figures to begin refining the analysis (Table 12).

Table 12. Index of gross value added per capita, nations and English regions, 1999–2018. UK = 100 at given dates

	1999	2014	2017
Northern Ireland	80	81	79
Scotland	89	95	92
Wales	74	73	73
England	103	103	103
North-east	74	74	72
North-west	86	87	88
Yorkshire and the Humber	84	80	79
East Midlands	88	81	80
West Midlands	89	83	84
East of England	97	90	93
London	165	176	177
South-east	114	110	107
South-west	92	88	87

Relative geographical stability rather than change is a clear feature of the devolutionary years, but more significant is how the UK has been continuously divided between the exceptional performance of London, aided and abetted by south-east England, and elsewhere. They have been the only parts of the UK to have above-average performance, while the whole of northern England, but more especially the north-east, is closer to the experience of Northern Ireland and Wales than other English regions. It is worth recalling here that, from the 1920s to the 1970s, London's share of the national population was in decline. But in the late 1980s that pattern reversed.[15] Such a division between London and its hinterland and the rest of the UK inevitably raises the question of which should be considered the norm and how far it is a consequence of the seat of central government favouring its own backyard.

Behind these figures are two main changes. First, deindustrialization, in all its complexities, has persisted since the peak of manufacturing employment was passed in 1965. Here the UK compares badly with its main Western competitors, shedding large amounts of labour and expanding output only slightly.[16] Although coal is an extractive industry, its final collapse in Britain symbolized this change – the bitter and prolonged miners' strike of 1984–5 was its death rattle – with the UK becoming a net importer of coal for the first time in its history in 2000. What has marked London and the south-east apart is that, as before, the region's economy was successfully repurposed, this time based more squarely on services and globalization. Its symbolic turning point was the 'Big Bang' of 1986, which ended restrictive practices on the London Stock Exchange.

A predictable consequence of devolution is that, as in the creation of the Scottish and Welsh offices before, it created interests within the political system whose *raison d'être* was to seek both greater political freedom and, nonetheless, more resources from central government, generating obvious enough questions about accountability. This key tension is best explored in relation to a renewed articulation of a north–south divide in England and calls to revise the Barnett Formula, especially in Wales.

SOME CHALLENGES OF DEVOLUTION

London has for centuries been a global city but, enabled by its location between Asian and American time zones, after the Big Bang this was taken to a new level by its thriving financial, commercial, managerial and legal services. Simultaneously its fortunes have also become tied to the wider knowledge economy, including at the most basic level the growing international significance of the English language. Its universities, research institutes and fertile cultural industries have thrived. This has rested on a distinctive population. In 2009, 34 per cent had a university degree, more than twice the UK average. A rising share of its workforce has been born outside the UK, reaching 45 per cent in 2018, twice the figure for England as a whole, nearly four times that of Scotland and five times that of Northern Ireland and Wales.[17] Accurately enough, 'In terms of sheer scale, depth and breadth of specialization, and strength of international connections, London seems to be in a league of its own.'[18] As it prospered, its regional influence expanded.[19]

Maintaining London's global role in the era of devolution has depended upon communications and connectivity, involving some very big-ticket items. The Channel Tunnel was opened in 1994 at a cost of £4.5 billion, linked fully to London by a high-speed rail link in 2007 (HS1) at a further cost of £6.8 billion. The cost of extending this to Birmingham, Manchester and Leeds (HS2) was put at up to £88.7 billion in 2019. It would be a pleasant surprise if it came in on budget. As London has grown since 1980, so have the difficulties of moving people around it. In 2003 a congestion charge helped to cut motor traffic in its central area, with the net income (exceeding £150 million in recent years) used to invest in transport in the capital.[20] In 2008 central government gave the go-ahead to Crossrail, a new east–west rail link between Berkshire and Essex designed to relieve pressure on key central London underground lines. It is expected to open fully, several years late, in 2021 and, inevitably, over-budget at £18.3 billion, though partly funded by a levy on new building in London.[21] Recent proposals for a third runway at Heathrow and for Crossrail 2 (running from Surrey to Hertfordshire) are evidence of the continuing ambition to enhance the capital's infrastructure, though the global pandemic that began in 2020 has, at least for a time, undercut their rationale.

Such lavish spending bears witness to perceptions of London's importance within central government, including to the wider UK, as well as to the power of London's own voice. The Mayor of the Greater London Authority has become a national figure, with Boris Johnson, in office from 2008 to 2016, using the position as a stepping stone to the premiership. London has continued to benefit from much of the UK's media being produced in London, while London First, a pro-growth and pro-business lobby, was established in 1992, pushing hard for many developments, including the London Olympics, staged in 2012.[22] Unsurprisingly, this has led to criticisms that since the 1980s public finances have unduly favoured London: even, with a neat inversion, that it was the real subsidy junkie.[23] Unquestionably, in recent years public expenditure per head has been higher in London than any other part of the Union – even without counting the costs of the bailout of the banks in 2008 and of the Olympics, because formally they were general UK expenditure. But this rests, as Table 12 showed, on an unusually buoyant economy, producing considerable tax receipts there, such that the capital appears to be a hefty net contributor to the public purse – though some of this is through the benefits of national and international businesses having their registered offices in London.[24] In 1998 this even led Ken Livingstone, soon to be London's first elected mayor, to suggest that some of the public expenditure in Scotland should be diverted to London, and in 2003 the London Chamber of Commerce complained that such a 'burden placed on the capital's economy is an inequitable one', while others have likened London to a golden goose, benefiting distant regions.[25] Relative to gross value added, public expenditure in London is the lowest in the UK, while at the other extreme are northeast England, Northern Ireland, Scotland and Wales.[26]

Heightening regional inequality within the UK has been linked to these developments. London is Europe's richest region – though inequality within London is also very high – but in the 2010s the UK had six of northern Europe's ten poorest regions, 'making the UK the continent's most geographically unbalanced economy'.[27] Moreover, in 2013, after a good deal of devolution had occurred, the UK remained one of the most fiscally centralized of states, with central government collecting 95 per cent of all public revenue and responsible for 75 per cent of all public expenditure (Table 13). Put another way, local government in total, including the devolved administrations, collected just 5 per cent of all UK public revenue and managed just 25 per cent of all public expenditure.

Table 13. Central government finances relative to all public finances, 2013, %

	Revenue	Spending
UK	95	75
France	87	70
Germany	71	61
US	63	52
Canada	50	33

A key response to these twin evils has been utilizing a 'North' of England as a 'gestural term', making claims for greater public resources to fund a trajectory of economic change better suited to its, rather than London's, conditions.[28] Traditional northern values of plain-speaking common sense sometimes continue to be set against those of an effete, decadent and corrupt South, proved to some by heavy public-finance investment in the latter.[29] It has been claimed that 'For decades, the Treasury has pump-primed London and the south-east almost exclusively', with 'decades of central government underinvestment' in the regions, especially regarding transport.[30]

The creation of devolved metropolitan authorities in England's north from 2011 meant that such views, redolent of those earlier voiced by the Highlands and Islands Development Board, began to have some purchase. In 2010 the newly elected Conservative prime minister, David Cameron, spoke publicly of the inequity of the UK's unbalanced economic geography – as did the SNP leader, Nicola Sturgeon, and a leading Liberal Democrat, Vince Cable, who likened London to a giant suction engine.[31] Turning their back on Thatcherite views of regional aid, the Conservatives looked to promote local deals for economic generation, climaxing in 2014 with George Osborne, the Chancellor of the Exchequer, conceptualizing a 'Northern power-house', endorsing, in passing, a 'dreadful monster' view of London.[32] This was clearly not the view of every Conservative – Osborne's sacking by Theresa May in 2016 led to a lull in regional initiatives – but it appears to have become reasonably embedded within central government's mindset. A key part of the Conservative strategy in the general election of 2019 was to argue for the 'levelling up' of poorer regions, though, then again, Margaret Thatcher had said something similar after winning her third general election in June 1987.[33]

The second area of the public finances of devolution to be explored is the operation of the Barnett Formula. Although devolution left it and tax-raising powers much as before, this was bound to come under renewed scrutiny under the new dispensation. Moreover, to improve the fiscal accountability of the settlements both the Treasury and the devolved administrations had to improve their annual published accounts. Not that the statistics were necessarily produced either disinterestedly or perfectly. But, more accurately than ever before, they helped to relate national and regional patterns of taxing, spending and economic performance. In any case, it quickly became apparent that patterns of public expenditure across the UK were diverging under devolution. Health and old-age care in England incurred many charges, but in Scotland virtually none. A system of tuition fees was introduced for English but not Scottish universities, creating the bizarre and discriminatory situation that English, Northern Irish and Welsh students in Scotland paid fees despite being in the EU, while other EU and Scottish students did not.

Public finance statistics were periodically seized on in the early years of devolution, usually by English commentators querying higher levels of spending in the devolved administrations, but came under more sustained scrutiny towards the end of the 2000s. Commissions of the Welsh and Scottish governments were established in 2008 and 2009 respectively and in 2009 a House of Lords Committee considered the workings of the Barnett Formula. All three particularly explored issues around accountability, fiscal independence and the operation of the formula.

Much the most insightful study was made by the Holtham Commission into Welsh public finances, named after its chairman, Professor Gerry Holtham. Carefully piecing together evidence and fully thinking through some of the key principles, the commission particularly explored how the 'Barnett squeeze' was eroding funding from London, threatening to go beneath levels of actual need. That squeeze, an unintended operational consequence of the formula, would, if other things remained as before, gradually lower per capita expenditure in Northern Ireland, Scotland and Wales to English levels, as the calculations leading to the final column in this example from the Holtham Report of 2009 shows (Table 14). In practice, while the squeeze had been worried about for some time, it was significant only in Wales under devolution. Holtham demonstrated that expenditure per head in Wales had been 25 per cent higher than in England in 1994, but had fallen to 13 per cent and was trending towards just 2 per cent, well beneath an estimated need for a 15 per cent uplift.[34]

Three features of this were important. First, the absence of a needs element within the Barnett Formula made the UK internationally

Table 14. Hypothetical example of the Barnett squeeze

	England		Wales		
Population	50 million		3 million		
Public expenditure	£bn	£ per head	£bn	£ per head	Wales as % of England per capita
Baseline	100.0	2,000	7.2	2,400	120
Increase	30.0	600	1.8	600	
New budget	130.0	2,600	9.0	3,000	115

unique, providing more evidence of an unwillingness at the very top of government to make rational arrangements.[35] Second, the Treasury and Scottish government (before and after devolution) claimed that calculating need was so imperfect as to be worthless. This was very unconvincing given needs assessments had since 1958 played a part in central government grants to local authorities, including fairly complex funding formula from 1974, and the Holtham Commission managed to do it for Wales easily enough by using a few readily available social indicators.[36] (In passing, they used the same method to show that Northern Ireland needed 21 per cent more spending per head than England, and Scotland 5 per cent, well beneath what they actually received.[37]) Finally, the UK government accepted the recommendation that for Wales a needs factor should be added to the Barnett Formula. But, adding another layer of muddle to devolution's existing confusions, no such adjustment was made for Northern Ireland or Scotland as it would have reduced their funding, provoking an unwanted political storm.

Clearly, Barnett was not set in stone. Its current form – amended for Wales, but not for Northern Ireland or Scotland – speaks of the fiscal generosity of central government in London to ease the work of the devolved administrations as well as to provide more public goods to their people. This reflects a recognition that those societies' distinctive circumstances require more such spending, but it is also underwritten by the feeling that such generosity is a necessary price for buttressing pro-Union sentiment in an era of rising separatism. Yet it has not ended calls for independence in the devolved administrations, especially in Scotland.

SCOTTISH INDEPENDENCE, 2014

Since devolution, Scottish electors have worked hard, going to the polls six times for general elections to Westminster and five times (in significantly fewer numbers) for those to Holyrood, in the process lending great support to the SNP. In the 2001 Westminster general election, the SNP secured just 5 of the 72 seats in Scotland. This showing did not change significantly until the general election in 2015, when it won 56 of the 59 seats – the number had been cut to reduce, though not completely eliminate, Scotland's over-representation at Westminster. Ever since, the SNP has dominated Scottish seats at Westminster. The SNP's successes in elections to the Scottish parliament began at a higher level – at a little over a quarter in 1999 – and grew less spectacularly to a peak in 2011 when it won 69 of the 129 seats, giving it an overall majority in the additional-member voting system designed to prevent such an outcome. Although the turnout was only 51 per cent, this made the party's call for independence impossible for the Conservative government in London to ignore, with a referendum held in September 2014. On an exceptionally high turnout of 84 per cent, 55 per cent voted for Scotland to remain in the Union.

An impressive feature of the debate around the Scottish independence referendum was the commitment to constitutional methods, reason and evidence. Perhaps, as the proudly Anglophobic Scottish nationalist poet Hugh MacDiarmid remarked long before, 'Scotland's worst disease is its appalling love for and dependence on the calculable.'[38] Passions certainly warmed on issues of identity politics, but discussion did not descend to the depths of illegality and dishonesty that characterized the Vote Leave campaign in the 2016 EU referendum. In keeping with the ideals of the Scottish Enlightenment, civil society functioned well.

In a core work published in 2013, the Scottish government of the SNP spelt out its analysis and arguments in over 600 pages, buttressed by a further 100-plus pages from a fiscal commission whose members included two Nobel laureates in economics (James Mirrlees and Joseph Stiglitz).[39] If repetitive, the Scottish government was moderate in tone, making clear its assumptions, principles and proofs.

Public finances were foregrounded in this, coming to play a central role in the unfolding debate. It was argued that it was impossible to fulfil Scotland's full potential under a union which 'locked it in to one of the most unequal economic models in the developed world'.[40] Its interests had been sacrificed to those of England in general and London in particular – including getting a very low share of EU funding. Scotland was said to be wealthy, and not just in oil, producing abundant public revenues to pay for what it believed it needed, including shifting some spending from defence to social welfare. It was asserted that it more than paid its way within the Union and would pay its share of the UK national debt after independence. Independence provided the opportunity to replace the bloated tax code currently weighing upon it – Mirrlees had chaired an independent review of the UK tax system in 2011.[41] But, because the EU's euro had been badly tainted by the 2008 financial crisis, it argued for a formal Sterling Area: 'The pound is Scotland's currency just as much as it is the rest of the UK's.'[42]

In a similar spirit, if more concisely, the UK government set out its opposition in two main documents: a general one on the benefits of the Union from the Secretary of State for Scotland; and the Treasury's response to the proposed currency union. Here the UK, as a 'family of nations', was said to be 'one of the most successful monetary, fiscal and political unions in history', with Scottish priorities and needs well met by a thriving devolution of responsibilities.[43] The benefits of an integrated and coordinated economy were stressed, as was the £45.5 billion in support from UK taxpayers for the Royal Bank of Scotland in 2008.[44] The Treasury detailed what it saw as the disadvantages of any shared currency arrangement, making clear that under independence Scotland would have little or no voice over monetary policy made in London. (Gordon Brown, who played a prominent role in opposing Scottish independence just before the referendum, had once vainly hoped that the Bank of England be renamed to take account of its UK-wide role.[45]) In the event, the Conservative government ruled out a currency union completely.

Such position papers were, despite their claims to authority, obviously political and interested, establishing thickets of disagreement rather than clearings of truth. Betraying their different initial assumptions, the UK government claimed that each person in Scotland would annually be £1,400 better off by continuing within the Union, while the Scottish government valued the independence dividend at £1,000 per person.[46] This was all played out in a more partisan way in the press and elsewhere, but such myth-making was carefully scrutinized by a number of influential independent voices, including experts such as Gavin McCrone and think tanks in Scotland and London.

The Scottish government sought independence with the clear objectives of raising prosperity while heightening redistribution to reduce inequality. But, despite its celebration of Scotland's potential, clear weaknesses in its case were exposed during the referendum debate that proved significant to the outcome. The plan for a currency union raised questions about how meaningful independence would actually be, while its rejection in London exposed just how unattractive were the alternatives. Joining the EU's currency union looked risky given the severe damage inflicted by the 2008 financial crisis on both the EU and Scotland. In any case, independence involved seceding from the EU, with any future membership depending on many things, including countries such as Spain not wishing to do anything to encourage their own separatist movements.[47] It was, however, the sustainability of Scotland's public finances that more immediately seriously weakened independence calls.

Public expenditure in Scotland exceeded taxes collected there. Indeed, Scotland's deficit was larger relative to its GDP than the UK's and looked hard to manage going forward.[48] The Scottish government thought future economic growth would right things, but in the meantime a heavy dependence on North Sea revenues left it exposed because production was gradually declining and prices were highly variable – peaking in 2012–13, but falling away sharply thereafter; as I write, they have plummeted again because of the coronavirus pandemic. (In 2011–12 duties on North Sea oil and gas accounted for 19 per cent of Scotland's public revenues, but only 2 per cent of the UK's.[49]) The well-respected Institute for Fiscal Studies concluded that independence would require much more belt tightening in Scotland than the UK, in part because of its significantly weaker demographic prospects. 'Scotland's debt-to-GDP ratio is projected to increase unsustainably over the next fifty years', according to the Institute, meaning that years of austerity lay ahead before it would meet the criteria for membership of the EU or be able fund its proposed re-distribution policies.[50] That, in 2016, Scotland's SNP First Minister, Nicola Sturgeon, created the Sustainable Growth Commission to report on how Scotland's public finances might be improved in the future suggests that such judgements had gained purchase.[51]

One thing that became clear during these debates was that, in terms of the balance of revenue and expenditure, Scotland did relatively well out of the UK as a fiscal compact. Indeed, it did better than some English regions, undermining a simple narrative of two nations facing one another. As was pointed out in two publications of the Edinburgh-based David Hume Institute, the economic performance of Scotland and England shared more similarities than differences, while amounts of redistribution within the UK exceeded the average for OECD countries.[52] Of course, this meant that fiscally Scotland was some-what dependent upon the rest of the UK and its policies, constraining, even under devolution, Scotland's freedom of action. But this also helps to explain the critical fact that what the SNP sought was not, in fact, complete independence, but a cooperative political economy with both the rest of the UK and the EU. In part this tension reflected public opinion surveys that showed more support for greater fiscal autonomy for Scotland – 'devo max', a quasi-federal arrangement – than full independence.[53] But the position also implicitly recognized some of Scotland's limitations when it came to public finances. In contrast, the UK Conservative government understood independence for Scotland in absolute terms. As was nicely pointed out at the time, 'To a good degree these are the differences of approach of a big, power-ful country used to a leading international role and a small, would-be country which would pursue its interests through co-operation with others.'[54]

In the weeks before the referendum, opinion polls showed signifi-cant growth in support for independence, leading to panic in Downing Street and promises that devolution would be significantly extended should independence be rejected. As usual, this was based on the pol-itics of concession and step-by-step change rather than anything more substantially principled. But significant changes have resulted, with much greater financial powers granted to both the Scottish and Welsh governments. In Scotland's case, it now (2021) raises around 40 per cent of its revenue, for Wales 30 per cent, including full devolution of income tax and business rates.[55] This marks a major step change to devolution, arguably 'unprecedented internationally and certainly within the UK'.[56] Yet this was unlikely to satisfy the SNP, while the outcome of the EU referendum in 2016, when all of Scotland's electoral districts voted to remain (though, overall, 38 per cent voted to leave), gave it some grounds to claim that the independence question could be vigorously pursued again. But, in the meantime, Scotland's public finances have remained challenging because the economic environment for exploiting North Sea resources are increasingly difficult, while the population continues to age more quickly than England's, making the fiscal case for independence harder to sustain.[57] Consequently, it is to the advantage of unionists to perpetuate Scottish funding under the Barnett Formula without paying significant attention to measured need, while simultaneously the SNP would not want Scotland's higher funding to be put at risk. Without grasping this nettle, it looks doubtful that the SNP will be able to convince sufficient numbers in Scotland that its plans for public finance under independence are credible. This is related to a dilemma, common to devolved or newly seceded states, between wanting autonomy while at least maintaining comparable standards of living with its closest neighbours.[58] If it was clear that the price of independence was a lower standard of living than that achieved in the rump of the UK, this would be honest and thoughtful, but it would also probably mean the SNP losing any future referendum.

FINAL REFLECTIONS

All polities of any extent have to confront fiscal dilemmas of the kind explored earlier, particularly the difficulties around balancing equality and equity while providing value for money (economy) and limiting the toll on efficiency. No formula can determine the best mix: it requires the application of values to politics. From generation to generation, it is for every society to choose what balance to strike. But so much depends upon how the choice is made amid altering circumstances, where long-term developments may take rather a long time to see and then be hard to address because of the short-term horizons of much day-to-day politics. This book has sought to show the difficulties involved in making decisions on this basis, of how different ideas, information and reckoning have worked out. Yet, whatever its limitations, the British fiscal state has endured, indeed often flourished.

Looking back over more than three centuries, it is clear that the mid-Victorian years were pivotal to the fiscal dilemmas of the UK. Until then, equity led to parts of the Union escaping some duties altogether or being subjected to others at lower levels. Such diversity may have been fiscally insignificant overall, but it was an important part of the politics of exaction by helping to legitimate control from London. The public-finance dimensions of the 1707 Union left unsettled how to reconcile the different objectives of equality and equity. A significant amount of refinement was subsequently needed. While this might have helped the framing of the 1801 Union, even more serious mistakes were made then. A new order was forged in 1817, aided by a diminution of the state's taxes, duties and debts. This opened the opportunity for profound changes subsequently. Critically for our story, from the 1850s, at least until very recently, central government taxation was very largely applied equally everywhere, though of course the progressive principle meant that taxes sought to bear more heavily upon richer individuals, a point that became increasingly important in the first half of the twentieth century as the income tax became ubiquitous. Pure uniformity was for a time held to be right and proper. Only in the 2010s, with fuller fiscal devolution, has the principle of universality been significantly compromised, including even reductions of fuel duties, a reserved power, in parts of Scotland's Highlands and Islands as well as several districts in England.[59]

A significant consequence of the change of direction in UK tax policy in the 1850s was to encourage complaints of fiscal injustice in Ireland, helping to underpin calls for Home Rule. That 'overtaxation' seemed calculable gave such complaints real point and potency, but it also prompted Scottish Home Rulers to argue that their voice was too weak in London, not least given the productivity of the Scottish tax base between 1840 and 1914. Creating the Scottish Office in 1885 led inexorably to claims for territorial preferential treatment regarding public finances – already in 1897 the Office was being called 'pertinacious' at the Treasury.[60] A form of geographical fiscal competitiveness set in, mainly in a struggle for bigger slices of total public expenditure, though it took decades for Northern Ireland to be given an institutional voice and decades more for Wales. What we have seen is that generally these nations have often successfully negotiated with central government in London for more funding – because they are able to detail why their circumstances are different and needy in ways difficult for the Treasury to challenge and because politicians in London often see largesse as politically useful to their often rather casual and under-theorized unionism.

It was also from 1870 that public expenditure on civil items became increasingly significant. The statutory requirement that certain public goods such as policing and education had to be provided by local authorities inevitably led to poorer areas receiving more central funding to top them up than richer ones. By contrast, new welfare provision by central government out of general taxation, such as pensions, unemployment benefits and healthcare, had less obvious territorial consequences. But there were two major consequences relevant here. First, they helped to legitimate the principle of uniform taxation and have involved expanding the empire of needs and rights common to all members of the Union. Second, the expansion of welfare provision had unintended implications for the geography of economic activity by helping to cushion some places against the forces of decline. This raised the question of the objectives of central aid to those in declining areas: should it seek to revive their fortunes or to manage their fall from grace? Not that, in an age of mass democracy, have many been prepared to ask it so bluntly – though in 1981 Thatcher's government privately considered allowing Liverpool simply to wither rather than spending large sums to, in the words of the Chancellor, Geoffrey Howe, 'pump water uphill'.[61] More often discussion has been framed in terms of the causes and consequences of a dependency culture.

Like many societies, over the last century or so the UK has become much governed. The state now manages many more resources, requiring considerable expertise and administrative complexity. Inevitably this has involved centralization. After all, the principle of sharing risks that is at the core of arguments for composite states requires at least some resources to be accumulated by and distributed from the capital. Such pressures were dramatically heightened to deal with world wars and interwar depression, but were taken much further by nationalization under the Labour party after 1945. Oddly, while the Thatcher revolution of the 1980s sought through privatization to limit the economic role of the state, her government's distrust of much local government made it a great centralizer in other ways, straining the Union in the process: what it gave with one hand it took back with the other. Devolution has been the major response to all these developments since the late twentieth century, but if outside England significant steps have now been made towards decentralization, within England they have not. To an extent not widely recognized, not least because of the SNP's successes in recent decades, this is a major flaw in the constitution of the UK.

Over the centuries centralization has been due to more than the inherent logic of the growth of a composite state. Two features must be stressed here. First, it has reflected wider developments in economic geography, particularly the repeated ability of London to refresh itself as a remarkably potent economic region. If demographically it trod water in the eighteenth century relative to national population trends, its economic base flourished sufficiently that it was not put in the shade by the early stirrings of the first industrial revolution on Britain's coalfields. That it was able to be far and away the most important node of the emerging railway network from the 1830s was a product of that, in itself encouraging some centralization. In very different circumstances, successful transformations of London's economy took place both between the two world wars and, after a period of decline, from the 1980s. Many other parts of the UK have struggled similarly to reinvent themselves economically, prospering with early industrialization, but finding adjusting to growing international competition very challenging. It is unmistakably the case that a city that did not exist in the eighteenth century and prospered because of industrialization in the nineteenth and early twentieth century might well have no plausible function at all in the twenty-first century. Some of London's relative success in such processes undoubtedly is due to its role as a capital city, feeding the 'dreadful monster' myth in the process, but many other capital cities have been unable to repeat the trick: not to anything like the same extent in The Hague or Berlin, Paris or Madrid, Washington, DC, or Ottawa. There is more to it than simply being a capital. In particular, London has built upon the benefits of its geography, facing into the heartlands of southern England with its agricultural strengths, up England's east coast as far as the once mighty coalfields of the north-east, as well as towards valuable markets in nearby continental Europe. Clearly, the nature of the British fiscal state has been heavily influenced by London's varied roles: the state has helped London and London has helped the state.

Secondly, states have to have a centre, acting as an umpire between rival claims of its territories and redistributing resources from one part to another to meet risks and ensure fairness. Only central government can produce equity between devolved administrations, whose preoccupations with difference and diversity unavoidably lead to inequalities between them.[62] Nonetheless, those beyond the centre must question whether the flows are right and proper and how this relates to perceptions of dependence and freedom. This has been fed by the increasing significance of England within the Union and London's part in both. In such circumstances, complaints that public finances were constructed according to English assumptions and interests were inevitable, often tied to a belief that politicians and officials in London were ignorant of the Union's distant parts: because of the 'Westminster bubble', in modern journalese. This has been a repeated refrain. In the early nineteenth century Walter Scott asserted that the 'English act on the principle that everything English is right and that anything in Scotland which is not English must therefore be wrong'.[63] In 1868 the political economist Nassau William Senior complained that 'the people of England are prone, more perhaps than any other equally intelligent nation, to transfer to other countries their own notions; to suppose that they have the same wants and the same powers; to believe, in short, that their social system resembles ours even in its details.'[64]

Some truth lay behind these views, particularly in those periods where uniformity was treasured – from the 1830s to the 1880s and from 1939 to 1997. Even so, ministers and officials in London often tried, from an early date, to get more information with which to tailor major policies to the circumstances of distant parts, in the process recognizing that some regions required particularly distinctive treatment, most frequently the Highlands and Islands. An important feature of this was the willingness of many distant from London to engage positively with the British state in the hope of influencing policies, a trend that was clearly noticeable from the late eighteenth century in Scotland and in some Home Rulers in late nineteenth-century Ireland. This was about manpower, of course, from soldiers to administrators to, in Scotland's case, prime ministers, but it is also notable that Scottish political economy was unusually influential in the century after 1776. (It is striking that voices in nineteenth-century Ireland complained about the influence there of Scottish policies, administrators and politicians.) This also speaks to a certain openness in central government, complicating simplistic views of the dependence and powerlessness of those beyond the centre.[65]

A further complication here is to make explicit what this book has often only implied – that within the national frame complaints from Wales have been much less forthcoming than those from Scotland or Ireland, despite enduring much the same system of public finances. This suggests the need to go beyond seeing tensions in the geography of public finances in binary core and periphery terms. Certainly there have been complaints of Wales being 'swallowed up entirely in the English State machine' or 'treated merely as a province of England', particularly as Plaid Cymru attained some prominence in the middle of the twentieth century.[66] But these have been fewer and quieter than elsewhere. Explaining an absence can never be certain, but the greater age and completeness of the Anglo-Welsh union has surely been a factor. For centuries, Wales has been less distinct and distant, despite the much greater resilience of its language than Gaelic in Scotland. With the industrialization of south Wales, including some migration there from England, a rising share of the national population came to live near England: in 2010 nearly one-half lived within twenty-five miles of the border, compared to just one-twenty-fifth in Scotland.[67]

Complaints over a dreadful monster and poor relations were often therefore rhetorical flourishes, a means of simplifying more complex relationships. Two further aspects of this need stressing. First, differences between the two myths have repeatedly been unresolvable, with regional or national deficits used as evidence for views of the Union as both extractive (negative) and resource sharing (positive). Surpluses can just as easily be used by some to show that greater autonomy or independence is possible, yet to others surpluses indicate that close union is working well.[68] This is also tied to the resort to counterfactuals: that other policies would have produced better outcomes, sometimes attached to a belief in unrealized or wasted potential. Necessarily this can only ever be speculative and uncertain. Moreover, a simple metric of territorial fiscal balance defies clear conceptualization, while those that have been developed are confronted by the vagaries of changing flows and quality of information on which to hazard some meaningful assessments. This is not, however, to suggest that such rhetoric is unimportant. It has provided key terms of reference for debate and assessment, though not for those who believe that where political self-determination is involved 'You cannot answer a poem with a balance sheet.'[69] Yet it remains the case that considering the geography of public finances remains what it has long been, a central means of judging the value of the Union to its people.

Debates over the territoriality of public finances also demonstrate that all but the smallest states are composite and, like nations, invented. It follows that there is no right or natural size of a state: states, large and small, have to make choices and trade-offs between the economies and diseconomies of scale discussed in Chapter 1. Equally, the UK as a state has no inherent right to exist any more than any other territory within the British Isles, though clearly its particular form since 1707 gave it more resources than the alternatives, allowing different ambitions to be pursued. It (and now the devolved administrations) have to prove their worth, in part with reference to the fiscal dilemmas examined above: of the impossibility of reconciling the rival claims to equality and equity, economy and efficiency, autonomy and accountability. Were, for example, Scotland and Wales to become independent, their capitals would in time, like London, come to seem by some as distant, self-centred and extractive. What suits Edinburgh or Cardiff may well not suit the Northern Isles or Anglesey.

If such fiscal dilemmas are usually inescapable, there can be a lot of variation in how well they are met. A key point has been the longevity of a highly centralized English state. Established in the two centuries after 1066, it was refashioned with Henry VIII's break from the Catholic Church in Rome and in the revolutions of the seventeenth century. Significant rival centres of power had been quashed in the process, most obviously great aristocratic landowners, and local government divided between 39 counties and around 10,000 parishes. This was a drastically different outcome from, say, the German-speaking lands in the same period. Critically for subsequent developments was the fact that provincial government, introduced into Ireland in the early seventeenth century, was avoided in the English case. This centralized English state, albeit often delegating authority to local elites in matters of day-to-day administration, was the bedrock upon which the unions of 1707 and 1801 were built.[70] It has proved remarkably resilient.

In the eighteenth century, the public finances of the British state were dramatically expanded – Scotland and Wales contributed very little – allowing it to project power globally. But at home this required it to extract resources from its people much more effectively than in rival powers, prompting two leading modern historians to conclude that 'Suddenly Britain looks rather more German or Prussian than we realized.'[71] Or, in a sense, more absolutist than had been thought. Enthusiasm for a strong centre weakened in the nineteenth century because of the importance of economy, the attachment to free trade and the need for local government to administer efforts to mitigate some of the worst consequences of industrialization and urbanization. But such choices were not permanent. In the twentieth century, pressures for centralization in politics and business mounted. Local government gradually lost a huge amount of leverage and effectiveness. It need not have done: a different balance between central and local government could have been struck. But local government reforms (of 1835, 1888 and 1974 in particular) failed to grasp the need for regions or provinces with which to disaggregate England while allowing some administrative scale economies to be reaped.[72] This would have set the challenge of defining regions and building their identities, but it is a challenge other nations have risen to, notably in Germany. Devolution has helped to address that in places; but much of England remains tightly governed from Whitehall. Decentralization has been reluctantly granted – concessive, piecemeal and disordered. If, in the eighteenth century, the British state was more 'Germanic' than is often thought, it is now very much less so.

Necessarily, this history of the territoriality of the public finances of the UK has been preoccupied with moments of stress and strain, of the sources of discontent, disagreement and discord. But as some leading historians and political scientists have pointed out, it is important not to underestimate the survival of the Union, albeit in attenuated form, recognizing its achievements and the strengths of unionism.[73] It has survived because it has evolved through expansion and retreat. Even in Ireland, where the retreat has been the greatest, London was previously able to extract surprisingly large amounts of revenue and came to spend much more money there than in other parts of the Union. Advocates of parliamentary sovereignty such as Burke and Dicey might ascribe this to what has been called the 'plasticity' of the compacts.[74] Far from the unions of 1707 and 1801 being untouchable fundamental laws, preserved in aspic, they have been significantly altered, both at headline moments of disunion and devolution and more quietly through the daily workings of the state. Yet in the process parliamentary sovereignty has been divided and Britain is now a quasi-federal state, even if enthusiasts for parliamentary sovereignty would be loath to admit as much.

Perhaps this is a sensibility that dares not speak its name or a sign of a certain schizophrenia in British political thought. After all, Britain has helped to establish federal governments around the world, including in parts of what was its empire. As the German foreign minister Hans-Dietrich Genscher, in office from 1974 to 1992, wryly observed, 'You were so generous you British – you gave us a decentralised federal structure and a proportional system of election so that never again could we concentrate power at the centre but you took neither of these for yourselves.'[75]

This book has identified several factors behind the preference for centralization within the UK and why this tendency endured for so long. Most simply, the malleability of the constitution allowed it to be changed relatively easily. The political scientist Iain McLean has observed that 'Since 1886, the fiscal constitution of the UK has contained only one rule: *what is politically acceptable is fair*', but the same could be said for the whole period since 1707.[76] Escaping the worst effects of the great European wars and revolutions, the UK has not had to redraw its constitution as fundamentally as Germany and France have had to from time to time. Even the American and Irish revolutions required thoroughgoing constitutional overhauls. Throughout there has been an unwillingness by leading politicians to think more strategically and structurally – though in fairness because they have rarely had to do so. Richard Crossman, a Labour MP (1945–74) and one-time Oxford classics don, reflected on this predilection for muddling through unsystematically. More originally and significantly, he suggested that 'In a very profound sense ... British political thought is dialectical in character. It is always part of a controversy, and therefore it is only intelligible in the context of conflict which gave rise to it.'[77] The dreadful monster and its poor relations need to be seen as part and parcel of such dialectical thinking.

Clearly Britain's constitution, including its fiscal element, is not working well now. Brexit confused a crisis within the Conservative party and press as one within society at large, whose resolution involved significant illegality. It has put Northern Ireland and Scotland profoundly at odds with England and Wales and the English at odds with themselves. No less significantly, the coronavirus pandemic of 2020 has exposed the economic fragility of an economy that is London-centric, highly globalized and service based, along with serious shortcomings of government capacity and the incoherence of devolution, both between the territories of the UK and between English devolved administrations and the centre.

It is not for a historian to suggest what might be done to rectify this mess, though I hope that this book has helped explain why the fiscal dilemmas of composite states are so tricky to resolve. One option, of course, is for the Union to fracture and for its four territories to go their separate ways. That at least would be a moment of opportunity to rationalize things. It would be difficult and costly to all, as the debate around the Scottish independence referendum in 2014 showed. But they are soluble problems and clearly many outside England (and inside, one suspects) think the costs are worth bearing. That, though, has the danger of leaving unresolved the 'English question' that has clearly emerged as a key weakness within the UK. Indeed that is a key reason why moving towards an explicitly federal UK is highly unlikely.[78] Too much political capital, especially in the Conservative party, is invested in maintaining the power of central government and the unity of England. In hindsight, the Labour landslide victory of 1997 was a major opportunity to tackle the 'English question'. But it was missed through an understandable view that the problems of the Union to be addressed were much more acute in Northern Ireland, Scotland and Wales.

If the Union is to continue there is, nonetheless, plenty of clearing up that should be done. The devolution settlements of the late 1990s should be made more consistent, though of course Northern Ireland's is rightly distinctive because of the role given there to the Irish Republic. More realistically, therefore, the nub of the soluble problem is the confusion of combined administrations within England and the many definitions of regions used for different activities of government there and across the UK: NHS regions are not, for example, those for economic planning. There is simply no logic for only one-third of people in England falling within combined authorities, giving them a voice denied to the other two-thirds. Greater consistency and coherence in the definitions of nations and regions should be tied to employing a common needs-based formula in their funding, which should also be extended from Wales to Northern Ireland and Scotland – that is, abandoning Barnett – while shifting resources from central to local government on a significant scale in England. There are instructive examples from around the world here – most obviously in Canada, Germany and Australia.[79] It may well also be the time, as has been recently argued, for higher taxation to be levied on those who have benefited most from agglomeration, in London particularly. These should be considered as national taxes, to be redistributed to aid the development of the poorest areas.[80] Current invocations of addressing regional economic imbalances by levelling up will be inadequate without significant redistribution. As this supposes, if the Union is to be more content with itself, the benefits of the sharing of risk and resources across its extent, organized centrally, have to be celebrated, with the language of 'subsidy' consigned to the rubbish bin of history and less presumption that what seems right for England must be right for the rest of the UK.

Addressing such complexities will certainly require a huge effort of political will and change management; it will not be quick, easy or cheap. But the costs of the democratic deficit of current arrangements should not be underestimated. Unless citizens can see clearly how they are governed, including why they are taxed as they are and the types of public expenditure that affects them, then the current cynicism, malaise and polarization coursing through the UK's politics will only worsen. People need to be able more easily to understand the hard choices I have discussed. Muddling along as at present will almost certainly happen, but there are better less-travelled roads to take.

Abbreviations

The following abbreviations appear in references throughout the book, including the Notes, Bibliography and source details for the figures, tables and maps.

Add. MSS	Additional Manuscripts
BL	British Library
BPP	British Parliamentary Papers
'Millennium of data'	Bank of England, 'A millennium of macroeconomic data', at https://www.bankofengland.co.uk/statistics/research-datasets, accessed 1 July 2020
NRS	National Records of Scotland, Edinburgh
ONS	Office for National Statistics
TNA	The National Archives, Kew, London

Notes

In the following notes, place of publication is London unless stated otherwise.

PREFACE

1. Edmund Burke, *Reflections on the revolution in France* (1790), 127.
2. Gavin McCrone, *Scottish independence: weighing up the economics* (Edinburgh, 2014).
3. Alexis de Tocqueville, *The old regime and the revolution*, ed. François Furet and Françoise Mélonio, 2 vols ([1856], Chicago, IL, 1998), I, 157.
4. https:// en.wikipedia.org/wiki/Death_and_taxes_(idiom), accessed 5 March 2020.
5. Brutus, 'Letter 5', in Alexander Hamilton, James Madison and John Jay, *The Federalist, with letters of 'Brutus'*, ed. Terence Ball (Cambridge, 2003), 469.
6. Nigel Dodds, https://twitter.com/NigelDoddsDUP, 18 October 2019.
7. Anon., *A Scots excise-man described* ([Edinburgh, 1707?]).
8. Citizen of Edinburgh, *A vindication of Scottish rights addressed to both Houses of Parliament* (Edinburgh, 1854), 6.
9. These are the words of Charles Lamb from an 1818 essay, 'Poor relations', quoted, tellingly, in Arthur Warren Samuels, *Home Rule finance: an examination of the financial bearings of the Government of Ireland Bill, 1912* (Dublin, 1912), 74.
10. Invention of the term in the 1980s appears to originate with junior members of the Thatcher government: Richard J. Finlay, 'Unionism and the dependency culture: politics and state intervention in Scotland, 1918–1997', in Catriona M. M. Macdonald (ed.), *Unionist Scotland, 1800–1997* (Edinburgh, 1998), 100–116, at 100. See also John Quiggin, *Zombie economics: how dead ideas still walk among us* (Princeton, NJ, 2012).

11. ONS, *Country and regional public sector finances: financial year ending March 2019* (2019), 19.
12. Major contributions to the vast literature include P. J. Cain and A. G. Hopkins, *British imperialism: 1688–2015* (3rd edn, 2015), and Lance E. Davis and Robert A. Huttenback, *Mammon and the pursuit of empire: the political economy of British imperialism* (Cambridge, 1987).

1. INTRODUCTION

1. J. H. Elliott, 'A Europe of composite monarchies', *Past and Present*, 137 (1992), 48–71; Aleksandar Pavković with Peter Radan, *Creating new states: theory and practice of secession* (Aldershot, 2007).
2. David Reynolds, *Island stories: Britain and its history in the age of Brexit* (2019), 116.
3. J. H. Elliott, *Scots and Catalans: union and disunion* (New Haven, CT, 2018).
4. See, for instance, Linda Colley, *Britons: forging the nation, 1707–1837* (New Haven, CT, 1992); Alvin Jackson, *The two unions: Ireland, Scotland, and the survival of the United Kingdom, 1707–2007* (Oxford, 2012); Vernon Bogdanor, *Devolution in the United Kingdom* (updated edn, Oxford, 2001).
5. Christophe Guilluy, *La France périphérique: comment on a sacrifié les classes populaires* (Paris, 2014).
6. Benedict Anderson, *Imagined communities: reflections on the origin and spread of nationalism* (1983).
7. Alexis de Tocqueville, *Democracy in America*, ed. Eduardo Nolla, 2 vols ([1835], Indianapolis, IN, 2010), I, 260.
8. In general, see: John Kendle, *Federal Britain: a history* (1997); Bernard Burrows and Geoffrey Denton, *Devolution or federalism? Options for a United Kingdom* (1980), 3; Robert Schütze and Stephen Tierney (eds), *The United Kingdom and the federal idea* (Oxford, 2018). On the German case, see Wolfgang Renzsch, 'German federalism in historical perspective: federalism as a substitute for a national state', *Publius*, 19.4 (1989), 17–33.
9. William H. Riker, *Federalism: origin, operation, significance* (Boston, MA, 1964).
10. Wallace E. Oates, *Fiscal federalism* (New York, 1972); Robin Boadway and Anwar Shah, *Fiscal federalism: principles and practices of multi-order governance* (New York, 2009).

11. John Robertson, 'Empire and union: two concepts of the early modern European political order', in John Robertson (ed.), *A union for empire: political thought and the British union of 1707* (Cambridge, 1995), 3–36.

12. Brian P. Levack, *The formation of the British state: England, Scotland, and the Union, 1603–1707* (Oxford, 1987); Colin Kidd, *Union and unionisms: political thought in Scotland, 1500–2000* (Cambridge, 2008), ch. 2.

13. James Kelly, 'The origins of the Act of Union: an examination of unionist opinion in Britain and Ireland, 1650–1800', *Irish Historical Studies*, 25 (1987), 236–63; Viola Florence Barnes, *The Dominion of New England: a study in British colonial policy* (New Haven, CT, 1923); Alison Gilbert Olson, 'The British government and colonial union, 1754', *William and Mary Quarterly*, 17.1 (1960), 22–34; Timothy J. Shannon, *Indians and colonists at the crossroads of empire: the Albany Congress of 1754* (Ithaca, NY, 2000).

14. Linda Colley, 'Empires of writing: Britain, America and constitutions, 1776–1848', *Law and History Review*, 32.2 (2014), 237–66.

15. Elizabeth R. Varon, *Disunion! The coming of the American Civil War, 1789–1859* (Chapel Hill, NC, 2008).

16. Lauren Benton and Lisa Ford, *Rage for order: the British Empire and the origins of international law, 1800–1850* (Cambridge, MA, 2016).

17. Bogdanor, *Devolution*; Vernon Bogdanor, *Beyond Brexit: towards a British constitution* (2019), ch. 2.

18. Scottish Government, *Scotland's right to choose: putting Scotland's future in Scotland's hands* (Edinburgh, 2019), 5; Neil MacCormick, *Questioning sovereignty: law, state and nation in the European commonwealth* (Oxford, 1999); Colin Kidd, 'Sovereignty and the Scottish constitution before 1707', *Juridical Review*, 3 (2004), 225–36.

19. Amartya Sen, *Inequality reexamined* (Oxford, 1992); R. H. Tawney, *Equality* (1931); Keith Joseph and Jonathan Sumption, *Equality* (1979); William Letwin (ed.), *Against equality: readings on economic and social policy* (1983); James M. Buchanan and Richard A. Musgrave, *Public finance and public choice: two contrasting visions of the state* (Cambridge, MA, 1999); Richard Wilkinson and Kate Pickett, *The spirit level: why more equal societies almost always do better* (2009); Arthur M. Okun, *Equality and efficiency: the big tradeoff* (Washington, DC, 1975), 6.

20. Lynn Hunt, *Inventing human rights: a history* (New York, 2007); Peter Jones, *Rights* (Basingstoke, 1994); Micheline R. Ishay (ed.), *The human*

rights reader: major political writings, essays, speeches, and documents from the Bible to the present (1997).

21. E. H. Hunt, *Regional wage variations in Britain, 1850–1914* (Oxford, 1973); C. H. Lee, *Regional economic growth in the United Kingdom since the 1880s* (1971).

22. David Heald, *Territorial equity and public finances: concepts and confusion* (Strathclyde, 1980); R. J. Bennett, 'Individual and territorial equity', *Geographical Analysis*, 15 (1983), 50–57.

23. Joseph A. Schumpeter, *Capitalism, socialism and democracy* (New York, 1942).

24. Evidence of Frederick Maclagan in 'Report from the committee upon distilleries in Scotland' (1798), in *Reports from the Committees of the House of Commons*, vol. 11: *1782–1799* (1803), 319–510, at 427.

25. Quoted in Ron Martin and Ben Gardiner, 'Reviving the "Northern Powerhouse" and spatially rebalancing the British economy: the scale of the challenge', in Craig Berry and Arianna Giovannini (eds), *Developing England's north: the political economy of the Northern Powerhouse* (Cham, Switzerland, 2018), 23–58, at 47.

26. Howard Glennerster, John Hills and Tony Travers with Ross Hendry, *Paying for health, education, and housing: how does the centre pull the purse strings?* (Oxford, 2000), 11; David Wiggins, *Needs, values, truth: essays in the philosophy of value* (3rd edn, Oxford, 1998).

27. Quoted in Wiggins, *Needs, values, truth*, 5.

28. Okun, *Equality and efficiency*.

29. A. B. Atkinson and T. Piketty (eds), *Top incomes over the twentieth century: a contrast between continental European and English-speaking countries* (Oxford, 2007); Thomas Piketty, *Capital in the twenty-first century* (Cambridge, MA, 2014).

30. José Harris, 'English ideas about community: another case of "made in Germany"?', in Rudolf Muhs, Johannes Paulmann and Willibald Steinmetz (eds), *Aneignung und Abwehr: interkultureller Transfer zwischen Deutschland und Großbritannien im 19. Jahrhundert* (Bodenheim, 1998), 143–58.

31. J. A. King and M. A. King, *The British tax system* (Oxford, 1978), 208.

32. David Heald, *Public expenditure: its defence and reform* (Oxford, 1983), 239.

33. James C. Scott, *Seeing like a state: how certain schemes to improve the human condition have failed* (New Haven, CT, 1999).

34. Kevin Theakston, *Winston Churchill and the British constitution* (2003), ch. 3; Fabian Society, *Municipalization by provinces*, New Heptarchy

Series, no. 1 (1905); C. B. Fawcett, *Provinces of England: a study of some geographical aspects of devolution* (1919).

35. YouGov, 'Perceptions of how tax is spent differ widely from reality', at https://yougov.co.uk/news/2014/11/09/public-attitudes-tax-distribution/, accessed 15 November 2017.

36. James Anderson, *Observations on the effects of the coal duty upon the remote and thinly peopled coasts of Britain* (Edinburgh, 1792), 11.

37. Vanessa S. Williamson, *Read my lips: why Americans are proud to pay taxes* (Princeton, NJ, 2017).

38. British Social Attitudes, http://www.bsa-data.natcen.ac.uk, accessed 15 November 2017.

39. Stephen Smith, *Taxation: a very short introduction* (Oxford, 2015), 4. Similarly, Louis Eisenstein, *The ideologies of taxation* ([1961], Cambridge, MA, 2010), 6.

40. Anon., *The constitutional right of the legislature of Great Britain, to tax the British colonies in America, impartially stated* (1768), 5.

41. W. M. Herries, *A letter addressed to the Dumfries and Galloway Courier on the subject of the tax upon property and income* (Dumfries, 1816), 4. Better known is the view from 1927 of the American jurist Oliver Wendell Holmes that 'Taxes are what we pay for civilized society', at https://caselaw.findlaw.com/us-supreme-court/275/87.html, accessed 14 November 2017.

42. Steven M. Sheffrin, *Tax fairness and folk justice* (Cambridge, 2014), 162; David F. Burg, *A world history of tax rebellions: an encyclopedia of tax rebels, revolts, and riots from antiquity to the present* (New York and London, 2004), xxix–xxxiv, lists eighteen clear instances of tax resistance in the UK, though omitting the Scottish malt tax riots of 1725.

43. E. P. Hennock, *British social reform and German precedents: the case of social insurance, 1880–1914* (Oxford, 1987).

44. John Brewer, *The sinews of power: war, money and the English state, 1688–1783* (1989); Martin Daunton, *Trusting Leviathan: the politics of taxation in Britain, 1799–1914* (Cambridge, 2001).

45. Ireland has been best dealt with, with a good introduction provided by Douglas Kanter and Patrick Walsh (eds), *Taxation, politics and protest in Ireland, 1662–2016* (Cham, Switzerland, 2019).

46. Iain McLean and Alistair McMillan, *State of the Union: unionism and the alternatives in the United Kingdom since 1707* (Oxford, 2005); James Mitchell, *The Scottish question* (Oxford, 2014); John Short, *Public expenditure and taxation in the UK regions* (Farnborough, 1981); Heald, *Territorial equity.*

47. Sijbren Cnossen, *Excise systems: a global study of the selective taxation of goods and services* (Baltimore, MD, 1977), 2.

48. [Benjamin Heath], *The case of the county of Devon, with respect to the consequences of the new excise duty on cyder and perry* (1763), 3.

49. Adam Smith, *An inquiry into the nature and causes of the wealth of nations*, ed. R. H. Campbell and A. S. Skinner, 2 vols ([1776], Oxford, 1976), II, 825–7.

50. The classic study of the development of the idea of the ability to pay is Edwin R. A. Seligman, *The income tax: a study of the history, theory, and practice of income tax at home and abroad* (2nd edn, New York, 1914).

51. R. A. Musgrave, 'A brief history of fiscal doctrine', in Alan J. Auerbach and Martin Feldstein (eds), *Handbook of public economics*, vol. 1 (Amsterdam, 1985), 1–59, at 7; Jeffrey Schoenblum, 'Taxation, the state, and the community', in Ellen Frankel, Fred D. Miller Jnr and Jeffrey Paul (eds), *Taxation, economic prosperity, and distributive justice* (Cambridge, 2006), 210–34, at 211.

52. Joseph Massie, *Observations on the new cyder-tax, so far as the same may affect our woollen manufactures, Newfoundland fisheries, &c.* ([1764?]), 8.

53. Smith, *Wealth of nations*, II, 825.

54. Samuel Fleischacker, *A short history of distributive justice* (Cambridge, MA, 2004), 62–8.

55. James E. Cronin, *The politics of state expansion: war, state and society in twentieth-century Britain* (1991); David Edgerton, *Warfare state: Britain, 1920–1970* (Cambridge, 2006); Roger Middleton, *Government versus the market: the growth of the public sector, economic management and British economic performance, c.1890–1979* (Cheltenham, 1996).

56. HM Treasury, *The green book: central government guidance on appraisal and evaluation* (2018); Duncan Campbell-Smith, *Follow the money: the Audit Commission, public money and the management of public services, 1983–2008* (2008); Amartya Sen, 'The discipline of cost-benefit analysis', *Journal of Legal Studies*, 29 (2000), 931–52; G. H. Peters, *Cost-benefit analysis and public expenditure* (3rd edn, 1973).

57. Linda Colley, '"This small island": Britain, size and empire', *Proceedings of the British Academy*, 121 (2002), 171–90.

58. The spans in miles are: Britain, Penzance to Thurso, 591; France, Biarritz to Calais, 541; Spain, Algeciras to San Sebastian, 530. The Scilly Isles are over 760 miles from the Shetland Isles.

59. Alberto Alesina and Enrico Spolaore, *The size of nations* (Cambridge, MA, 2003), 3–6; Stein Rokkan and Derek K. Urwin, *Economy, territory, identity: politics of western European peripheries* (1983), 2–3.

60. Geoff Jenkins, Matthew Perry and John Prior, *The climate of the United Kingdom and recent trends* (Exeter, 2009).

61. A. S. Goudie and D. Brunsden, *The environment of the British Isles* (Oxford, 1994), 22.

62. Jim Bulpitt, *Territory and power in the United Kingdom: an interpretation* (Manchester, 1983), 77.

63. E. A. Wrigley, *Continuity, chance and change: the character of the industrial revolution in England* (Cambridge, 1988).

64. Liám Kennedy and Leslie A. Clarkson, 'Birth, death and exile: Irish population history, 1700–1921', in B. J. Graham and L. J. Proudfoot (eds), *An historical geography of Ireland* (1993), 158–84.

65. David Coleman and John Salt, *The British population: patterns, trends, and processes* (Oxford, 1992), 86.

66. I. D. Whyte, 'Scottish and Irish urbanisation in the seventeenth and eighteenth centuries: a comparative perspective', in S. J. Connolly, R. A. Houston and R. J. Morris (eds), *Conflict, identity and economic development: Scotland and Ireland, 1600–1939* (Preston, 1995), 14–28, at 16; Richard Lawton and Colin G. Pooley, *Britain, 1740–1950: an historical geography* (1992), 91; C. M. Law, 'The growth of urban population in England and Wales, 1801–1911', *Transactions of the Institute of British Geographers*, 41 (1967), 125–43, at 135; Harold Carter and C. Roy Lewis, *An urban geography of England and Wales in the nineteenth century* (1990), 56–7.

67. Whyte, 'Scottish and Irish urbanisation', 16.

68. David Barnett, *London, hub of the industrial revolution: a revisionary history, 1775–1825* (1998).

69. Nick Buck, Ian Gordon and Ken Young, *The London employment problem* (Oxford, 1986).

70. Philip Loft, 'Litigation, the Anglo-Scottish Union, and the House of Lords as the High Court, 1660–1875', *Historical Journal*, 61.4 (2018), 943–67.

71. T. M. Devine, *The Scottish clearances: a history of the dispossessed, 1600–1900* (2018); E. A. Wrigley, *The path to sustained growth: England's transition from an organic economy to an industrial revolution* (Cambridge, 2016), 129; William Cobbett, *Rural rides* (1830).

72. Coleman and Salt, *The British population*, 90–91.

73. 'Millennium of data', Table A8.

74. Ibid.; C. T. Sandford, *Economics of public finance: an economic analysis of government expenditure and revenue in the United Kingdom* (4th edn, Oxford, 1992), 24–6; B. R. Mitchell, *British historical statistics* (Cambridge, 1988), 578–80, 587–97, 606–42. GDP estimates before the mid nineteenth century involve considerable guesswork.

75. Julian Hoppit, 'Checking the Leviathan, 1688–1832', in Donald Winch and Patrick K. O'Brien (eds), *The political economy of British historical experience, 1688–1914* (Oxford, 2002), 267–94.

76. Brewer, *The sinews of power*, 66; Earl of Dunraven, *The outlook in Ireland: the case for devolution and conciliation* (Dublin, 1907), 157; Jim Tomlinson, 'De-industrialization not decline: a new meta-narrative for post-war British history', *Twentieth Century British History*, 27.1 (2016), 76–99, at 91.

77. Fiscal Commission Working Group, *Principles for a modern and efficient tax system in an independent Scotland* (Edinburgh, 2013), 24.

78. See, for example: Andrew Mackillop, *'More fruitful than the soil': army, empire and the Scottish Highlands, 1715–1815* (East Linton, 2000); James Walvin, *Fruits of empire: exotic produce and British taste, 1660–1800* (Basingstoke, 1997); Catherine Hall and Sonya O. Rose (eds), *At home with the empire: metropolitan culture and the imperial world* (Cambridge, 2006).

2. 1707–1801: SCOTLAND'S CHALLENGE

1. Julian Hoppit, *A land of liberty? England, 1689–1727* (Oxford, 2000); Julian Hoppit, *Britain's political economies: parliament and economic life, 1660–1800* (Cambridge, 2017).

2. D'Maris Coffman, *Excise taxation and the origins of public debt* (Basingstoke, 2013); C. D. Chandaman, *The English public revenue, 1660–1688* (Oxford, 1975).

3. Karen J. Cullen, *Famine in Scotland: the 'ill years' of the 1690s* (Edinburgh, 2010), 188–91.

4. Douglas Watt, *The price of Scotland: Darien, Union and the wealth of nations* (Edinburgh, 2007).

5. Laura A. M. Stewart, 'The "rise" of the state?', in T. M. Devine and Jenny Wormald (eds), *The Oxford handbook of modern Scottish history* (Oxford, 2012), 220–35, at 233.

6. BPP, 1868–9, XXXV (366), part 2, 357.

7. [William Black], *A short view of our present trade and taxes, compared with what these taxes may amount to after the Union* ([Edinburgh,

1706?]), 6; [William Black], *Remarks upon a pamphlet, intitled, The considerations in relation to trade considered, and a short view of our present trade and taxes reviewed* ([Edinburgh?], 1706). See, in general, Karin Bowie, *Scottish public opinion and the Anglo-Scottish Union, 1699–1707* (Woodbridge, 2007).

8. [Daniel Defoe], *The state of the excise after the Union, compared with what it is now* ([Edinburgh?], 1706); Anon., *Considerations in relation to trade considered, and A short view of our present trade and taxes, compared with what these taxes may amount to after the Union, &c. Reviewed* ([Edinburgh?], 1706).

9. Quoted in John Clerk, *History of the Union of Scotland and England by Sir John Clerk of Penicuik*, ed. Douglas Duncan (Edinburgh, 1993), 141. On Scottish unionist ideas, see Kidd, *Union and unionisms*, ch. 2.

10. In practice, this meant that the maximum land tax collected in Scotland would be £48,000 per annum, whereas the figure for England and Wales would be £1.9 million, i.e. Scotland contributed 2.5 per cent of the British total.

11. For a cogent and convincing overview of the terms of the Union, see Christopher A. Whatley, *The Scots and the Union: then and now* (Edinburgh, 2014). Another important interpretation is Allan I. Macinnes, *Union and empire: the making of the United Kingdom in 1707* (Cambridge, 2007).

12. Paul Slack, *The invention of improvement: information and material progress in seventeenth-century England* (Oxford, 2015); Davis D. McElroy, *Scotland's age of improvement: a survey of eighteenth-century literary clubs and societies* (Pullman, WA, 1969), 5.

13. Joanna Innes, 'The distinctiveness of the English poor laws, 1750–1850', in Donald Winch and Patrick K. O'Brien (eds), *The political economy of British historical experience, 1688–1914* (Oxford, 2002), 381–407; Joanna Innes, 'The state and the poor: eighteenth-century England in European perspective', in John Brewer and Eckhart Hellmuth (eds), *Rethinking Leviathan: the eighteenth-century state in Britain and Germany* (Oxford, 1999), 225–80; David Feldman, 'Migrants, immigrants and welfare from the old poor law to the welfare state', *Transactions of the Royal Historical Society*, 13 (2003), 79–104.

14. *Calendar of state papers, colonial series, 1706–1708, June*, ed. Cecil Headlam (1916), 431.

15. Brewer, *The sinews of power*.

16. J. F. Mitchell, 'Englishmen in the Scottish excise department, 1707–1823', *Scottish Genealogist*, 13.2 (1966), 16–28.

17. Julian Hoppit, 'Reforming Britain's weights and measures, 1660–1824', *English Historical Review*, 108 (1993), 82–104.

18. [Robert Freebairn], *The miserable state of Scotland, since the Union, briefly represented* (Perth, 1716), 1.

19. BL, Add. MSS, 70047, f. 83.

20. Linda Colley, *Britons: forging the nation, 1707–1837* (New Haven, CT, 1992), 39; J. F. Bosher, *The single duty project: a study of the movement for a French customs union in the eighteenth century* (1964); Jeff Horn, *Economic development in early modern France: the privilege of liberty, 1650–1820* (Cambridge, 2015); Mark Dincecco, *Political transformations and public finances: Europe, 1650–1913* (Cambridge, 2011), 16.

21. Christopher A. Whatley, 'How tame were the Scottish Lowlanders during the eighteenth century?', in T. M. Devine (ed.), *Conflict and Stability in Scottish Society, 1700–1850* (Edinburgh, 1990), 1–30, at 6. Rates of duties are not the same as duties collected, a distinction often subsequently lost in, for example, Amy Watson, 'Patriotism and partisanship in post-Union Scotland, 1724–37', *Scottish Historical Review*, 97.1 (2018), 57–84, at 60–61, and T. M. Devine, *Independence or Union: Scotland's past and Scotland's present* (2017), 31.

22. More fully discussed in Julian Hoppit, 'Scotland and the taxing union, 1707–1815', *Scottish Historical Review*, 98.1 (2019), 45–70.

23. Excise: BL, Harleian MSS, 4227; Sandon Hall, Harrowby Trust MSS, 525; TNA, PRO 30/8/288, ff. 18 and 56; NRS, E26/12/2, E554/3. Customs: BL, Add. MSS, 8133A; NRS, E231/9/3, E501/43 and 73.

24. For the land tax, see Anon., *Land tax at 4s in ye pound paid by England & Wales in 1702, & 1704* (1745); BL, Harleian MSS, 4226, ff. 15–16.

25. J. Marshall, *Digest of all the accounts* (1834), [part 2], 29.

26. Brewer, *The sinews of power*; William Ashworth, *The industrial revolution: the state, knowledge and global trade* (2017), 120. The importance of London and the south-east to direct taxation was recognized in E. J. Buckatzsch, 'The geographical distribution of wealth in England, 1086–1843: an experimental study of certain tax assessments', *Economic History Review*, 3.2 (1950), 180–202.

27. Julian Hoppit, 'Taxing London and the British fiscal state, 1660–1815', in Julian Hoppit, Adrian Leonhard and Duncan Needham (eds), *Money and markets: essays in honour of Martin Daunton* (Woodbridge, 2019), 19–33.

28. Anderson, *Observations on the effects of the coal duty*, 6–7.

29. Based on the years 1752, 1776, 1801 and 1815, NRS, E555/1, 24, 26, 40.

30. Based on the years 1734–1815, NRS, E501/27–111.

31. Harrowby Trust MSS 525; TNA, PRO30/8/288, f. 19; NRS, E555/1–40; BL, Add. MSS, 8133.

32. Using decennial figures from 1710 to 1780 inclusive, perhaps 14 per cent of gross receipts were spent in this way: NRS, E231/9/3, 501/27–111; BL, Add. MSS, 8133. After 1801 accounting conventions improved, though by then drawbacks and bounties were far less important.

33. NRS, E231/9/3, 501/33, 43, 53, 63, 73.

34. NRS, E231/9/3, 501/27–111; BL, Add. MSS, 8133. On drawbacks in Scotland, see Philipp Robinson Rössner, *Scottish trade in the wake of the Union (1700–1760): the rise of a warehouse economy* (Stuttgart, 2008).

35. Hoppit, *Britain's political economies*, ch. 8. For a stimulating interpretation, see Andrew Mackillop, 'Subsidy state or drawback province? Eighteenth-century Scotland and the British fiscal-military complex', in Aaron Graham and Patrick Walsh (eds), *The British fiscal-military states, 1660–c.1783* (Abingdon, 2016), 179–99.

36. Costs of collection from 1802 to 1815 were 4 per cent of gross receipts. Mitchell, *British historical statistics*, 587.

37. Hoppit, 'Scotland and the taxing union', 51.

38. Hoppit, *Britain's political economies*, 291.

39. Mitchell, *British historical statistics*, 578–80, 587. The unpersuasive claim that civil expenditure was significantly higher is made in Steve Pincus and James Robinson, 'Challenging the fiscal-military hegemony: the British case', in Aaron Graham and Patrick Walsh (eds), *The British fiscal-military states, 1660–c.1783* (2016), 229–61.

40. James Postlethwayt, *The history of the public revenue, from the Revolution in 1688, to Christmas 1753* (1759), 201–2.

41. Patrick A. Walsh, 'The fiscal state in Ireland, 1691–1769', *Historical Journal*, 56.3 (2013), 629–56.

42. Roger Knight and Martin Wilcox, *Sustaining the fleet, 1793–1815: war, the British navy and the contractor state* (Woodbridge, 2010), 144, 218.

43. Jonathan Coad, *Support for the fleet: architecture and engineering of the Royal Navy's bases, 1700–1914* (Swindon, 2013), ch. 1.

44. Chris Tabraham and Doreen Grove, *Fortress Scotland and the Jacobites* (1995), 92–5. See also Andrew Mackillop, 'Confrontation, negotiation and accommodation: garrisoning the burghs in post-Union Scotland', *Journal of Early Modern History*, 15.1–2 (2011), 159–83.

45. Renaud Morieux, *The society of prisoners: Anglo-French wars and incarceration in the eighteenth century* (Oxford, 2019), 366.

46. James Douet, *British barracks, 1600–1914: their architecture and role in society* (1998), 61. Ireland also had many barracks at that time, not

always occupied; see Charles Ivar McGrath, *Ireland and empire, 1692–1770* (2012), ch. 4.

47. Andrew Saunders, *Fortress Britain: artillery fortifications in the British Isles and Ireland* (Liphook, 1989), 141–3, 152.

48. Douet, *British barracks*, 70.

49. Mackillop, '*More fruitful than the soil*'; Christopher Duffy, 'The Jacobite wars, 1708–46', and Charles J. Esdaile, 'The French Revolutionary and Napoleonic Wars, 1793–1815', in Edward M. Spiers, Jeremy A. Crang and Matthew J. Strickland (eds), *A military history of Scotland* (Edinburgh, 2014), 348–82 and 407–35 respectively, especially 412.

50. William Taylor, *The military roads in Scotland* (revised edn, Colonsay, 1996).

51. Patrick Colquhoun, *A treatise on the wealth, power, and resources, of the British Empire* (1814), 228; BPP, 1868–9 (366), XXXV, part 1, 147–89, 446–9.

52. Taylor, *Military roads*, 109–14.

53. Jo Guldi, *Roads to power: Britain invents the infrastructure state* (Cambridge, MA, 2012), significantly exaggerates its case; BPP, 1868–9, XXXV (366), part 1, 109–37, 165–75.

54. P. G. M. Dickson, *The financial revolution in England: a study in the development of public credit, 1688–1756* (1967), part 3.

55. Ranald C. Michie, *The London stock exchange: a history* (Oxford, 1999), 32–3.

56. H. V. Bowen, *The business of empire: the East India Company and imperial Britain, 1756–1833* (Cambridge, 2006), 111. There are very few Scottish addresses or Scottish-sounding names listed in Bank of England, *The names and descriptions of the proprietors of unclaimed dividends on Bank stock, and on the public funds* ([1791]).

57. A. J. Durie, *The Scottish linen industry in the eighteenth century* (Edinburgh, 1979), 23, 164; R. H. Campbell (ed.), *States of the annual progress of the linen manufacture, 1727–1754* (Edinburgh, 1964).

58. Julian Hoppit, 'Compulsion, compensation and property rights in Britain, 1688–1833', *Past and Present*, 210 (2011), 93–28.

59. Annette M. Smith, *Jacobite estates of the forty-five* (Edinburgh, 1982), 211–12, 221.

60. A. D. Cameron, *The Caledonian Canal* (4th edn, Edinburgh, 2005).

61. Hoppit, 'Compulsion', 121–2; [Thomas Smith], *Case of the Lowland distillers in Scotland, humbly submitted to the consideration of the Committee of the Honourable the House of Commons, appointed to inquire into the state of that manufacture* ([Edinburgh, 1798?]), 47.

62. TNA, SP 54/15/47.

63. Horace Walpole, *Memoirs of King George II*, ed. John Brooke, 3 vols (New Haven, CT, 1985), I, 184, and 185 for the Earl of Bath in a similar vein in the same debate.

64. *Parliamentary Register* (1790), 466–7.

65. NRS, CE8/3/87–92.

66. NRS, CE8/1/34, CE8/2/45–7, 160–62.

67. John Houghton, *An account of the acres & houses, with the proportional tax, &c., of each county in England and Wales* (1693); Charles Davenant, *An essay upon ways and means of supplying the war* (1695), table between 76 and 77.

68. L. G. Schwoerer, 'No standing armies!': the antiarmy ideology in seventeenth-century England* (Baltimore, MD, 1974); J. R. Western, *The English militia in the eighteenth century: the story of a political issue, 1660–1802* (1965).

69. Paul Langford, *The excise crisis: society and politics in the age of Walpole* (Oxford, 1975).

70. William Cobbett (ed.), *The parliamentary history of England, from the earliest period to the year 1803*, 36 vols (1806–20), XV, 1307–8.

71. J. R. Breihan, 'Economical reform, 1785–1810' (University of Cambridge PhD thesis, 1977); E. A. Reitan, 'Edmund Burke and economic reform, 1779–83', *Studies in Eighteenth-Century Culture*, 14 (1985), 129–58.

72. Stephen Dowell, *A history of taxation and taxes in England*, 4 vols (2nd edn, 1888), II, 261.

73. John Brewer, 'The misfortunes of Lord Bute: a case-study in eighteenth-century political argument and public opinion', *Historical Journal*, 16.1 (1973), 3–43; Paul Langford, 'South Britons' reception of North Britons, 1707–1820', in T. C. Smout (ed.), *Anglo-Scottish relations from 1603 to 1900*, Proceedings of the British Academy, 127 (Oxford, 2005), 143–69.

74. [Heath], *The case of the county of Devon*, 3.

75. [William Dowdeswell], *An address to such of the electors of Great-Britain as are not makers of cyder and perry* (2nd edn 1763), 10.

76. Patrick Woodland, 'Extra-parliamentary political organization in the making: Benjamin Heath and the opposition to the 1763 cider excise', *Parliamentary History*, 4 (1985), 115–36.

77. Cobbett (ed.), *Parliamentary history*, XXIV, 1231.

78. See, for example, Robert A. Becker, *Revolution, reform, and the politics of American taxation, 1763–1783* (Baton Rouge, LA, 1980).

79. Jack P. Greene, *Peripheries and center: constitutional development in the extended polities of the British Empire and the United States, 1607–1788* (New York, 1986).

80. The best studies of ideas about taxation in the period are William Kennedy, *English taxation, 1640–1799: an essay on policy and opinion* (1913), and Shane Horwell, 'Taxation in British political and economic thought, 1733–1816' (UCL PhD thesis, 2019).

81. Jonathan Swift, 'An answer to a paper called "A memorial for the poor inhabitants, tradesmen and labourers of the Kingdom of Ireland"' [1728], in his *Irish political writings after 1725: a modest proposal and other works*, ed. D. W. Hayton and Adam Rounce (Cambridge, 2018), 27–41, at 34–5.

82. Hoh-Cheung Mui and Lorna H. Mui, 'Smuggling and the British tea trade before 1784', *American Historical Review*, 74.1 (1968), 44–73; Hoh-Cheung Mui and Lorna H. Mui, 'William Pitt and the enforcement of the Commutation Act, 1784–1788', *English Historical Review*, 76 (1961), 447–65.

83. Cobbett (ed.), *Parliamentary history*, XXV, 586.

84. Thomas Jefferson in a letter to James Madison, 28 October 1785, when discussing issues about inequality, at https://founders.archives.gov/documents/Madison/01-08-02-0202, accessed 3 March 2020.

85. Christopher A. Whatley, 'Order and disorder', in Elizabeth Foyster and Christopher A. Whatley (eds), *A history of everyday life in Scotland, 1600 to 1800* (Edinburgh, 2010), 191–216, at 203. See also Whatley, 'How tame were the Scottish Lowlanders during the eighteenth century?'

86. Walter Scott, *The heart of Mid-Lothian*, ed. David Hewitt and Alison Lumsden ([1818], Edinburgh, 2004), 22. See also H. T. Dickinson and Kenneth Logue, 'The Porteous riot: a study of the breakdown of law and order in Edinburgh, 1736–1737', *Scottish Labour History Society Journal*, 10 (1976), 21–40.

87. Andrew Fletcher, *Political works*, ed. John Robertson (Cambridge, 1997), 213.

88. [James Thomson Callender], *The political progress of Britain; or, an impartial account of the principal abuses in the government of this country, from the revolution in 1688* (Edinburgh, [1792]), 3, 7, 9, 11–12. An anonymous pamphlet, said by the *Oxford dictionary of national biography* to be by Callender, had previously argued for the oppressiveness in Scotland of the excise laws in *An impartial account of the conduct of the excise towards the breweries in Scotland* (Edinburgh, 1791).

89. Reay Sabourn, *Oppression exposed, or liberty and property maintained: being an enquiry into the several mismanagements of persons concerned in the revenues of customs and excise in Scotland* (Edinburgh, 1729).

Sabourn defended the Union in *The Scotch prophecy: or, the Lord Bel-haven's remarkable speech before the Union, examin'd and compar'd with the articles afterwards concluded, and now subsisting. Wherein the advantages accruing to Scotland by the Union, are discovered* (1737).

90. [Andrew Hamilton], *An inquiry into the principles of taxation* (1790).

91. N. T. Phillipson, 'Culture and society in the 18th century province: the case of Edinburgh and the Scottish Enlightenment', in Lawrence Stone (ed.), *The university in society*, vol. 2 (Princeton, NJ, 1975), 407–48; Colin Kidd, 'The Phillipsonian Enlightenment', *Modern Intellectual History*, 11.1 (2014), 175–90; Kidd, *Union and unionisms*.

92. Henry Home, Lord Kames, *Sketches of the history of man*, ed. James A. Harris, 3 vols ([1774], Indianapolis, IN, 2006), II, 432–85; Smith, *Wealth of nations*, II, 825–906, at 842.

93. David Hume, *Essays moral, political and literary*, ed. Eugene F. Miller ([1741–76], Indianapolis, IN, 1987), 349–65; Smith, *Wealth of nations*, II, 907–7; [Alexander Montgomerie, Earl of Eglinton], *An inquiry into the original and consequences of the public debt* (Edinburgh, 1753); [Patrick Murray, Lord Elibank], *Thoughts on money, circulation and paper currency* (Edinburgh, 1758); John Dalrymple, Earl of Stair, *The state of the national debt, the national income, and the national expenditure* (1776); William Pulteney, *Considerations on the present state of public affairs, and the means of raising the necessary supplies* (1779). Some of this literature is considered in Istvan Hont, *Jealousy of trade: international competition and the nation-state in historical perspective* (Cambridge, MA, 2005), ch. 4; Donald Winch, 'The political economy of public finance in the "long" eighteenth century', in John Maloney (ed.), *Debt and deficits: an historical perspective* (Cheltenham, 1998), 8–26.

94. Hont, *Jealousy of trade*, ch. 3.

95. General Assembly of the Church of Scotland, *An act for preventing the running of goods, and perjuries in custom-houses* (Edinburgh, 1719); Act of parliament, 5 George I, c. 11.

96. Alexander Murdoch, *'The people above': politics and administration in mid-eighteenth-century Scotland* (Edinburgh, 1980), 124.

97. *The correspondence of Adam Smith*, ed. Ernest Campbell Mossner and Ian Simpson Ross (2nd edn, Oxford, 1987), 290; Gary M. Anderson, William F. Shughart II and Robert D. Tollison, 'Adam Smith in the customhouse', *Journal of Political Economy*, 93.4 (1985), 740–59. Smith's father had been a customs officer and a number of his other relatives worked for the revenue services.

98. Colin Kidd, *Subverting Scotland's past: Scottish Whig historians and the creation of an Anglo-British identity, 1689–c.1830* (Cambridge, 1993), ch. 9; Andrew Mackillop, 'The political culture of the Scottish Highlands from Culloden to Waterloo', *Historical Journal*, 46.3 (2003), 511–32.

99. James Anderson, *An account of the present state of the Hebrides, and western coasts of Scotland* (Edinburgh, 1785). This was a version of a report submitted to the Treasury in 1784, a copy of which is in the Scottish papers of William Pitt the Younger: TNA, PRO 30/8/317, part 3. Anderson reflected more generally on Scotland's economic potential and the impact of political economy in *Observations on the means of exciting a spirit of national industry; chiefly intended to promote the agriculture, commerce, manufactures, and fisheries of Scotland* (Edinburgh, 1777).

100. Anderson, *Observations on the effects of the coal duty*, 17. Other Scots also discussed coal duties and the linked question of duties on salt.

101. Rosalind Mitchison, 'Anderson, James (1739–1808)', *Oxford dictionary of national biography*, online edn.

102. John Sinclair, *A history of the public revenue of the British Empire* (3rd edn, 1803–4), III, 127–51, at 143.

103. Michael Fry, *The Dundas despotism* (Edinburgh, 1992), 63, 65.

104. George Skene Keith, *A general view of the taxes on malt, as imported both in England and in Scotland* (Edinburgh, 1803), 2–3.

105. Geoffrey Holmes and Clyve Jones, 'Trade, the Scots and the parliamentary crisis of 1713', *Parliamentary History*, 1.1 (1982), 47–77.

106. Anon., *A dialogue between a brewer and a gager concerning the malt tax* ([Edinburgh, 1713?]), 1. See also: Anon., *A letter from a brewer in the city, to a justice of the peace in the country, concerning the malt tax* (Edinburgh, 1713); Donald Goodale, *Scotland's complaint against the malt-tax: in a letter from a Scots farmer* ([Edinburgh?], 1718).

107. George Lockhart, *The Lockhart papers: containing memoirs and correspondence upon the affairs of Scotland from 1702 to 1715*, 2 vols (1817), I, 414.

108. Alexander Pennecuik, 'Dialogu[e] betwixt a Glasgow malt-man and an English excise-ma[n]' ([Edinburgh, 1725?]), from the online English Broadside Ballad Archive.

109. TNA, SP/54/15/26.

110. L. D. L., *A letter from a Fyfe gentleman at present in Edinburgh, to the chief magistrate of a burgh in Fyfe, upon our present situation, with regard to the malt-tax* (Edinburgh, 1725), 4. One observer from Elgin in May 1725 believed that 'the whole nation in generall is enraged': TNA, SP/54/15/1.

111. Anon., *Memorial concerning the malt-tax* (Edinburgh, 1726), 1.

112. Anon., *An historical account of the Union betwixt the Egyptians and Israelites* ([Edinburgh, 1725?]), which was branded 'seditious' by the authorities in London: TNA, SP/54/15/1.

113. Anon., *Broad Scotch, address'd to all true Scots men* (2nd edn, Edinburgh, 1734), 6–7.

114. TNA, SP/54/15/55a, SP/54/16/99a, 105d; Anon., *Memorial concerning the malt-tax*, 2; *Journals of the House of Commons*, 20 (1722–7), 594–6, 598, 604.

115. Well studied in T. M. Devine, 'The rise and fall of illicit whisky-making in northern Scotland, *c.*1780–1840', *Scottish Historical Review*, 54.2 (1975), 155–77, and V. E. Dietz, 'The politics of whisky: Scottish distillers, the excise, and the Pittite state', *Journal of British Studies*, 36.1 (1997), 35–69.

116. On output, see Michael S. Moss and John R. Hume, *The making of Scottish whisky: a history of the Scotch whisky distilling industry* (Edinburgh, 2000), 249.

117. Anon., *An apology for whisky* (Edinburgh, 1759).

118. Robert Burns, 'Scotch drink' (1785); NRS, CE8/1/60.

119. See, in general, 'Report from the committee upon the distilleries in Scotland' (1798), but on the specific points made, see 319, 321, 405, 418, 452, 474; 'Report from the committee upon the distilleries in Scotland' (1799), 515.

120. He is not to be confused with John Dalrymple, Earl of Stair, mentioned earlier.

121. John Dalrymple, *Address from Sir John Dalrymple, Bart. one of the Barons of Exchequer in Scotland, to the landholders of England, upon the interest they have in the state of the distillery laws* (Edinburgh, 1786), 4–7.

122. Anon., *Resolutions of the landed interest of Scotland respecting the distillery* (Edinburgh, 1786).

123. [Smith], *Case of the Lowland distillers*, 47.

124. Robert Burns, 'The author's earnest cry and prayer' (1786): 'Freedom an' whisky gang thegither!'

125. Anon., *Case of the Lowland distillers* (1798), 4–6; J. A. Chartres, 'Spirits in the north-east? Gin and other vices in the long eighteenth century', in Helen Berry and Jeremy Gregory (eds), *Creating and consuming culture in north-east England, 1660–1830* (Aldershot, 2004), 37–56, at 53; John Philipson, 'Whisky smuggling on the border in the early nineteenth century', *Archaeologia Aeliana*, 4th Series, 39 (1961), 151–63.

126. 'Report from the committee upon the distilleries in Scotland' (1798), 418.

127. Anon., *Answer to the defence of the Perthshire resolutions* (Edinburgh, 1785), 25.

128. Anon., *Considerations on the impolicy of local exemptions from the payment of excise duties on the distillation of spirits in Scotland* (1797), 83; see 22 for a commitment to the principle of universality.

129. Anon., *Case of the Lowland distillers*, 15.

130. For universalist positions, see Anon., *The distilleries considered, in their connection with the agriculture, commerce, and revenue of Britain* (Edinburgh, 1797), 32; Anon., *Importance of the brewery stated* (Edinburgh, 1797), 4.

131. NRS, E554/3; TNA, PRO30/8/288, f. 56.

132. Discussed in more detail in Hoppit, 'Taxing London'. See also W. J. Hausman, *Public policy and the supply of coal to London, 1700–1770* (New York, 1981).

133. Colley, *Britons*, 64.

134. Arthur Young, *Travels in France during the Years 1787, 1788 and 1789*, ed. Constantia Maxwell (Cambridge, 1929), 16, 49, 72.

135. Jacques Necker, *A treatise on the administration of the finances of France*, trans. Thomas Mortimer, 3 vols (1785), III, 275.

136. Sinclair, *History of the public revenue*, III, 140–41; TNA, CUST17/21.

137. Hansard, *Commons debates*, 16 February 1810, 438.

138. E. H. Hunt, 'Industrialization and regional inequality: wages in Britain, 1760–1914', *Journal of Economic History*, 46.4 (1986), 935–66, at 941.

139. David Macpherson, *Annals of commerce, manufactures, fisheries, and navigation*, 4 vols (1805), III–IV; Michael W. Flinn, *The history of the British coal industry*, vol. 2: *1700–1830: the industrial revolution* (Oxford, 1984), 26; John Ginarlis and Sidney Pollard, 'Roads and waterways, 1750–1850', in Charles H. Feinstein and Sidney Pollard (eds), *Studies in capital formation in the United Kingdom, 1750–1920* (Oxford, 1988), 182–224, at 198–9, 206; Edward Baines, *History of the cotton manufacture in Great Britain* (2nd edn, 1966), 283; Charles K. Hyde, *Technological change and the British iron industry, 1700–1870* (Princeton, NJ, 1977), 123.

140. J. C. Stamp, *British incomes and property: the application of official statistics to economic problems* (1916), 516.

141. In other words, $^{11}/_{15}$ is 73 per cent. The size of the numerator is critical here: if, for example, Scotland's economy was 10 or 12 per cent of Britain's, then its productivity would have been 67 or 80 per cent.

142. Mitchell, 'Englishmen in the Scottish excise department'.

143. TNA, CUST17/21.

144. Harrowby Trust MSS, 525, ff. 1–50; NRS, GD1/54/10. NRS, E555/ 1–40 lists salaries and other expenses of excise collection from 1752. Six years have been sampled, 1752, 1760, 1770, 1776, 1801 and 1815, with tacksmen noted at the first four but not the last two years (E555/1, 18, 24, 26, 40).

145. Anon., *Considerations on the Union between England and Scotland, and on some commercial matters in both kingdoms* (1790), 66.

146. BL, Add. MSS, 33050, ff. 110–87; William Coxe (ed.), *Memoirs of the administration of the Right Honourable Henry Pelham*, 2 vols (1829), II, 412–17, 439–40; Privy Council Office, 'List of charters granted', at https://privycouncil.independent.gov.uk/royal-charters/list-of-charters-granted/, accessed 9 July 2020; Ros Stott, 'Revolution? What revolution? Some thoughts about revestment', *Proceedings of the Isle of Man Natural and Antiquarian Society*, 11 (2003–5), 541–52; NRS, CE8/1, ff. 58, 76–85, CE8/2, ff. 32, 59–60.

147. NRS, E555/40, Tables 23 and 24. See also Table 26.

148. NRS, GD113/4/141/6, 9, 42, 72, 110.

149. From Dumfries in 1749 it was stated that 'Midsummer and Martinmass are the only season when money is to be found in the country, by the returns of cattle from England': NRS, GD113/5/196/4. On slow land tax payments in northern England, see J. V. Beckett, 'Local custom and the "new taxation" in the seventeenth and eighteenth centuries: the example of Cumberland', *Northern History*, 12 (1976), 105–26, at 107.

150. NRS, GD113/5/196/1–34; *Memoirs of the life of Sir John Clerk of Penicuik, Baronet, Baron of the Exchequer, extracted by himself from his own journals, 1676–1755*, ed. John M. Gray, Publications of the Scottish Historical Society, 13 (Edinburgh, 1898), 206.

151. On the lack of JPs, see: *Calendar of Treasury books, October 1706 to December 1707*, vol. 21, part 2, ed. William A. Shaw (1952), 260–61 and 368; Rosalind Mitchison, 'The government and the Highlands, 1707–1745', in N. T. Phillipson and Rosalind Mitchison (eds), *Scotland in the age of improvement: essays in Scottish history in the eighteenth century* (Edinburgh, 1970), 24–46, at 26. On juries, see TNA, SP54/16/70.

152. Duncan Forbes, *Some considerations on the present state of Scotland* (3rd edn, Edinburgh, 1744), 15.

153. Anderson, *Observations*, 460; Colonel David Stewart, *Sketches of the character, manners, and present state of the Highlanders of Scotland*, 2 vols (Edinburgh, 1822), I, 192.

154. [Robert Orr], *An address to the people of Ireland, against an union* (Dublin, 1799), 27–8.

155. John J. W. Jervis, *A letter addressed to the gentlemen of England and Ireland, on the inexpediency of a federal-union between the two kingdoms* (1798), 32.

156. John Foster, *Speech of the Right Honourable John Foster, Speaker of the House of Commons of Ireland ... 11th day of April, 1799* (Dublin, 1799), 104–5.

157. [Colonel Tittler], *Ireland profiting by example; or, the question, whether Scotland has gained, or lost, by an union with England, fairly discussed* (Dublin, 1799), 33; Rev. Dr Clarke [T. B. Clarke], *Misconceptions of facts, and mistatements [sic] of the public accounts, by the Right Hon. John Foster ... proved & corrected according to the official documents and authentic evidence of the Inspector General of Great Britain* (1799).

158. Important context is provided by Alexander Murdoch, 'Henry Dundas, Scotland and the Union with Ireland, 1792–1801', in Bob Harris (ed.), *Scotland in the age of the French Revolution* (Edinburgh, 2005), 125–39.

159. [John Bruce], *Report on the events and circumstances, which produced the Union of the kingdoms of England and Scotland; on the effects of this great national event, on the reciprocal interests of both kingdoms; and on the political and commercial influence of Great-Britain, in the balance of power in Europe*, 2 vols ([1799]).

160. Peter King and Richard Ward, 'Rethinking the Bloody Code in eighteenth-century Britain: capital punishment at the centre and on the periphery', *Past and Present*, 228 (2015), 159–205, at 204–5.

161. Joanna Innes, 'Legislating for three kingdoms: how the Westminster parliament legislated for England, Scotland and Ireland, 1707–1830', in Julian Hoppit (ed.), *Parliaments, nations and identities in Britain and Ireland, 1660–1850* (Manchester, 2003), 15–47.

3. 1801–1914: IRELAND'S CHALLENGE

1. The titles of three important surveys: Asa Briggs, *The age of improvement, 1783–1867* (1959); G. Kitson Clark, *An expanding society: Britain 1830–1900* (Cambridge, 1967); David Cannadine, *Victorious century: the United Kingdom, 1800–1906* (2017).

2. 'Millennium of data', Table A29.

3. Cobbett, *Rural rides*, 83.

4. Norman Gash, 'Cheap government, *1815–1874*', in his *Pillars of government and other essays on state and society, c.1770–c.1880* (1986), 43–54; Philip Harling, *The waning of 'old corruption': the politics of economical reform in Britain, 1779–1846* (Oxford, 1996); Hoppit, 'Checking the Leviathan'.

5. John Morley, *The life of William Ewart Gladstone*, 3 vols (1903), II, 62.

6. Edwin Cannan, *The history of local rates in England in relation to the proper distribution of the burden of taxation* (2nd edn, 1912), 173.

7. Thomas Carlyle, *Selected writings*, ed. Alan Shelston (Harmondsworth, 1980), 67.

8. See, for example, Henry Parnell, *On financial reform* (3rd edn, 1831), 49.

9. Norman Gash, *Mr. Secretary Peel: the life of Sir Robert Peel to 1830* (2nd edn, Harlow, 1985), 226. On the context, see M. J. Cullen, *The statistical movement in early Victorian Britain: the foundations of empirical social research* (Hassocks, 1975).

10. For some suggestive thinking on this, see: Davis and Huttenback, *Mammon and the pursuit of empire*, ch. 5; C. A. Bayly, 'Returning the British to South Asian history: the limits of colonial hegemony', *South Asia*, 17.2 (1994), 1–25; Miles Taylor, 'The 1848 revolutions and the British Empire', *Past and Present*, 166 (2000), 146–80; Martin Daunton, *State and market in Victorian Britain: war, welfare and capitalism* (Woodbridge, 2008), 128–46. On amounts of taxes collected, see Ewout Frankema, 'Raising revenue in the British empire, 1870–1940: how "extractive" were colonial taxes?', *Journal of Global History*, 5.3 (2010), 447–77.

11. A. V. Dicey, *England's case against Home Rule* (3rd edn, 1887), 83.

12. John Prest, *Liberty and locality: parliament, permissive legislation, and ratepayers' democracies in the nineteenth century* (Oxford, 1990); Joanna Innes, 'Forms of "government growth", 1780–1830', in David Feldman and Jon Lawrence (eds), *Structures and transformations in modern British history* (Cambridge, 2011), 74–99.

13. Devine, *The Scottish clearances*; Barbara Lewis Solow, *The land question and the Irish economy, 1870–1903* (Cambridge, MA, 1971), 55.

14. Mitchell, *British historical statistics*, 9–10; Kennedy and Clarkson, 'Birth, death and exile: Irish population history, 1700–1921', 173.

15. Ernest Gellner, *Nations and nationalism* (Oxford, 1983); E. J. Hobsbawm, *Nations and nationalism since 1780: programme, myth, reality* (Cambridge, 1990).

16. T. W. Moody, *Davitt and Irish revolution, 1846–82* (Oxford, 1981), 26.

17. David Armitage, 'Greater Britain: a useful category of historical analysis?', *American Historical Review*, 104.2 (1999), 427–45.

18. Quoted in I. G. C. Hutchison, 'Anglo-Scottish political relations in the nineteenth century, c.1815–1914', in T. C. Smout (ed.), *Anglo-Scottish relations from 1603 to 1900*, Proceedings of the British Academy, 127 (2005), 247–66, at 252.

19. Matthew Arnold, *English literature and Irish politics: the complete prose works of Matthew Arnold* (Ann Arbor, MI, 1973), 277.

20. Léonce de Lavergne, *The rural economy of England, Scotland, and Ireland* (Edinburgh, 1855), 361.

21. Alice Effie Murray, *A history of the commercial and financial relations between England and Ireland from the period of the Restoration* (1903). In general, see: Pauric Travers, 'The financial relations question, 1800–1914', in F. B. Smith (ed.), *Ireland, England, and Australia: essays in honour of Oliver MacDonagh* (Sydney and Cork, 1990), 41–69; Kanter and Walsh (eds), *Taxation, politics, and protest in Ireland*.

22. The standard histories are G. C. Bolton, *The passing of the Irish Act of Union* (Oxford, 1966), and Patrick M. Geoghegan, *The Irish Act of Union: a study in high politics, 1798–1801* (Dublin, 1999). Neither gives much consideration to the financial terms, for which see Trevor McCavery, 'Politics, public finance and the British-Irish Act of Union of 1801', *Transactions of the Royal Historical Society*, 10 (2000), 353–75.

23. Julian Hoppit, 'Introduction', in Julian Hoppit (ed.), *Parliaments, nations and identities in Britain and Ireland, 1660–1850* (Manchester, 2003), 1–14, at 4–5.

24. Lord Byron, *The complete works of Lord Byron* (Paris, 1835), 930. This, probably unknowingly, refashioned Robert Blair's comment of 1652 on the Cromwellian Anglo-Scottish union: 'the embodying of Scotland with England, it will be as when the poor bird is embodied in the hawk that hath eaten it up.' Quoted in Arthur C. Turner, *Scottish Home Rule* (Oxford, 1952), 51.

25. McGrath, *Ireland and empire*; Patrick Walsh, 'Enforcing the fiscal state: the army, the revenue and the Irish experience of the fiscal-military state, 1690–1769', in Aaron Graham and Patrick Walsh (eds), *The British fiscal-military states, 1660–c.1783* (Abingdon, 2016), 131–58; Walsh, 'The fiscal state in Ireland, 1691–1769'.

26. BPP 1868–9, XXXV (366).

27. Julian Hoppit, 'The nation, the state and the first industrial revolution', *Journal of British Studies*, 50.2 (2011), 313; Patrick Walsh, 'Patterns of taxation in eighteenth-century Ireland', in Kanter and Walsh (eds), *Taxation, politics, and protest in Ireland*, 89–119.

28. Duke of Portland to Lord Cornwallis, 25 November 1798: Robert Stewart, Viscount Castlereagh, *Memoirs and correspondence of Viscount Castlereagh*, ed. Charles Vane, Marquess of Londonderry, 12 vols (1848–53), II, 22.

29. Including, for example, Public Record Office of Northern Ireland, Castlereagh papers, D3030/35, 60, 79–85, 87, 1169F–G, 1148/7, 9, 10, 14, 16, 20–22.

30. William Playfair, *The commercial and political atlas; representing, by means of stained copper-plate charts ... the national debt, and other public accounts* (1786); R. V. Clarendon, *A sketch of the revenue and finances of Ireland and of the appropriated funds, loans, and debt of the nation* (London and Dublin, 1791), appendix, liv–lv.

31. Roger Knight, *Britain against Napoleon: the organization of victory, 1793–1815* (2013).

32. Public Record Office of Northern Ireland, T3229/2/35.

33. Jervis, *A letter addressed to the gentlemen of England and Ireland*, 23.

34. Cobbett (ed.), *Parliamentary history*, XXXIV, 689.

35. David Dickson, 'Taxation and disaffection in late eighteenth-century Ireland', in Samuel Clark and James S. Donnelly Jnr (eds), *Irish peasants: violence and political unrest, 1780–1914* (Manchester, 1983), 37–63. On earlier tax riots in Ireland, see Timothy D. Watt, 'Taxation riots and the culture of popular protest in Ireland, 1714–1740', *English Historical Review*, 130 (2015), 1418–48.

36. Nicholas Robinson, 'Marriage against inclination: the Union and caricature', in Dáire Keogh and Kevin Whelan (eds), *Acts of Union: the causes, contexts and consequences of the Act of Union* (Dublin, 2001), 140–58; Roy Douglas, Liam Harte and Jim O'Hara, *Drawing conclusions: a cartoon history of Anglo-Irish relations, 1798–1998* (Belfast, 1998).

37. Foster, *Speech of the Right Honourable John Foster*, 57.

38. Henry Grattan, *The speeches of the Right Honourable Henry Grattan, in the Irish, and in the imperial parliament*, ed. Henry Grattan [Jnr], 4 vols (1822), IV, 11.

39. *Journals of the House of Lords* [Ireland], 8 (1798–1800), 385–6.

40. Trevor McCavery, 'Finance and politics in Ireland, 1801–17', in Kanter and Walsh (eds), *Taxation, politics, and protest in Ireland*, 121–50, at 124–6.

41. Some aspects of this, though not the fiscal dimensions, are discussed in Ron Weir, 'The Scottish and Irish unions: the Victorian view in perspective', in S. J. Connelly (ed.), *Kingdoms united? Great Britain and Ireland since 1500: integration and diversity* (Dublin, 1999), 56–66.

42. Murray, *Commercial and financial relations*, 375.

43. The argument that Ireland's government would become more liberal after the Union was made by Sir Robert Peel Snr: Cobbett (ed.), *Parliamentary history*, XXXIV, 478. On the role of Scottish ideas, see James Stafford, 'The Scottish Enlightenment and the British-Irish Union of 1801', in Naomi Lloyd-Jones and Margaret M. Scull (eds), *Four nations approaches to modern 'British' history: a (dis)United Kingdom?* (2018), 111–34.

44. On the political wrangling involved, see Trevor Robert McCavery, 'Finance and politics in Ireland, 1801–1817' (Queen's University Belfast PhD thesis, 1980).

45. This can be put within the context of an important general assessment by K. Theodore Hoppen, *Governing Hibernia: British politicians and Ireland, 1800–1921* (Oxford, 2016). For a matter-of-fact account of developments, see R. B. McDowell, *The Irish administration, 1801–1914* (1964).

46. Figures have been collected for every tenth year. For 1861, 1871 and 1891, they are taken from J. Morrison Davidson, *Scotia rediviva: Home Rule for Scotland* ([1904]), 45–6; all other years are from BPP: 1812, VIII (125); 1812, VIII (110); 1822, XVI (112); 1831–2, XXVI (310); 1842, XXVI (135); 1852, XXVIII (196); 1892, XLVIII (274); 1902, LV (256); 1912–13, XLIX (190). For population, see Mitchell, *British historical statistics*, 9–10.

47. Rev. Edward Chichester, *Oppressions and cruelties of Irish revenue officers: being the substance of a letter to a British member of parliament* (1818), replied to by an excise official in Aeneas Coffey, *Observations on the Rev. Edward Chichester's pamphlet, entitled Oppressions and cruelties of Irish revenue officers* (1818). See also *Second report from Select Committee on Illicit Distillation in Ireland*, BPP, 1816, IX (490).

48. E. B. McGuire, *Irish whiskey: a history of distilling, the spirit trade, and excise controls in Ireland* (Dublin, 1973), chs 4 and 6; K. H. Connell, 'Illicit distillation: an Irish peasant industry', *Historical Studies*, 3 (1961), 58–91; Robert Shipkey, 'Problems in alcohol production and control in early nineteenth-century Ireland', *Historical Journal*, 16.2 (1973), 291–302; Norma M. Dawson, 'Illicit distillation and the revenue police in Ireland in the eighteenth and nineteenth centuries', *Irish Jurist*, 12.2 (1977), 282–94; James R. Barrett, 'Why Paddy drank: the social importance of whiskey in pre-famine Ireland', *Journal of Popular Culture*, 11.1 (1977), 155–66; Andy Bielenberg, 'The Irish distilling industry under the Union', in David Dickson & Cormac Ó Gráda (eds), *Refiguring Ireland: essays in honour of L. M. Cullen* (Dublin, 2013), 290–315.

49. T. W. H. Crosland, *The wild Irishman* (1905), 29.

50. Murray, *Commercial and financial relations*, 372–3; BPP, 1868–9, XXXV (366), 440–41; BPP, 1814–15, VI (214), 4; BPP, 1849, XXX (423), 2.

51. William James MacNeven and Thomas Emmet, *Pieces of Irish history, illustrative of the Catholics in Ireland* (New York, 1807), 253.

52. Quoted in Martin McElroy, 'The 1830 budget and repeal: parliament and public opinion in Ireland', *Irish Historical Studies*, 36 (2008), 38–52, at 49.

53. Hansard, *Commons debates*, 22 April 1834, 1143.

54. BPP, 1843, XXX (573), 1.

55. Peter Mathias, *The brewing industry in England, 1700–1830* (Cambridge, 1959), 242–3; Eric Tenbus, 'A draught of discontentment: national identity and nostalgia in the Beerhouse Act of 1830', *Brewery History*, 161 (2015), 2–9, ignores Irish and Scottish reactions.

56. Daunton, *Trusting Leviathan*, 191.

57. Hansard, *Commons debates*, 19 February 1845, 789.

58. Robert Peel, *The speeches of the late Right Honourable Sir Robert Peel, Bart. Delivered in the House of Commons*, 4 vols (1853), I, 208.

59. A. O'Neill Daunt, 'The financial relations between Great Britain and Ireland', *Westminster Review*, 147.4 (April, 1897), 379.

60. Hansard, *Commons debates*, 19 February 1845, 769–70.

61. R. M. Martin, *Ireland before and after the Union with Great Britain* (1843), 241.

62. Hansard, *Commons debates*, 19 February 1845, 764.

63. W. N. Calkins, 'A Victorian free trade lobby', *Economic History Review*, 13.1 (1960), 90–104; Stephen Utz, 'Chartism and the income tax', *British Tax Review* (2013), 192–221; Eugenio F. Biagini, 'Popular liberals, Gladstonian finance, and the debate on taxation, 1860–1874', in Eugenio F. Biagini and Alastair J. Reid (eds), *Currents of radicalism: popular radicalism, organised labour and party politics in Britain, 1850–1914* (Cambridge, 1991), 134–62.

64. *Reports of the Select Committee of the House of Commons on public petitions, 1852–3* ([1853?]), appendix, 7.

65. Donal A. Kerr, *Peel, priests, and politics: Sir Robert Peel's administration and the Roman Catholic Church in Ireland, 1841–1846* (Oxford, 1982).

66. W. Neilson Hancock, *Three lectures on the questions, should the principles of political economy be disregarded at the present crisis? And if not, how can they be applied towards the discovery of measures of relief?* (Dublin, 1847). A good recent summary of political economy in Ireland during the Famine years is Tadhg Foley, *Death by discourse? Political economy and the Great Irish Famine* (Hamden, CT, 2016). For

context, see: R. D. Collison Black, *Economic thought and the Irish question, 1817–1870* (Cambridge, 1960); Thomas Boylan and Timothy P. Foley, *Political economy and colonial Ireland: the propagation and ideological function of economic discourse in the nineteenth century* (1992); James Malcolm Stafford, 'Political economy and the reform of empire in Ireland, 1776–1845' (University of Cambridge PhD thesis, 2016).

67. Quoted in Cannadine, *Victorious century*, 173.

68. Quoted in Maurice Wright, *Treasury control of the civil service, 1854–1874* (Oxford, 1969), xx.

69. Hansard, *Commons debates*, 18 April 1853, 1393; J. R. McCulloch, *Observations on the duty on sea-borne coal; and on the peculiar duties and charges on coal, in the Port of London* (1830), 13. Douglas Kanter, 'The politics of Irish taxation, 1842–53', *English Historical Review*, 127 (2012), 1121–55.

70. H. C. G. Matthew, 'Disraeli, Gladstone, and the politics of mid-Victorian budgets', *Historical Journal*, 22.3 (1979), 615–43. In general, see: Francis W. Hirst, *Gladstone as financier and economist* (1931); John Maloney, 'Gladstone and sound Victorian finance', in John Maloney (ed.), *Debt and deficits: an historical perspective* (Cheltenham, 1998), 27–46.

71. Hansard, *Commons debates*, 28 April 1853, 693.

72. *The Economist*, 30 April 1853.

73. Hansard, *Commons debates*, 28 April 1853, 707–8.

74. Hansard, *Commons debates*, 19 April 1858, 1290–91; P. R. Ghosh, 'Disraelian conservatism: a financial approach', *English Historical Review*, 99 (1984), 268–96.

75. Douglas Kanter, 'The campaign against over-taxation, 1863–65: a reappraisal', in Kanter and Walsh (eds), *Taxation, politics, and protest in Ireland*, 227–52.

76. Thomas Kennedy, *A history of the Irish protest against over-taxation, from 1853 to 1897* (Dublin, 1897), 4; *The Times*, 5 January 1897, 11.

77. Joseph M'Kenna in *The Times*, 16 March 1875, 10.

78. Mitchell Henry in *The Times*, 1 May 1883, 10.

79. Kennedy, *Irish protest*, 6.

80. *The Times*, 17 December 1896, 9.

81. *The Times*, 15 September 1896, 7.

82. Kennedy, *Irish protest*, xii.

83. Robert Giffen, 'The economic value of Ireland to Great Britain', *Nineteenth Century*, 19 (1886), 329–45.

84. BPP, 1896, XXXIII (Cmd 8262).

85. *The Times*, 10 September 1896, 7.

86. Quoted in T. M. Kettle, *Home Rule finance: an experiment in justice* (Dublin, 1911), 59.

87. W. Mitchell, *Is Scotland to be sold again? Home Rule for Scotland* (Edinburgh, [1893]), 7.

88. Edgar Crammond, 'The economic position of Scotland and her financial relations with England and Ireland', *Journal of the Royal Statistical Society*, 75.2 (1912), 157–75, at 162.

89. BPP, 1896, XXXIII (Cmd 8262), 24.

90. Frank Geary and Tom Stark, 'Comparative output and growth in the four countries of the United Kingdom, 1861–1911', in Connelly (ed.), *Kingdoms united?*, 153–68.

91. C. H. Lee, *Regional economic growth in the United Kingdom since the 1880s* (1971), chs 3 and 7.

92. Liám Kennedy and Philip Ollerenshaw (eds), *An economic history of Ulster, 1820–1940* (Manchester, 1985).

93. BPP, 1830, XXV (221), 2–3; BPP, 1835, XLVIII (233), 2; BPP, 1847, XXXIV (388), 2; Anon., *The parliamentary gazetteer of Ireland*, 3 vols (Dublin, 1844), I, cviii; BPP, 1857 session 1, III (2186), 135; BPP, 1877, XXVI (Cmd 1791), 94–5; BPP, 1911, LXXV (Cmd 5852), 371.

94. Edward Wakefield, *An account of Ireland, statistical and political*, 2 vols (1812), II, 267.

95. Grattan, *The speeches of Grattan*, I, 10.

96. BPP, 1857 session 1, III (2186), 39.

97. William Webb, *Coastguard! An official history of HM Coastguard* (1976), 14–23.

98. NRS, CE7/12, f. 13.

99. Dawson, 'Illicit distillation'; Jim Herlihy, *The Irish Revenue Police: a short history and genealogical guide to the 'poteen hussars'* (Dublin, 2018).

100. BPP, 1854, X (53), 234–6.

101. George Cornewall Lewis, *On local disturbances in Ireland; and on the Irish Church question* (1836). See also Gash, *Mr. Secretary Peel*, 167–8; Virginia Crossman, *Politics, law and order in nineteenth-century Ireland* (Dublin, 1996).

102. Cornewall Lewis, *On local disturbances in Ireland*, 1.

103. Samuels, *Home Rule finance*, 34; John D. Brewer, *The Royal Irish Constabulary: an oral history* (Belfast, 1990), 24. (I am grateful to Tim Wilson for the latter reference.)

104. José Harris, 'The transition to high politics in English social policy, 1880–1914', in Michael Bentley and John Stevenson (eds), *High and low politics in modern Britain: ten studies* (Oxford, 1983), 58–79, at 60.

105. G. J. Goschen, *Laissez-faire and government interference* (1883).

106. NRS, BR/CCL/1/1, 16.

107. Anon., 'Caledonian Canal', *Blackwood's Edinburgh Magazine*, 7 (July 1820), 427–36; A. D. Cameron, *The Caledonian Canal* (4th edn, Edinburgh, 2005), 100.

108. *The Times*, 24 July 1828, 3.

109. Alexander Somerville, *Letters from Ireland during the Famine of 1847*, ed. K. D. M. Snell (Dublin, 1994), 157; H. J. Hanham, 'The creation of the Scottish Office, 1881–87', *Juridical Review*, 10 (1965), 205–44, at 233.

110. Ian Webster, 'The Public Works Loan Board and the growth of the state in nineteenth-century England', *Economic History Review*, 71.3 (2018), 887–908; McDowell, *The Irish administration*, 203.

111. William F. Bailey, *Local and centralized government in Ireland: a sketch of the existing system* (London and Dublin, 1888), 56.

112. E. P. Hennock, 'Finance and politics in urban local government in England, 1835–1900', *Historical Journal*, 6.2 (1963), 212–25; G. C. Baugh, 'Government grants in aid of the rates in England and Wales, 1889–1990', *Historical Research*, 65 (1992), 215–37; Robert Millward and Sally Sheard, 'The urban fiscal problem, 1870–1914: government expenditure and finance in England and Wales', *Economic History Review*, 48.3 (1995), 501–35; Christine Bellamy, *Administering central-local relations, 1871–1919: the Local Government Board in its fiscal and cultural context* (Manchester, 1998), especially 89 for local debt.

113. Quoted in John Percival Day, *Public administration in the Highlands and Islands of Scotland* (1918), 346. See also J. Watson Grice, *National and local finance: a review of relations between the central and local authorities in England, France, Belgium, and Prussia during the nineteenth century* (1910), 3–6.

114. NRS, GD325/1/461, appendix 1.

115. Charles Read, 'Taxation and the economics of nationalism in 1840s Ireland', in Kanter and Walsh (eds), *Taxation, politics, and protest in Ireland*, 199–225, at 218.

116. Mel Cousins, 'Resistance to the collection of rates under the poor law, 1842–44', in Kanter and Walsh (eds), *Taxation, politics, and protest in Ireland*, 173–98.

117. *The Times*, 2 March 1909, 19; Erskine Childers, *The framework of Home Rule* (1911), 181; Lord Welby, 'Irish finance', in J. H. Morgan (ed.), *The new Irish constitution: an exposition and some arguments* (1912), 112–56, at 141; Cormac Ó Gráda, '"The greatest blessing of

all": the old age pension in Ireland', *Past and Present*, 175 (2002), 124–61; BPP, 1911, XV (Cmd 5827), 80.

118. Joel Mokyr, *Why Ireland starved: a quantitative and analytical history of the Irish economy, 1800–1850* (1983).

119. Foley, *Death by discourse?*; Melissa Fegan, *Literature and the Irish Famine, 1845–1919* (Oxford, 2003); Roy Foster, *Paddy and Mr Punch: connections in Irish and English history* (1993), ch. 9. Fegan and Foster are correcting L. P. Curtis Jnr, *Anglo-Saxons and Celts: a study of anti-Irish prejudice in Victorian England* (Bridgeport, CT, 1968).

120. *The Times*, 15 May 1844, 6; 27 February 1846, 5; 10 March 1847, 5.

121. Hansard, *Commons debates*, 2 March 1849, 110.

122. The charge of genocide can be traced back to the nationalist, republican and racist John Mitchel, in his *The last conquest of Ireland (perhaps)* (Glasgow, 1861). A modern iteration is Tim Pat Coogan, *The famine plot: England's role in Ireland's greatest tragedy* (Basingstoke, 2012). Better works on government policy in Ireland are: Thomas P. O'Neill, 'The organisation and administration of relief, 1845–52', in R. Dudley Edwards and T. Desmond Williams (eds), *The Great Famine: studies in Irish history, 1845–52* (Dublin, 1956), 209–60; Christine Kinealy, *This great calamity: the Irish Famine, 1845–52* (Dublin, 1994); Peter Gray, *Famine, land and politics: British government and Irish society, 1843–1850* (Dublin, 1999).

123. T. M. Devine, *The great Highland famine: hunger, emigration and the Scottish Highlands in the nineteenth century* (Edinburgh, 1988).

124. *The Times*, 10 February 1849, 4; James S. Donnelly Jnr, '"Irish property must pay for Irish poverty": British public opinion and the Great Irish Famine', in Chris Morash and Richard Hayes (eds), *'Fearful realities': new perspectives on the famine* (Dublin, 1996), 60–76.

125. Peter Gray, 'The Great Famine, 1845–1850', in James Kelly (ed.), *The Cambridge history of Ireland*, vol. 3: *1730–1880* (Cambridge, 2018), 639–65, at 655; Charles Read, 'Laissez-faire, the Irish Famine, and British financial crisis', *Economic History Review*, 69.2 (2016), 411–34.

126. Jennifer Hart, 'Sir Charles Trevelyan at the Treasury', *English Historical Review*, 75 (1960), 92–110; a well-evidenced defence of Trevelyan is Robin Haines, *Charles Trevelyan and the Great Irish Famine* (Dublin, 2004).

127. Neilson Hancock, *Three lectures*.

128. National Association for the Vindication of Scottish Rights, *Justice to Scotland. Report of the first public meeting of the National Association for the Vindication of Scottish Rights, held ... November 2, 1853* (Edinburgh, 1853), especially 23–7. For a modern assessment of the

movement, see Graeme Morton, 'Scottish rights and "centralisation" in the mid-nineteenth century', *Nations and Nationalism*, 2.2 (1996), 257–79.

129. [W. Aytoun], 'Scotland since the Union', *Blackwood's Edinburgh Magazine*, 74.455 (September 1853), 266–83, at 283.

130. On unionism in Scotland in the period, see Kidd, *Union and unionisms*, 268–72.

131. Hugh Scott, *The progress of the Scottish national movement* (Edinburgh, 1853); Citizen of Edinburgh, *A vindication of Scottish rights*, 5.

132. Robert Christie, *Injustice to Scotland exposed; in a letter to the Scottish representatives in the Commons' House of Parliament* (Edinburgh, 1854).

133. Dunraven, *The outlook in Ireland*, 157.

134. M. H. Port, *Imperial London: civil government building in London, 1851–1915* (New Haven, CT, 1995), 37.

135. K. Theodore Hoppen, 'Gladstone, Salisbury and the end of Irish assimilation', in Mary E. Daly and K. Theodore Hoppen (eds), *Gladstone: Ireland and beyond* (Dublin, 2011), 45–63, at 59; Edgar Crammond, 'The financial difficulties of Home Rule', *Nineteenth Century*, 70 (1911), 601–26, at 612.

136. Nathan Foley-Fisher and Eoin McLaughlin, 'Capitalising on the Irish land question: land reform and state banking in Ireland, 1891–1938', *Financial History Review*, 23.1 (2016), 71–109, at 74, 89; Martin Daunton, 'Thomas Gibson Bowles v the Bank of England (1913): a modern John Hampden?', in John Snape and Dominic de Cogan, *Landmark cases in revenue law* (Oxford, 2019), 91–118, at 100; Avner Offer, 'Empire and social reform: British overseas investment and domestic politics, 1908–1914', *Historical Journal*, 26.1 (1983), 119–38, at 134.

137. NRS, GD40/16/53, 39r.

138. Catherine B. Shannon, *Arthur J. Balfour and Ireland, 1874–1922* (Washington, DC, 1988), 52. On the Irish Board, see Ciara Breathnach, *The Congested Districts Board, 1891–1923: poverty and development in the west of Ireland* (Cork, 2005); William L. Micks, *An account of the constitution, administration and dissolution of the Congested Districts Board for Ireland from 1891 to 1923* (Dublin, 1925). On the Scottish Board, see Ewen A. Cameron, *Land for the people? The British government and the Scottish Highlands, c.1880–1925* (East Linton, 1996); Alexander S. Mather, 'The Congested Districts Board for Scotland', in William Ritchie, Jeffrey C. Stone and Alexander S. Mather (eds), *Essays for Professor R. E. H. Mellow* (Aberdeen, 1986), 196–204; Percival Day, *Public administration in the Highlands and Islands*.

139. Naomi Lloyd-Jones, 'Liberalism, Scottish nationalism and the Home Rule crisis, *c.*1886–93', *English Historical Review*, 129 (2014), 862–87.

140. 'Year by year England and the British Empire have passed more and more under the sway of the all-conquering Scot': Dunraven, *The outlook in Ireland*, 183–4.

141. Convention of the Royal Burghs of Scotland, *The national meeting in favour of the creation of a separate department of state for Scotland, held within the Free Assembly Hall, Edinburgh on 16th January 1884* (1890); Anon., 'The Union of 1707 viewed financially', *Scottish Review*, 10 (October 1887), 213–34.

142. *The Times*, 4 August 1883, 9; Hanham, 'The creation of the Scottish Office'.

143. Hansard, *Commons debates*, 8 April 1886, 1052.

144. James Mitchell, *Governing Scotland: the invention of administrative devolution* (Houndmills, 2003), ch. 8.

145. Mitchell, *British historical statistics*, 33–4.

146. Hansard, *Commons debates*, 12 May 1892, 794–807.

147. Welby, 'Irish finance'; Patricia Jalland, 'Irish Home-Rule finance: a neglected dimension of the Irish question, 1910–14', *Irish Historical Studies*, 23 (1983), 233–53.

148. Crammond, 'Financial difficulties of Home Rule', 616; *The Times*, 30 April 1912, 7.

149. Crammond, 'Financial difficulties of Home Rule', 623. Similarly, Samuels, *Home Rule finance*, 18.

150. Quoted in Bernard Mallet, *British budgets, 1887–88 to 1912–13* (1913), 29.

151. *The Times*, 5 July 1898, 9.

152. Dicey, *England's case against home rule*, 84.

153. Jackson, *The two unions*.

154. Francis Russell Hart and J. B. Pick, *Neil M. Gunn: a Highland life* (1981), 47.

155. NRS, AD56/127.

156. Samuels, *Home Rule finance*, 81.

157. Thomas Carlyle, 'Occasional discourse on the negro question', *Fraser's Magazine for Town and Country*, 40.240 (1849), 672.

158. Reproduced in the *Wexford Independent*, 24 October 1846.

159. Childers, *Framework of Home Rule*, 262.

160. Wright, *Treasury control*.

161. Stefan Collini, John Burrow and Donald Winch, *That noble science of politics: a study in nineteenth-century intellectual history* (Cambridge,

1983), ch. 8; G. M. Koot, *English historical economics, 1870–1926: the rise of economic history and neomercantilism* (Cambridge, 1987). For intellectual developments more specifically in relation to Irish matters, see: Clive Dewey, 'Celtic agrarian legislation and the Celtic revival: historicist implications of Gladstone's Irish and Scottish Land Acts, 1870–1886', *Past and Present*, 64 (1974), 30–70; Tom Dunne, '*La trahison des clercs*: British intellectuals and the first home-rule crisis', *Irish Historical Studies*, 23 (1982), 134–73; W. C. Lubenow, 'The Liberals and the national question: Irish Home Rule, nationalism, and their relationship to nineteenth-century liberalism', *Parliamentary History*, 13 (1994), 119–42.

162. Hansard, *Commons debates*, 8 April 1886, 1057.

163. H. C. G. Matthew, *Gladstone: 1875–1898* (Oxford, 1995), 215.

164. Hansard, *Commons debates*, 3 April 1871, 1116.

4. 1914–1999: REGIONS AND NATIONS

1. Jim Tomlinson, *Managing the economy, managing the people: narratives of economic life in Britain from Beveridge to Brexit* (Oxford, 2017).

2. Joel Barnett, *Inside the Treasury* (1982).

3. 'Millennium of data', Tables A27 and A29.

4. Catherine Nash, Bryonie Reid and Brian Graham, *Partitioned lives: the Irish borderlands* (Farnham, 2013), 29–33, 50–56.

5. Joan R. Roses and Nikolaus Wolf, 'Aggregate growth, 1913–1950', in Stephen Broadberry and Kevin H. O'Rourke (eds), *The Cambridge economic history of modern Europe*, vol. 2 (Cambridge, 2012), 190.

6. Graham Butler and Gavin Barrett, 'Europe's "other" open-border zone: the Common Travel Area under the shadow of Brexit', *Cambridge Yearbook of European Legal Studies*, 20 (2018), 252–86.

7. Eoin McLaughlin, 'The Irish Revolution and its aftermath: the economic dimension', in John Crowley, Donal Ó Drisceoil, Mike Murphy and John Borgonovo (eds), *Atlas of the Irish Revolution* (Cork, 2017), 762–9; Angus Maddison, *The world economy: a millennial perspective* (Paris, 2001), 185.

8. Thomas Jones, *Whitehall diary*, vol. 3: *Ireland 1918–1925*, ed. Keith Middlemas (Oxford, 1971), 121.

9. Kevin O'Rourke, 'Burn everything British but their coal: the Anglo-Irish economic war of the 1930s', *Journal of Economic History*, 51.2 (1991), 357–66; Ronan Fanning, *The Irish Department of Finance, 1922–58* (Dublin, 1978), 162 and ch. 7.

10. Kevin O'Rourke, *A short history of Brexit: from Brentry to backstop* (2019), ch. 7.

11. Graham Walker, 'Scotland, Northern Ireland, and devolution, 1945–1979', *Journal of British Studies*, 49.1 (2010), 117–42.

12. Arthur S. Quekett, *The constitution of Northern Ireland. Part 1: The origin and development of the constitution* (Belfast, 1928), 31, 43–8.

13. Patrick Buckland, *The factory of grievances: devolved government in Northern Ireland, 1921–39* (Dublin, 1979), 82.

14. R. J. Lawrence, *The government of Northern Ireland: public finance and public services, 1921–1964* (Oxford, 1965), 76.

15. Henry Harrison, *Ulster and the British Empire, 1939: help or hindrance?* (1939), 107.

16. Arthur Berriedale Keith, *The constitution of England from Queen Victoria to George VI*, 2 vols (1940), II, 199.

17. W. S. Armour, *Ulster, Ireland and Britain: a forgotten trust* (1938), 181.

18. Turner, *Scottish Home Rule*, 72.

19. Mitchell, *The Scottish question*; Andrew Marr, *The battle for Scotland* (Harmondsworth, 1992); Alan Butt Philip, *The Welsh question: nationalism in Welsh politics, 1945–1970* (Cardiff, 1975).

20. Gwynfor Evans, President of Plaid Cymru from 1945 to 1981, commissioned the production of Welsh 'national accounts' in the 1950s. Gwynfor Evans, *For the sake of Wales: the memoirs of Gwynfor Evans*, translated from the Welsh by Meic Stephens (Cardiff, 1996), 140; Edward Nevin (ed.), *The social accounts of the Welsh economy, 1948 to 1952* (Aberystwyth, 1956).

21. 'Millennium of data', Table A27. Andrew Dilnot and Carl Emmerson, 'The economic environment', in A. H. Halsey and Josephine Webb (eds), *Twentieth-century British social trends* (Basingstoke, 2000), 324–57, at 340. For a highly informed overview, see Roger Middleton, 'The size and scope of the public sector', in S. J. D. Green and R. C. Whiting (eds), *The boundaries of the state in modern Britain* (Cambridge, 1996), 89–145, and, more exhaustively, Middleton, *Government versus the market*.

22. Dilnot and Emmerson, 'The economic environment', 340.

23. Sandford, *Economics of public finance*, 30; Dilnot and Emmerson, 'The economic environment', 334; R. J. Bennett, *Central government grants to local governments: the political and economic impact of the Rate Support Grant in England and Wales* (Cambridge, 1982), 44.

24. Edgerton, *Warfare state*.

25. Gavin McCrone, 'Scotland's public finances from Goschen to Barnett', *Fraser of Allander Quarterly Economic Commentary*, 24.2 (1999), 30–46, at 42, 44.

26. Peter Robson, 'Appendix: standards of public expenditure in Northern Ireland', in Thomas Wilson (ed.), *Ulster under Home Rule* (1955), 216–17; McCrone, 'Scotland's public finances', 46.

27. Nicholas Crafts, 'The British economy', in Francesca Carnevali and Julie-Marie Strange (eds), *Twentieth-century Britain: economic, cultural and social change* (Harlow, 2007), 7–25, at 10; Clive Lee, *Scotland and the United Kingdom: the economy and the Union in the twentieth century* (Manchester, 1995), 53.

28. Wal Hannington, *The problem of the distressed areas* (1937), 19.

29. Hugh Dalton, *The fateful years: memoirs, 1931–1945* (1957), 463.

30. James A. Bowie, *The future of Scotland: a survey of the present position with some proposals for future policy* (1939), 30; Edwin Muir, *Scottish journey* (1935), 3, a companion volume to J. B. Priestley's well-known *English journey* (1934); Mitchell, *British historical statistics*, 9.

31. Lee, *Scotland and the United Kingdom*, 142.

32. George Malcolm Thomson, *Scotland: that distressed area* (Edinburgh, 1935), 7.

33. Jim Tomlinson, 'De-industrialization not decline: a new meta-narrative for post-war British history', *Twentieth Century British History*, 27.1 (2016), 76–99, at 78.

34. Short, *Public expenditure and taxation*, 34–7, 72–5.

35. Martin Daunton, *Just taxes: the politics of taxation in Britain, 1914–1979* (Cambridge, 2002), 46.

36. *The Times*, 25 March 1931, 15.

37. King and King, *The British tax system*, 19.

38. Institute for Fiscal Studies, *The structure and reform of direct taxation, report of a committee chaired by Professor J. E. Meade* (1978), 89, 98; Daunton, *Just taxes*, 337.

39. Daunton, *Just taxes*, 46, 140, 175, 187, 278, 338.

40. M. J. Daunton, 'Payment and participation: welfare and state-formation in Britain, 1900–1951', *Past and Present*, 150 (1996), 170.

41. Surveyed in Green and Whiting (eds), *The boundaries of the state*. For a comparative overview of the growth of public spending, see Peter Lindert, *Growing public: social spending and economic growth since the eighteenth century*, 2 vols (Cambridge, 2004).

42. Martin Chick, 'Discounting time', in Julian Hoppit, Duncan Needham and Adrian Leonard (eds), *Money and markets: essays in honour of Martin Daunton* (Woodbridge, 2019), 251–62.

43. Ian Levitt (ed.), *Treasury control and public expenditure in Scotland, 1885–1979*, Records of Social and Economic History, New Series, 54 (Oxford, 2014), 179.

44. William Plowden, *The motor car and politics, 1896–1970* (1971).

45. Levitt (ed.), *Treasury control*, 174.

46. Ian Levitt, 'The Scottish Office and St. Kilda, 1885–1930: a steamer too far', in J. Randall (ed.), *The decline and fall of St. Kilda* (Port of Ness, 2006), 51–63.

47. Auditor General [Scotland], 'Transport Scotland's ferry services: impact report' (2019), at https://www.audit-scotland.gov.uk/uploads/docs/report/2017/ir_190919_ferry_services.pdf, accessed 20 July 2020.

48. Highland and Islands Development Board, *Roads to the isles: a study of sea freight charges in the Highlands and Islands* ([Inverness?], 1974); Roy Pedersen, *Who pays the ferryman? The great Scottish ferries swindle* (Edinburgh, 2013), 10–11, 48–50.

49. Levitt (ed.), *Treasury control*, 42.

50. C. de B. Murray, *How Scotland is governed* (Edinburgh, 1938), 5; quote from *The Scotsman*, 10 August 1939 – clipping in NRS, DD15/5/6.

51. Ian Levitt (ed.), *The Scottish Office: depression and reconstruction, 1919–1959*, Scottish History Society, 5th Series, vol. 5 (1992), 97.

52. Quoted in James G. Kellas and Peter Madgwick, 'Territorial ministries: the Scottish and Welsh Offices', in Peter Madgwick and Richard Rose (eds), *The territorial dimension in United Kingdom politics* (1982), 9–33, at 20; Colin Thain and Maurice Wright, *The Treasury and Whitehall: the planning and control of public expenditure, 1976–1993* (Oxford, 1993), ch. 14.

53. Quoted in John Stewart, 'The National Health Service in Scotland, 1947–74: Scottish or British?', *Historical Research*, 76 (2003), 389–410, at 404.

54. Levitt (ed.), *Treasury control*, 203.

55. Patrick Geddes and Victor Branford, 'General Editors' introduction' to C. B. Fawcett, *Provinces of England: a study of some geographical aspects of devolution* (1919), ii–iii.

56. Fawcett, *Provinces of England*, 231 and 264.

57. BPP, 1933–4, XIII (Cmd 4728), 107; Dalton, *The fateful years*, 442; Lord Hailsham, *The door wherein I went* (1975), 210.

58. *The Times*, 20–22 March 1934, 15–16 in each case.

59. Hansard, *Commons debates*, 17 November 1936, 1663.

60. Daniel Ritschel, *The politics of planning: the debate on economic planning in Britain in the 1930s* (Oxford, 1997).

61. Quoted in Nicholas Deakin (ed.), *Origins of the welfare state*, 9 vols (2000), I, xv.

62. BPP, 1964–5, XXX (Cmd 2764).

63. See, for example, G. D. H. Cole and M. I. Cole, *The condition of Britain* (1937).

64. Peter Scott, *The triumph of the south: a regional economic history of early twentieth century Britain* (Aldershot, 2007), 99.

65. S. R. Dennison, *The location of industry and the depressed areas* (Oxford, 1939), 73.

66. Labour Party, *Labour and the Distressed Areas: a programme of immediate action. Interim report of the Labour Party's Commission of Enquiry into the Distressed Areas* (1937), 7.

67. Bowie, *The future of Scotland*, 176.

68. Scottish Committee Communist Party, *A people's plan for Scotland* (Glasgow, [1945?]), 9.

69. David Edgerton, *The rise and fall of the British nation: a twentieth century history* (2018).

70. Ellen Wilkinson, *The town that was murdered: the life-story of Jarrow* (1939), 283.

71. Andrew Dewar Gibb, *Scotland in eclipse* (Edinburgh, 1930), 72.

72. James A. A. Porteous, *Scotland and the south: economic and financial relations* (Stirling, 1947), 28; Herbert Morrison, *Socialisation and transport: the organisation of socialised industries with particular reference to the London Passenger Transport Bill* (1933).

73. D. J. Davies, *Towards Welsh freedom: twenty-seven articles*, ed. Ceinwen Thomas (Cardiff, 1958), 91; Marshall E. Dimock, *British public utilities and national development* (1933).

74. *Aberdeen Press and Journal*, 9 August 1939, letter from 'Man o' Buchan': clipping in NRS, DD15/5/6; Hansard, *Commons debates*, 16 December 1936, 2559–63.

75. Peter Clarke, 'The Treasury's analytical model of the British economy between the wars', in Mary O. Furner and Barry Supple (eds), *The state and economic knowledge: the American and British experiences* (Cambridge, 1990), 171–207, at 173; Thomas L. Heath, *The Treasury* (1927), 1.

76. *Daily Mail*, 29 January 1921, 7; Christopher Hood and Rozana Himaz, *A century of fiscal squeeze politics: 100 years of austerity, politics, and bureaucracy in Britain* (Oxford, 2017), 46–50.

77. Quoted in G. C. Peden, 'The "Treasury view" on public works and employment in the interwar period', *Economic History Review*, 37.2 (1984), 167–81, at 169.

78. Winston S. Churchill, *Great contemporaries* (New York, 1937), 254–5.

79. *The Times*, 4 March 1931, 8.

80. BPP, 1930–31, XVI (Cmd 3920), 13, 20, 220 and quote at 12. The committee was chaired by Sir George May, who had recently retired from spending his career working for the Prudential Assurance Company.

81. The words of the Scottish County Councils Association from 1937, quoted in Richard Saville, 'The industrial background to the post-war Scottish economy', in Richard Saville (ed.), *The economic development of modern Scotland, 1950–1980* (Edinburgh, 1985), 18.

82. G. R. Searle, *The quest for national efficiency: a study in British politics and British political thought, 1899–1914* (Oxford, 1971); J. M. Winter, *The Great War and the British people* (1986); Arthur L. Bowley, *Some economic consequences of the Great War* (1930).

83. Quoted in Ritschel, *The politics of planning*, 26.

84. J. M. Keynes, 'The end of laissez-faire', in his *Essays in persuasion*, ed. Donald Moggridge (Cambridge, 1972), 272–94, at 287.

85. M. J. Daunton, *A property-owning democracy? Housing in Britain* (1987), chs 2 and 3.

86. Marian Bowley, *Housing and the state, 1919–1944* (1945), vi.

87. Levitt (ed.), *The Scottish Office*, 266.

88. Joan Robinson, *The new mercantilism* (Cambridge, 1966); Harry G. Johnson (ed.), *The new mercantilism: some problems in international trade, money and investment* (Oxford, 1974). Quote from J. M. Keynes, *The general theory of employment, interest and money*, ed. Donald Moggridge (Cambridge, 1973), 335.

89. B. Chatterji, 'Business and politics in the 1930s: Lancashire and the making of the Indo-British trade agreement, 1939', *Modern Asian Studies*, 15.3 (1981), 527–73.

90. R. H. Campbell, 'The Scottish Office and the Special Areas in the 1930s', *Historical Journal*, 22.1 (1979), 167–83, at 174; Fredric M. Miller, 'The unemployment policy of the National Government, 1931–1936', *Historical Journal*, 19.2 (1976), 453–76, at 469.

91. Huw T. Edwards, *What I want for Wales* (Carmarthen, 1949), 6.

92. Wayne Parsons, *The political economy of British regional policy* (1988), 189.

93. James Griffiths, *Pages from memory* (1969), 181 and 203.

94. Parsons, *British regional policy*.

95. Dennison, *The location of industry*, 177, 187, 190–92; W. R. Garside, *British unemployment, 1919–1939: a study in public policy* (Cambridge, 1990), ch. 9; Scott, *Triumph of the south*, 219.

96. Dennison, *The location of industry*, 84.

97. BPP, 1930–31, XVI (Cmd 3920), 19.

98. Thomson, *Scotland: that distressed area*, 96.

99. Hannington, *Distressed areas*, 26–7, 217; Anon., 'The betrayal of the Special Areas', *Spectator*, 13 November 1936, 840.

100. Lachlan Grant, *A new deal for the Highlands* ([Oban], 1935), 18, 25, 30.

101. Hansard, *Commons debates*, 16 December 1936, 2520, 2534.

102. [Ruaraidh Hilleary], *The Highlands and Islands of Scotland. A review of the economic conditions with recommendations for improvement* (1938), 17, 25, 28, 63, 75. This is usually called the Hilleary Report, after its chairman.

103. There is a useful collection of newspaper clippings responding to both the report and the government's reaction in NRS, DD15/5/6. Hansard, *Commons debates*, 4 August 1939, 2919.

104. NRS, DD5/558, letter from J. Alston to ?, 16 November 1925. Similarly, see in the same file the letter from R. E. Muirhead to A. D. McInnes Shaw, MP, 14 June 1926. On the national breakdowns of public finances, see Hansard, *Commons debates*, 3 February 1926, 141 written answers. *Aberdeen Press and Journal*, 9 January 1933: clipping in NRS, DD10/290.

105. NRS, GD325/1/153: memo by the Scottish Land and Property Federation to Lord Colwyn's committee on national debt and taxation, October 1924; *Glasgow Herald*, 2 March 1933, report on Scottish National Development Council.

106. *Scotsman*, 6 April 1939: clipping in NRS, AF43/343.

107. Paul Addison, *The road to 1945: British politics and the Second World War* (1975).

108. BPP, 1942–3, VI (Cmd 6404), 6–7.

109. Sir Norman Chester, *The nationalisation of British industry, 1945–1951* (1957), 1017.

110. David Parker, *The official history of privatisation*, vol. 1: *The formative years, 1970–1987* (2009), 7.

111. This quote is widely repeated, but I have not found the original source.

112. Stewart, 'The National Health Service in Scotland'.

113. Richard Pryke, *Public enterprise in practice: the British experience of nationalization over two decades* (1971); Richard Pryke, *The nationalised*

industries: policies and performance since 1968 (Oxford, 1981); Parker, *Official history of privatisation*, vol. 1, 12–17.

114. Robert Bradley, 'Colliery closures since 1947', at http://www.healey hero.co.uk /rescue/individual /Bob_Bradley/PM-Closures.html, accessed 8 October 2019.

115. BPP, 1939–40, IV (Cmd 6153); Hansard, *Commons debates*, 21 March 1945, 838.

116. Alan Booth, 'The Second World War and the origins of modern regional policy', *Economy and Society*, 11.1 (1982), 1–21; Richard Toye, *The Labour party and the planned economy, 1931–1951* (Woodbridge, 2003).

117. John Tomaney, 'The idea of English regionalism', in Robert Hazell (ed.), *The English question* (Manchester, 2006), 158–73, at 167.

118. Patrick Abercrombie and Robert H. Matthew, *The Clyde Valley regional plan, 1946* (Edinburgh, 1949), 7; Ian Levitt, 'New towns, new Scotland, new ideology, 1937–57', *Scottish Historical Review*, 76.2 (1997), 229.

119. J. B. Cullingworth, *Environmental planning, 1939–1969*, vol. 3: *New towns policy* (1979), 46, 120 (Macmillan quote), 122, 125, 452, 530, 603–4.

120. Gwynfor Evans and Ioan Rhys, 'Wales', in Owen Dudley Edwards, Gwynfor Evans, Ioan Rhys and Hugh MacDiarmid, *Celtic nationalism* (1968), 213–98, at 274–5.

121. Anon., 'North to Elizabetha', *The Economist*, 8 December 1962, 989–90.

122. Kim Swales, 'Civil service dispersal – a long time coming', *Fraser of Allander Quarterly Economic Commentary*, 8.1 (1982), 38–41.

123. Evans, *For the sake of Wales*, 186.

124. Arthur Geddes, *The Highlands and Islands: their regional planning* (Edinburgh, 1949), 45, 53; Arthur Geddes, *The Isle of Lewis and Harris: a study in British community* (Edinburgh, 1955).

125. R. H. Law, 'Highland development: a strategic appreciation', NRS, SEP4/1929.

126. Highlands and Islands Development Board, *First report, 1 November 1965 to 31 December 1966* (Inverness, 1967), unpaginated 'Foreword'.

127. Highlands and Islands Development Board, *Fifth report 1970* (Inverness, 1971), 5.

128. Highlands and Islands Development Board, *25th annual report 1990* ([Inverness, 1990?]), iii–iv.

129. Sir Kenneth Alexander, 'The Highlands and Islands Development Board', in Saville (ed.), *Economic development of modern Scotland*,

231; Scottish Government, *Highlands and Islands Scotland: European Regional Development Fund, 2007–2013* (Edinburgh, 2008), 11.

130. Sean Straw and John W. Young, 'The Wilson government and the demise of TSR-2, October 1964–April 1965', *Journal of Strategic Studies*, 20.4 (1997), 18–44, at 22, 26.

131. Peter Hall, *Great planning disasters* (1980), ch. 4.

132. James Grassie, *Highland experiment: the story of the Highlands and Islands Development Board* (Aberdeen, 1983).

133. Graham Brownlow, 'Soft budget constraints and regional industrial policy: reinterpreting the rise and fall of DeLorean', Queen's University Centre for Economic History, Working Paper 14-09, 2014.

134. Amanda Root, 'Transport and communications', in Halsey and Webb (eds), *Twentieth-century British social trends*, 437–68.

135. David Heald, 'Accounting for the Severn Bridge', *Financial Accountability and Management*, 7.4 (1991), 267–9.

136. Nicholas Crickhowell, *Westminster, Wales and water* (Cardiff, 1999), 141 and 145.

137. Sir Ernest Benn, 'The case against planning', *Today and Tomorrow*, 3.1 (1932), 46–52, at 50.

138. Mancur Olson, *The logic of collective action: public goods and the theory of groups* (Cambridge, MA, 1965).

139. James G. Kellas and Peter Madgwick, 'Territorial ministries: the Scottish and Welsh Offices', in Madgwick and Rose (eds), *The territorial dimension*, 9–33, at 18–19.

140. John Jewkes, *Ordeal by planning* (1948), viii.

141. Quoted in Matthew Cragoe, ' "We like local patriotism": the Conservative party and the discourse of decentralization, 1947–51', *English Historical Review*, 122 (2007), 965–85, at 980.

142. George Allen, 'The geography of liberty', in George Watson (ed.), *The unservile state: essays in liberty and welfare* (1957), 131–47, at 136.

143. John Kendle, *Federal Britain: a history* (1997), x. For the quote, see G. D. H. Cole, 'Plan for living', in G. D. H. Cole et al., *Plan for Britain: a collection of essays prepared for the Fabian Society* (1943), 1–33, at 26; also Aneurin Bevan, 'The claim of Wales: a statement', *Wales, the national magazine*, 7.27 (December, 1947), 151–3, at 151. A mid-Victorian debate over centralization is well summarized by K. Theodore Hoppen, *The mid-Victorian generation, 1846–1886* (Oxford, 1998), 104–8.

144. May L. Dhonau, *Decentralisation in government departments* (1938), 15.

145. Chester, *The nationalisation of British industry*, 1034.

In the end decentralisation to be significant implies a right to take a
decision on one's own responsibility without getting higher approval.
When these rights are exercised by a number of boards or individuals
it has to be accepted that diversity will follow – that the attitude
taken in Scotland will differ from that taken in Wales or Lancashire.
But diversity is not always a convenient state of affairs for Ministers
and senior civil servants – coordination, leading to agreed attitudes,
is the less embarrassing administrative arrangement.

146. Thomas Johnston, *Memories* (1952), 166.
147. Graham Brownlow, 'The causes and consequences of rent-seeking in
     Northern Ireland, 1945–72', *Economic History Review*, 60.1 (2007),
     70–96, at 71.
148. Kendle, *Federal Britain*, 162–7; Hansard, *Commons debates*, 13 Janu-
     ary 1976, 216, 237.
149. Matthew Keep, 'The Barnett Formula', House of Commons Library,
     Briefing Paper 7386, 23 January 2018.
150. McCrone, 'Scotland's public finances'; Arthur Midwinter, 'The Barnett
     Formula and public spending in Scotland: policy and practice', *Scottish
     Affairs*, 28 (1999), 83–92; McLean and McMillan, *State of the Union*;
     Mitchell, *The Scottish question*, 233–5; BPP, 1997–8, HC 341.
151. HM Treasury, *Needs assessment study – report* (1979), 4; Kellas and
     Madgwick, 'Territorial ministries', 22.
152. NRS, SOE6/1/1708–9, with the quote at 1708, 14 August 1984.
153. Christopher Harvie, *Fool's gold: the story of North Sea oil* (1994);
     David Heald, *Financing devolution within the United Kingdom: a study
     of the lessons from failure* (Canberra, 1980), 76.
154. Alex Kemp, *The official history of North Sea oil and gas*, vol. 1: *The
     growing dominance of the state* (2012), ch. 2.
155. Scottish National Party, *Scotland pays her way* (n.p., 1996); Nigel Law-
     son, *The view from No. 11: memoirs of a Tory radical* (1992), 989.
156. [Scottish National Party], *The new Scotland* (n.p., [1972?]).
157. EEC, 'Treaty of Rome', at https://ec.europa.eu/romania/sites/romania/
     files/tratatul_de_la_roma.pdf, accessed 18 September 2019.
158. Raphael Samuel, 'Mrs Thatcher and Victorian values', in his *Island
     stories: unravelling Britain* (1998), 330–48.
159. Margaret Thatcher, *The collected speeches of Margaret Thatcher*, ed.
     Robin Harris (1997), 297.
160. David Torrance, *'We in Scotland': Thatcherism in a cold climate* (Edin-
     burgh, 2009), 107–11; Finlay, 'Unionism and the dependency culture',
     100; Ewen A. Cameron, 'The stateless nation and the British state since

1918', in T. M. Devine and Jenny Wormald (eds), *The Oxford handbook of modern Scottish history* (Oxford, 2012), 620–34.

161. Thatcher, *Collected speeches*, 306.

162. Ian Gilmour, *Dancing with dogma: Britain under Thatcherism* (1992), 212–20; Cragoe, '"We like local patriotism"', 980.

163. Sam Wetherell, 'Freedom planned: enterprise zones and urban non-planning in post-war Britain', *Twentieth Century British History*, 27.2 (2016), 266–89; Otto Saumarez Smith, 'Action for cities: the Thatcher government and inner-city policy', *Urban History*, 47 (2020), 274–91; Jeppe Mulich, *In a sea of empires: networks and crossings in the revolutionary Caribbean* (Cambridge, 2020), ch. 2.

164. Tony Travers, *The politics of local government finance* (1986), 5.

165. Thatcher, *Collected speeches*, 301–2.

166. David Butler, Andrew Adonis and Tony Travers, *Failure in British government: the politics of the poll tax* (Oxford, 1994), 167.

167. Danny Burns, *Poll tax rebellion* (Stirling, 1992), 55.

168. Lawson, *The view from No. 11*, 584; Gilmour, *Dancing with dogma*, 218–19.

169. Dennison, *The location of industry*, 104; McCrone, 'Scotland's public finances', 30–31.

170. Marr, *The battle for Scotland*, 152.

171. Margaret Thatcher, 'Interview for *Woman's Own*', at https://www.margaretthatcher.org/document/106689, accessed 15 October 2019; Norbert Elias, *The society of individuals*, ed. Michael Schröter, trans. Edmund Jephcott (Oxford, 1991), vii.

5. 1999–2020: CONCLUSION

1. David McCrone, *Understanding Scotland: the sociology of a nation* (New York and London, 2001), 90–93; Fiscal Commission Working Group, *Principles*, 110; McLean and McMillan, *State of the Union*, 196.

2. For a summary, after leaving office, see John Major, 'Say no to this doomed enterprise', *The Times*, 30 August 1997, 20.

3. Jim Sillars, *Scotland: the case for optimism* (Edinburgh, 1986), 1, 106.

4. Evans and Rhys, 'Wales', 213–98.

5. Tony Blair, *A journey* (2010), 251; the standard account of devolution is Bogdanor, *Devolution*.

6. Selina Chen and Tony Wright (eds), *The English question*, Fabian Society (2000); Robert Hazell (ed.), *The English question* (Manchester,

2006); Richard Weight, *Patriots: national identity in Britain 1940–2000* (2002), 726.

7. Mark Sandford (ed.), *The northern veto* (Manchester, 2009).

8. Hansard, *Commons debates*, 3 April 1871, 1116.

9. Craig Berry and Arianna Giovannini, 'Introduction: powerhouse politics and economic development in the north', in Craig Berry and Arianna Giovannini (eds), *Developing England's north: the political economy of the Northern Powerhouse* (Cham, Switzerland, 2018), 1–19, at 7.

10. Liesbet Hooghe, Gary Marks, Arjan H. Schakel, Sara Niedzwiecki, Sandra Chapman Osterkatz and Sarah Shair-Rosenfield, *Measuring regional authority: a postfunctionalist theory of governance*, vol. 1 (Oxford, 2016), 409.

11. Civil Service, 'Introduction to devolution' ([2017?]), 6, at https://assets.pub lishing.service.gov.uk/government/uploads/system/uploads/attachment_data/file/770300/IntroductionToDevolution.pdf, accessed 20 April 2020.

12. Bogdanor, *Devolution*, 235.

13. Ben Deaner and David Phillips, *Government spending on public services in Scotland: current patterns and future issues*, Institute for Fiscal Studies (2013), 3; David Bell and Alex Christie, 'Finance – the Barnett Formula: nobody's child?', in Alan Trench (ed.), *The state of the nations* (2001), 135–51, at 140.

14. David B. Smith, 'Historical trends in the government spending and tax ratios', in Philip Booth (ed.), *Taxation, government spending and economic growth*, Institute of Economic Affairs (2016), 48–65, at 64.

15. LSE, *London's place in the UK economy, 2009–10* (2009), 17.

16. Michael Kitson and Jonathan Michie, 'The de-industrial revolution: the rise and fall of UK manufacturing, 1870–2010', in Roderick Floud, Jane Humphries and Paul Johnson (eds), *The Cambridge economic history of modern Britain*, vol. 2: *1870 to present* (Cambridge, 2014), 302–29; Paul N. Balchin, *Regional policy in Britain: the north–south divide* (1990), 13, 16.

17. Oxford Economics, *London's competitive place in the UK and global economies* (2011), 3, 9, 32, 33; ONS, 'Population of the UK by country of birth and nationality', at https://www.ons.gov.uk/peoplepopulation andcommunity/populationandmigration/internationalmigration/bulletins /ukpopulationbycountryofbirthandnationality/july2018tojune2019/re lateddata, Table 1.2, accessed 8 April 2020.

18. LSE, *London's place, 2009–10*, 28.

19. Daniel Dorling and Bethan Thomas, *People and places: a 2001 census atlas of the UK* (Bristol, 2004), 183.

20. Transport for London, 'Annual report and statement of accounts, 2018/19', at http://content.tfl.gov.uk/board-20190724–agenda-item08–annual-report-and-accounts.pdf, 118, accessed 8 April 2020.

21. BBC, 'Crossrail Delay: line will not open until 2021 as costs increase', at https://www.bbc.co.uk/news/business-50345344, accessed 14 April 2020; Transport for London, 'Mayoral community infrastructure levy', at https://tfl.gov.uk/info-for/urban-planning-and-construction/planning-applications/community-infrastructure-levy#on-this-page-6, accessed 14 April 2020.

22. London First, https://www.londonfirst.co.uk/about-us/our-achievements, accessed 14 April 2020.

23. Joan McAlpine, 'Real subsidy junkies are in the south-east', *Daily Record*, 3 December 2013, at https://www.dailyrecord.co.uk/news/politics/joan-mcalpine-real-subsidy-junkies-2877045, accessed 4 July 2019; Iain Deas, Graham Haughton and Stephen Hincks, 'Size matters? London – the subsidy junky', at https://citiesmcr.wordpress.com /2014/03/24/size-matters-london-the-subsidy-junky, accessed 9 July 2019.

24. Jim Gallagher, 'The ghost in the machine? The government of England', in Michael Kenny, Iain McLean and Akash Paun (eds), *Governing England: English identity and institutions in a changing United Kingdom*, Proceedings of the British Academy, 217 (Oxford, 2018), 69–90; and, in the same volume, Iain McLean, 'England in a changing fiscal union', 227–44.

25. Bogdanor, *Devolution*, 248; LSE, *London's place in the UK economy* (2002), 56–61; LSE, *London's place, 2009–10*, 108; Oxford Economics, *London's competitive place*, 3; Doreen Massey, *World city* (Cambridge, 2007), 123, 131.

26. Oxford Economics, *Regional winners and losers in UK public finances* (2008), 9; Smith, 'Historical trends in the government spending and tax ratios', 63.

27. Institute for Public Policy Research Commission on Economic Justice, *Prosperity and justice: a plan for the new economy* (Cambridge, 2018), 18–19; John Bachtler, 'Regional disparities in the United Kingdom', in Helmut Karl and Philippe Rollet (eds), *Employment and regional development policy: market efficiency versus policy intervention* (Hanover, 2004), 36–49. On London's Gini coefficient, a way of measuring inequality, see David Bell, David Eiser and Michael McGoldrick, *Inequality in Scotland: new perspectives*, David Hume Institute (Stirling, 2014), 13.

28. Ash Amin, Doreen Massey and Nigel Thrift, *Decentering the nation: a radical approach to regional inequality* (2003), 8.

29. David Russell, *Looking north: Northern England and the national imagination* (Manchester, 2004), xi; Ronald L. Martin, 'The contemporary debate over the north–south divide: images and realities of regional inequality in late-twentieth-century Britain', in Alan R. H. Baker and Mark Billinge (eds), *Geographies of England: the north–south divide, material and imagined* (Cambridge, 2004), 15–43.

30. Luke Raikes, Arianna Giovannini and Bianca Getzel, *Divided and connected: regional inequalities in the north, the UK and the developed world. State of the north 2019*, Institute for Public Policy Research (Manchester, 2019), 8.

31. Martin and Gardiner, 'Reviving the "Northern Powerhouse"', 25.

32. George Osborne, 'We need a Northern powerhouse', speech in Manchester, 23 June 2014, at https://www.gov.uk/government/speeches/chancellor-we-need-a-northern-powerhouse, accessed 21 June 2019.

33. Boris Johnson, htttps://www.politicshome.com/news/article/read-in-full-boris-johnsons-speech-to-the-2019–conservative-party-conference, accessed 14 April 2020; Margaret Thatcher, 'Remarks returning to Central Office', 12 June 1987, at https:// www.margaretthatcher.org/document/106653, accessed 14 April 2020.

34. Independent Commission on Funding & Finance for Wales, *First report. Funding devolved government in Wales: Barnett & beyond* (2009), 23; Independent Commission on Funding & Finance for Wales, *Final report. Fairness and accountability: a new funding settlement for Wales: full text* (2010).

35. Bell and Christie, 'Finance', 139.

36. G. C. Baugh, 'Government grants in aid of the rates in England and Wales, 1889–1990', *Historical Research*, 65 (1992), 215–37, at 221.

37. Independent Commission on Funding & Finance for Wales, *Fairness and accountability*, 21–2.

38. Quoted in Alexander Malcolm MacEwen, *The thistle and the rose: Scotland's problem to-day* (Edinburgh, 1932), 6.

39. Scottish Government, *Scotland's future: your guide to an independent Scotland* (Edinburgh, 2013); Fiscal Commission Working Group, *Principles*.

40. Scottish Government, *Scotland's future*, 5.

41. Institute for Fiscal Studies, *Tax by design: the Mirrlees review* (Oxford, 2011).

42. Scottish Government, *Scotland's future*, 7.

43. HM Government, *Scotland analysis: devolution and the implications of Scottish independence* (2013), Cmd 8554, 5; HM Treasury, *Scotland analysis: currency and monetary policy* (2013), Cmd 8594, 5.

44. HM Government, *Scotland analysis*, 21.

45. Gordon Brown, *My life, our times* (2018), 121.

46. Charlie Jeffery and Ray Perman, 'Introduction' to Charlie Jeffery and Ray Perman (eds), *Scotland's decision: 16 questions to think about for the referendum on 18 September* (Edinburgh, 2014), 2–3, at 2.

47. Iain McLean, Jim Gallagher and Guy Lodge, *Scotland's choices: the referendum and what happens afterwards* (Edinburgh, 2013), 41.

48. David Phillips, 'Question 3: What would the picture for the Scottish government's finances be if Scotland votes yes? What if it votes no?', in Jeffery and Perman (eds), *Scotland's decision*, 18–21, at 19.

49. Michael Amior, Rowena Crawford and Gemma Tetlow, *Fiscal sustainability of an independent Scotland*, Institute for Fiscal Studies (2013), 9.

50. Ibid., 37.

51. Sustainable Growth Commission, *Scotland – the new case for optimism: a strategy for inter-generational economic renaissance* ([Edinburgh], 2018).

52. David Bell, 'Question 1: What would the outlook for Scotland's economy be if the vote is Yes/if the vote is No?', in Jeffery and Perman (eds), *Scotland's decision*, 9–13, at 12; Bell, Eiser and McGoldrick, *Inequality in Scotland*, 25.

53. BBC, 'BBC survey indicates support for Scottish "devo-max"', at https://www.bbc.co.uk/news/uk-scotland-scotland-politics-15610909, accessed 20 April 2020; David McCrone, 'Scotland out of the Union? The rise and rise of the nationalist agenda', *Political Quarterly*, 83.1 (2012), 69–76, at 74.

54. Jeffery and Perman, 'Introduction', 2.

55. Fraser of Allander Institute, *Scotland's budget – 2016* (Strathclyde, 2016), 38–9; Guto Ifan and Ed Gareth Poole, *The Welsh tax base: risks and opportunities after fiscal devolution*, Wales Centre for Public Policy (Cardiff, 2018), 4.

56. Fraser of Allander Institute, *Scotland's budget*, iii.

57. David Phillips, 'GERS shows that Scotland's fiscal position continues to be weak but tells us much more as well' (2018) at https:// www.ifs.org.uk/publications/13287, accessed 2 November 2019.

58. Bernard Burrows and Geoffrey Denton, *Devolution or federalism? Options for the United Kingdom* (1980), 47.

59. HM Revenue and Customs, 'Rural fuel duty relief' (2015), at https://assets.publishing.service.gov.uk/government/uploads/system/uploads/attachment_data/file/395158/Rural_Fuel_Duty_Relief_-_TIIN.pdf, accessed 28 April 2020.

60. Levitt (ed.), *Treasury control*, 80.

61. Alan Travers, 'Thatcher government toyed with evacuating Liverpool after 1981 riots', *Guardian*, 30 December 2011.

62. David Walker, *In praise of centralism: a critique of the new localism* (2002).

63. Quoted in Paul Henderson Scott, *'The boasted advantages': the consequences of the Union of 1707* (Edinburgh, 1999), 5.

64. Nassau William Senior, *Journals, conversations and essays relating to Ireland*, 2 vols (1868), I, 216.

65. An influential work on conceptualizing peripheries is Rokkan and Urwin, *Economy, territory, identity*.

66. Davies, *Towards Welsh freedom*, 85; Edgar L. Chappell, *Wake up Wales! A survey of Welsh Home Rule activities* (1943), 7.

67. Independent Commission on Funding & Finance for Wales, *Fairness and accountability*, 37.

68. Jim Cuthbert and Margaret Cuthbert, 'GERS: where now?', in Donald MacKay (ed.), *Scotland's economic future*, Reform Scotland (Edinburgh, 2011), 35–44, at 40.

69. Bob Kernohan, Director of Scottish Conservative Central Office, quoted in Ian Lang, *Blue remembered years: a political memoir* (2002), 198. Similarly, Turner, *Scottish Home Rule*, 52.

70. G. E. Aylmer, 'The peculiarities of the English state', *Journal of Historical Sociology*, 3.2 (1990), 91–108; Martin Loughlin, 'Evolution and *gestalt* of the state in the United Kingdom', in Armin von Bogdandy, Peter M. Huber Sabino Cassese and (eds), *The administrative state* (Oxford, 2017), 451–92; Philip Corrigan and Derek Sayer, *The great arch: English state formation as cultural change* (Oxford, 1985).

71. John Brewer and Eckhart Hellmuth, 'Introduction: rethinking Leviathan', in John Brewer and Eckhart Hellmuth (eds), *Rethinking Leviathan: the eighteenth-century state in Britain and Germany* (Oxford, 1999), 1–21, at 9.

72. Jack Brand, *Local government reform in England, 1888–1974* (1974).

73. Jackson, *The two unions*; Kidd, *Union and unionisms*; McLean and McMillan, *State of the Union*.

74. David Eastwood, Laurence Brockliss and Michael John, 'From dynastic union to unitary state: the European experience', in Laurence Brockliss and David Eastwood (eds), *A union of multiple identities: The British Isles, c.1750–c.1850* (Manchester, 1997), 193–212, at 195.

75. Quoted in David Steele, 'A new union for today's world', *David Hume Institute Occasional Papers*, 97 (Edinburgh, 2013), 10.

76. Iain McLean, 'A fiscal constitution for the UK', in Chen and Wright (eds), *The English question*, 80.
77. R. H. S. Crossman, *Planning for freedom* (1965), 3.
78. Bogdanor, *Beyond Brexit*, 185–9.
79. Iain McLean, *The fiscal crises of the United Kingdom* (Basingstoke, 2005).
80. Paul Collier, *The future of capitalism: facing the new anxieties* (2019), ch. 7.

Bibliography

Place of publication in the references included in this bibliography, and in source details for the figures, tables and maps, is London unless stated otherwise.

MANUSCRIPT SOURCES
British Library

Add. MSS, 8133, Musgrave papers
Add. MSS, 33050, Newcastle papers
Add. MSS 70047, Portland papers
Harleian MSS, 4226–7

The National Archives, Kew

CUST 17/21, States of navigation, commerce and revenue
CUST 145/4–13: European State Finance Database, at https://www.esfdb. org/table.aspx?resourceid=12801, accessed 16 August 2015
PRO 30/8/288, 317, Pitt papers
SP 54/15–16, State papers Scotland
T 64/236, Treasury: miscellaneous records of Scotland. Interim report of the Commissioners of the Equivalent

National Records of Scotland

AD 56/127, Inland Revenue: correspondence relating to customs and excise – general

AF43/343, Forth Road Bridge
BR/CCL/1, Caledonian Canal
CE7/12, Scottish Excise Board: letter books
CE8/1–3, Scottish Excise Board
DD10/290, Industrial development
DD5/558, Local government files: taxation in Scotland; imperial taxation; comparisons of English and Scottish grants
DD15/5/6, Highland development files: Highland Development Committee
E26/12/2–4, Exchequer records: Treasury accounts
E231/9/3, Gross and net produce of customs, 1707–34
E501/27–111, Customs: general accounts
E554/3–4, Exchequer records: states of accounts
E555/1–40, Exchequer records: collectors' states of accounts
GD1/54/10, Haddington documents and miscellaneous papers
GD40/16/53, Political and official papers of Schomberg Henry Kerr, 9th Marquess of Lothian, Secretary of State for Scotland
GD113/4/141, GD113/5/196/1–34, Papers of George Innes
GD325/1/461, 'Local taxation: its relations to imperial taxation', by James T. Sellar
GD325/1/153, Scottish Landowners' Federation: correspondence subject files
SEP4/1929, Regional industrial promotion and development files
SOE6/1/1708–9, Local government and general files: needs assessment study

Public Record Office of Northern Ireland

D3030, Castlereagh papers
T3229/2/35, Photocopy of Sneyd MSS at Keele

Sandon Hall, Staffordshire

Harrowby Trust MSS, 525, Employment of excise

GOVERNMENT PUBLICATIONS, INCLUDING OF THE DEVOLVED ADMINISTRATIONS
British Parliamentary Papers, in chronological order

1805, VI (56): *Finance accounts of Great Britain, for the year ended fifth January 1805*

1812, VIII (125): *Finance accounts of Great Britain, for the year ended fifth January 1812*

1812, VIII (110): *Finance accounts of Ireland, for the year ended 5th January 1812*

1814–15, VI (214): *Report from the Select Committee on the public income and expenditure of Ireland*

1816, IX (490): *Second report from Select Committee on illicit distillation in Ireland*

1822, XVI (112): *The finance accounts, I–VIII of the United Kingdom of Great Britain and Ireland, for the year ended fifth January 1822*

1830, XXV (221): *Customs and excise duties (Ireland.) Accounts of the amount of duties of customs and excise, in each of the last ten years, in the several revenue districts of Ireland; distinguishing the years and the districts*

1831–2, XXVI (310): *The finance accounts I–VIII of the United Kingdom of Great Britain and Ireland, for the year 1831, ended fifth January 1832*

1835, XLVIII (233): *Customs and excise duties, (Ireland.) An account of the amount of duties of customs and excise collected in each revenue district in Ireland, in each year since 1828*

1842, XXVI (135): *The finance accounts I–VIII of the United Kingdom of Great Britain and Ireland, for the year 1841, ended fifth January 1842*

1843, XXX (573): *Taxation. Statement, showing the total amount of taxation which has been reduced or repealed in Great Britain and Ireland respectively, since 1st January 1814*

1847, XXXIV (388): *Customs duty. An account of the gross and net amount of customs duty received at each port of the United Kingdom, during the years ending the 5th day of January 1846 and 1847*

1849, XXX (423): *Accounts of the debt, income and expenditure of Ireland, from the Union to 1848 inclusive*

1852, XXVIII (196): *The finance accounts I–VIII of the United Kingdom of Great Britain and Ireland, for the year 1851, ended fifth January 1852*

1854, X (53): *Report from the Select Committee of the House of Lords, appointed to consider the consequences of extending the functions of the constabulary in Ireland to the suppression or prevention of illicit distillation*

1857 session 1, III (2186): *First report of the Commissioners of Her Majesty's Customs on the customs*

1868–9, XXXV (366): *Accounts of net public income and expenditure of Great Britain and Ireland, 1688–1800; Receipts and issues from Exchequer; Accounts of gross public income and expenditure, 1801–69*

1877, XXVI (Cmd 1791): *Twenty-first report of the Commissioners of Her Majesty's Customs on the customs (for the year ended 31st December 1876)*

1892, XLVIII (274): *Finance accounts of the United Kingdom of Great Britain and Ireland, for the financial year 1891–92, ended 31st March 1892*

1896, XXXIII (Cmd 8262): *Royal commission on the financial relations between Great Britain and Ireland. Final report by Her Majesty's Commissioners appointed to inquire into the financial relations between Great Britain and Ireland*

1902, LV (256): *Revenue and expenditure (England, Scotland, and Ireland). Return showing, for the year ended 31st March 1902*

1911, XV (Cmd 5827): *Second report of the Commissioners of His Majesty's Customs and Excise. (For the year ended 31st March, 1911.)*

1911, LXXV (Cmd 5852): *Annual statement of the trade of the United Kingdom with foreign countries and British possessions. 1910 compared with the four preceding years*

1912–13, XLIX (190): *Revenue and expenditure (England, Scotland, and Ireland). Return showing, for the year ended the 31st day of March 1912*

1930–31, XVI (Cmd 3920): *Committee on national expenditure. Report*

1933–4, XIII (Cmd 4728): *Ministry of Labour. Reports of investigations into the industrial conditions in certain depressed areas*

1939–40, IV (Cmd 6153): *Royal commission on the distribution of the industrial population. Report*

1942–3, VI (Cmd 6404): *Social insurance and allied services*

1964–5, XXX (Cmd 2764): *The National Plan*

1997–8, HC 341: *Treasury Committee. Second report. The Barnett Formula*

Other government publications, in chronological order

Calendar of Treasury books, October 1706 to December 1707, vol. 21, part 2, ed. William A. Shaw (1952)

Calendar of state papers, colonial series, 1706–1708, June, ed. Cecil Headlam (1916)

Journals of the House of Commons, 20 (1722–7)

Journals of the House of Lords [Ireland], 8 (1798–1800)

'Report from the committee upon the distilleries in Scotland' (1798), in *Reports from the committees of the House of Commons*, vol. 11: *1782–1799* (1803), 319–510

'Report from the committee upon the distilleries in Scotland' (1799), in *Reports from the committees of the House of Commons*, vol. 11: *1782–1799* (1803), 511–804

Hansard, *Commons debates* (1803–), online at https://api.parliament.uk/
historic-hansard/index.html

Reports of the Select Committee of the House of Commons on public peti-
tions, 1852–3 ([1853?])

HM Treasury, *Needs assessment study – report* (1979)

Scottish Government, *Highlands and Islands Scotland: European Regional*
Development Fund, 2007–2013 (Edinburgh, 2008)

Independent Commission on Funding & Finance for Wales, *First report.*
Funding devolved government in Wales: Barnett & beyond (2009)

Independent Commission on Funding & Finance for Wales, *Final report.*
Fairness and accountability: a new funding settlement for Wales: full
text (2010)

Fiscal Commission Working Group, *Principles for a modern and efficient tax*
system in an independent Scotland (Edinburgh, 2013)

HM Government, *Scotland analysis: devolution and the implications of Scot-*
tish independence (2013), Cmd 8554

HM Treasury, *Scotland analysis: currency and monetary policy* (2013), Cmd
8594

Scottish Government, *Scotland's future: your guide to an independent Scot-*
land (Edinburgh, 2013)

HM Revenue and Customs, 'Rural fuel duty relief' (2015), at https://assets.
publishing.service.gov.uk/government/uploads/system/uploads/attachment
_data/file/395158/Rural_Fuel_Duty_Relief_-_TIIN.pdf, accessed 28 April
2020

Civil Service, 'Introduction to devolution' ([2017?]), at https://assets.publish-
ing.service.gov.uk/government/uploads/system/uploads/attachment_data/file
/770300/IntroductionToDevolution.pdf, accessed 20 April 2020

HM Revenue and Customs, *A disaggregation of HMRC tax receipts between*
England, Wales, Scotland and Northern Ireland (2018)

HM Treasury, *The green book: central government guidance on appraisal*
and evaluation (2018)

ONS, 'Population of the UK by country of birth and nationality', at https://
www.ons.gov.uk/peoplepopulationandcommunity/populationandmigration/
internationalmigration/bulletins/ukpopulationbycountryofbirthandnation
ality/july2018tojune2019/relateddata, accessed 8 April 2020

Sustainable Growth Commission, *Scotland – the new case for optimism: a*
strategy for inter-generational economic renaissance ([Edinburgh], 2018)

Auditor General [Scotland], 'Transport Scotland's ferry services: impact
report' (2019), at https://www.audit-scotland.gov.uk/uploads/docs/report/
2017/ir_190919_ferry_services.pdf, accessed 20 July 2020

ONS, *Country and regional public sector finances: financial year ending March 2019* (2019)

Scottish Government, *Scotland's right to choose: putting Scotland's future in Scotland's hands* (Edinburgh, 2019)

ONS, 'Regional gross value added (balanced) per head and income components', at https://www.ons.gov.uk/economy/grossvalueaddedgva/datasets/nominalregionalgrossvalueaddedbalancedperheadandincomecomponents, accessed 8 April 2020

——, 'Public sector finances, UK: July 2020', at https://www.ons.gov.uk/economy/governmentpublicsectorandtaxes/publicsectorfinance/datasets/publicsectorfinancesappendixatables110, accessed 26 August 2020

Privy Council Office, 'List of charters granted', at https://privycouncil.independent.gov.uk/royal-charters/list-of-charters-granted/, accessed 9 July 2020

OTHER SOURCES

Patrick Abercrombie and Robert H. Matthew, *The Clyde Valley regional plan, 1946* (Edinburgh, 1949)

Aberdeen Press and Journal

Paul Addison, *The road to 1945: British politics and the Second World War* (1975)

Alberto Alesina and Enrico Spolaore, *The size of nations* (Cambridge, MA, 2003)

Sir Kenneth Alexander, 'The Highlands and Islands Development Board', in Richard Saville (ed.), *The economic development of modern Scotland, 1950–1980* (Edinburgh, 1985), 214–32

George Allen, 'The geography of liberty', in George Watson (ed.), *The unservile state: essays in liberty and welfare* (1957), 131–47

Ash Amin, Doreen Massey and Nigel Thrift, *Decentering the nation: a radical approach to regional inequality* (2003)

Michael Amior, Rowena Crawford and Gemma Tetlow, *Fiscal sustainability of an independent Scotland*, Institute for Fiscal Studies (2013)

Benedict Anderson, *Imagined communities: reflections on the origin and spread of nationalism* (1983)

Gary M. Anderson, William F. Shughart II and Robert D. Tollison, 'Adam Smith in the customhouse', *Journal of Political Economy*, 93.4 (1985), 740–59

James Anderson, *An account of the present state of the Hebrides, and western coasts of Scotland* (Edinburgh, 1785)

——, *Observations on the effects of the coal duty upon the remote and thinly peopled coasts of Britain* (Edinburgh, 1792)

——, *Observations on the means of exciting a spirit of national industry; chiefly intended to promote the agriculture, commerce, manufactures, and fisheries of Scotland* (Edinburgh, 1777).

Anon., *An apology for whisky* (Edinburgh, 1759)

——, *Answer to the defence of the Perthshire resolutions* (Edinburgh, 1785)

——, *Broad Scotch, address'd to all true Scots men* (2nd edn, Edinburgh, 1734)

——, 'Caledonian Canal', *Blackwood's Edinburgh Magazine*, 7 (July 1820), 427–36

——, *Case of the Lowland distillers* (1798)

——, *Considerations in relation to trade considered, and A short view of our present trade and taxes, compared with what these taxes may amount to after the Union, &c. Reviewed* ([Edinburgh?], 1706).

——, *Considerations on the impolicy of local exemptions from the payment of excise duties on the distillation of spirits in Scotland* (1797)

——, *Considerations on the Union between England and Scotland, and on some commercial matters in both kingdoms* (1790)

——, *The constitutional right of the legislature of Great Britain, to tax the British colonies in America, impartially stated* (1768)

——, *A dialogue between a brewer and a gager concerning the malt tax* ([Edinburgh, 1713?])

——, *The distilleries considered, in their connection with the agriculture, commerce, and revenue of Britain* (Edinburgh, 1797)

——, *An historical account of the Union betwixt the Egyptians and Israelites* ([Edinburgh, 1725?])

——, *Importance of the brewery stated* (Edinburgh, 1797)

——, *Land tax at 4s in ye pound paid by England & Wales in 1702, & 1704* (1745)

——, *A letter from a brewer in the city, to a justice of the peace in the country, concerning the malt tax* (Edinburgh, 1713)

——, *Memorial concerning the malt-tax* (Edinburgh, 1726)

——, *The parliamentary gazetteer of Ireland*, 3 vols (Dublin, 1844)

——, *Resolutions of the landed interest of Scotland respecting the distillery* (Edinburgh, 1786)

——, *A Scots excise-man described* ([Edinburgh, 1707?])

——, 'The Union of 1707 viewed financially', *Scottish Review*, 10 (October 1887), 213–34

David Armitage, 'Greater Britain: a useful category of historical analysis?', *American Historical Review*, 104.2 (1999), 427–45

W. S. Armour, *Ulster, Ireland and Britain: a forgotten trust* (1938)

Matthew Arnold, *English literature and Irish politics; the complete prose works of Matthew Arnold* (Ann Arbor, MI, 1973)

William Ashworth, *The industrial revolution: the state, knowledge and global trade* (2017)

A. B. Atkinson and T. Piketty (eds), *Top incomes over the twentieth century: a contrast between continental European and English-speaking countries* (Oxford, 2007)

G. E. Aylmer, 'The peculiarities of the English state', *Journal of Historical Sociology*, 3.2 (1990), 91–108

[W. Aytoun], 'Scotland since the Union', *Blackwood's Edinburgh Magazine*, 74.455 (September 1853), 266–83

John Bachtler, 'Regional disparities in the United Kingdom', in Helmut Karl and Philippe Rollet (eds), *Employment and regional development policy: market efficiency versus policy intervention* (Hanover, 2004), 36–49

William F. Bailey, *Local and centralized government in Ireland: a sketch of the existing system* (London and Dublin, 1888)

Edward Baines, *History of the cotton manufacture in Great Britain* (2nd edn, 1966)

Paul N. Balchin, *Regional policy in Britain: the north–south divide* (1990)

Bank of England, 'A millennium of macroeconomic data', at https://www.bankofengland.co.uk/statistics/research-datasets, accessed 1 July 2020

——, *The names and descriptions of the proprietors of unclaimed dividends on Bank stock, and on the public funds* ([1791])

Viola Florence Barnes, *The Dominion of New England: a study in British colonial policy* (New Haven, CT, 1923)

David Barnett, *London, hub of the industrial revolution: a revisionary history, 1775–1825* (1998)

Joel Barnett, *Inside the Treasury* (1982)

James R. Barrett, 'Why Paddy drank: the social importance of whiskey in pre-famine Ireland', *Journal of Popular Culture*, 11.1 (1977), 155–66

G. C. Baugh, 'Government grants in aid of the rates in England and Wales, 1889–1990', *Historical Research*, 65 (1992), 215–37

C. A. Bayly, 'Returning the British to South Asian history: the limits of colonial hegemony', *South Asia*, 17.2 (1994), 1–25

BBC, 'BBC survey indicates support for Scottish "devo-max"', at https://www.bbc.co.uk/news/uk-scotland-scotland-politics-15610909, accessed 20 April 2020

——, 'Crossrail delay: line will not open until 2021 as costs increase', at https://www.bbc.co.uk/news/business-50345344, accessed 14 April 2020

Robert A. Becker, *Revolution, reform, and the politics of American taxation, 1763–1783* (Baton Rouge, LA, 1980)

J. V. Beckett, 'Local custom and the "new taxation" in the seventeenth and eighteenth centuries: the example of Cumberland', *Northern History*, 12 (1976), 105–26

David Bell, 'Question 1: What would the outlook for Scotland's economy be if the vote is Yes/if the vote is No?', in Charlie Jeffery and Ray Perman (eds), *Scotland's decision: 16 questions to think about for the referendum on 18 September* (Edinburgh, 2014), 9–13

David Bell and Alex Christie, 'Finance – the Barnett Formula: nobody's child?', in Alan Trench (ed.), *The state of the nations* (2001), 135–51

David Bell, David Eiser and Michael McGoldrick, *Inequality in Scotland: new perspectives*, David Hume Institute (Stirling, 2014).

Christine Bellamy, *Administering central–local relations, 1871–1919: the Local Government Board in its fiscal and cultural context* (Manchester, 1998)

Sir Ernest Benn, 'The case against planning', *Today and Tomorrow*, 3.1 (1932), 46–51

R. J. Bennett, *Central government grants to local governments: the political and economic impact of the Rate Support Grant in England and Wales* (Cambridge, 1982)

——, 'Individual and territorial equity', *Geographical Analysis*, 15 (1983), 50–57

Lauren Benton and Lisa Ford, *Rage for order: the British Empire and the origins of international law, 1800–1850* (Cambridge, MA, 2016)

Arthur Berriedale Keith, *The constitution of England from Queen Victoria to George VI*, 2 vols (1940)

Craig Berry and Arianna Giovannini, 'Introduction: powerhouse politics and economic development in the north', in Craig Berry and Arianna Giovannini (eds), *Developing England's north: the political economy of the Northern Powerhouse* (Cham, Switzerland, 2018), 1–19

Aneurin Bevan, 'The claim of Wales: a statement', *Wales, the national magazine*, 7, no. 27 (December, 1947), 151–3

Eugenio F. Biagini, 'Popular liberals, Gladstonian finance, and the debate on taxation, 1860–1874', in Eugenio F. Biagini and Alastair J. Reid (eds), *Currents of radicalism: popular radicalism, organised labour and party politics in Britain, 1850–1914* (Cambridge, 1991), 134–62

Andy Bielenberg, 'The Irish distilling industry under the Union', in David Dickson and Cormac Ó Gráda (eds), *Refiguring Ireland: essays in honour of L. M. Cullen* (Dublin, 2013), 290–315

[William Black], *Remarks upon a pamphlet, intitled, The considerations in relation to trade considered, and a short view of our present trade and taxes reviewed* ([Edinburgh?], 1706)

——, *A short view of our present trade and taxes, compared with what these taxes may amount to after the Union* ([Edinburgh, 1706?])

Tony Blair, *A journey* (2010)

Robin Boadway and Anwar Shah, *Fiscal federalism: principles and practices of multiorder governance* (New York, 2009)

Vernon Bogdanor, *Beyond Brexit: towards a British constitution* (2019)

——, *Devolution in the United Kingdom* (Oxford, 2001)

G. C. Bolton, *The passing of the Irish Act of Union* (Oxford, 1966)

Alan Booth, 'The Second World War and the origins of modern regional policy', *Economy and Society*, 11.1 (1982), 1–21

Philip Booth, *Federal Britain: the case for decentralisation*, Institute of Economic Affairs (2015)

J. F. Bosher, *The single duty project: a study of the movement for a French customs union in the eighteenth century* (1964)

H. V. Bowen, *The business of empire: the East India Company and imperial Britain, 1756–1833* (Cambridge, 2006)

James A. Bowie, *The future of Scotland: a survey of the present position with some proposals for future policy* (1939)

Karin Bowie, *Scottish public opinion and the Anglo-Scottish Union, 1699–1707* (Woodbridge, 2007)

Arthur L. Bowley, *Some economic consequences of the Great War* (1930)

Marian Bowley, *Housing and the state, 1919–1944* (1945)

Thomas Boylan and Timothy P. Foley, *Political economy and colonial Ireland: the propagation and ideological function of economic discourse in the nineteenth century* (1992)

Robert Bradley, 'Colliery closures since 1947', at http://www.healeyhero.co.uk/rescue/individual/Bob_Bradley/PM-Closures.html, accessed 8 Oct 2019

Jack Brand, *Local government reform in England, 1888–1974* (1974)

Ciara Breathnach, *The Congested Districts Board, 1891–1923: poverty and development in the west of Ireland* (Cork, 2005)

J. R. Breihan, 'Economical reform, 1785–1810' (University of Cambridge PhD thesis, 1977)

John Brewer, 'The misfortunes of Lord Bute: a case-study in eighteenth-century political argument and public opinion', *Historical Journal*, 16.1 (1973), 3–43

——, *The sinews of power: war, money and the English state, 1688–1783* (1989)

John Brewer and Eckhart Hellmuth, 'Introduction: rethinking Leviathan', in John Brewer and Eckhart Hellmuth (eds), *Rethinking Leviathan: the eighteenth-century state in Britain and Germany* (Oxford, 1999), 1–21

John D. Brewer, *The Royal Irish Constabulary: an oral history* (Belfast, 1990)

Asa Briggs, *The age of improvement, 1783–1867* (1959)

British Social Attitudes, http://www.bsa-data.natcen.ac.uk, accessed 15 November 2017

Gordon Brown, *My life, our times* (2018)

Graham Brownlow, 'The causes and consequences of rent-seeking in Northern Ireland, 1945–72', *Economic History Review*, 60.1 (2007), 70–96

——, 'Soft budget constraints and regional industrial policy: reinterpreting the rise and fall of DeLorean', Queen's University Centre for Economic History, Working Paper 14–09, 2014

[John Bruce], *Report on the events and circumstances, which produced the Union of the kingdoms of England and Scotland; on the effects of this great national event, on the reciprocal interests of both kingdoms; and on the political and commercial influence of Great-Britain, in the balance of power in Europe*, 2 vols ([1799])

James M. Buchanan and Richard A. Musgrave, *Public finance and public choice: two contrasting visions of the state* (Cambridge, MA, 1999)

Nick Buck, Ian Gordon and Ken Young, *The London employment problem* (Oxford, 1986)

E. J. Buckatzsch, 'The geographical distribution of wealth in England, 1086–1843: an experimental study of certain tax assessments', *Economic History Review*, 3.2 (1950), 180–202

Patrick Buckland, *The factory of grievances: devolved government in Northern Ireland, 1921–39* (Dublin, 1979)

Jim Bulpitt, *Territory and power in the United Kingdom: an interpretation* (Manchester, 1983)

David F. Burg, *A world history of tax rebellions: an encyclopedia of tax rebels, revolts, and riots from antiquity to the present* (New York and London, 2004)

Edmund Burke, *Reflections on the revolution in France* (1790)

Danny Burns, *Poll tax rebellion* (Stirling, 1992)

Robert Burns, 'The author's earnest cry and prayer' (1786)

——, 'Scotch drink' (1785)

Bernard Burrows and Geoffrey Denton, *Devolution or federalism? Options for a United Kingdom* (1980)

David Butler, Andrew Adonis and Tony Travers, *Failure in British government: the politics of the poll tax* (Oxford, 1994)

Graham Butler and Gavin Barrett, 'Europe's "other" open-border zone: the Common Travel Area under the shadow of Brexit', *Cambridge Yearbook of European Legal Studies*, 20 (2018), 252–86

Lord Byron, *The complete works of Lord Byron* (Paris, 1835)

P. J. Cain and A. G. Hopkins, *British imperialism: 1688–2015* (3rd edn, 2015)

W. N. Calkins, 'A Victorian free trade lobby', *Economic History Review*, 13.1 (1960), 90–104

[James Thomson Callender?], *An impartial account of the conduct of the excise towards the breweries in Scotland* (Edinburgh, 1791)

[James Thomson Callender], *The political progress of Britain; or, an impartial account of the principal abuses in the government of this country, from the revolution in 1688* (Edinburgh, [1792])

A. D. Cameron, *The Caledonian Canal* (4th edn, Edinburgh, 2005)

Ewen A. Cameron, *Land for the people? The British government and the Scottish Highlands, c.1880–1925* (East Linton, 1996)

——, 'The stateless nation and the British state since 1918', in T. M. Devine and Jenny Wormald (eds), *The Oxford handbook of modern Scottish history* (Oxford, 2012), 620–34

R. H. Campbell, 'The Scottish Office and the Special Areas in the 1930s', *Historical Journal*, 22.1 (1979), 167–83

——(ed.), *States of the annual progress of the linen manufacture, 1727–1754* (Edinburgh, 1964)

Duncan Campbell-Smith, *Follow the money: the Audit Commission, public money and the management of public services, 1983–2008* (2008).

David Cannadine, *Victorious century: the United Kingdom, 1800–1906* (2017)

Edwin Cannan, *The history of local rates in England in relation to the proper distribution of the burden of taxation* (2nd edn, 1912)

Thomas Carlyle, 'Occasional discourse on the negro question', *Fraser's Magazine for Town and Country*, 40 (240) (1849), 670–79

——, *Selected writings*, ed. Alan Shelston (Harmondsworth, 1980)

Harold Carter and C. Roy Lewis, *An urban geography of England and Wales in the nineteenth century* (1990)

Robert Stewart, Viscount Castlereagh, *Memoirs and correspondence of Viscount Castlereagh*, ed. Charles Vane, Marquess of Londonderry, 12 vols (1848–53)

C. D. Chandaman, *The English public revenue, 1660–1688* (Oxford, 1975)

Edgar L. Chappell, *Wake up Wales! A survey of Welsh Home Rule activities* (1943)

J. A. Chartres, 'Spirits in the north-east? Gin and other vices in the long-eighteenth century', in Helen Berry and Jeremy Gregory (eds), *Creating and consuming culture in north-east England, 1660–1830* (Aldershot, 2004)

B. Chatterji, 'Business and politics in the 1930s: Lancashire and the making of the Indo-British trade agreement, 1939', *Modern Asian Studies*, 15.3 (1981), 527–73

Selina Chen and Tony Wright (eds), *The English question*, Fabian Society (2000)

Sir Norman Chester, *The nationalisation of British industry, 1945–1951* (1957)

Rev. Edward Chichester, *Oppressions and cruelties of Irish revenue officers: being the substance of a letter to a British member of parliament* (1818)

Martin Chick, 'Discounting time', in Julian Hoppit, Duncan Needham and Adrian Leonard (eds), *Money and markets: essays in honour of Martin Daunton* (Woodbridge, 2019), 251–62

Erskine Childers, *The framework of Home Rule* (1911)

Robert Christie, *Injustice to Scotland exposed; in a letter to the Scottish representatives in the Commons' House of Parliament* (Edinburgh, 1854)

Winston S. Churchill, *Great contemporaries* (New York, 1937)

Citizen of Edinburgh, *A vindication of Scottish rights addressed to both Houses of Parliament* (Edinburgh, 1854)

R. V. Clarendon, *A sketch of the revenue and finances of Ireland and of the appropriated funds, loans, and debt of the nation* (London and Dublin, 1791)

Peter Clarke, 'The Treasury's analytical model of the British economy between the wars', in Mary O. Furner and Barry Supple (eds), *The state and economic knowledge: the American and British experiences* (Cambridge, 1990), 171–207

Rev. Dr Clarke [T. B. Clarke], *Misconceptions of facts, and mistatements* [*sic*] *of the public accounts, by the Right Hon. John Foster ... proved & corrected according to the official documents and authentic evidence of the Inspector General of Great Britain* (1799).

John Clerk, *History of the Union of Scotland and England by Sir John Clerk of Penicuik*, ed. Douglas Duncan (Edinburgh, 1993)

——, *Memoirs of the life of Sir John Clerk of Penicuik, Baronet, Baron of the Exchequer, extracted by himself from his own journals, 1676–1755*, ed. John M. Gray, Publications of the Scottish Historical Society, 13 (Edinburgh, 1898)

Sijbren Cnossen, *Excise systems: a global study of the selective taxation of goods and services* (Baltimore, MD, 1977).

Jonathan Coad, *Support for the fleet: architecture and engineering of the Royal Navy's bases, 1700–1914* (Swindon, 2013)

William Cobbett (ed.), *The parliamentary history of England, from the earliest period to the year 1803*, 36 vols (1806–20)

——, *Rural rides* (1830)

Aeneas Coffey, *Observations on the Rev. Edward Chichester's pamphlet, entitled Oppressions and cruelties of Irish revenue officers* (1818)

D'Maris Coffman, *Excise taxation and the origins of public debt* (Basingstoke, 2013)

G. D. H. Cole, 'Plan for living', in G. D. H. Cole et al., *Plan for Britain: a collection of essays prepared for the Fabian Society* (1943), 1–33

G. D. H. Cole and M. I. Cole, *The condition of Britain* (1937)

David Coleman and John Salt, *The British population: patterns, trends, and processes* (Oxford, 1992)

Linda Colley, *Britons: forging the nation, 1707–1837* (New Haven, CT, 1992)

——, 'Empires of writing: Britain, America and constitutions, 1776–1848', *Law and History Review*, 32.2 (2014), 237–66

——, '"This small island": Britain, size and empire', *Proceedings of the British Academy*, 121 (2002), 171–90

Paul Collier, *The future of capitalism: facing the new anxieties* (2019)

Stefan Collini, John Burrow and Donald Winch, *That noble science of politics: a study in nineteenth-century intellectual history* (Cambridge, 1983)

R. D. Collison Black, *Economic thought and the Irish question, 1817–1870* (Cambridge, 1960)

Patrick Colquhoun, *A treatise on the wealth, power, and resources, of the British Empire* (1814)

K. H. Connell, 'Illicit distillation: an Irish peasant industry', *Historical Studies*, 3 (1961), 58–91

Convention of the Royal Burghs of Scotland, *The national meeting in favour of the creation of a separate department of state for Scotland, held within the Free Assembly Hall, Edinburgh on 16th January 1884* (1890)

Tim Pat Coogan, *The famine plot: England's role in Ireland's greatest tragedy* (Basingstoke, 2012)

George Cornewall Lewis, *On local disturbances in Ireland; and on the Irish Church question* (1836)

Philip Corrigan and Derek Sayer, *The great arch: English state formation as cultural change* (Oxford, 1985)

Mel Cousins, 'Resistance to the collection of rates under the poor law, 1842–44', in Douglas Kanter and Patrick Walsh (eds), *Taxation, politics, and protest in Ireland, 1662–2016* (Cham, Switzerland, 2019), 173–98

William Coxe (ed.), *Memoirs of the administration of the Right Honourable Henry Pelham*, 2 vols (1829)

Nicholas Crafts, 'The British economy', in Francesca Carnevali and Julie-Marie Strange (eds), *Twentieth-century Britain: economic, cultural and social change* (Harlow, 2007), 7–25

Matthew Cragoe, '"We like local patriotism": the Conservative party and the discourse of decentralization, 1947–51', *English Historical Review*, 122 (2007), 965–85

Edgar Crammond, 'The economic position of Scotland and her financial relations with England and Ireland', *Journal of the Royal Statistical Society*, 75.2 (1912), 157–75

——, 'The financial difficulties of Home Rule', *Nineteenth Century*, 70 (1911), 601–26

Nicholas Crickhowell, *Westminster, Wales and water* (Cardiff, 1999)

James E. Cronin, *The politics of state expansion: war, state and society in twentieth-century Britain* (1991)

T. W. H. Crosland, *The wild Irishman* (1905)

R. H. S. Crossman, *Planning for freedom* (1965)

Virginia Crossman, *Politics, law and order in nineteenth-century Ireland* (Dublin, 1996)

Karen J. Cullen, *Famine in Scotland: the 'ill years' of the 1690s* (Edinburgh, 2010)

M. J. Cullen, *The statistical movement in early Victorian Britain: the foundations of empirical social research* (Hassocks, 1975)

J. B. Cullingworth, *Environmental planning, 1939–1969*, vol. 3: *New towns policy* (1979)

L. P. Curtis Jnr, *Anglo-Saxons and Celts: a study of anti-Irish prejudice in Victorian England* (Bridgeport, CT, 1968)

Jim Cuthbert and Margaret Cuthbert, 'GERS: where now?', in Donald MacKay (ed.), *Scotland's economic future*, Reform Scotland (Edinburgh, 2011), 35–44

Daily Mail

Daily Record

John Dalrymple, *Address from Sir John Dalrymple, Bart. one of the Barons of Exchequer in Scotland, to the landholders of England, upon the interest they have in the state of the distillery laws* (Edinburgh, 1786)

John Dalrymple, Earl of Stair, *The state of the national debt, the national income, and the national expenditure* (1776)

Hugh Dalton, *The fateful years: memoirs, 1931–1945* (1957)

A. O'Neill Daunt, 'The financial relations between Great Britain and Ireland', *Westminster Review*, 147.4 (April, 1897)

M. J. Daunton, 'Payment and participation: welfare and state-formation in Britain, 1900–1951', *Past and Present*, 150 (1996), 169–216

——, *A property-owning democracy? Housing in Britain* (1987)

Martin Daunton, *Just taxes: the politics of taxation in Britain, 1914–1979* (Cambridge, 2002)

——, *State and market in Victorian Britain: war, welfare and capitalism* (Woodbridge, 2008)

——, 'Thomas Gibson Bowles v the Bank of England (1913): a modern John Hampden?', in John Snape and Dominic de Cogan, *Landmark cases in revenue law* (Oxford, 2019), 91–118

——, *Trusting Leviathan: the politics of taxation in Britain, 1799–1914* (Cambridge, 2001)

Charles Davenant, *An essay upon ways and means of supplying the war* (1695)

D. J. Davies, *Towards Welsh freedom: twenty-seven articles*, ed. Ceinwen Thomas (Cardiff, 1958)

Lance E. Davis and Robert A. Huttenback, *Mammon and the pursuit of empire: the political economy of British imperialism* (Cambridge, 1987)

Norma M. Dawson, 'Illicit distillation and the revenue police in Ireland in the eighteenth and nineteenth centuries', *Irish Jurist*, 12.2 (1977), 282–94

Nicholas Deakin (ed.), *Origins of the welfare state*, 9 vols (2000)

Ben Deaner and David Phillips, *Government spending on public services in Scotland: current patterns and future issues*, Institute for Fiscal Studies (2013)

Iain Deas, Graham Haughton and Stephen Hincks, 'Size matters? London – the subsidy junky', at citiesmcr.wordpress.com/2014/03/24/size-matters-london-the-subsidy-junky, accessed 9 July 2019

[Daniel Defoe], *The state of the excise after the Union, compared with what it is now* ([Edinburgh?],1706)

S. R. Dennison, *The location of industry and the depressed areas* (Oxford, 1939)

T. M. Devine, *The great Highland famine: hunger, emigration and the Scottish Highlands in the nineteenth century* (Edinburgh, 1988)

——, *Independence or Union: Scotland's past and Scotland's present* (2017)

——, 'The rise and fall of illicit whisky-making in northern Scotland, *c.*1780–1840', *Scottish Historical Review*, 54.2 (1975), 155–77

——, *The Scottish clearances: a history of the dispossessed, 1600–1900* (2018)

Clive Dewey, 'Celtic agrarian legislation and the Celtic revival: historicist implications of Gladstone's Irish and Scottish Land Acts, 1870–1886', *Past and Present*, 64 (1974), 30–70

May L. Dhonau, *Decentralisation in government departments* (1938)

A. V. Dicey, *England's case against Home Rule* (3rd edn, 1887)

H. T. Dickinson and Kenneth Logue, 'The Porteous riot: a study of the breakdown of law and order in Edinburgh, 1736–1737', *Scottish Labour History Society Journal*, 10 (1976), 21–40

David Dickson, 'Taxation and disaffection in late eighteenth-century Ireland', in Samuel Clark and James S. Donnelly Jnr (eds), *Irish peasants: violence and political unrest, 1780–1914* (Manchester, 1983), 37–63

P. G. M. Dickson, *The financial revolution in England: a study in the development of public credit, 1688–1756* (1967)

V. E. Dietz, 'The politics of whisky: Scottish distillers, the excise, and the Pittite state', *Journal of British Studies*, 36 (1997), 35–69

Andrew Dilnot and Carl Emmerson, 'The economic environment', in A. H. Halsey and Josephine Webb (eds), *Twentieth-century British social trends* (Basingstoke, 2000), 324–57

Marshall E. Dimock, *British public utilities and national development* (1933)

Mark Dincecco, *Political transformations and public finances: Europe, 1650–1913* (Cambridge, 2011)

Nigel Dodds, https://twitter.com/NigelDoddsDUP, 18 October 2019

James S. Donnelly Jnr, '"Irish property must pay for Irish poverty": British public opinion and the Great Irish Famine', in Chris Morash and Richard Hayes (eds), *'Fearful realities': new perspectives on the famine* (Dublin, 1996), 60–76

Daniel Dorling and Bethan Thomas, *People and places: a 2001 census atlas of the UK* (Bristol, 2004)

James Douet, *British barracks, 1600–1914: their architecture and role in society* (1998)

Roy Douglas, Liam Harte and Jim O'Hara, *Drawing conclusions: a cartoon history of Anglo-Irish relations, 1798–1998* (Belfast, 1998)

[William Dowdeswell], *An address to such of the electors of Great-Britain as are not makers of cyder and perry* (2nd edn 1763)

Stephen Dowell, *A history of taxation and taxes in England*, 4 vols (2nd edn, 1888)

Christopher Duffy, 'The Jacobite wars, 1708–46', in Edward M. Spiers, Jeremy A. Crang and Matthew J. Strickland (eds), *A military history of Scotland* (Edinburgh, 2014), 348–82

Tom Dunne, '*La trahison des clercs*: British intellectuals and the first home-rule crisis', *Irish Historical Studies*, 23 (1982), 134–73

Earl of Dunraven, *The outlook in Ireland: the case for devolution and conciliation* (Dublin, 1907)

A. J. Durie, *The Scottish linen industry in the eighteenth century* (Edinburgh, 1979)

David Eastwood, Laurence Brockliss and Michael John, 'From dynastic union to unitary state: the European experience', in Laurence Brockliss and David Eastwood (eds), *A union of multiple identities: The British Isles, c.1750–c.1850* (Manchester, 1997), 193–212

The Economist

David Edgerton, *The rise and fall of the British nation: a twentieth century history* (2018)

——, *Warfare state: Britain, 1920–1970* (Cambridge, 2006)

Huw T. Edwards, *What I want for Wales* (Carmarthen, 1949)

EEC, 'Treaty of Rome', at https://ec.europa.eu/romania/sites/romania/files/tratatul_de_la_roma.pdf, accessed 18 September 2019

Louis Eisenstein, *The ideologies of taxation* ([1961], Cambridge, MA, 2010)

Norbert Elias, *The society of individuals*, ed. Michael Schröter, trans. Edmund Jephcott (Oxford, 1991)

J. H. Elliott, 'A Europe of composite monarchies', *Past and Present*, 137 (1992), 48–71

——, *Scots and Catalans: union and disunion* (New Haven, CT, 2018)

Charles J. Esdaile, 'The French Revolutionary and Napoleonic Wars, 1793–1815', in Edward M. Spiers, Jeremy A. Crang and Matthew J. Strickland (eds), *A military history of Scotland* (Edinburgh, 2014), 407–35

Gwynfor Evans, *For the sake of Wales: the memoirs of Gwynfor Evans*, trans. from the Welsh by Meic Stephens (Cardiff, 1996)

Gwynfor Evans and Ioan Rhys, 'Wales', in Owen Dudley Edwards, Gwynfor Evans, Ioan Rhys and Hugh MacDiarmid, *Celtic nationalism* (1968), 213–98

Fabian Society, *Municipalization by provinces*, New Heptarchy Series, no. 1 (1905)

Ronan Fanning, *The Irish Department of Finance, 1922–58* (Dublin, 1978)

C. B. Fawcett, *Provinces of England: a study of some geographical aspects of devolution* (1919)

Melissa Fegan, *Literature and the Irish Famine, 1845–1919* (Oxford, 2003)

David Feldman, 'Migrants, immigrants and welfare from the old poor law to the welfare state', *Transactions of the Royal Historical Society*, 13 (2003), 79–104

Richard J. Finlay, 'Unionism and the dependency culture: politics and state intervention in Scotland, 1918–1997', in Catriona M. M. Macdonald (ed.), *Unionist Scotland, 1800–1997* (Edinburgh, 1998), 100–116

Samuel Fleischacker, *A short history of distributive justice* (Cambridge, MA, 2004)

Andrew Fletcher, *Political works*, ed. John Robertson (Cambridge, 1997)

Michael W. Flinn, *The history of the British coal industry*, vol. 2: *1700–1830: the industrial revolution* (Oxford, 1984)

Tadhg Foley, *Death by discourse? Political economy and the Great Irish famine* (Hamden, CT, 2016)

Nathan Foley-Fisher and Eoin McLaughlin, 'Capitalising on the Irish land question: land reform and state banking in Ireland, 1891–1938', *Financial History Review*, 23.1 (2016), 71–109

Duncan Forbes, *Some considerations on the present state of Scotland* (3rd edn, Edinburgh, 1744)

John Foster, *Speech of the Right Honourable John Foster, Speaker of the House of Commons of Ireland . . . 11th day of April, 1799* (Dublin, 1799)

Roy Foster, *Paddy and Mr Punch: connections in Irish and English history* (1993)

Ewout Frankema, 'Raising revenue in the British empire, 1870–1940: how "extractive" were colonial taxes?', *Journal of Global History*, 5.3 (2010), 447–77

Fraser of Allander Institute, *Scotland's budget – 2016* (Strathclyde, 2016)

[Robert Freebairn], *The miserable state of Scotland, since the Union, briefly represented* (Perth, 1716)

Michael Fry, *The Dundas despotism* (Edinburgh, 1992)

Jim Gallagher, 'The ghost in the machine? The government of England', in Michael Kenny, Iain McLean and Akash Paun (eds), *Governing England: English identity and institutions in a changing United Kingdom*, Proceedings of the British Academy, 217 (Oxford, 2018), 69–90

W. R. Garside, *British unemployment, 1919–1939: a study in public policy* (Cambridge, 1990)

Norman Gash, 'Cheap government, 1815–1874', in his *Pillars of government and other essays on state and society, c.1770–c.1880* (1986), 43–54

——, *Mr Secretary Peel: the life of Sir Robert Peel to 1830* (2nd edn, Harlow, 1985)

Frank Geary and Tom Stark, 'Comparative output and growth in the four countries of the United Kingdom, 1861–1911', in S. J. Connelly (ed.), *Kingdoms united? Great Britain and Ireland since 1500: integration and diversity* (Dublin, 1999), 153–68

Arthur Geddes, *The Highlands and Islands: their regional planning* (Edinburgh, 1949)

——, *The Isle of Lewis and Harris: a study in British community* (Edinburgh, 1955)

Patrick Geddes and Victor Branford, 'General Editors' introduction' to C. B. Fawcett, *Provinces of England: a study of some geographical aspects of devolution* (1919)

Ernest Gellner, *Nations and nationalism* (Oxford, 1983)

General Assembly of the Church of Scotland, *An act for preventing the running of goods, and perjuries in custom-houses* (Edinburgh, 1719)

Patrick M. Geoghegan, *The Irish Act of Union: a study in high politics, 1798–1801* (Dublin, 1999)

P. R. Ghosh, 'Disraelian conservatism: a financial approach', *English Historical Review*, 99 (1984), 268–96

Andrew Dewar Gibb, *Scotland in eclipse* (Edinburgh, 1930)

Robert Giffen, 'The economic value of Ireland to Great Britain', *Nineteenth Century*, 19 (1886), 329–45

Ian Gilmour, *Dancing with dogma: Britain under Thatcherism* (1992)

John Ginarlis and Sidney Pollard, 'Roads and waterways, 1750–1850', in Charles H. Feinstein and Sidney Pollard (eds), *Studies in capital formation in the United Kingdom, 1750–1920* (Oxford, 1988), 182–224

Glasgow Herald

Howard Glennerster, John Hills and Tony Travers with Ross Hendry, *Paying for health, education, and housing: how does the centre pull the purse strings?* (Oxford, 2000)

Donald Goodale, *Scotland's complaint against the malt-tax: in a letter from a Scots farmer* ([Edinburgh?], 1718)

G. J. Goschen, *Laissez-faire and government interference* (1883)

A. S. Goudie and D. Brunsden, *The environment of the British Isles* (Oxford, 1994)

Lachlan Grant, *A new deal for the Highlands* ([Oban], 1935)

James Grassie, *Highland experiment: the story of the Highlands and Islands Development Board* (Aberdeen, 1983)

Henry Grattan, *The speeches of the Right Honourable Henry Grattan, in the Irish, and in the imperial parliament*, ed. Henry Grattan [Jnr], 4 vols (1822)

Peter Gray, *Famine, land and politics: British government and Irish society, 1843–1850* (Dublin, 1999)

——, 'The Great Famine, 1845–1850', in James Kelly (ed.), *The Cambridge history of Ireland*, vol. 3: *1730–1880* (Cambridge, 2018), 639–65

S. J. D. Green and R. C. Whiting (eds), *The boundaries of the state in modern Britain* (Cambridge, 1996)

Jack P. Greene, *Peripheries and center: constitutional development in the extended polities of the British Empire and the United States, 1607–1788* (New York, 1986)

James Griffiths, *Pages from memory* (1969)

Guardian

Christophe Guilluy, *La France périphérique: comment on a sacrifié les classes populaires* (Paris, 2014)

Jo Guldi, *Roads to power: Britain invents the infrastructure state* (Cambridge, MA, 2012)

Lord Hailsham, *The door wherein I went* (1975)

Robin Haines, *Charles Trevelyan and the Great Irish Famine* (Dublin, 2004)

Catherine Hall and Sonya O. Rose (eds), *At home with the empire: metropolitan culture and the imperial world* (Cambridge, 2006)

Peter Hall, *Great planning disasters* (1980)

Graham Hallett, Peter Randall and E. G. West, *Regional policy for ever? Essays on the history, theory and political economy of forty years of regionalism*, Institute of Economic Affairs (1973)

Alexander Hamilton, James Madison and John Jay, *The Federalist, with letters of 'Brutus'*, ed. Terence Ball (Cambridge, 2003)

[Andrew Hamilton], *An inquiry into the principles of taxation* (1790)

H. J. Hanham, 'The creation of the Scottish Office, 1881–87', *Juridical Review*, 10 (1965), 205–44

Wal Hannington, *The problem of the distressed areas* (1937)

Philip Harling, *The waning of 'old corruption': the politics of economical reform in Britain, 1779–1846* (Oxford, 1996)

José Harris, 'English ideas about community: another case of "made in Germany"?', in Rudolf Muhs, Johannes Paulmann and Willibald Steinmetz (eds), *Aneignung und Abwehr: interkultureller Transfer zwischen Deutschland und Großbritannien im 19. Jahrhundert* (Bodenheim, 1998), 143–58

——, 'The transition to high politics in English social policy, 1880–1914', in Michael Bentley and John Stevenson (eds), *High and low politics in modern Britain: ten studies* (Oxford, 1983), 58–79

Henry Harrison, *Ulster and the British Empire, 1939: help or hindrance?* (1939)

Jennifer Hart, 'Sir Charles Trevelyan at the Treasury', *English Historical Review*, 75 (1960), 92–110

Christopher Harvie, *Fool's gold: the story of North Sea oil* (1994)

W. J. Hausman, *Public policy and the supply of coal to London, 1700–1770* (New York, 1981)

Robert Hazell (ed.), *The English question* (Manchester, 2006)

David Heald, 'Accounting for the Severn Bridge', *Financial Accountability and Management*, 7.4 (1991), 267–9

——, *Financing devolution within the United Kingdom: a study of the lessons from failure* (Canberra, 1980)

——, *Public expenditure: its defence and reform* (Oxford, 1983)

——, *Territorial equity and public finances: concepts and confusion* (Strathclyde, 1980).

[Benjamin Heath], *The case of the county of Devon, with respect to the consequences of the new excise duty on cyder and perry* (1763)

Thomas L. Heath, *The Treasury* (1927)

E. P. Hennock, *British social reform and German precedents: the case of social insurance, 1880–1914* (Oxford, 1987)

——, 'Finance and politics in urban local government in England, 1835–1900', *Historical Journal*, 6.2 (1963), 212–25

Jim Herlihy, *The Irish Revenue Police: a short history and genealogical guide to the 'poteen hussars'* (Dublin, 2018)

W. M. Herries, *A letter addressed to the Dumfries and Galloway Courier on the subject of the tax upon property and income* (Dumfries, 1816)

Highland and Islands Development Board, *Roads to the isles: a study of sea freight charges in the Highlands and Islands* ([Inverness?], 1974)

——, *First report, 1 November 1965 to 31 December 1966* (Inverness, 1967)

——, *Fifth report 1970* (Inverness, 1971)

——, *25th annual report 1990* ([Inverness, 1990?])

[Ruaraidh Hilleary], *The Highlands and Islands of Scotland. A review of the economic conditions with recommendations for improvement* (1938)

Francis W. Hirst, *Gladstone as financier and economist* (1931)

E. J. Hobsbawm, *Nations and nationalism since 1780: programme, myth, reality* (Cambridge, 1990)

Geoffrey Holmes and Clyve Jones, 'Trade, the Scots and the parliamentary crisis of 1713', *Parliamentary History*, 1.1 (1982), 47–77

Oliver Wendell Holmes, https://caselaw.findlaw.com/us-supreme-court/275/87.html, accessed 14 November 2017

Henry Home, Lord Kames, *Sketches of the history of man*, ed. James A. Harris, 3 vols ([1774], Indianapolis, IN, 2006)

Istvan Hont, *Jealousy of trade: international competition and the nation-state in historical perspective* (Cambridge, MA, 2005)

Christopher Hood and Rozana Himaz, *A century of fiscal squeeze politics: 100 years of austerity, politics, and bureaucracy in Britain* (Oxford, 2017)

Liesbet Hooghe, Gary Marks, Arjan H. Schakel, Sara Niedzwiecki, Sandra Chapman Osterkatz and Sarah Shair-Rosenfield, *Measuring regional authority: a postfunctionalist theory of governance*, vol. 1 (Oxford, 2016)

K. Theodore Hoppen, 'Gladstone, Salisbury and the end of Irish assimilation', in Mary E. Daly and K. Theodore Hoppen (eds), *Gladstone: Ireland and beyond* (Dublin, 2011), 45–63

——, *Governing Hibernia: British politicians and Ireland, 1800–1921* (Oxford, 2016)

——, *The mid-Victorian generation, 1846–1886* (Oxford, 1998)

Julian Hoppit, *Britain's political economies: parliament and economic life, 1660–1800* (Cambridge, 2017)

——, 'Checking the Leviathan, 1688–1832', in Donald Winch and Patrick K. O'Brien (eds), *The political economy of British historical experience, 1688–1914* (Oxford, 2002), 267–94

——, 'Compulsion, compensation and property rights in Britain, 1688–1833', *Past and Present*, 210 (2011), 93–28

——, 'Introduction', in Julian Hoppit (ed.), *Parliaments, nations and identities in Britain and Ireland, 1660–1850* (Manchester, 2003), 1–14

——, *A land of liberty? England, 1689–1727* (Oxford, 2000)

——, 'The nation, the state and the first industrial revolution', *Journal of British Studies*, 50.2 (2011), 307–31

——, 'Reforming Britain's weights and measures, 1660–1824', *English Historical Review*, 108 (1993), 82–104

——, 'Scotland and the taxing union, 1707–1815', *Scottish Historical Review*, 98.1 (2019), 45–70

——, 'Taxing London and the British fiscal state, 1660–1815', in Julian Hoppit, Adrian Leonhard and Duncan Needham (eds), *Money and markets: essays in honour of Martin Daunton* (Woodbridge, 2019), 19–33

Jeff Horn, *Economic development in early modern France: the privilege of liberty, 1650–1820* (Cambridge, 2015)

Shane Horwell, 'Taxation in British political and economic thought, 1733–1816' (UCL PhD thesis, 2019)

John Houghton, *An account of the acres & houses, with the proportional tax, &c., of each county in England and Wales* (1693)

David Hume, *Essays moral, political and literary*, ed. Eugene F. Miller ([1741–76], Indianapolis, IN, 1987)

E. H. Hunt, 'Industrialization and regional inequality: wages in Britain, 1760–1914', *Journal of Economic History*, 46 (1986), 935–66

——, *Regional wage variations in Britain, 1850–1914* (Oxford, 1973)

Lynn Hunt, *Inventing human rights: a history* (New York, 2007)

I. G. C. Hutchison, 'Anglo-Scottish political relations in the nineteenth century, c.1815–1914', in T. C. Smout (ed.), *Anglo-Scottish relations from 1603 to 1900*, Proceedings of the British Academy, 127 (2005), 247–66

Charles K. Hyde, *Technological change and the British iron industry, 1700–1870* (Princeton, NJ, 1977)

Guto Ifan and Ed Gareth Poole, *The Welsh tax base: risks and opportunities after fiscal devolution*, Wales Centre for Public Policy (Cardiff, 2018)

Joanna Innes, 'The distinctiveness of the English poor laws, 1750–1850', in Donald Winch and Patrick K. O'Brien (eds), *The political economy of British historical experience, 1688–1914* (Oxford, 2002), 381–407

——, 'Forms of "government growth", 1780–1830', in David Feldman and Jon Lawrence (eds), *Structures and transformations in modern British history* (Cambridge, 2011), 74–99

——, 'Legislating for three kingdoms: how the Westminster parliament legislated for England, Scotland and Ireland, 1707–1830', in Julian Hoppit (ed.), *Parliaments, nations and identities in Britain and Ireland, 1660–1850* (Manchester, 2003), 15–47

——, 'The state and the poor: eighteenth-century England in European perspective', in John Brewer and Eckhart Hellmuth (eds), *Rethinking Leviathan: the eighteenth-century state in Britain and Germany* (Oxford, 1999), 225–80

Institute for Fiscal Studies, *The structure and reform of direct taxation, report of a committee chaired by Professor J. E. Meade* (1978)

——, *Tax by design: the Mirrlees review* (Oxford, 2011)

Institute for Public Policy Research Commission on Economic Justice, *Prosperity and justice: a plan for the new economy* (Cambridge, 2018)

Micheline R. Ishay (ed.), *The human rights reader: major political writings, essays, speeches, and documents from the Bible to the present* (1997)

Alvin Jackson, *The two unions: Ireland, Scotland, and the survival of the United Kingdom, 1707–2007* (Oxford, 2012)

Patricia Jalland, 'Irish Home-Rule finance: a neglected dimension of the Irish question, 1910–14', *Irish Historical Studies*, 23 (1983), 233–53

Thomas Jefferson, 'To James Madison, 28 October 1785', at https://founders.archives.gov/documents/Madison/01-08-02-0202, accessed 3 March 2020

Charlie Jeffery and Ray Perman, 'Introduction' to Charlie Jeffery and Ray Perman (eds), *Scotland's decision: 16 questions to think about for the referendum on 18 September* (Edinburgh, 2014), 2–3

Geoff Jenkins, Matthew Perry and John Prior, *The climate of the United Kingdom and recent trends* (Exeter, 2009)

John J. W. Jervis, *A letter addressed to the gentlemen of England and Ireland, on the inexpediency of a federal-union between the two kingdoms* (1798)

John Jewkes, *Ordeal by planning* (1948)

Boris Johnson, https://www.politicshome.com/news /article/read-in-full-boris-johnsons-speech-to-the-2019–conservative-party-conference, accessed 14 April 2020

Harry G. Johnson (ed.), *The new mercantilism: some problems in international trade, money and investment* (Oxford, 1974)

Thomas Johnston, *Memories* (1952)

Peter Jones, *Rights* (Basingstoke, 1994)

Thomas Jones, *Whitehall diary*, vol. 3: *Ireland 1918–1925*, ed. Keith Middlemas (Oxford, 1971)

Keith Joseph and Jonathan Sumption, *Equality* (1979)

Douglas Kanter, 'The campaign against over-taxation, 1863–65: a reappraisal', in Douglas Kanter and Patrick Walsh (eds), *Taxation, politics, and protest in Ireland, 1662–2016* (Cham, Switzerland, 2019), 227–52

——, 'The politics of Irish taxation, 1842–53', *English Historical Review*, 127 (2012), 1121–55

Douglas Kanter and Patrick Walsh (eds), *Taxation, politics, and protest in Ireland, 1662–2016* (Cham, Switzerland, 2019)

Matthew Keep, 'The Barnett Formula', *House of Commons Library*, Briefing Paper 7386, 23 January 2018

George Skene Keith, *A general view of the taxes on malt, as imported both in England and in Scotland* (Edinburgh, 1803)

James G. Kellas and Peter Madgwick, 'Territorial ministries: the Scottish and Welsh Offices', in Peter Madgwick and Richard Rose (eds), *The territorial dimension in United Kingdom politics* (1982), 9–33

James Kelly, 'The origins of the Act of Union: an examination of unionist opinion in Britain and Ireland, 1650–1800', *Irish Historical Studies*, 25 (1987), 236–63

Alex Kemp, *The official history of North Sea oil and gas*, vol. 1: *The growing dominance of the state* (2012)

John Kendle, *Federal Britain: a history* (1997).

Liám Kennedy and Leslie A. Clarkson, 'Birth, death and exile: Irish population history, 1700–1921', in B. J. Graham and L. J. Proudfoot (eds), *An historical geography of Ireland* (1993), 158–84

Liám Kennedy and Philip Ollerenshaw (eds), *An economic history of Ulster, 1820–1940* (Manchester, 1985)

Thomas Kennedy, *A history of the Irish protest against over-taxation, from 1853 to 1897* (Dublin, 1897)

William Kennedy, *English taxation, 1640–1799: an essay on policy and opinion* (1913)

Donal A. Kerr, *Peel, priests, and politics: Sir Robert Peel's administration and the Roman Catholic Church in Ireland, 1841–1846* (Oxford, 1982)

T. M. Kettle, *Home Rule finance: an experiment in justice* (Dublin, 1911)

J. M. Keynes, 'The end of laissez-faire', in his *Essays in persuasion*, ed. Donald Moggridge (Cambridge, 1972), 272–94

——, *The general theory of employment, interest and money*, ed. Donald Moggridge (Cambridge, 1973).

Colin Kidd, 'The Phillipsonian Enlightenment', *Modern Intellectual History*, 11.1 (2014), 175–90

——, 'Sovereignty and the Scottish constitution before 1707', *Juridical Review*, 3 (2004), 225–36

——, *Subverting Scotland's past: Scottish Whig historians and the creation of an Anglo-British identity, 1689–c.1830* (Cambridge, 1993)

——, *Union and unionisms: political thought in Scotland, 1500–2000* (Cambridge, 2008)

Christine Kinealy, *This great calamity: the Irish Famine, 1845–52* (Dublin, 1994)

J. A. King and M. A. King, *The British tax system* (Oxford, 1978)

Peter King and Richard Ward, 'Rethinking the Bloody Code in eighteenth-century Britain: capital punishment at the centre and on the periphery', *Past and Present*, 228 (2015), 159–205

Michael Kitson and Jonathan Michie, 'The de-industrial revolution: the rise and fall of UK manufacturing, 1870–2010', in Roderick Floud, Jane Humphries and Paul Johnson (eds), *The Cambridge economic history of modern Britain*, vol. 2: *1870 to present* (Cambridge, 2014), 302–29

G. Kitson Clark, *An expanding society: Britain 1830–1900* (Cambridge, 1967)

Roger Knight, *Britain against Napoleon: the organization of victory, 1793–1815* (2013)

Roger Knight and Martin Wilcox, *Sustaining the fleet, 1793–1815: war, the British navy and the contractor state* (Woodbridge, 2010)

G. M. Koot, *English historical economics, 1870–1926: the rise of economic history and neomercantilism* (Cambridge, 1987)

L. D. L., *A letter from a Fyfe gentleman at present in Edinburgh, to the chief magistrate of a burgh in Fyfe, upon our present situation, with regard to the malt-tax* (Edinburgh, 1725)

Labour Party, *Labour and the Distressed Areas: a programme of immediate action. Interim report of the Labour Party's Commission of Enquiry into the Distressed Areas* (1937)

Ian Lang, *Blue remembered years: a political memoir* (2002)

Paul Langford, *The excise crisis: society and politics in the age of Walpole* (Oxford, 1975)

——, 'South Britons' reception of North Britons, 1707–1820', in T. C. Smout (ed.), *Anglo-Scottish relations from 1603 to 1900*, Proceedings of the British Academy, 127 (Oxford, 2005), 143–69

Léonce de Lavergne, *The rural economy of England, Scotland, and Ireland* (Edinburgh, 1855)

C. M. Law, 'The growth of urban population in England and Wales, 1801–1911', *Transactions of the Institute of British Geographers*, 41 (1967), 125–43.

R. J. Lawrence, *The government of Northern Ireland: public finance and public services, 1921–1964* (Oxford, 1965)

Nigel Lawson, *The view from No. 11: memoirs of a Tory radical* (1992)

Richard Lawton and Colin G. Pooley, *Britain, 1740–1950: an historical geography* (1992)

C. H. Lee, *Regional economic growth in the United Kingdom since the 1880s* (1971)

Clive Lee, *Scotland and the United Kingdom: the economy and the Union in the twentieth century* (Manchester, 1995)

William Letwin (ed.), *Against equality: readings on economic and social policy* (1983)

Brian P. Levack, *The formation of the British state: England, Scotland, and the Union, 1603–1707* (Oxford, 1987)

Ian Levitt, 'New towns, new Scotland, new ideology, 1937–57', *Scottish Historical Review*, 76.2 (1997), 222–38

——, 'The Scottish Office and St. Kilda, 1885–1930: a steamer too far', in J. Randall (ed.), *The decline and fall of St. Kilda* (Port of Ness, 2006), 51–63

—— (ed.), *The Scottish Office: depression and reconstruction, 1919–1959*, Scottish History Society, 5th Series, vol. 5 (1992)

—— (ed.), *Treasury control and public expenditure in Scotland, 1885–1979*, Records of Social and Economic History, New Series, 54 (Oxford, 2014)

Peter Lindert, *Growing public: social spending and economic growth since the eighteenth century*, 2 vols (Cambridge, 2004)

Naomi Lloyd-Jones, 'Liberalism, Scottish nationalism and the Home Rule crisis, c.1886–93', *English Historical Review*, 129 (2014), 862–87

George Lockhart, *The Lockhart papers: containing memoirs and correspondence upon the affairs of Scotland from 1702 to 1715*, 2 vols (1817)

Philip Loft, 'Litigation, the Anglo-Scottish Union, and the House of Lords as the High Court, 1660–1875', *Historical Journal*, 61.4 (2018), 943–67

London First, https://www.londonfirst.co.uk/about-us/our-achievements, accessed 14 April 2020

Martin Loughlin, 'Evolution and *gestalt* of the state in the United Kingdom', in Armin von Bogdandy, Peter M. Huber and Sabino Cassese (eds), *The administrative state* (Oxford, 2017), 451–92

LSE, *London's place in the UK economy* (2002)

——, *London's place in the UK economy, 2009–10* (2009)

W. C. Lubenow, 'The Liberals and the national question: Irish Home Rule, nationalism, and their relationship to nineteenth-century liberalism', *Parliamentary History*, 13 (1994), 119–42

Neil MacCormick, *Questioning sovereignty: law, state and nation in the European commonwealth* (Oxford, 1999)

Alexander Malcolm MacEwen, *The thistle and the rose: Scotland's problem to-day* (Edinburgh, 1932)

Allan I. Macinnes, *Union and empire: the making of the United Kingdom in 1707* (Cambridge, 2007)

Andrew Mackillop, 'Confrontation, negotiation and accommodation: garrisoning the burghs in post-Union Scotland', *Journal of Early Modern History*, 15.1–2 (2011), 159–83

——, *'More fruitful than the soil': army, empire and the Scottish Highlands, 1715–1815* (East Linton, 2000)

——, 'The political culture of the Scottish Highlands from Culloden to Waterloo', *Historical Journal*, 46.3 (2003), 511–32

——, 'Subsidy state or drawback province? Eighteenth-century Scotland and the British fiscal-military complex', in Aaron Graham and Patrick Walsh (eds), *The British fiscal-military states, 1660–c.1783* (2016), 179–99

William James MacNeven and Thomas Emmet, *Pieces of Irish history, illustrative of the Catholics in Ireland* (New York, 1807)

David Macpherson, *Annals of commerce, manufactures, fisheries, and navigation*, 4 vols (1805)

Angus Maddison, *The world economy: a millennial perspective* (Paris, 2001)

Bernard Mallet, *British budgets, 1887–88 to 1912–13* (1913)

John Maloney, 'Gladstone and sound Victorian finance', in John Maloney (ed.), *Debt and deficits: an historical perspective* (Cheltenham, 1998), 27–46

Andrew Marr, *The battle for Scotland* (Harmondsworth, 1992)

J. Marshall, *Digest of all the accounts* (1834)

R. M. Martin, *Ireland before and after the Union with Great Britain* (1843)

Ron Martin and Ben Gardiner, 'Reviving the "Northern Powerhouse" and spatially rebalancing the British economy: the scale of the challenge', in Craig Berry and Arianna Giovannini (eds), *Developing England's north:*

the political economy of the Northern Powerhouse (Cham, Switzerland, 2018), 23–58.

Ronald L. Martin, 'The contemporary debate over the north–south divide: images and realities of regional inequality in late-twentieth-century Britain', in Alan R. H. Baker and Mark Billinge (eds), *Geographies of England: the north–south divide, material and imagined* (Cambridge, 2004), 15–43

Doreen Massey, *World city* (Cambridge, 2007)

Joseph Massie, *Observations on the new cyder-tax, so far as the same may affect our woollen manufacturies, Newfoundland fisheries, &c.* ([1764?])

Alexander S. Mather, 'The Congested Districts Board for Scotland', in William Ritchie, Jeffrey C. Stone and Alexander S. Mather (eds), *Essays for Professor R. E. H. Mellow* (Aberdeen, 1986), 196–204

Peter Mathias, *The brewing industry in England, 1700–1830* (Cambridge, 1959)

H. C. G. Matthew, 'Disraeli, Gladstone, and the politics of mid-Victorian budgets', *Historical Journal*, 22.3 (1979), 615–43

——, *Gladstone: 1875–1898* (Oxford, 1995)

Trevor McCavery, 'Finance and politics in Ireland, 1801–17', in Douglas Kanter and Patrick Walsh (eds), *Taxation, politics, and protest in Ireland, 1662–2016* (Cham, Switzerland, 2019), 121–50

——, 'Politics, public finance and the British-Irish Act of Union of 1801', *Transactions of the Royal Historical Society*, 10 (2000), 353–75

Trevor Robert McCavery, 'Finance and politics in Ireland, 1801–1817' (Queen's University of Belfast PhD thesis, 1980)

David McCrone, 'Scotland out of the Union? The rise and rise of the nationalist agenda', *Political Quarterly*, 83.1 (2012), 69–76

——, *Understanding Scotland: the sociology of a nation* (New York and London, 2001)

Gavin McCrone, 'Scotland's public finances from Goschen to Barnett', *Fraser of Allander Quarterly Economic Commentary*, 24.2 (1999), 30–46

——, *Scottish independence: weighing up the economics* (Edinburgh, 2014)

J. R. McCulloch, *Observations on the duty on sea-borne coal; and on the peculiar duties and charges on coal, in the Port of London* (1830)

R. B. McDowell, *The Irish administration, 1801–1914* (1964)

Davis D. McElroy, *Scotland's age of improvement: a survey of eighteenth-century literary clubs and societies* (Pullman, WA, 1969)

Martin McElroy, 'The 1830 budget and repeal: parliament and public opinion in Ireland', *Irish Historical Studies*, 36 (2008), 38–52

Charles Ivar McGrath, *Ireland and empire, 1692–1770* (2012)

E. B. McGuire, *Irish whiskey: a history of distilling, the spirit trade, and excise controls in Ireland* (Dublin, 1973)

Eoin McLaughlin, 'The Irish Revolution and its aftermath: the economic dimension', in John Crowley, Donal Ó Drisceoil, Mike Murphy and John Borgonovo (eds), *Atlas of the Irish Revolution* (Cork, 2017), 762–9

Iain McLean, 'England in a changing fiscal union', in Michael Kenny, Iain McLean and Akash Paun (eds), *Governing England: English identity and institutions in a changing United Kingdom*, Proceedings of the British Academy, 217 (Oxford, 2018), 227–44

——, 'A fiscal constitution for the UK', in Selina Chen and Tony Wright (eds), *The English question*, Fabian Society (2000), 80–95

——, *The fiscal crises of the United Kingdom* (Basingstoke, 2005)

Iain McLean and Alistair McMillan, *State of the Union: unionism and the alternatives in the United Kingdom since 1707* (Oxford, 2005)

Iain McLean, Jim Gallagher and Guy Lodge, *Scotland's choices: the referendum and what happens afterwards* (Edinburgh, 2013)

Ranald C. Michie, *The London stock exchange: a history* (Oxford, 1999)

William L. Micks, *An account of the constitution, administration and dissolution of the Congested Districts Board for Ireland from 1891 to 1923* (Dublin, 1925)

Roger Middleton, *Government versus the market: the growth of the public sector, economic management and British economic performance, c.1890–1979* (Cheltenham, 1996)

——, 'The size and scope of the public sector', in S. J. D. Green and R. C. Whiting (eds), *The boundaries of the state in modern Britain* (Cambridge, 1996), 89–145

Arthur Midwinter, 'The Barnett Formula and public spending in Scotland: policy and practice', *Scottish Affairs*, 28 (1999), 83–92

Fredric M. Miller, 'The unemployment policy of the National Government, 1931–1936', *Historical Journal*, 19.2 (1976), 453–76

Robert Millward and Sally Sheard, 'The urban fiscal problem, 1870–1914: government expenditure and finance in England and Wales', *Economic History Review*, 48.3 (1995), 501–35

John Mitchel, *The last conquest of Ireland (perhaps)* (Glasgow, 1861)

B. R. Mitchell, *British historical statistics* (Cambridge, 1988)

J. F. Mitchell, 'Englishmen in the Scottish excise department, 1707–1823', *Scottish Genealogist*, 13.2 (1966), 16–28

James Mitchell, *Governing Scotland: the invention of administrative devolution* (Houndmills, 2003)

——, *The Scottish question* (Oxford, 2014)

W. Mitchell, *Is Scotland to be sold again? Home Rule for Scotland* (Edinburgh, [1893])

Rosalind Mitchison, 'Anderson, James (1739–1808)', *Oxford dictionary of national biography*, online edn

——, 'The government and the Highlands, 1707–1745', in N. T. Phillipson and Rosalind Mitchison (eds), *Scotland in the age of improvement: essays in Scottish history in the eighteenth century* (Edinburgh, 1970), 24–46

Joel Mokyr, *Why Ireland starved: a quantitative and analytical history of the Irish economy, 1800–1850* (1983)

[Alexander Montgomerie, Earl of Eglinton], *An inquiry into the original and consequences of the public debt* (Edinburgh, 1753)

T. W. Moody, *Davitt and Irish revolution, 1846–82* (Oxford, 1981)

Renaud Morieux, *The society of prisoners: Anglo-French wars and incarceration in the eighteenth century* (Oxford, 2019)

John Morley, *The life of William Ewart Gladstone*, 3 vols (1903)

Herbert Morrison, *Socialisation and transport: the organisation of socialised industries with particular reference to the London Passenger Transport Bill* (1933)

J. Morrison Davidson, *Scotia rediviva: Home Rule for Scotland* ([1904])

Graeme Morton, 'Scottish rights and "centralisation" in the mid-nineteenth century', *Nations and Nationalism*, 2.2 (1996), 257–79

Michael S. Moss and John R. Hume, *The making of Scottish whisky: a history of the Scotch whisky distilling industry* (Edinburgh, 2000)

Hoh-Cheung Mui and Lorna H. Mui, 'Smuggling and the British tea trade before 1784', *American Historical Review*, 74.1 (1968), 44–73

——, 'William Pitt and the enforcement of the Commutation Act, 1784–1788', *English Historical Review*, 76 (1961), 447–65

Edwin Muir, *Scottish journey* (1935)

Jeppe Mulich, *In a sea of empires: networks and crossings in the revolutionary Caribbean* (Cambridge, 2020)

Alexander Murdoch, 'Henry Dundas, Scotland and the Union with Ireland, 1792–1801', in Bob Harris (ed.), *Scotland in the age of the French Revolution* (Edinburgh, 2005), 125–39

——, *'The people above': politics and administration in mid-eighteenth-century Scotland* (Edinburgh, 1980)

Alice Effie Murray, *A history of the commercial and financial relations between England and Ireland from the period of the Restoration* (1903)

C. de B. Murray, *How Scotland is governed* (Edinburgh, 1938)

[Patrick Murray, Lord Elibank], *Thoughts on money, circulation and paper currency* (Edinburgh, 1758)

R. A. Musgrave, 'A brief history of fiscal doctrine', in Alan J. Auerbach and Martin Feldstein (eds), *Handbook of public economics*, vol. 1 (Amsterdam, 1985), 1–59

Catherine Nash, Bryonie Reid and Brian Graham, *Partitioned lives: the Irish borderlands* (Farnham, 2013)

National Association for the Vindication of Scottish Rights, *Justice to Scotland. Report of the first public meeting of the National Association for the Vindication of Scottish Rights, held ... November 2, 1853* (Edinburgh, 1853)

Jacques Necker, *A treatise on the administration of the finances of France*, trans. Thomas Mortimer, 3 vols (1785)

W. Neilson Hancock, *Three lectures on the questions, should the principles of political economy be disregarded at the present crisis? And if not, how can they be applied towards the discovery of measures of relief?* (Dublin, 1847)

Edward Nevin (ed.), *The social accounts of the Welsh economy, 1948 to 1952* (Aberystwyth, 1956)

Cormac Ó Gráda, '"The greatest blessing of all": the old age pension in Ireland', *Past and Present*, 175 (2002), 124–61

Wallace E. Oates, *Fiscal federalism* (New York, 1972)

Avner Offer, 'Empire and social reform: British overseas investment and domestic politics, 1908–1914', *Historical Journal*, 26.1 (1983), 119–38

Arthur M. Okun, *Equality and efficiency: the big tradeoff* (Washington, DC, 1975)

Alison Gilbert Olson, 'The British government and colonial union, 1754', *William and Mary Quarterly*, 17.1 (1960), 22–34

Mancur Olson, *The logic of collective action: public goods and the theory of groups* (Cambridge, MA, 1965)

Thomas P. O'Neill, 'The organisation and administration of relief, 1845–52', in R. Dudley Edwards and T. Desmond Williams (eds), *The Great Famine: studies in Irish history, 1845–52* (Dublin, 1956), 209–60

Kevin O'Rourke, 'Burn everything British but their coal: the Anglo-Irish economic war of the 1930s', *Journal of Economic History*, 51.2 (1991), 357–66

——, *A short history of Brexit: from Brentry to backstop* (2019)

[Robert Orr], *An address to the people of Ireland, against an union* (Dublin, 1799)

George Osborne, 'We need a Northern powerhouse', speech in Manchester 23 June 2014, at https://www.gov.uk/government/speeches/chancellor-we-need-a-northern-powerhouse; accessed 21 June 2019

Oxford dictionary of national biography, online edn

Oxford Economics, *London's competitive place in the UK and global economies* (2011)

——, *Regional winners and losers in UK public finances* (2008)

David Parker, *The official history of privatisation*, vol. 1: *The formative years, 1970–1987* (2009)

Parliamentary Register (1790)

Henry Parnell, *On financial reform* (3rd edn, 1831)

Wayne Parsons, *The political economy of British regional policy* (1988)

Aleksandar Pavković with Peter Radan, *Creating new states: theory and practice of secession* (Aldershot, 2007)

G. C. Peden, 'The "Treasury view" on public works and employment in the interwar period', *Economic History Review*, 37.2 (1984), 167–81

Roy Pedersen, *Who pays the ferryman? The great Scottish ferries swindle* (Edinburgh, 2013)

Robert Peel, *The speeches of the late Right Honourable Sir Robert Peel, Bart. Delivered in the House of Commons*, 4 vols (1853)

Alexander Pennecuik, 'Dialogu[e] betwixt a Glasgow malt-man and an English excise-ma[n]', ([Edinburgh, 1725?]), from the online English Broadside Ballad Archive

John Percival Day, *Public administration in the Highlands and Islands of Scotland* (1918)

G. H. Peters, *Cost-benefit analysis and public expenditure* (3rd edn, 1973)

Alan Butt Philip, *The Welsh question: nationalism in Welsh politics, 1945–1970* (Cardiff, 1975)

John Philipson, 'Whisky smuggling on the border in the early nineteenth century', *Archaeologia Aeliana*, 4th Series, 39 (1961), 151–63

David Phillips, 'GERS shows that Scotland's fiscal position continues to be weak but tells us much more as well' (2018), at https://www.ifs.org.uk/publications/13287, accessed 2 November 2019

——, 'Question 3: What would the picture for the Scottish government's finances be if Scotland votes yes? What if it votes no?', in Charlie Jeffery and Ray Perman (eds), *Scotland's decision: 16 questions to think about for the referendum on 18 September* (Edinburgh, 2014), 18–21

N. T. Phillipson, 'Culture and society in the 18th century province: the case of Edinburgh and the Scottish Enlightenment', in Lawrence Stone (ed.), *The university in society*, vol. 2 (Princeton, NJ, 1975), 407–48

Thomas Piketty, *Capital in the twenty-first century* (Cambridge, MA, 2014)

Steve Pincus and James Robinson, 'Challenging the fiscal-military hegemony: the British case', in Aaron Graham and Patrick Walsh (eds), *The British fiscal-military states, 1660–c.1783* (Abingdon, 2016), 229–61

William Playfair, *The commercial and political atlas; representing, by means of stained copper-plate charts … the national debt, and other public accounts* (1786)

William Plowden, *The motor car and politics, 1896–1970* (1971)

M. H. Port, *Imperial London: civil government building in London, 1851–1915* (New Haven, CT, 1995)

James A. A. Porteous, *Scotland and the south: economic and financial relations* (Stirling, 1947)

James Postlethwayt, *The history of the public revenue, from the Revolution in 1688, to Christmas 1753* (1759)

John Prest, *Liberty and locality: parliament, permissive legislation, and ratepayers' democracies in the nineteenth century* (Oxford, 1990)

J. B. Priestley, *English journey* (1934)

Richard Pryke, *The nationalised industries: policies and performance since 1968* (Oxford, 1981)

——, *Public enterprise in practice: the British experience of nationalization over two decades* (1971)

William Pulteney, *Considerations on the present state of public affairs, and the means of raising the necessary supplies* (1779)

Arthur S. Quekett, *The constitution of Northern Ireland. Part 1: The origin and development of the constitution* (Belfast, 1928)

John Quiggin, *Zombie economics: how dead ideas still walk among us* (Princeton, NJ, 2012)

Luke Raikes, Arianna Giovannini and Bianca Getzel, *Divided and connected: regional inequalities in the north, the UK and the developed world. State of the north 2019*, Institute for Public Policy Research (Manchester, 2019)

Charles Read, 'Laissez-faire, the Irish Famine, and British financial crisis', *Economic History Review*, 69.2 (2016), 411–34

——, 'Taxation and the economics of nationalism in 1840s Ireland', in Douglas Kanter and Patrick Walsh (eds), *Taxation, politics, and protest in Ireland, 1662–2016* (Cham, Switzerland, 2019), 199–225

E. A. Reitan, 'Edmund Burke and economic reform, 1779–83', *Studies in Eighteenth-Century Culture*, 14 (1985), 129–58

Wolfgang Renzsch, 'German federalism in historical perspective: federalism as a substitute for a national state', *Publius*, 19.4 (1989), 17–33

David Reynolds, *Island stories: Britain and its history in the age of Brexit* (2019)

William H. Riker, *Federalism: origin, operation, significance* (Boston, MA, 1964)

Daniel Ritschel, *The politics of planning: the debate on economic planning in Britain in the 1930s* (Oxford, 1997)

John Robertson, 'Empire and union: two concepts of the early modern European political order', in John Robertson (ed.), *A union for empire: political thought and the British union of 1707* (Cambridge, 1995), 3–36

Joan Robinson, *The new mercantilism* (Cambridge, 1966)

Nicholas Robinson, 'Marriage against inclination: the Union and caricature', in Dáire Keogh and Kevin Whelan (eds), *Acts of Union: the causes, contexts and consequences of the Act of Union* (Dublin, 2001), 140–58

Peter Robson, 'Appendix: standards of public expenditure in Northern Ireland', in Thomas Wilson (ed.), *Ulster under Home Rule* (1955), 216–17

Stein Rokkan and Derek K. Urwin, *Economy, territory, identity: politics of western European peripheries* (1983)

Amanda Root, 'Transport and communications', in A. H. Halsey and Josephine Webb (eds), *Twentieth-century British social trends* (Basingstoke, 2000), 437–68

Richard Rose, *Understanding the United Kingdom: the territorial dimension in government* (1982)

Joan R. Roses and Nikolaus Wolf, 'Aggregate growth, 1913–1950', in Stephen Broadberry and Kevin H. O'Rourke (eds), *The Cambridge economic history of modern Europe*, vol. 2 (Cambridge, 2012), 181–207

Philipp Robinson Rössner, *Scottish trade in the wake of the Union (1700–1760): the rise of a warehouse economy* (Stuttgart, 2008)

David Russell, *Looking north: Northern England and the national imagination* (Manchester, 2004)

Francis Russell Hart and J. B. Pick, *Neil M. Gunn: a Highland life* (1981)

Reay Sabourn, *Oppression exposed, or liberty and property maintained: being an enquiry into the several mismanagements of persons concerned in the revenues of customs and excise in Scotland* (Edinburgh, 1729)

——, *The Scotch prophecy: or, the Lord Belhaven's remarkable speech before the Union, examin'd and compar'd with the articles afterwards concluded, and now subsisting. Wherein the advantages accruing to Scotland by the Union, are discovered* (1737).

Raphael Samuel, 'Mrs Thatcher and Victorian values', in his *Island stories: unravelling Britain* (1998), 330–48

C. T. Sandford, *Economics of public finance: an economic analysis of government expenditure and revenue in the United Kingdom* (4th edn, Oxford, 1992)

Mark Sandford (ed.), *The northern veto* (Manchester, 2009)

Otto Saumarez Smith, 'Action for cities: the Thatcher government and inner-city policy', *Urban History*, 47 (2020), 274–91

Andrew Saunders, *Fortress Britain: artillery fortifications in the British Isles and Ireland* (Liphook, 1989)

Richard Saville, 'The industrial background to the post-war Scottish economy', in Richard Saville (ed.), *The economic development of modern Scotland, 1950–1980* (Edinburgh, 1985), 1–46

Jeffrey Schoenblum, 'Taxation, the state, and the community', in Ellen Frankel, Fred D. Miller Jnr and Jeffrey Paul (eds), *Taxation, economic prosperity, and distributive justice* (Cambridge, 2006), 210–34

Joseph A. Schumpeter, *Capitalism, socialism and democracy* (New York, 1942)

Robert Schütze and Stephen Tierney (eds), *The United Kingdom and the federal idea* (Oxford, 2018)

L. G. Schwoerer, *'No standing armies!': the antiarmy ideology in seventeenth-century England* (Baltimore, MD, 1974)

The Scotsman

Hugh Scott, *The progress of the Scottish national movement* (Edinburgh, 1853)

James C. Scott, *Seeing like a state: how certain schemes to improve the human condition have failed* (New Haven, CT, 1999)

Paul Henderson Scott, *'The boasted advantages': the consequences of the Union of 1707* (Edinburgh, 1999)

Peter Scott, *The triumph of the south: a regional economic history of early twentieth century Britain* (Aldershot, 2007)

Walter Scott, *The heart of Mid-Lothian*, ed. David Hewitt and Alison Lumsden ([1818], Edinburgh, 2004)

Scottish Committee Communist Party, *A people's plan for Scotland* (Glasgow, [1945?])

[Scottish National Party], *The new Scotland* (n.p., [1972?])

Scottish National Party, *Scotland pays her way* (n.p., 1996)

G. R. Searle, *The quest for national efficiency: a study in British politics and British political thought, 1899–1914* (Oxford, 1971)

Edwin R. A. Seligman, *The income tax: a study of the history, theory, and practice of income tax at home and abroad* (2nd edn, New York, 1914)

Amartya Sen, 'The discipline of cost-benefit analysis', *Journal of Legal Studies*, 29 (2000), 931–52

——, *Inequality reexamined* (Oxford, 1992)

Nassau William Senior, *Journals, conversations and essays relating to Ireland*, 2 vols (1868)

Catherine B. Shannon, *Arthur J. Balfour and Ireland, 1874–1922* (Washington, DC, 1988)

Timothy J. Shannon, *Indians and colonists at the crossroads of empire: the Albany Congress of 1754* (Ithaca, NY, 2000)

Steven M. Sheffrin, *Tax fairness and folk justice* (Cambridge, 2014)

Robert Shipkey, 'Problems in alcohol production and control in early nineteenth-century Ireland', *Historical Journal*, 16.2 (1973), 291–302

John Short, *Public expenditure and taxation in the UK regions* (Farnborough, 1981)

Jim Sillars, *Scotland: the case for optimism* (Edinburgh, 1986)

John Sinclair, *A history of the public revenue of the British Empire* (3rd edn, 1803–4)

Paul Slack, *The invention of improvement: information and material progress in seventeenth-century England* (Oxford, 2015)

Adam Smith, *The correspondence of Adam Smith*, ed. Ernest Campbell Mossner and Ian Simpson Ross (2nd edn, Oxford, 1987)

——, *An inquiry into the nature and causes of the wealth of nations*, ed. R. H. Campbell and A. S. Skinner, 2 vols ([1776], Oxford, 1976)

Annette M. Smith, *Jacobite estates of the forty-five* (Edinburgh, 1982)

David B. Smith, 'Historical trends in the government spending and tax ratios', in Philip Booth (ed.), *Taxation, government spending and economic growth*, Institute of Economic Affairs (2016), 48–65

Stephen Smith, *Taxation: a very short introduction* (Oxford, 2015)

[Thomas Smith], *Case of the Lowland distillers in Scotland, humbly submitted to the consideration of the Committee of the Honourable the House of Commons, appointed to inquire into the state of that manufacture* ([Edinburgh, 1798?])

Barbara Lewis Solow, *The land question and the Irish economy, 1870–1903* (Cambridge, MA, 1971)

Alexander Somerville, *Letters from Ireland during the Famine of 1847*, ed. K. D. M. Snell (Dublin, 1994)

Spectator

James Malcolm Stafford, 'Political economy and the reform of empire in Ireland, 1776–1845' (University of Cambridge PhD thesis, 2016)

James Stafford, 'The Scottish Enlightenment and the British-Irish Union of 1801', in Naomi Lloyd-Jones and Margaret M. Scull (eds), *Four nations approaches to modern 'British' history: a (dis)United Kingdom?* (2018), 111–34

J. C. Stamp, *British incomes and property: the application of official statistics to economic problems* (1916)

David Steele, 'A new union for today's world', *David Hume Institute Occasional Papers*, 97 (Edinburgh, 2013), 10

Colonel David Stewart, *Sketches of the character, manners, and present state of the Highlanders of Scotland*, 2 vols (Edinburgh, 1822)

John Stewart, 'The National Health Service in Scotland, 1947–74: Scottish or British?', *Historical Research*, 76 (2003), 389–410

Laura A. M. Stewart, 'The "rise" of the state?', in T. M. Devine and Jenny Wormald (eds), *The Oxford handbook of modern Scottish history* (Oxford, 2012), 220–35

Ros Stott, 'Revolution? What revolution? Some thoughts about revestment', *Proceedings of the Isle of Man Natural and Antiquarian Society*, 11 (2003–5), 541–52

Sean Straw and John W. Young, 'The Wilson government and the demise of TSR-2, October 1964–April 1965', *Journal of Strategic Studies*, 20.4 (1997), 18–44

Kim Swales, 'Civil service dispersal – a long time coming', *Fraser of Allander Quarterly Economic Commentary*, 8.1 (1982), 38–41

Jonathan Swift, 'An answer to a paper called "A memorial for the poor inhabitants, tradesmen and labourers of the Kingdom of Ireland"' [1728], in his *Irish political writings after 1725: a modest proposal and other works*, ed. D. W. Hayton and Adam Rounce (Cambridge, 2018), 27–41

Chris Tabraham and Doren Grove, *Fortress Scotland and the Jacobites* (1995)

R. H. Tawney, *Equality* (1931)

Miles Taylor, 'The 1848 revolutions and the British Empire', *Past and Present*, 166 (2000), 146–80

William Taylor, *The military roads in Scotland* (revised edn, Colonsay, 1996)

Eric Tenbus, 'A draught of discontentment: national identity and nostalgia in the Beerhouse Act of 1830', *Brewery History*, 161 (2015), 2–9

Colin Thain and Maurice Wright, *The Treasury and Whitehall: the planning and control of public expenditure, 1976–1993* (Oxford, 1993)

Margaret Thatcher, *The collected speeches of Margaret Thatcher*, ed. Robin Harris (1997)

——, 'Interview for *Woman's Own*', at www.margaretthatcher.org/document/106689, accessed 15 October 2019

——, 'Remarks returning to Central Office', at https://www.margaretthatcher.org/document/106653, accessed 14 April 2020

Kevin Theakston, *Winston Churchill and the British constitution* (2003)

George Malcolm Thomson, *Scotland: that distressed area* (Edinburgh, 1935)

The Times

[Colonel Tittler], *Ireland profiting by example; or, the question, whether Scotland has gained, or lost, by an union with England, fairly discussed* (Dublin, 1799)

Alexis de Tocqueville, *Democracy in America*, ed. Eduardo Nolla, 2 vols ([1835], Indianapolis, IN, 2010)

——, *The old regime and the revolution*, ed. François Furet and Françoise Mélonio, 2 vols ([1856], Chicago, IL, 1998)

John Tomaney, 'The idea of English regionalism', in Robert Hazell (ed.), *The English question* (Manchester, 2006), 158–73

Jim Tomlinson, 'De-industrialization not decline: a new meta-narrative for post-war British history', *Twentieth Century British History*, 27.1 (2016), 76–99

——, *Managing the economy, managing the people: narratives of economic life in Britain from Beveridge to Brexit* (Oxford, 2017)

David Torrance, *'We in Scotland': Thatcherism in a cold climate* (Edinburgh, 2009)

Richard Toye, *The Labour party and the planned economy, 1931–1951* (Woodbridge, 2003)

Transport for London, 'Annual report and statement of accounts, 2018/19', at http://content.tfl.gov.uk/board-20190724–agenda-item08–annual-report-and-accounts.pdf, 118, accessed 8 April 2020

——, 'Mayoral community infrastructure levy', at https://tfl.gov.uk/info-for/urban-planning-and-construction/planning-applications/community-infrastructure-levy#on-this-page-6, accessed 14 April 2020

Pauric Travers, 'The financial relations question, 1800–1914', in F. B. Smith (ed.), *Ireland, England, and Australia: essays in honour of Oliver MacDonagh* (Sydney and Cork, 1990), 41–69

Tony Travers, *The politics of local government finance* (1986)

Arthur C. Turner, *Scottish Home Rule* (Oxford, 1952)

Stephen Utz, 'Chartism and the income tax', *British Tax Review* (2013), 192–221

Elizabeth R. Varon, *Disunion! The coming of the American Civil War, 1789–1859* (Chapel Hill, NC, 2008)

Edward Wakefield, *An account of Ireland, statistical and political*, 2 vols (1812)

David Walker, *In praise of centralism: a critique of the new localism* (2002)

Graham Walker, 'Scotland, Northern Ireland, and devolution, 1945–1979', *Journal of British Studies*, 49.1 (2010), 117–42

Horace Walpole, *Memoirs of King George II*, ed. John Brooke, 3 vols (New Haven, CT, 1985).

Patrick Walsh, 'Enforcing the fiscal state: the army, the revenue and the Irish experience of the fiscal-military state, 1690–1769', in Aaron Graham and Patrick Walsh (eds), *The British fiscal-military states, 1660–c.1783* (Abingdon, 2016), 131–58

——, 'Patterns of taxation in eighteenth-century Ireland', in Douglas Kanter and Patrick Walsh (eds), *Taxation, politics, and protest in Ireland, 1662–2016* (Cham, Switzerland, 2019), 89–119

Patrick A. Walsh, 'The fiscal state in Ireland, 1691–1769', *Historical Journal*, 56.3 (2013), 629–56

James Walvin, *Fruits of empire: exotic produce and British taste, 1660–1800* (Basingstoke, 1997)

Arthur Warren Samuels, *Home Rule finance: an examination of the financial bearings of the Government of Ireland Bill, 1912* (Dublin, 1912)

Amy Watson, 'Patriotism and partisanship in post-Union Scotland, 1724–37', *Scottish Historical Review*, 97.1 (2018), 57–84.

J. Watson Grice, *National and local finance: a review of relations between the central and local authorities in England, France, Belgium, and Prussia during the nineteenth century* (1910)

Douglas Watt, *The price of Scotland: Darien, Union and the wealth of nations* (Edinburgh, 2007)

Timothy D. Watt, 'Taxation riots and the culture of popular protest in Ireland, 1714–1740', *English Historical Review*, 130 (2015), 1418–48

William Webb, *Coastguard! An official history of HM Coastguard* (1976)

Ian Webster, 'The Public Works Loan Board and the growth of the state in nineteenth-century England', *Economic History Review*, 71.3 (2018), 887–908

Richard Weight, *Patriots: national identity in Britain 1940–2000* (2002)

Ron Weir, 'The Scottish and Irish unions: the Victorian view in perspective', in S. J. Connelly (ed.), *Kingdoms united? Great Britain and Ireland since 1500: integration and diversity* (Dublin, 1999), 56–66

Lord Welby, 'Irish finance', in J. H. Morgan (ed.), *The new Irish constitution: an exposition and some arguments* (1912), 112–56

J. R. Western, *The English militia in the eighteenth century: the story of a political issue, 1660–1802* (1965)

Sam Wetherell, 'Freedom planned: enterprise zones and urban non-planning in post-war Britain', *Twentieth Century British History*, 27.2 (2016), 266–89

Wexford Independent

Christopher A. Whatley, 'How tame were the Scottish Lowlanders during the eighteenth century?', in T. M. Devine (ed.), *Conflict and stability in Scottish society, 1700–1850* (Edinburgh, 1990), 1–30

——, 'Order and disorder', in Elizabeth Foyster and Christopher A. Whatley (eds), *A history of everyday life in Scotland, 1600–1800* (Edinburgh, 2010), 191–216

——, *The Scots and the Union: then and now* (Edinburgh, 2014)

I. D. Whyte, 'Scottish and Irish urbanisation in the seventeenth and eighteenth centuries: a comparative perspective', in S. J. Connolly, R. A. Houston and R. J. Morris (eds), *Conflict, identity and economic development: Scotland and Ireland, 1600–1939* (Preston, 1995), 14–28

David Wiggins, *Needs, values, truth: essays in the philosophy of value* (3rd edn, Oxford, 1998)

Wikipedia, https://en.wikipedia.org/wiki/Death_and_taxes_(idiom), accessed 5 March 2020

——, https://en.wikipedia.org/wiki/Demography_of_England/Ireland/Northern Ireland/Scotland/London (details of separate websites combined into one), accessed 24 October 2017 and 15 January 2020

Ellen Wilkinson, *The town that was murdered: the life-story of Jarrow* (1939)

Richard Wilkinson and Kate Pickett, *The spirit level: why more equal societies almost always do better* (2009)

Vanessa S. Williamson, *Read my lips: why Americans are proud to pay taxes* (Princeton, NJ, 2017)

Donald Winch, 'The political economy of public finance in the "long" eighteenth century', in John Maloney (ed.), *Debt and deficits: an historical perspective* (Cheltenham, 1998), 8–26

J. M. Winter, *The Great War and the British people* (1986)

Patrick Woodland, 'Extra-parliamentary political organization in the making: Benjamin Heath and the opposition to the 1763 cider excise', *Parliamentary History*, 4 (1985), 115–36

Maurice Wright, *Treasury control of the civil service, 1854–1874* (Oxford, 1969)

E. A. Wrigley, *Continuity, chance and change: the character of the industrial revolution in England* (Cambridge, 1988)

——, *The path to sustained growth: England's transition from an organic economy to an industrial revolution* (Cambridge, 2016)

YouGov, 'Perceptions of how tax is spent differ widely from reality', at https://yougov.co.uk/news/2014/11/09/public-attitudes-tax-distribution/, accessed 15 November 2017

Arthur Young, *Travels in France during the Years 1787, 1788 and 1789*, ed. Constantia Maxwell (Cambridge, 1929)

Acknowledgements

I could not have written this book as I did without the award of a Major Research Fellowship by the Leverhulme Trust that allowed me to undertake three years of research free from teaching and administrative duties between 2016 and 2019. I am very much in the Trust's debt, as well as to the characteristic generosity of my colleagues at UCL's History Department who had to shoulder additional burdens during my prolonged absence from normal duties. For enabling this I am very grateful to two heads of department during my absence, Jason Peacey and Eleanor Robson, and the department manager, Claire Morley.

I must also warmly thank three historians who supported my fellowship application. John Morrill enthused me as an undergraduate – some of the concerns of this book echo his preoccupations at the time – and he has generously encouraged me ever since. Paul Slack's work was important to me at the start of my academic career and it has been a great pleasure (and further education) to get to know him personally over the last decade. And Colin Kidd's commitment to careful research to answer challenging questions about the Union has set standards that others can only grope towards.

That the book has been finished in good time owes enormously to the wonderful staff at Addenbrooke's and Royal Papworth hospitals who got me going again after an accident in 2017. Even so, I had for months to depend even more than usual upon my wife, Karin, which she bore lovingly.

Many friends have provided help and advice while I worked on this book, including Richard Fisher, Aaron Graham, Bob Harris, Joanna Innes, Adrian Leonard, Renaud Morieux, Duncan Needham, Jon

Parry, Hamish Scott, Koji Yamamoto and Patrick Walsh. Renaud, Jon and my colleague Florence Sutcliffe-Braithwaite also commented helpfully on draft chapters. Philipp Rössner generously provided me with data he had collected from Scottish customs records. I owe an especially large debt to Martin Daunton, dating back to 1986 when he sat on the committee which appointed me at UCL. His studies of taxation in the UK were inspirational and he kindly commented with great care and insight on a complete draft of this book, helping me to address some of its limitations. Audiences in Belfast, Cambridge, Dublin, London, Oxford, Paris and Toulouse provided useful feedback on my developing ideas.

Most of the research for this book was undertaken at the British Library, Cambridge University Library, National Library of Scotland, the National Archives (Kew) and the National Records of Scotland. I have made frequent calls on their staff's expertise and energy and never been disappointed. These are beacons of light where it is a pleasure to work, often despite the efforts of today's holders of the purse strings.

Finally, it has been a real pleasure to publish this book with Penguin, where my editor, Simon Winder, has been a generous and wise supporter, and Eva Hodgkin helped with the illustrations, maps, figures and tables. The text has been considerably improved through the meticulous copy-editing of Kate Parker.

Julian Hoppit
Cockayne Hatley, Bedfordshire, July 2020

Index